SOCIAL PROBLEMS IN AMERICA

SOCIAL PROBLEMS IN AMERICA

JONATHAN H. TURNER

University of California, Riverside

HARPER & ROW, PUBLISHERS
New York   Hagerstown   San Francisco   London

Sponsoring Editor: Dale Tharp
Project Editor: Karla B. Philip
Designer: T. R. Funderburk
Production Supervisor: Stefania J. Taflinska
Photo Researcher: Myra Schachne
Compositor: Progressive Typographers, Inc.
Printer: The Murray Printing Company
Binder: Halliday Lithograph Corporation
Art Studio: Vantage Art, Inc.

SOCIAL PROBLEMS IN AMERICA

Copyright © 1977 by Jonathan H. Turner

Library of Congress Cataloging in Publication Data

Turner, Jonathan H
    Social problems in America.

    Bibliography: p.
    Includes index.
    1. Social problems.   2. United States—Social
conditions—1960-   I. Title.
HN59.T87   309.1'73'092   76-50656
ISBN 0-06-046717-7

To my children,
Patricia, Donna, and Jon

CONTENTS

PART II
PROBLEMS IN THE INSTITUTIONAL SYSTEM

PREFACE

In this text I have sought to communicate that social problems are related to the values, beliefs, and structural arrangements of a society. The sources of social problems reside in these arrangements; thus, it is in the culture and structure of a society that we must analyze what people consider problematic.

I have selected problems to study that both students and instructors will consider relevant and important. I offer no "scientific" reason for selecting these particular problems—there is no science of problem selecting. Problems are defined by people's beliefs and values about what is good and bad, and as we can all observe, different people hold different conceptions of the good and bad in a society. One person's anathema is another's paradise.

Lacking a scientific definition of problems, however, does not require us to throw out science. Once we define a condition as a problem—even if it is a problem only from our personal point of view—we can study the problem objectively. Science cannot identify our problems for us, but it can enable us to understand them.

Social Problems in America is organized into five sections. Part I introduces the reader to the sociology of social problems. Part II analyzes problems in our basic institutions. Part III discusses problems in the distribution of scarce resources and the creation of a stratification system. Part IV looks at the problems of community, including the ecological community. Finally, Part V discusses the problems of deviance, most notably the structured reaction to, and attempts at regulation of, deviance. In each chapter of the text the cultural and structural sources of problems are discussed. By looking at their cultural and structural roots, we can better visualize the interrelationships among social problems. For example, Watergate, the CIA, domestic spying, and the decline of congressional power are not separate problems of government (assuming, of course, that one defines these as problems). Rather, they are related because they arise from *the same set of social and cultural arrangements.* Similarly, the problems of the aged and of rising divorce rates are related because they are the result of fundamental changes of the culture and structure of kinship. Thus, a structural approach allows us to see the threads—cultural and structural—connecting social problems.

In this book, then, I use the available data on the culture and structure of American society to analyze those social problems associated with the structure of social institutions, the stratification system, the organization of community, and the deviance-regulating system in America. Hopefully, students will come to better understand the culture and structure of their society by studying what they define as problematic.

PHOTOGRAPH CREDITS

Below are listed the pages on which photographs appear by special permission. We appreciate the right to reproduce the following photographs:

Chapter 1
4, Baldwin-Watriss, Woodfin Camp; **6,** Charles Gatewood; **6,** Charles Gatewood; **7,** Charles Gatewood; **7,** Anderson, Woodfin Camp; **7,** Charles Gatewood; **8,** Marion Bernstein; **8,** George Gardner; **9,** UPI; **11,** Johnson, Woodfin Camp; **11,** Charles Gatewood; **11,** Charles Gatewood; **12,** Charles Gatewood.

Chapter 2
16, Charles Gatewood; **20,** Holland, Stock, Boston; **20,** Combs, FreeVision; **20,** Combs, FreeVision; **20,** UPI; **22,** George Gardner; **23,** George Gardner; **24,** American Airlines; **24,** George Gardner; **26,** George Gardner; **26,** Baldwin-Watriss, Woodfin Camp; **33,** Albertson, Stock, Boston; **33,** Charles Gatewood; **36,** George Gardner; **36,** Eagan, Woodfin Camp; **37,** Eagan, Woodfin Camp; **39,** George Gardner; **40,** Charles Gatewood; **41,** Anderson, Woodfin Camp; **47,** Dietz, Stock, Boston.

Chapter 3
52, Marion Bernstein; **54,** Culver; **56,** Menzel, Stock, Boston; **58,** George Gardner; **62,** Combs, FreeVision; **62,** Combs, FreeVision; **62,** George Gardner; **63,** George Gardner; **65,** Dietz, Stock, Boston; **79,** Combs, FreeVision; **80,** Crews, Jeroboam.

Chapter 4
86, UPI; **90,** Culver; **90,** Culver; **99,** UPI; **101,** Charles Gatewood; **104,** Davidson, Magnum; **106,** Crews, Jeroboam; **109,** Carlson, Stock, Boston; **117,** Charles Gatewood.

Chapter 5
122, George Gardner; **125,** Powers, Jeroboam; **126,** George Gardner; **129,** Lebo, Jeroboam; **133** (*top left and right*), UPI; **133** (*bottom left*), Culver; **133** (*bottom right*), UPI; **137,** UPI; **140,** UPI; **144,** UPI; **145,** Control Data Corporation.

Chapter 6
150, George Gardner; **159,** Franken, Stock, Boston; **161,** UPI; **165,** Charles Gatewood; **167,** Culver; **168,** Culver; **171,** Wide World; **171,** Morrow, Stock, Boston; **171,** Powers, Jeroboam.

Chapter 7
186, Charles Gatewood; **193,** Prelutsky, Stock, Boston; **193,** Graves, Jeroboam; **196,** Shumsky, Jeroboam; **196,** George Gardner; **198,** George Gardner; **204,** Joel Gordon; **211,** Wolinsky, Stock, Boston; **215,** Combs, FreeVision.

Chapter 8
222, Joel Gordon; **226,** George Gardner; **230,** Christelow, Jeroboam; **234,** George Gardner; **236,** George Gardner; **238,** Herwig, Stock, Boston; **245,** Finch, Stock, Boston; **247,** UPI; **247,** Combs, FreeVision.

Chapter 9
254, George Gardner; **257,** Culver; **263,** Abbell, Stock, Boston; **264,** Berndt, Stock, Boston; **271,** George Gardner; **282,** Patterson, Stock, Boston.

Chapter 10
290, Powers, Jeroboam; **293,** Joel Gordon; **296,** Grace, Stock, Boston; **298,** Berndt, Stock, Boston; **299,** Combs, FreeVision; **299,** Powers, Jeroboam; **308,** Berndt, Stock, Boston; **312,** Wide World; **313,** Stewart, Jeroboam; **315,** Virginia Hamilton.

Chapter 11
326, George Gardner; **329,** Culver; **334,** Wide World; **334,** Mazzacki, Stock, Boston; **336,** Wide World; **338,** Miller, DPI; **339,** Virginia Hamilton; **339,** Charles Gatewood; **342,** Combs, FreeVision; **348,** Vilms, Jeroboam; **348,** Lowering, Stock, Boston; **350,** Combs, FreeVision; **357,** Southwick, Stock, Boston.

Chapter 12
362, Charles Gatewood; **376,** Hamlin, Stock, Boston; **377,** Charles Gatewood; **379,** Vilms, Jeroboam; **381,** Charles Gatewood; **383,** Combs, FreeVision; **385,** George Gardner; **387,** UPI; **389,** Gross, Stock, Boston.

Chapter 13
398, Charles Gatewood; **406,** Bodin, Stock, Boston; **407,** Monroe, DPI; **407,** Charles Gatewood; **409,** George Gardner; **414,** Charles Gatewood; **417,** George Gardner; **422,** George Gardner; **426,** Charles Gatewood; **431,** Combs, FreeVision.

Chapter 14
437, Strickler, Monkmeyer; **442,** George Gardner; **455,** Charles Gatewood; **455,** Charles Gatewood; **460,** George Gardner; **461,** Southwick, Stock, Boston; **463,** Wolinsky, Stock, Boston; **463,** Wolinsky, Stock, Boston; **466,** Wide World; **467,** Charles Gatewood; **477,** Preuss, Jeroboam.

Chapter 15
484, Combs, FreeVision; **488,** Joel Gordon; **489,** Combs, FreeVision; **489,** Combs, Free-Vision; **489,** Combs, FreeVision; **491,** Krathwohl, Stock, Boston; **496,** Culver; **501,** Charles Gatewood; **501,** Charles Gatewood.

Chapter 16
506, George Gardner; **509,** Beckwith Sudios; **514,** Charles Gatewood; **516,** Culver; **517,** Culver; **519,** Culver; **521,** Albertson, Stock, Boston; **523,** Culver; **524,** George Gardner.

I

INTRODUCTION TO SOCIAL PROBLEMS

PROLOGUE 1: CONVERSATION WITH A STUDENT

Student: I still don't know how to define a social problem.

Instructor: A social problem is whatever you, or anyone else, defines as a "problematic" or "bad" condition in society.

Student: But . . . don't sociologists have some objective way to define social problems? What good are you if you can't tell us this?

Instructor: Sociologists do not objectively know what a "good" society is, nor do we know what a "pathological" society is. Like you or anyone, we have opinions, but these are not any more scientific or objective than yours or someone else's.

Student: You still haven't told us what you sociologists are good for, then.

Instructor: We have no way to scientifically define a social problem, but we can do this: We can help you understand, with the tools of science, the causes and reasons for the existence of a social problems that you, a politician, or a housewife define as "bad."

Student: Is that all? Aren't you obligated to tell us what is wrong with society and what to do about its problems?

Instructor: If you know the causes of an event, or problem, then you are in a position to suggest solutions. Sociologists cannot tell you what is "bad" in society, we can only inform people about the causes of matters considered problematic, and this information can be used to construct solutions.

Student: O.K. I'll reserve judgment for a few weeks on what sociologists are good for.

In the late 1960s, during the peak of student unrest, I was often confronted this way at the end of my first lecture in a social problems course. This conversation focuses on the key issues we must approach in the study of social problems: (1) Science cannot be used to determine what is "wrong" with society. (2) Science can, however, help us understand the causes of conditions that some people for whatever reason, define as a "problem."

1

APPROACHING THE STUDY
OF SOCIAL PROBLEMS

PROBLEMS IN DEFINING SOCIAL PROBLEMS

Sociology originally emerged as a self-conscious discipline because thinkers were concerned about the social world around them. For once people began to seek secular interpretations of events, they began to ask: What is wrong with society? How can society be changed for the better? Sociologists still ask these questions. Like all members of a society, they are concerned about the conditions of their society. Often the only difference between the professional sociologist and the "person on the street" is that sociologists seek to objectively study the facts surrounding "problematic" events.

To study objectively and scientifically a condition defined as a "problem" does not mean, however, that all people will agree on what conditions are problematic. One person's problem can be another's paradise. Even among sociologists there is disagreement over the problems of American society. While sociologists may all agree to study societal problems objectively, they will often choose different features of the society to study. For example, twenty-five years ago very few people viewed the ecosystem and environment as a problem area. Today the topic can hardly be ignored. Who, to take another obvious example, considered sexual discrimination and inequality a problem twenty years ago? But who today could not see sexism as a problem? Even when problems do not suddenly emerge from "nowhere," there are subtle shifts in what are defined as major problem

Sociologists and objectivity

Thirty years ago these were not considered to be social problems by most, but rather as signs of "progress and prosperity." Today many would see these as social problems.

areas. In the 1960s, the "ghetto" and the associated racial turmoil were a major problem. Now this situation is viewed as less "troublesome," despite the fact that ghetto conditions remain the same. Or, student activism was a major problem just a few years ago, but today student *in*activism over social and moral issues is viewed by some as a problem.

What is evident, then, is that defining social problems is an illusive task. We might all agree that conditions that cause harm to people and society are problems, but we would probably disagree over what is "harmful." Is marijuana harmful? prostitution? gambling? homosexuality? divorce? capitalism? inequality? welfare? Our answers would vary, and for a simple reason: It is often difficult to determine if a practice or condition is harmful to either individuals or society. And sometimes we are placed in the situation of determining if one "harm" is worse than another. For example, is a recession or its cure, high unemployment, more harmful? Or, is the loss of jobs more harmful than environmental controls that limit construction and production? The answer to these questions would vary depending on whom one asked.

What is harmful to society?

Thus, we are left with a "problem" in studying social problems: What do we study? And what criteria should be used in selecting problems for study? Some possible criteria include:

1. those conditions that violate a majority's sense of right and wrong,
2. those conditions that a majority of social scientists agree are "bad" for individuals and society,

Criteria for identifying social problems

3. those conditions that politicians regard as bad for individuals and society,
4. those conditions that a highly vocal minority regards as bad,
5. those conditions that the powerful regard as bad,
6. those conditions that college students regard as bad,
7. those conditions the media regard as bad,
8. those conditions that the author of a social problems text regards as bad, and so on, for any group, person, or segment of the society.

   If we choose any one of the above criteria, we would ignore many conditions that other people regard as bad. If we took only those problems defined as such by a majority of the population, many conditions defined as problematic by others—including most social scientists—would be ignored. If the majority ruled, for example, inequality, sexual discrimination, poverty, racism, and environment, would not, by recent opinion polls, be defined as major problems. The reverse would be true for many citizens if only conditions selected by social scientists were regarded as problems.

   For this reason, sociologists often open their texts with lengthy discussions on scientific criteria for isolating the problematic from the nonproblematic. Such discussions perpetuate an illusion—the belief that we know what is "good" and "bad" in society. We do not. Science can enable us to study problems objectively, but it cannot select our problems for us. This we must do as members of our society. Thus, the coverage of social problems in this book will use illdefined criteria for selecting the problematic, but scientific criteria for gath-

Science cannot define a social problem

Are these social problems? How would they be defined as such? By whom? If their actions are defined as problematic, then the cause of the problem resides in the social situation, not the individual.

ering and reporting the evidence will guide the analysis of the topics selected for study. A combination of the criteria previously listed has been used to select problem-area topics: (1) the author thinks a condition is "bad," (2) the author perceives from opinion polls that the general public believes some condition is "problematic," (3) the author believes from discussions with students that they see some condition as "bad" or "problematic," and (4) the author thinks that most social scientists will agree that the conditions selected are problematic. This definition of social problems is not as academic as that found in other texts, but it is more honest. Most importantly, it recognizes that *the selection of social problems for study is ultimately a subjective assessment.* But once selected, subjectivity can be suspended. It is the desire of social scientists to suspend subjectivity when analyzing social conditions. Their objectivity separates them from the "person on the street" and enables them to reach insights and conclusions about the causes of events that others might not see.

PRELUDE TO THE SOCIOLOGICAL PERSPECTIVE

Americans live in an "individualized" culture. We tend to see events as the result of individual motivations, of individual moralities, or of individual failings. This individualization of the world leads to the following kinds of conclusions: People are poor because they do not

Only little over a decade ago Americans "discovered" the poverty of the inner city—the slum and the deteriorating school—but today most Americans rarely think about these conditions.

want to work. Corrupt politicians have created an unresponsive system of government. Individuals must all pitch in and stop polluting in order to solve environmental problems. Marriages do not work out because people do not try hard enough. Industry is unresponsive to social needs because industrialists are greedy people.

We often reason this way in everyday conversations. We seek answers to problems in the individual psychology of the participant instead of in possible societal influences. Sociologists do not ignore individual psychology, but they ask two interesting questions: (1) What makes individuals act the way they do? (2) What makes people appear, by some moral yardstick, greedy, lazy, corrupt, or unre-

Whose actions are the more "problematic"? Is the urban protester a problem? Or, is the harsh police reaction a problem? Or both? People's answers to these questions will vary because they are a matter of subjective assessment.

solved? When we ask such questions we are beginning to approach a topic sociologically. We are asking, in effect: Do social conditions make people what they are? Sociologists answer this question by developing concepts and theories about the way culture and social structure shape human conduct. They tend to view most human thought and action as carried out within boundaries and constraints imposed by culture and society. Thus, people appear evil, corrupt, or lazy because they are forced to act in a cultural and social system that limits their options and induces or constrains them to act in certain ways. Considering this perspective, the causes of social problems do not reside in individual psychologies (although they certainly affect individual lives), but in a system of cultural and structural arrangements.

Social problems do not reside in individuals

When we identify a social condition as a problem, we are saying that something is wrong with the structure and culture of society. For a condition to be sufficiently prominent to be labeled a problem by the public, students, or social scientists, it must be rooted in the basic culture and structure of American society. For example, if pollution is defined as a problem, its causes are not the "evil profit motives" of industrial capitalists or "insensitive and job-hungry hard hats." Rather, the causes are in a *system* of beliefs and practices that force industries to seek profits and communities to dump sewage, regardless of environmental consequences, and that provide workers with few work alternatives for income outside environmentally harmful activities. Or, if poverty is viewed as a problem, its causes do not lie in the "laziness" of the poor, nor in the malevolence of the rich. Its causes reside in a *system* of beliefs and established practices which deny economic and educational opportunities to certain groups in the society. Or, if rising divorce rates are defined as a problem, the cause is not a loosening of individual morality, but a change of values and structural arrangements in the institution of the family.

Social problems are thus conditions whose cause inhere in cultural and social arrangements. Often, these problem-producing arrangements are defined as "good" or "necessary" by a majority of Americans. Social problems are therefore not always the result of structures that people would define as bad. For example, while many would view poverty as a severe problem of American society, they would not see the political and economic structure, as well as the cherished beliefs associated with these structures, as bad. And yet, the causes of poverty may lie within these structures and beliefs. While most Americans viewed Watergate abuses, as well as spying on citizens by the FBI, IRS, Pentagon, and CIA, as bad, few are ready to reject the American political system. But in point of fact, it was the

Are these people's problems—loneliness, poverty, and despair—"their own fault"? Or, is it "the system" that forces them to live a life without meaning?

political *system*, not just immoral incumbents, that was the cause of these problematic events.

At this stage, of course, no evidence has been introduced to support the theme that social problems inhere in those cultural and structural arrangements which most Americans cherish. Yet, the basic principle of the sociological approach to social problems must be stated early, before we begin to examine specific problems: *Social problems are caused by social and cultural arrangements in society.* And because people believe in the cultural values that legitimize the social structures that shape their lives, they are often reluctant to see them

Social problems are caused by social and cultural arrangements

Individuals are influenced by groups. Their actions are the result of group forces, even actions that appear to assert "individuality." The person above is able to make this statement to a hostile public because of the support recieved from a group.

changed. For this reason, a corollary to the previously stated approach can be offered: *Social problems are difficult to eliminate because their solution will often require a change—usually a great change—in people's beliefs, values, and daily lives.* It is for this reason that sociological treatments of social problems often appear both "radical" and "impractical." People understandably do not want to have their values, beliefs, and daily routines viewed as the causes of evils in the society. Nor do they wish to change a society that, for the majority in America, has brought "the good life."

Few sociologists are political radicals; few are political conservatives; most lie somewhere between. Thus, a sociological analysis which appears radical does so not from political motivations, but from the simple truth that social problems reside in what for most people are "good" social arrangements. And thus, if we are to understand social problems, we must be willing to suspend our commitments to existing cultural and social arrangements. Unless we are willing to do this, we would abandon the scientific goal of understanding the causes of those events and conditions that are defined, by various criteria and by different people, as social problems.

Sociology and politics

And thus, a sociological perspective on social problems must ask: What is the nature of culture? What is social structure? And for our purposes, what is the nature of culture and social structure in American society? To answer these questions, we must suspend our tendency toward "individualizing the world." We must be willing to look beyond specific people and examine the social and cultural forces that often constrain the individual, for it is in these broader forces that the causes of social problems are to be found.

SUMMARY

Defining a "social problem" presents the difficulty of selecting criteria to be used to define a condition or event as a problem. Sociologists who write social problems text sometimes pretend that there are objective scientific reasons for determining the problematic. This is not true. But once selected, by whatever and whoever's criteria, social problems can be studied objectively. In this book we have selected problems that concern the public, students, instructors, and this author.

Available data and evidence are presented for understanding the causes of these selected problems. To present the data and employ a sociological perspective means that we must resist the temptation to individualize events. Social problems are caused by social and cultural arrangements. People may often view these arrangements as good, but we must also recognize that they also pose problems that people define as bad. Sociologists are not necessarily political radicals who criticize the good society; rather, they simply seek to understand the cultural and structural causes of events that become social problems.

REVIEW QUESTIONS

1. Can scientific methods be used to define social problems for people?
2. Are one set of criteria for defining social problems better than another set?
3. What distinguishes the social scientist's examination of social problems from the average person on the street?
4. Why do analyses of social problems by sociologists often appear "radical" or "too extreme?"
5. What is meant by the term *individualization* of social problems and what is the sociological alternative?

PROLOGUE 2: THE DIFFICULT QUESTION

People often ask: What is sociology? The answer is superficially simple, and yet it has extensive implications that cannot be communicated in a few sentences. My answer is: Sociologists study the structure and processes of society and culture. Some people appear satisfied by this answer, others become frustrated. But in order to answer them fully, it would be necessary to define culture and society, indicate their nature, discuss the relationship between culture and society, and indicate how they affect, and are affected by, people. And to talk intelligently about these matters, one must invoke new terms and concepts—that is, jargon—which would quickly bring on a blank stare.

Studying social problems presents the same dilemmas: We need some tools or concepts to understand our topic. We need to understand the basic nature of culture and social structure as well as their relationship to each other and to the individual person. We also need to invoke some jargon to describe culture and society. In Chapter 2, the discussion is kept as simple as possible and the jargon is limited in an effort to avoid the "blank stare" phenomenon. Chapter 2 is also analytical and it seeks to provide a framework for understanding the individual, culture, and society. With this understanding, we will be better able to appreciate, and with less difficulty the reasons for the existence of social problems. Thus, with some analytical background as a framework, we can simplify our task for the remainder of the book.

2

THE SOCIOLOGY OF SOCIAL PROBLEMS

Before exploring specific social problems, it is necessary to examine in more detail the sociological perspective. For if social problems are caused by cultural and social structures, then we must learn more about these forces. In this way it will be possible to approach the study of social problems with conceptual tools that can provide insights into why social problems exist and persist in American society.

CULTURE AND SOCIAL PROBLEMS

For sociologists, *culture* refers to the systems of symbols—such as language, values, beliefs, technologies, religious doctrines, art, and music—created and transmitted by humans living in society. Humans are unique in their ability to surround themselves in a world of symbols that are used as resources to guide their behaviors and organize themselves in societies. The social world of humans would be impossible without our ability to create and use symbol systems to regulate our affairs.

    Sociologists tend to be most interested in those features of culture that guide and regulate patterns of interaction and social organization. While art, music, literature, and language influence human interaction and organization, sociological analysis typically focuses on systems of symbols which have more direct consequences for regulating and guiding everyday human affairs. This focus is often re-

Culture

17

ferred to as the study of "idea systems." Sociologists are most interested in how interacting humans create ideas that, in turn, feed back and shape the course of their interaction. While humans are not highly "programmed" by instincts, they tend to create their own programming, and it is this cultural programming that gives a regularity and predictability to human behaviors. Three types of ideas are considered to be most important in influencing human interaction and conduct: (1) values, (2) beliefs, and (3) norms.

1. *Values* are highly abstract criteria that the people of a society share about what is a good, bad, appropriate, or inappropriate action. Values provide the standards by which people judge all actions—their own and those of others. And as such, values represent a powerful force in shaping human thought and action in society. Indeed, the dominant structures in a society—the economy, family, religions, communities—are likely to reflect people's concepts about what is appropriate.

Values

2. While values transcend all situations in a society, *beliefs* apply to specific situations. Beliefs are less general, applying to such concrete situations as the work place, the school, the government, the economy, the church, and any of the many social situations that people in a complex society encounter. Values, in contrast, apply to all these situations and provide the abstract criteria for judging what is "good" and "bad" in these situations. Some beliefs say what *ought* to exist in a specific situation and thus represent the concrete application of more general values to the particular social context. For example: "Welfare cheaters ought to be put to work" is a *belief* held by some about what should or ought to be done about welfare. Or, to take another example: "People should have jobs" is a *belief* about what should occur in the economic sphere. Both of these beliefs reflect more abstract values about "being active" and trying to "master your destiny." Notice how these *values* are very general and can be applied to any situation, while the beliefs represent concrete applications of these values to a specific situation, such as welfare and the economic sphere. Other beliefs do not indicate what should be, but rather, what actually *does exist* in a specific situation. They say what does or what is, not what should be. For example, "many people on welfare cheat" indicates what actually does exist; or, "most people work" indicates a conception of what is. Such beliefs do not necessarily have to be accurate—many are not, as is the case with the belief that most people on welfare cheat. People often hold inaccurate conceptions about the world around them. Such inaccuracy is the result of many forces: they do not have enough information; values about what is "good" distort their perceptions; or, beliefs about what should exist in a particular situation similarly bias their understanding of what actually is. Be-

Beliefs

liefs are thus a very complex system of ideas. They link values to specific contexts when they indicate what ought to or what should exist; values also reflect what is, although often in a distorted manner. What is important to recognize at this juncture in our analysis is that beliefs are a powerful force in shaping human conduct and are, thus, intimately involved in the definition and substance of social problems.

3. *Norms* are specific instructions about how people in various social contexts should behave. Norms are tied to social situations. They indicate how people are to play roles, such as the roles of father, mother, student, child, worker, voter, legislator. Norms are often defined in formal laws and administrative codes of conduct but equally often they are informal, yet "understood" by all. Norms reflect the actual requirements of a situation, but norms also conform to basic values and beliefs about *how* tasks should be performed. For example, norms can specify the technical aspects of how to put windshields into cars on an assemblyline, but they also reflect values and beliefs about the manner, such as the efficiency, speed, or quality, in which the job should be done.

Norms

IDEAS AND THE DEFINITION OF SOCIAL PROBLEMS

Most human conduct is guided by a complex system of ideas which sociologists commonly label values, beliefs, and norms. The institutions, communities, and organizations of human society are likewise shaped by this complex of ideas. In many ways humans are slaves to their own symbolic creations. Ideas not only say how we should behave, but they legitimize the structures shaping our lives and make them seem right and proper. There are exceptions, however. There is never a perfect consensus over ideas, and people do not always "give in" to the dominant ideas of a society. This fact will help us understand how social problems arise, or at least, become defined. For indeed, in a society where everyone accepted the same cultural values, shared the same beliefs, and conformed to the same norms, social problems could not exist. Everyone would agree on what was right; all would perceive the same things; and all would behave as required. But in reality people often do not "see eye to eye." While most Americans share certain common values and beliefs, and while most seem willing to conform to crucial norms, we can still identify certain conditions as violating our interpretation of values and beliefs. Or, we can see deviations from norms as being too extreme or as quite tolerable. For example, Americans can have intense and even violent disagreement over the "problemness" of school busing to achieve racial integration. For some busing is necessary to realize cherished values of equality and beliefs that all children should have an equal oppor-

Ideas (symbols) influence what people view as problematic

tunity. For others, busing is seen to violate the deeply rooted values of freedom of choice and beliefs in "local autonomy and control." Thus, the application of separate sets of criteria, as well as values, beliefs, to a particular situation can lead to entirely different definitions of the "problemness" of that situation.

IDEAS AND THE SUBSTANCE OF SOCIAL PROBLEMS

Cultural ideas influence more than just the definition of social problems. They influence the actual substance or existence of a problem. For example, the violence that has been associated with busing is a result of people's refusal to let their basic values and

Ideas are a powerful force in shaping human thought and action. People's ideas influence what they see as "wrong" with the world, while at the same time channeling their actions in directions that may be defined by others, holding different ideas, as "problems."

beliefs be violated. Thus, parents and children have been moved to violence, while the courts and police have been forced to respond repressively. Each group operates under a different system of values and beliefs, creating the violence that has become a problem.

Culture can therefore influence both the *definition* and *existence* of conditions which become defined as problematic. This is why social scientists must be alerted to culture and its influence on human conduct. For our purposes in this introductory chapter, then, we must recognize that many social problems are the result of cultural arrangements, especially of contradictions among values, beliefs, norms, and social structure. Stated in such an abstract way, it is perhaps difficult to visualize just what these contradictions might be and just how they generate social problems. In each of the remaining chapters of this book where a specific set of social problems is discussed, it will be our task to analyze these cultural arrangements in an effort to see how they can help us understand the definition and substance of social problems. But cultural arrangements present only part of the picture. A cultural analysis of social problems would be incomplete. We must also understand the nature of our social structure and its relationship to culture.

Culture and human conduct

SOCIAL STRUCTURE AND SOCIAL PROBLEMS

The concept of structure denotes stable relationships among components. This can apply to positions occupied by people. The organizational chart of a business corporation represents one way of visualizing structure. It outlines positions—such as president, vice president, comptroller, payroll manager—while specifying the relationship of authority among them. But as those studying business, or any type of organization, have discovered, this formal structure does not reveal the full extent of informal relations among the people who occupy the positions. Thus, a *social structure* is the totality of relations among positions within a social context. It indicates the way in which positions occupied by people are related to each other. Stated in the most static terms possible, a social structure is a map that relates positions within society to each other. But, of course, real social structures are dynamic, filled with processes occurring among interacting people. In studying society, we must be attuned to both dynamic and stabilizing processes as people create, maintain, and change the way they organize themselves.

Social structure

The structuring of human affairs is possible because we can create and use symbols. Symbols allow humans to communicate with each other and to regulate their affairs. Social structure is then a "structure" because people elaborate ideas, called norms, to govern their concrete relations and then elaborate additional ideas, termed beliefs and values, to justify and legitimize their patterns of regulation. In this way people can "see" much the same world, they can believe in the same goals, and they can view action from the same standards of appropriateness and inappropriateness. The word *same* is, of course, an overstatement because "similar" is about as close as humans get to achieving a consensus of ideas. And as already noted, consensus is often fragile, easily degenerating into conflict and dissensus.

Symbols are basic to social structures

One of the remarkable outcomes of humans' symbol-using capacity is the diversity of ideas and structures that they create. Perhaps even more remarkable, however, is the similarity among social structures that humans have evolved. In fact, all human societies reveal three basic types of social structures: (1) institutional systems, (2) community systems, and (3) distributive systems. The term *system* merely underscores the structure or patterns among the parts of these basic forms of organization.

Types of social structures

1. *Social institutions* are those structures that organize conduct for the task of resolving the most fundamental problems facing humans: how to eat, how to govern, how to procreate, how to control tension, how to induce conformity, how to regularize sex, and how to coordi-

Social institutions

The institution of the family has changed dramatically, becoming a smaller, isolated unit.

The economy has become more industrialized, creating new work relationships for people.

nate activities. In most primitive societies these protein problems are dealt with by the institution of kinship, or in modern terms, the family. Such family institutions are much different from the ones familiar to us, but it is not a gross oversimplification to view most activity as being carried out in the familylike units. In more complex societies, however, separate institutions evolve to cope with different types of problems. The economy evolved to deal with problems of securing resources from the environment and converting them into life-maintaining commodities. Government became separated from kinship to deal with the problems of allocating power to organize and control societywide action. Laws emerged to regulate and coordinate activities, at the same time sanctioning certain forms of deviance. Educational institutions assume many of the socialization functions formally performed by parents in the family. Modern societies like the United States, then, will reveal many separate institutions—family, economy, government, education, law—for dealing with universal dilemmas facing humans.

Naturally, institutions are highly interrelated, and this is what enables us to call them an institutional *system*. For indeed, what happens in the economy affects family patterns, and vice versa. What government does reverberates throughout society. What occurs in all institutions has consequences for events in others.

As the society has grown government has become a huge bureaucracy.

The school has assumed many of the functions formerly performed by the family.

2. *Communities* are geographical units which provide people with a place to live and carry out their diverse activities. Just *how* these activities are carried out, however, is influenced by institutions. For example, how one lives in a home is affected by the institution of the family; how one works is determined by the economy; how one is governed by the polity; how one is socialized by family and education. The fact that institutions are involved in community processes raises the question: Are communities a separate type of structure? Sociologists generally answer yes to this question because communities can, independently of institutions, determine *where* and *in what pattern* people will reside and act. The influence of institutions on geographical or spatial patterning underscores an important facet of human organization: Structures interpenetrate and influence each other. For example, just as the economy may affect the way people work and transport themselves, the patterns of the community (its zoning laws, tax base, size, road system, and composition of citizens) will influence the types of economic organizations that can exist.

Many social problems inhere in *interpenetration*. For example, the conflict between workers in search of construction jobs and environmentalists in pursuit of control over land use often represent two forces: the workers an economic force, the environmentalists a community force. One group wants economic expansion, the other wants greater community control over land use. Thus, in studying social problems, we must be attuned to problems *within* and *between* institutions and communities. Even though institutions and communities are highly interdependent, if we did not separate the two, we could miss much insight into the causes of social problems.

3. All societies, except perhaps the most simple and primitive, unequally distribute valued resources such as money, power, and prestige. The most salient feature of the *distributive system* in a society is its "social class" structure. Social classes are relatively homogeneous groupings of people in a society who possess a similar share of scarce resources. When we talk about the "working class," the "middle class," the "rich," or the "poor," we are distinguishing large groupings of people in terms of their share of the valued resources—money, prestige, and power.

Distributive systems, institutions, and communities also interpenetrate. Government, for example, influences the distribution of power, and the economy the distribution of money. Communities, in determining where people live, can affect people's access to valued resources, such as money-earning work opportunities, or educational opportunities, or perhaps, political participation and the opportunities to acquire power. While the profile of distributive systems is shaped by community and institutional forces, the reverse is also

Communities

Distributive systems

true. The structure of a social class and the kinds of resources possessed by its members influences basic institutions and the patterning of communities. For example, residential patterns in communities are often a reflection of people's access to resources and of their class position. Residential ghettos are, for instance, clear manifestations of the distributive system in a society.

The organization of the community is diverse, but its structure sets the pattern for how people live and work.

Inhering in the distributive system are many social problems in America—poverty and racism being two of the most obvious. Much of the tension and conflict between members of the society occurs over how resources are to be distributed. Ghetto riots, hard hat protests, wildcat strikes, taxpayer's revolts, women's liberation, and the like are the result of the unequal distribution of scarce resources.

In sum, human societies reveal three basic structures: institutional systems, community systems, and distributive systems. These structures evidence very complex patterns of interdependence. The arrows connecting the three types of structures in Figure 1 denote this mutual interdependence. Within the institutional system, the family, economy, religion, government, law, and education have their own internal structures. These institutions also comprise a system of institutions with a highly complex network of interrelations, represented in Figure 1 by the "social ties" connecting the basic institutions. Communities reveal their own structure of residential patterns, transportation networks, recreational facilities, schools, work areas, and the like. Such patterns vary for each community and yet, as is represented by the community system in Figure 1, communities in America have many common features. Social classes can be isolated within the distributive system, ranging from upper to middle, middle to working, and working to poverty. These classes have their own internal life-styles, but equally important, there are relations between social classes.

The structures of a society are highly complex, especially a society as advanced and large as America. It is this complexity *within* the institutional, distributive, and community systems as well as *between* these systems that makes the understanding of social problems so difficult. Moreover, we must remember that all facets of these structures, and their multitude of relations, influence and are influenced by cultural values, beliefs, and norms. Thus, in studying social problems in America we must examine the incredibly complex relations among, within, and between the components of culture and society. It is here that social problems originate—in their cultural and structural bases.

AMERICAN CULTURE AND SOCIETY

In order to place our discussion in context with later chapters, it is necessary to outline some of the most prominent features of American culture and society. In particular, it is desirable to profile basic American values that provide the "core ideas" influencing the forma-

Figure 1 **The Basic Structure of Society**

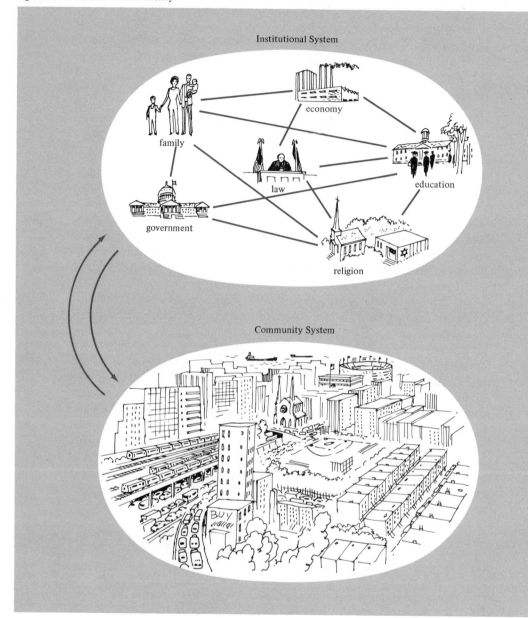

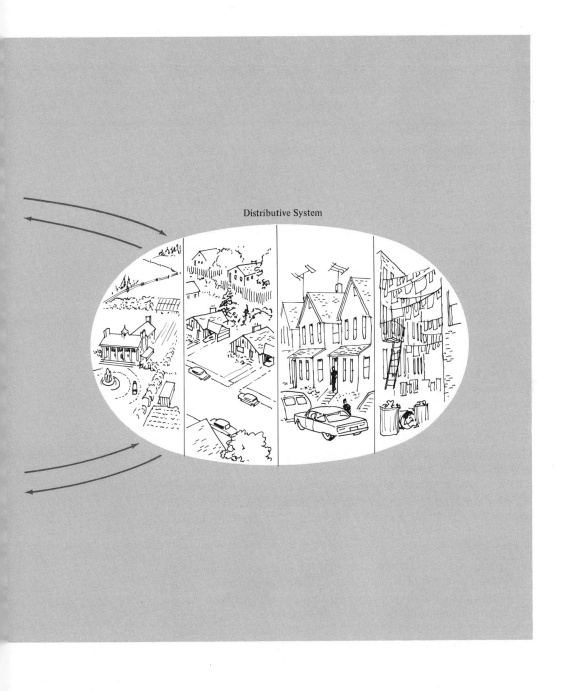

Distributive System

tion of beliefs. Later, as we delve into specific problems associated with a concrete social structure, we can discuss how these values become translated into beliefs and norms influencing people's thoughts and actions in society. And just as an understanding of the basic profile of American culture is necessary, we should also briefly sketch the basic features of American social structure—a sketch that will guide us in our analysis of specific social problems in later chapters.

CULTURE: THE CORE VALUES

As discussed earlier, values represent highly abstract and general standards among members of a society for assessing appropriate and inappropriate conduct in most social settings. Not all values are seen as relevant by people to each and every social setting, but almost all interaction in society is guided by several core values. Our task in this section is to isolate the most basic values of American culture. We must recognize, of course, that the list of values offered represents a simplification of the complex value processes occurring in people's minds. But as we will see, this kind of simplifying activity is necessary if we are to understand American culture and its consequences for social problems.

Core values

1. *Activism.* Americans value—that is, they think it proper—to take a manipulative stance toward the world around them. They value actively seeking to master situations in the most "rational" and "efficient" manner possible. It would be impossible to understand Americans or American society without appreciating the extent to which this value is embedded in our emotions and consciousness. How could we, for example, understand the energy and even frenzy with which Americans approach tasks, whether landing on the moon, increasing productivity, providing the material comforts of life, or hustling a date. Thus, much of the negative reaction of Americans to "laziness," "idleness," and "loafing" can only be appreciated when it is recognized that such activities are being judged by the value of activism.

2. *Achievement.* Americans value doing well and excelling. They also value winning in competition, whether it be for a promotion, a vicarious victory on the television football field, or in getting a good grade on an examination. Achievement and success are truly dominant orientations of Americans; we strive to be successful in virtually all spheres. We are, for example, desirous of being good students, successful breadwinners, successful parents, great lovers, winning "jocks," and in fact, it is very difficult in American society to find any

activity that is not viewed in terms of doing well, being successful, and where relevant, winning in the competition.

3. Materialism. Americans value accumulating material possessions and comforts. In many ways we believe that the spoils should go to the victors in "life's competition," since those who display material goods have been the most "active" in their lives. Unless we appreciated the extent to which materialism is a part of the American consciousness, we could not understand people's efforts to have "the good life" of cars, recreational vehicles, homes in suburbia, and all the other material symbols of "success" in America. Even among counterculture devotees, who supposedly have rejected materialism, it is possible to observe a concern with acquiring the "right" material possessions—the van, the wardrobe with just the proper elements of grub and chic, and the right living quarters, whether the "trippy" apartment or "far out" dome in the forest. Few Americans can escape their socialization into this value, despite some almost frantic attempts to escape it. But most Americans do not want to escape; they desire ever-increasing accumulations of material things, and while they may become concerned with "tastefully" displaying their material well-being, they nevertheless consider it appropriate to acquire and display their success and achievements through possessions.

4. Progress. Americans also think it appropriate that human efforts be directed toward improving existing conditions. In many ways we maintain that our efforts to be active, to achieve, and to acquire material well-being will improve both the individual and society. That is, they will progress. It is only recently that this value has been challenged by the recognition that progress, as it has traditionally been defined (economic growth and increased wages, for example), does not always lead to a better environment, increased levels of worker contentment, or escalating personal happiness. Yet, this recognition is not so much a rejection of the appropriateness of "progressive" actions, but an indictment that present actions have not led to the *real* progress of a clean environment, worker satisfaction, and personal contentment. Thus, even among those who claim to have rejected the value of progress, it insidiously appears to govern many of their actions. For indeed, progress is a dominant value in America, and despite varying definitions of what progress is, most Americans feel that it is appropriate and necessary to seek improvement of existing conditions.

5. Freedom. Americans value "freedom" from external controls and constraints. To be free from regulation is one of the most de-

sirable goals for Americans, and despite their inability to attain freedom in many spheres, such as the economic, most Americans fantasize and seek to be "freer" from constraints than they presently are. In many ways the compulsiveness with which Americans pursue "open road" recreation—campers, trailers, dirt motorcycles, dune buggies, skydiving, sailing, backwoods jeeps, and the like—is perhaps one indicator of the desire to adhere to a value which, in the urbanized, bureaucratized, and industrialized work world, they cannot realize. The value of freedom, however, extends into many spheres other than people's recreational habits as is the case, for example, when Americans value free elections, free enterprise, or freedom to seek opportunities. Freedom is highly related to other values since efforts to be active, to achieve, and to acquire material comforts lead to the most "progress" when they free individuals from the routines, controls, and constraints of everyday life. Freedom, then, is a core value of American culture.

6. Individualism. While Americans value freedom for many social units—corporations, communities, religious groups, for example— they place even more value on freedom for the individual. In fact, all other values are influenced by the emphasis placed upon the individual, as opposed to the group, in American society. It is the individual who is to be active, the individual who is to achieve, the individual who is to acquire material well-being, the individual who is to better his or her condition, and the individual who is to be free. Americans, then, think that it is appropriate for the individual to shoulder the burden of life, its achievements and its failings. Few societies value the individual as much as the United States, and few societies go to such lengths to assure at least the illusion of individual self-determination in most social matters. To restrict self-determination or to burst the illusion would, in the eyes of most Americans, violate a most important value, individualism.

7. Equality. Americans value equality, that is, the appropriateness of having the same chance to act and achieve in a social setting. Most important, people should be treated equally and should be given "equal opportunities" to realize other values such as activism, achievement, materialism, progress, freedom, and individualism. Few societies value equality as much as the United States, and despite the clear instances of inequality, Americans often delude themselves that there is equality of opportunities for all people. When Americans have been convinced that equality does not exist, they have responded vigorously. But equality is tempered by other values, for some it means equality to achieve and be successful, not

Inequality creates problems of poverty in the midst of affluence.

equality of means or income. It is this tempering of the value of equality that sometimes obscures people's perceptions of inequality. If people are failures, it is "their own fault" or "they did not take advantage of opportunities presented to them." It is only when the lack of equal opportunities can be demonstrated, and conclusively so, that Americans begin to perceive that the value of equality has been violated. To view matters otherwise would violate the values placed upon individual activity, achievement, and success.

8. Morality. Americans tend to view matters in absolute terms: there is a "right" and "wrong" in each situation. This tendency is a reflection of the morality value which makes it appropriate and desirable to determine the "rightness" and "wrongness" in each situation. Many overseas observers have noted this propensity of Americans to view matters in absolute terms, ignoring the many subtleties in, and "shades of gray between," various facets of social life. There are, to put the matter simply, "good guys" and "bad guys," "white hats," and "black hats." The appropriateness of a moral orientation to the social world gives added imperative to other values because to violate activism, achievement, progress, materialism, individualism, equality, and other values can be viewed as "absolutely wrong" and cause for severe judgements, if not punishments. The value of morality often changes the standards of what is "appropriate" to standards of what is "necessary," "right," and "imperative."

9. Humanitarianism. Americans think it appropriate to help those who have been less successful in the "game of life." Those who are unable to be active, to achieve, and to be self-determined, or those who have been denied equal opportunity, should be assisted. But humanitarianism is highly conditional, lest the moral imperative attached to other dominant values be violated. Thus, for those who can, but have chosen not to be active and to achieve, "society does not owe them a living." It is this highly conditional nature of humanitarianism that makes Americans, to outsiders, seem at the same time like the most generous and most punishing people on earth. But when the fact that humanitarianism is circumscribed by other values is recognized, this seeming contradiction becomes less difficult to understand. Americans are, under the "right" conditions, very generous to the less fortunate, but when conditions are "wrong," they can be niggardly. Such is the power the value humanitarianism has in American social life.

10. Conformity. Not all values are consistent and the value of conformity is an example of how people can hold what would appear to be contradictory values. Americans value conformity to dominant standards in any social situation; deviance is looked upon in negative, and moral, terms. Yet, Americans also value individualism and freedom—two values that would seem to dictate a tolerant attitude toward nonconformity. But such is not the case, although Americans are becoming more reconciled in recent decades to nonconformity in people's life-styles. But even in the so-called new or alternative life-styles, it can be noted that there is a considerable degree of conformity in dress, speech, hairstyles, and other features of the facades people display. As many commentators have noted, businessmen and "rock" stars look very much alike when compared to their respective cohorts. This similarity of appearances and actions in diverse subcultures perhaps attests to the operation of the value conformity, even in groups that have rejected the dominant standards for judging conformity. Americans thus value conformity, and it is for this reason that it is relatively easy, without much inquiry, to determine which "trip," "culture," "bag," or "scene" an individual in America is "in," "on," or "into."

This profile of core American values is obviously simplified, but does offer a beginning point for understanding American culture, especially as it influences social problems. As we will come to appreciate in the analysis of social problems in America, the definition and substance of each social problem is greatly influenced by the various combinations of values as they become translated into diverse beliefs and norms.

Values influence social problems

To take a simple example, "welfare" is often defined as a problem in America because in the eyes of many citizens it is seen as violating a "work ethic"—a dominant belief based on such core values as activism and achievement. If Americans did not hold these values, the "problemness" of welfare and welfare "cheaters" would not exist. But core values influence more than just the definition of a social problem, they are also involved in the substance of the problem. To illustrate, the poor are highly resentful of the welfare system that seems abusive and restrictive, and at times this resentment is translated into civil disorder, heated political debate, protests, and court battles. For the recipients, the problems of welfare "cheating" and "welfare abusers" are not the problems of recipients but those of the administrators of the system. The system reflects the highly conditional core value humanitarianism and is thus consonant with the majority of American values and beliefs. But, at the same time, the system generates conflicts and tension between recipients on the one hand and taxpayers–administrators on the other. These tensions make "the welfare mess" a highly complex problem—a problem whose definition and cause lie in the structure and culture of the general population, the welfare system, and the recipients of welfare.

It is this complex interplay among values, beliefs, and social structure that makes necessary, at the outset, an understanding of the core values and basic structures of American society. We now have some understanding of America's core values, and before analyzing concrete social problems, a brief sketch of the problems to be found in America's institutional, community, and distributive systems should be provided.

SOCIAL STRUCTURE: INSTITUTIONAL, DISTRIBUTIVE, AND COMMUNITY SYSTEMS

The Institutional System. Like other modern societies, American society reveals a highly differentiated institutional system composed of clearly separated institutions. The family, as we will emphasize in Chapter 3, is "nucleated" and composed of only parents and their offspring. This nuclear structure presents many problems in the modern world. Marriage and divorce become problematic; what to do with   Family
the aged and other "relatives" becomes an issue; who has authority in such a small unit becomes a question; how to raise children when so much socialization is done outside the family raises additional problems; what to do with adolescents—biologically adult but socially defined as children—increasingly becomes a problem; and, how men and women are to relate and divide their household labor when they both work is an issue for one-half of all families. Thus, in

Problems of family tension and the isolation of the elderly have grown with changes in the family.

contrast to the early American family where parents, children, and other relatives lived and worked together, and where marriage, authority, control, and the divisions of labor were unambiguous, the small, mobile contemporary family—for all its apparent freedom and flexibility—encounters a large number of problems.

As the family has given up more functions and become smaller, other institutions have taken on greater prominence. One of these is the educational system which has assumed much of the socialization burden previously performed by the family. As an agent of socialization, elementary schools in America present a spectrum of dilemmas: Who should control the schools? Who should finance them? What is

Educational systems

Dilemmas over how to educate have increased as the school assumes a more dominant role in determining how today's children will function as adults in tomorrow's societies.

the most humane way to education? Whose values should dominate educational socialization? Schools also perform gatekeeping functions: they give credentials that facilitate access to desired jobs. Surrounding secondary and college education are a host of issues which are the subject of constant controversy in America: Do the schools discriminate? If schools train for jobs, who should influence policies: government, industry, family, or community? As the centers of higher learning, what are the functions of the universities: to teach or to do research? Who should influence their policies: the public, the students, or the faculty? Thus, as the educational structure of American society has grown and assumed so many important functions that affect people's lives, it has confronted many problems and dilemmas, as we see in Chapter 4.

As the seat of power in society, government is always a center of controversy because ultimately government can regulate and control virtually all processes in society. There are many enduring controversies in America surrounding government: Who should control the controllers? Does the public have a voice? Are politicians responsive, corrupt, or violating people's privacy? What should our national priorities be? Who should set them? Who should have more power: Congress or the president? These and other prominent questions will bc addressed in Chapter 5.

Government

The economy as the institution responsible for securing resources, producing and distributing goods, as well as employing Americans, touches all other institutions and structures in the society. Many problems are evident in the economy, such as: How big should corporations be? How much political influence should they have? Should they seek to make the worker's life better if it means decreased profits? How are inflation and recession to be controlled? What should be the role of government in a capitalistic economic system? How are foreign cartels to be dealt with? These and other questions will be addressed in Chapter 6.

The economy

The Distributive System. There is a great inequality in the distribution of income and wealth in American society. A relatively small portion of the population (as little as 1%) controls 30 percent of all wealth, and 20 percent holds 76 percent of the wealth. The extent and consequences of such inequality will be thoroughly discussed in Chapter 7, with an eye to such questions as: Is inequality a problem in itself, and does it contribute to other problems?

Inequality

In Chapter 8, one facet of the distributive system is analyzed: the existence of a large poverty class in America. This poverty class, depending upon whose statistical definition of poverty is used, totals between 35 and 50 million people and represents one of the more enduring problems confronting America. Important questions which Chapter 8 will address include: Why does a poverty class exist in the most affluent land in the world? What perpetuates poverty? And what problems does it cause for American society?

Poverty

In Chapter 9 we will examine how inequality in America is compounded by another problem: racial and ethnic discrimination. Such discrimination has kept many "minorities" at the bottom of the social class system—a situation that has been a constant source of tension and conflict. How did this happen? Why does discrimination persist?

Racial and ethnic discrimination

Sexism and sexual discrimination are examined in Chapter 10. Fe-

males constitute a majority of the population, and yet, they have
been subjected to economic, legal, and political discrimination. They
have, as a group, been denied equal access to money, power, and
prestige. Why? What forces perpetuate this situation? Are there
changes in the wind?

Sexism

    The Community System. America is an urban society—the entire
population of 212 million is compressed into only 2 percent of the
land areas of this huge country. America is also a metropolitan society with a majority of the population residing in areas with a large
central city, surrounded by smaller suburban cities. How did this
come to pass? Why does this urban profile cause problems of financing, decision making, central city decay, racial and ethnic tensions,
and the other problems of the central city in metropolitan America?
These problems will be discussed in Chapter 11.

The central city

*America's system of inequality is compounded by racial and ethnic
tensions.*

America's industrial-urban system has created problems of pollution.

America's cities, communities, and metropolitan areas reveal another problem: segregation. Within any community blacks (and other "distinguishable" minorities) are segregated from whites; and within the entire metropolitan area, blacks are confined to the decaying core of the large central city, surrounded by affluent, white suburbs. How did this come to be? What tensions does it generate? How can the problem be solved, if at all? What does it foretell for the future of community life in America? Chapter 12 will examine these problems.

Segregation

A society is only a part of a much larger ecological community. Humans are, in the end, only one species in a complex network of other species and the life-sustaining substances of the physical environment. But humans are a very special population because their culture, institutions, and communities are structured in ways which could potentially destroy much of the ecosystem. Nowhere is this more of a problem than America, the world's greatest polluter. How could this be so? And why are ecological problems so difficult to resolve? Population, society and the ecological community are thus the topics of Chapter 13.

The ecological community

SOCIAL STRUCTURE AND DEVIATION

Despite values emphasizing conformity, deviations from dominant social patterns are inevitable, especially in a large and differentiated society like the United States. Much deviance becomes defined as a "problem" because it is seen as violating basic values and beliefs, as well as "normal" social structural arrangements. Much of the problemness with respect to deviance, however, stems not from deviant acts per se, but from the way society reacts to them. In fact, the societal reaction can generate more problems than the deviance itself. For example, the reaction of marijuana use for the last fifteen years

The societal reaction to deviance

Transvestites and users of drugs have often suffered from severe societal reactions—reactions that are often part of the problem.

has made criminals of millions of people who, in all other contexts, are law-abiding, while consuming police time and clogging the courts over a crime that does not hurt others or society (the issue of whether it hurts the user is unclear, but recent evidence indicates that the harm, if any, is not great). To take another example, efforts to control "hard" drugs makes them less available which, in turn, raises their price. The high costs of drugs such as heroin forces their users to steal in order to secure the large quantities of money needed to purchase the drugs, thus crime increases. Which is the greater problem: the biological effects of heroin on an individual's body or the increase in crime within society? There is no easy or straightforward answer to such a question, but it is evident that the reaction to deviance can create other problems.

Not only can the societal reaction cause additional problems, it can also aggravate the very problem it seeks to eliminate. For example, it has become clear that throwing criminals into jail does not cure them of their criminal tendencies; on the contrary, it makes them more committed and skilled criminals. Or, to illustrate further, there is evidence that *some* (not all) mental patients become more ill in mental hospitals than if they had not been committed. Again, deviance cannot be understood without examining the societal reaction, for in these reactions lie many problems.

In analyzing problems of deviance in America, then, we must be alerted not only to the causes of the problem per se, but also to the consequences of the reaction to the problem. In particular, we should note the impact of the reaction to deviance on the institutional, distributive, and community systems. Are deviants excluded from participation in institutions such as the economy and government? What consequences does this have for the deviant and the society? Are deviants denied access to scarce resources? Are they relegated to deprived social classes? Are deviants segregated in communities? Are they forced to endure discrimination in community housing, recreation, and education? These are the kinds of questions that a structural analysis of deviance forces us to ask. We must not merely seek the causes of deviance in particular structures, we must also understand the consequences (for social structures) of societal reactions to deviance.

In Chapter 14 we will examine crime. Attention will not focus on the causes of crime (these are unknown), but on the system of criminal justice designed to deal with crime. Important questions will include: Is the system fair? Does it help alleviate the problem or aggravate it?

Crime

Chapter 15 will examine drug use and abuse. What are the consequences of drugs for individuals? What are the consequences of the

Drug use

societal reaction? Has this reaction encouraged the spread of organized crime? And does organized crime encourage the use of drugs?

Chapter 16 focuses on mental illness. As with crime and most forms of deviance, little is known about the cause of adjustment problems facing millions of Americans. Thus, our concern must be on the consequences of the societal reaction. What do we do with the ill? Are people really mentally "sick"? Do our hospitals cure patients or do they aggravate emotional problems?

Mental illness

SUMMARY

This chapter reviewed how social problems inhere in cultural and social structural arrangements. *Culture* was defined as the systems of symbols created and transmitted by humans living in a society. Three types of symbol systems, or idea systems, are studied by sociologists: *values, beliefs,* and *norms.* The definition and substance of social problems is intimately connected to these systems. To help understand American culture, a profile of core values in America was discussed. These *core values* will be used in the analysis of beliefs and norms in subsequent chapters on specific social problems.

Social structure was defined as a relatively stable network of relations among the positions people occupy. The creation and elaboration of a social structure is only possible because of cultural ideas. Moreover, *cultural ideas* regulate and legitimize social structural arrangements. Three structures are universal to human societies: an *institutional system,* a *community system,* and a *distributive system.*

Finally, a section of chapters on the cultural and structural *reactions to deviance* was outlined. Just as problems inhere in basic cultural and structural arrangements, so they inhere in the way society reacts to deviance.

REVIEW QUESTIONS

1. Can you distinguish among cultural values, beliefs, and norms?
2. Can you define and distinguish among the institutional, community, and distributive systems?
3. Can you identify and define the ten core values of American society?
4. What is deviance? Can you explain how the societal reaction to deviance can be a social problem?

GLOSSARY

beliefs ideas about concrete situations or contexts which indicate what should and what does exist

community system geographical social structures where people live and carry out their daily activities

culture the system of symbols created and transmitted by humans and used to guide, regulate, and legitimize their conduct and organization

deviance actions that violate generally accepted norms of appropriate conduct

distributive system those social structures that influence the way valued resources—such as money, power, and prestige—are held by members of a society

idea (symbol) system that system of symbols that guides and regulates concrete patterns of social interaction

institutional system those societywide social structures organized to resolve the universal problems facing all humans

norms highly specific rules or instructions about how people in a particular social situation are to behave

social structure the pattern of relationships among positions occupied by people which persist or endure over time

societal reaction the way the forces of social control and the general public respond to and deal with deviant behaviors in society

values abstract criteria that the people of a society share about what is good, bad, appropriate, or inappropriate

II
PROBLEMS IN THE INSTITUTIONAL SYSTEM

Understanding American society would be impossible without inquiring into the nature of its basic institutions. Much of our social life is conducted within limits imposed by the economy, government, education, and family. These institutions are involved in dealing with the basic exigencies of our daily life—what to eat, how to secure shelter, how to raise our young, how to acquire necessary knowledge, how to maintain order, how to organize activity, and how to make decisions. Structures so intimately connected to people's affairs would obviously be the subject of intense feelings. For indeed, what we are and what we aspire to be are shaped by these basic institutions.

It is inevitable that the institutional arrangements of any society will systematically generate strains and tensions. One of the curious ironies of social life is that institutional structures so instrumental to human survival can pose profound problems for many citizens; and because of their importance to social life, institutions are a major source of problems.

Chapter 3, our first chapter on social institutions, focuses on the problems of family and kinship in America. In many ways, the problems of the American family are the result of the ascendance of separate economic, political, and educational institutions. As we come to appreciate, the family has given many of its functions to other institutions, and in so doing, questions over its structure and operation have arisen. These

questions pose many problems including the "proper" roles for males and females, the "proper" way to socialize the young, and the "proper" place of the aged in American society.

In Chapter 4 we will examine problems in the American educational system. As a major agent of socialization and as an institution determining people's life chances as adults, education is a constant source of turmoil in America. At the lower educational level, questions of who should control, finance, and administer the schools compound dilemmas over how to educate the young. At the higher educational level, questions of the goals and functions of colleges and universities in a modern society still prevail, despite the absence of student protests and violence on campus.

We will shift our attention to the government in Chapter 5, with particular emphasis on the related problems of establishing priorities and making decisions, and on the problem of government abuses and illegalities. These problems of governance have profound consequences on the capacity of American society to deal with any social problem, for if the centers of power and decision making in a society have difficulty in addressing social ills, then such incapacity to establish priorities and make decisions becomes a problem in itself. And as we will come to see throughout the remaining chapters of this book, there is a political dimension to all social problems in America.

Chapter 6 examines the structure of the American economy and its basic problems. Inflation, monopolization, price fixing, recession, "stagflation," coordination and control, nationalization, consumer fraud, worker alienation, and pollution will be viewed as outgrowths of the structure and culture of the economy. This analysis of the economy closes the part on institutional problems because so much of what occurs in American society is influenced by economics. It is, therefore, wise to understand the economy's operation and the inherent problems that it generates before leaving the study of social institutions. The background acquired in Chapter 6 will enable us to understand problems in noneconomic contexts that are, in part, influenced by economic processes.

Social institutions are basic to the functioning of American society and their problems of structure are important topics in their own right. But as will become increasingly clear in the chapters of Parts III, IV, and V, these institutions also determine the distribution of resources, the living patterns of Americans, and societal reactions to deviants. It is for this reason that this book opens with an institutional analysis. Such an analysis will provide a good foundation for examining all social problems in America.

PROLOGUE 3: THE LESS PLEASANT SIDE OF FAMILY LIFE IN AMERICA

In Riverside, California an old woman shuffles down the street in the skid row district. She is pulling a little wire cart with wheels and carrying a few groceries to a small room on the third floor of an old brick building. Along the way, she tells one panhandler and an equally old drunk to let her pass. This woman is alone; her children still live, but they seem to have forgotten about her.

In this same town, or any town in the United States, not too far from skid row in the downtown district, is a court house. In this court house a large number of divorce cases will occupy a bored judge's time. People are giving up and deciding that the romantic fantasies and dreams with which they started the great adventure of marriage have turned into nightmares of quarrels, bickering, and tension.

In some of the neighborhoods of Riverside, or any other town, divorce has not yet arrived. But parents seem unhappy. The husband resents his wife's efforts to "be somebody" and "to get out" of the household work. The wife is jealous, with a smoldering resentment that cannot yet find articulate expression, of her husband's meaningful life and freedom from household chores and the daily clamor of children. The husband can't understand his wife's problems

50

because, after all, he "supports her and the family" and "they never have to worry about food or money."

A teenage boy just had another argument with his father. He left the house in anger, jumped into a car, and sped away, wondering to himself when his father will "get off his case." His father is boiling in anger, not understanding the disrespect of his son. His mother worries that he will "pile up" the car and create more problems for himself and for his relations with his father.

This picture of family life does not correspond to that portrayed in the TV series, "The Waltons," but it is more real. It is the less happy side of family life in America. These events occur every day and it is in a rare family that this does not ring true at some time. They are what many people see as "wrong" with the family in America—an indictment that is made without much knowledge about how to cope with these problems. In Chapter 3 we will address the problems built into the structure of the American family. We will try to understand how the culture and structure of the family and its surrounding society operate to affect actual people, like you as you read this book. Certain problems are common to all families, and the reason for this commonality is that most Americans live within a broad but similar set of cultural and structural contexts. It is this broader context that will be explored in the pages to follow.

3

PROBLEMS IN FAMILY AND KINSHIP

The family is probably the oldest human institution. Indeed, among the first humans, family groupings and the society were one and the same thing. Religious, governmental, educational, and economic activities were carried out within a family. And even today, many preliterate societies do not reveal institutions other than family and kinship.

For most of human history social problems were family and kinship problems. But with industrialization, the family loses many of its functions; economic, political, and educational institutions become separated from the family and have an autonomy of their own. This process of separation between family and other institutions began at least ten thousand years ago. And yet, in many modern societies a clear separation of family has occurred only within the last few hundred years. Such is the case in America and, as we will see, many of the problems of the American family inhere in its rapid transformation from an economic and educational unit to one with fewer functions.

As we have emphasized, institutions are legitimized by values and beliefs. No where is this more likely than in the family since it deals with so many basic human issues—birth, death, children, sex, and companionship. Beliefs are usually more difficult to change, however, than the actual structure of kinship. In fact, beliefs about such a central institution die very hard, even when they contradict the actual operation of family life. Because American society in general, and kinship in particular, have changed rapidly within just the last

Loss of family functions

150 years, the family's functions and structure are often at odds with traditional beliefs about such basic issues as the sexual division of labor, the rearing of children, sexual relations prior to and during marriage, authority relations between males and females, the roles of parenthood, and many other family related activities. As we will begin to appreciate, many problems in the family reside in the conflict between belief and practice. Moreover, new beliefs reflecting alternative family practices now challenge the old, giving many family problems an almost ideological character as strongly held beliefs stand in sharp contrast to each other.

Beliefs and the family

To understand family problems, then, we must first examine the changes occurring in the structure and functions of the family. Then we must examine the cultural conflicts these changes have wrought, for they are intimately connected to the definition and substance of "family problems." And finally, with this broader perspective, we can analyze specific problem areas, including marriage and divorce, male–female roles, dilemmas of child rearing, and the aged.

THE CHANGING FAMILY IN AMERICA

Lineage and Descent In America. At birth a child inherits two separate bloodlines. This fact raises an important question that has profound consequences for family organization: Whose bloodline, or side

Changes in family structure

The traditional American family— several children, two generations of adults, strong male authority, a clear division of labor, and a prohibition against divorce.

of the family, is to be more important? Human societies have evolved three basic answers to this question, reflected in types of *descent* or *lineage norms:* (1) *patrilineal*, when the father's side of the family is defined as most important, (2) *matrilineal*, the mother's is most important, and (3) *bilateral*, both are weighed equally, but neither is of greater importance.

While it is difficult to typify all early American families, descent in preindustrial, rural Americans tended toward a patrilineal system. Loyalty was to the husband's parents; wives were brought to the husband's family farm; and economic activity revolved around the husband's side of the family. With industrialization and urbanization, however, this system quickly changed to a bilateral system of descent where both sides of the family were weighed equally. And with increasing mobility of children in industrial America, descent came to mean less and less as children began to "live their own lives." Thus, lineage is no longer organized around parents, grandparents, and other relatives, but around the marital bond, that is, around an autonomous husband and wife.

Family Residence. At one time, residence, or where husband and wife were to settle, tended to be dictated by descent: people settled with or near the husband's family. But the migration of Europeans who had often broken family ties, as well as the rapid urbanization of indigenous Americans and the subsequent "conquering of the Western frontier," created a normative climate where freedom of residence gradually became the dominant pattern. Families in America are free to move when and where they desire. Today, the average American family moves every five years—a highly mobile family that moves not as a reaction to kinship consideration but in response to economic opportunities.

Family Size and Composition. With the breakdown of lineage and the increased mobility of the urbanized family, the size and composition of the American family changed. In 1850, for example, the average family had almost six members, today less than three. These figures are low, of course, because they are averages of *all* household units, many of which have only one person. What is clear, though, is that family size has shrunk, and so has its composition: grandparents, aunts, uncles, cousins, and other kin have been excluded. These changes in size and composition reflect the urbanization of the population. Large families organized around lineage are not needed to perform farm labor in an urban setting. In fact, they are a liability, since it is harder to move a large family (with diverse kindred) in response to changing economic opportunities. Thus, the American

A modern version of the traditional farm family. Most now live in poverty, and yet they still rely upon their size and the labor that children can perform to survive in a modern, mechanized world.

family is now a small, isolated, conjugal unit that must support itself and that tends to exclude all kin except mother, father, and children.

Division of Labor. In early rural America, the division of labor was clear: women performed household chores—cooking, cleaning, child care; men performed economic tasks related to labor on the farm. With industrialization, however, women became employed outside the home in factories, especially in tasks that were considered "women's work," such as looming in textile mills. With increased industrialization, and the resulting bureaucratization of administrative tasks, women began to perform many clerical roles in the business economy. Today women have expanded their economic activities outside the home into many spheres, even some traditionally defined as "men's work," and around 40 percent of women now participate in the labor force.

The traditional division of labor between household and economic tasks for men and women has thus changed dramatically during the last century. This fact would indicate that the division of labor within the household unit is under pressure to change. Questions about who should do the housework, care for and feed the children, shop, and perform other household tasks are increasingly asked. And as we will see, the ambiguity over the appropriate answer to these questions represents a source of family conflict in America.

Authority in the Family. In a small, mobile conjugal family where the wife often works and where debate over household chores has increased, authority patterns become another arena for potential conflict. Such was not the case in preindustrial America where the husband dominated almost all decision making. One indicator of male dominance in the household was the lack of legal rights possessed by women: Women could not vote until 1920; they could not sit on juries in most states until after World War II; women could not own their own property in a marriage; and, women could not enter legal contracts without her husband's signature. Today women possess these rights and as they have become economic partners with males, the dominance of males in the family is often an issue, with more equal sharing of decision making clearly the trend. Yet, as we will see, the tradition of male dominance still prevails and can create many conflicts and tensions in the family.

Marriage and Divorce. In America, where extended kinship ties to other relatives are weak, the major family unit is not established, maintained, or changed by lineage or descent norms, but by marriage and divorce patterns. The small, isolated conjugal unit is created by marriage and it is altered or dissolved with divorce. In contrast, in preindustrial America the family unit existed prior to and after marriage and divorce since it embodied several generations of relatives who could "carry on" the family of a son or daughter that died, divorced, or remained single. The boundaries of the family in contemporary America are thus defined by the marriage and divorce patterns of the conjugal unit of husband and wife.

Since marriage is no longer a part of a larger kinship system, its control by other relatives has decreased. At one time the choice of a wife by a male was circumscribed by considerations of how she would fit into the larger network of kin, how she could manage a household, and whether her child-rearing potential could help carry on the family line. To some extent the female's selection of a husband was dictated by her family's feelings, but not to the same degree as the male's. Further, in a system where economic work and household activity were intimately connected to a larger cast of kin and to the maintenance of the family line, qualities such as health, reliability, morality, and family background were much more important criteria for mate selection than today.

Presently, as the family has become isolated from other kin and economically self-sufficient, mate selection is more open and free. Mates are selected for their appearance, personality, sexiness, and other qualities related to mutual compatibility. Whether or not the family approves or whether the female is a good homemaker have become less salient—not irrelevant, however—criteria of mate selection. Mate selection is thus a personal rather than kindred decision and it is based on a "love" relationship involving considerations of personal feelings and compatibility. But free choice in terms of vague, and sometimes unrealistic, criteria of "love" creates many problems of adjustment for the family as husbands and wives begin to cope with the practical problems of maintaining their own separate household. One result of the modern love-oriented marriage is an

The modern, extreme family, and perhaps the prototype of the future— more equal authority, one generation of adults, one child, a flexible division of labor, and little fear of divorce. While this couple is considered deviant today, the deviants of a society sometimes foretell the future.

Table 3.1 **The Changing American Family**

Kinship Pattern with Respect to:	Early American Pattern	Contemporary Pattern
Descent and lineage:	some patrilineal	weak and bilateral
Residence:	tendency toward patrilocal	free and open
Size and composition:	large, multi-generational	small, two generations (parents and children)
Division of labor:	clear male and female roles	in flux; ambiguity over male–female roles
Authority:	male-dominated	still male-dominated, but increasing egalitarianism
Marriage and divorce:	marriage regulated; divorce infrequent	marriage free; divorce frequent

increase in divorce. And because it occurs outside a broader kinship system, it presents many problems of adjustment for the couple and their children.

The changes in the structure of the family are summarized in Table 3.1 (Turner, 1972b:95). The American family has moved from a stable patrilineal system of large, multigenerational family units with patrilocal residence, a clear division of labor, and patriarchal authority to one that is a comparatively unstable, small, isolated, and mobile conjugal unit where the division of labor and household authority are increasingly ambiguous. These changes in structure are, in most respects, responses to the changing functions of the family in contemporary society. As tasks formerly performed by the family have been assumed by other institutions, such as the economy, government, and education, the functions of the family have changed.

Socialization Functions. At one time in America almost all socialization occurred in the family. By the early 1800s, however, many children were enrolled in either church or public schools, and today, over 98 percent of younger children go to school. The school has taken over many of the socialization functions that were once performed by the family. Many skills, especially those relating to future job opportunities, are now acquired almost exclusively outside of the home. While many critical aspects of children's personalities (such as their self-concepts, basic values, aspirations, and motives) still appear to be acquired primarily in the family, children still learn much outside of kinship. As a result, many uncertainties about how to reconcile

Changes in family functions

children's diverse socialization experiences prevail in the modern family.

Economic Functions. The family is no longer a productive group; it is now a consuming unit. As people left their family farms they began to work outside the home in autonomous industries where they earned wages that could be spent by family members. While this change in the family may appear obvious, it is nonetheless profound since virtually all family activity revolves around consuming. Moreover, much of the consumption is "individualized" as each family member spends much of his or her income (whether earned or received as an allowance) independently of other family members. For example, children spend their allowance and time with other children; fathers with other males; mothers by themselves for both personal and family needs. Such individualized consumption represents a dramatic change from the economic functions of the rural and even early industrial family where all pitched in to produce a living and where consumption was primarily a collective enterprise.

Procreation and Maintenance Functions. Today, as in past times, the family still provides for the regularization of birth and the maintenance of its members. Yet, the isolation of the modern conjugal family from other kin creates problems of how to support the old. While maintenance of the young is still a vital function, the old are often cast out into a society that makes few provisions for their health and well being.

Social Support. The impersonality of an urbanized, industrialized, and bureaucratized society has often been noted. Much emotion must be suppressed when working in a neutral, impersonal, and "rational" world, making the family one of the few structures in modern societies where emotion can be released and where personal feelings can be communicated. At times the family suffers "emotional overload" from the demands placed on it by its members because now a much smaller unit of mother, father, and children must absorb the emotions of, and provide support for, people who, by necessity, must participate in many neutral, impersonal, and frustrating situations outside the family. Thus, as the family has lost many of the functions it once performed, it has been required to assume increasing social support functions. And as a result, the small, isolated conjugal unit is often put under considerable strain because of this increased burden.

The family's structure and functions have undergone considerable alteration with urbanization and industrialization in America (Turner, 1972:112–116). The extensiveness and rate of this change

The family as emotional buffer

has created much ambiguity and uncertainty among family members about how they are to act. Such ambiguity is reflected in the cultural beliefs pertaining to family activities; the application of basic core values to family structures has created a system of beliefs that is at times outmoded and which no longer corresponds to the structural realities of family life. Moreover, as new beliefs more consonant with structural realities have become codified, they have come into conflict with the old. This situation of conflicting beliefs compounds and aggravates the American family's problems of structure.

THE CULTURE OF THE FAMILY

Beliefs about what the family is and should be are presently in such flux and conflict that it is difficult to discuss a unified "culture" of the family. Even for a particular family, we can often observe conflicting beliefs that are at odds with other people's basic values—attesting again to the human ability to segregate and, hence, tolerate inconsistent cognitions.

Much of the "problemness" of the family depends upon which set of beliefs individuals hold. For example, among those adhering to traditional beliefs, modern beliefs advocating free and equal sharing of economic and household tasks among men and women can spell the "destruction" of the family and thereby reveal what is "wrong" with the modern family. For those holding modern beliefs, traditional concerns with male economic dominance and female confinement to home and household chores represents "the enslavement and repression of women"—another conception of what is "wrong" with the family. Thus, what is problematic is ultimately a matter of personal belief and nowhere is there more conflict over definitions than with respect to the family.

Traditional versus modern beliefs

What are dominant family beliefs? We can isolate two systems of beliefs concerning the modern family: (1) those concerning marriage and divorce—that is the creation and dissolution of a family; and (2) those dealing with family relations or the "proper" roles of husbands, wives, and children.

MARRIAGE BELIEFS

In America, the initiation of the family unit is to be guided by "love" and "romance." While this may seem an obvious universal, other considerations often influence mate selection: wealth, family background, health, strength, and only after these considerations, love. In early America, this was often the case, although romantic

Romantic love

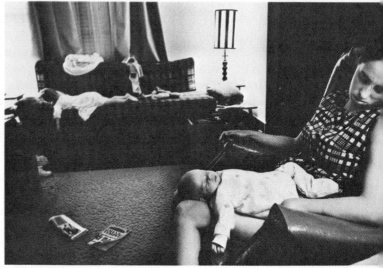

*Young couples are particularly likely to believe that their "oneness"
and "love" can make them immune to the problems of modern life,
but the romance and idealism surrounding the marriage ceremony
often contradict the hard realities of married life.*

love has always been a prominent consideration for those seeking marriage partners. The tenets of this belief provide the criteria for selecting mates as well as for forming conceptions about what marriage should and will be like (Turner, 1972b:103; Goode, 1963; Cavan, 1969):

1. Whether to marry is a decision those seeking mates must make, and other kin are not to make the partner selection.
2. Marriage partners are to be judged and assessed in terms of personal qualities and traits—appearance, personality, and responsiveness—and not in terms of utilitarian considerations—money, power, and social connections.
3. When partners are selected on the basis of their personal qualities, complete attraction and compatibility are more likely to result. Life together is seen as an unbroken sequence of compatibility, with conflicts and troubles easily ironed out.
4. Love is to be an emotional "oneness" in which the solitary and compatible couple insulate themselves from corrupting influences.
5. Sexual happiness and bliss are assured under the above conditions. Complete sexual attraction can only augment love, happiness, and compatibility.

Stated in this form these beliefs may appear naive but, in fact, most Americans seeking partners adhere to them. While they may be held in more sophisticated form by some and while they may be embellished with psychiatric and sensitivity group symbols, these basic beliefs remain intact. Such beliefs, in whatever form manifested, are compatible with both core values and evolving structural arrangements in the modern family. Values of individualism, activism, and achievement are consistent with individuals actively seeking to achieve marital harmony and compatibility. Moreover, the values of freedom and equality would dictate that those seeking partners should be free of constraints in selecting mates and that selection on the basis of personal qualities—not social class, money, and background—will assure greater equality and openness in the formation of family units. As we have discussed, the family has increasingly become a small, isolated, conjugal unit. Romantic love beliefs are thus consonant with such a small family unit since it is the marriage partners who must, in the end, form and maintain a relationship with each other (as opposed to other kindred). Such a concentrated relationship in a small unit would require considerable freedom for individuals to choose their partners in terms of qualities that they feel are desirable and that they "can live with."

Values and mate selection

An emphasis on romantic love, however, can pose problems: It can establish unrealistic expectations about the harmony of the small, conjugal family unit. Romantic love can mask many of the problems of a day to day, working marriage; it can create false expectations about sexual bliss; it provides few guidelines for resolving problems; and it overestimates the degree of isolation from external influences—work, finances, relatives, and the like. These problems, built into the tenets of romantic love beliefs, are further compounded by the ambiguities and conflicts in beliefs pertaining to how relations are to proceed once the family unit is formed.

FAMILY RELATIONS AND ROLE-PLAYING BELIEFS

In examining beliefs about "proper" family relationships, it is necessary to separate the beliefs of males and females and, after examining them independently, indicate the conflicts and ambiguities that they reveal.

Beliefs about the husband's role are relatively unambiguous (Turner, 1972b:97–98; Williams, 1970:69–75): Husbands are to (1) work steadily and provide an adequate income for the family; (2) express kindness and tenderness for the family; (3) "help out" around the house, but just what constitutes "helping" is ill defined—a fact that, as we will see, can cause conflict; and, (4) make major economic decisions and those pertaining to major purchases, but it is desirable

Beliefs about husband roles

that he consult with the family. These beliefs reflect basic values of activism and achievement in "providing for" the family, and to a limited extent, they exhibit some emphasis on equality in decisions and household chores. In many ways, however, the emphasis on husband control and dominance of "major" decisions and the vague definition of "helping out" underscores the fact that they also violate basic values of equality among people. Such becomes particularly clear when these beliefs are juxtaposed to those governing females and wives.

Three sets of beliefs concerning wives are presently evident in America (Turner, 1972b:99): (1) those beliefs emphasizing the wife-mother-homemaker role in which values of activism and achievement are to be realized in the narrow spheres of bearing and raising children and in the maintenance of the household for her husband and children; (2) beliefs emphasizing the companion role of wives who are to relinquish some child-rearing and household chores to others, such as schools, domestics, and day care centers, while being "active" and "achieving" in leisure and recreational activities. The wife can demand emotional responses and admiration from her husband, but there are limits to her "freedom" and "equality" since she must act in ways that facilitate her husband's economic and social

Beliefs about wife roles

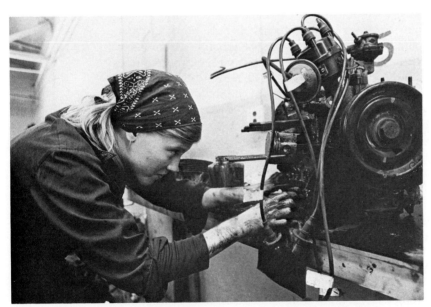

The realities of the working wife and mother have challenged traditional beliefs concerning the woman's role in the family.

dealings; and, (3) those beliefs, which have only recently gained wide acceptance, emphasizing the appropriateness of the wife as partner, actively seeking to achieve in the job sphere while "equally" sharing child-rearing and household responsibilities with her husband.

As can be seen, beliefs about women in the family are in conflict, and perhaps flux. At one time in America wife-mother beliefs dominated, even though they violated values of freedom and equality. Companionship beliefs became prevalent among the affluent middle classes, and while they allowed some "freedom" and some capacity to be active and achieve outside the household, they did so within rather narrow boundaries. Partner beliefs are, of course, reflections of the growing economic involvement of wives and the political activities of various women's groups; they are the most consistent with basic American values, but most in conflict with other beliefs concerning the woman's role and those dealing with the husband's household role. It is this conflict, along with (1) the realities of the working wife, (2) basic values of equality, freedom, individualism, activism, and achievement, and (3) long-standing beliefs about the proper family roles for men and women that poses one of the most difficult problems facing the American family.

Conflicting values and beliefs about women

DIVORCE BELIEFS

At one time in America, as recently as the last decade, marriage was to be permanent, with only death dissolving the marital union. Even in unhappy marriages it was considered more desirable for a couple to stay together, if only for "the sake of the children." Such beliefs were consistent with romantic love beliefs that preclude the possibility of marital discord. These beliefs also reflected the conditions of marriages in early America, where other kin were involved in mate selection; husbands, wives, and kin were economically interdependent; small communities exerted social pressure to remain married; religious sanctions against dissolution were high; and, the legal system made divorce difficult. The creation of the urban, economically self-sufficient, conjugal family, coupled with the reality of increasing divorce, changed beliefs dramatically. Although divorce is still considered regrettable, it is also accepted as "best" for the parents and children involved in an unhappy home. Yet, the older traditional beliefs have not disappeared; rather, they stand in conflict with more liberal beliefs about divorce. These new beliefs are, however, more consistent with dominant American values of freedom and individualism than traditional beliefs about divorce. They are less likely to pose cultural conflicts for marriage partners than highly restrictive traditional beliefs that emphasized conformity to the

Changing beliefs about divorce

tenets of romantic love and wife–husband roles, even if such conformity means sacrificing one's individualism and freedom.

In summary, the structure and culture of the American family contains the potential for many problems. Family structure is small, isolated, and involved in increased social support functions. At the same time, dominant beliefs create unrealistic expectations about what marriage and family life will bring, and they provide ambiguous and conflicting beliefs, many of which contradict basic values and the realities of the working wife. Coupled with new, liberalized beliefs about marital dissolution, the potential for family disruption and dissolution in America has increased. It is in this context that family problems in America must be analyzed since they are indeed problems of its culture and structure.

PROBLEMS OF FAMILY STRUCTURE

DIVORCE AND DISSOLUTION

Divorce Rates. One indicator of the cultural and structural strains on the American family is the rising divorce rate. In contrast to many popular commentaries, however, divorce is probably not "out of hand," nor is it even clear just how high divorce rates have become. Even today, the U.S. government does not collect complete data on divorce rates for all states in a given year. Every ten years on 0-numbered years (1940, 1950, 1960, and 1970, for example) questions about marital status are asked, but these concern only people's marital status at the time, not their status during the years since the last census. When these limitations on current data collection are coupled with the earlier reluctance of the government to collect *any* data on its citizens, it becomes very difficult to understand either long-range or short-range trends on divorce rates.

Even if complete data were collected each year, there are problems in presentation and interpretation. For example, one way to present divorce data is the number of divorces per 10,000 people in the population. From such data it is possible to discern that before the turn of the century there were about 3 to 4 divorces per 10,000 people, and 47 per 10,000 today. But neither children nor all adults are married, hence, variations in the marriage rate and age composition of the population make such statistics rather meaningless. The most popular way to report divorce data is the number of divorces per 100 marriages in a given year. Thus, in 1974 there were over 40 divorces per 100 marriages which, in the public's eyes, means a marriage has about a 40 percent chance of failing. Such is not necessarily the case,

Inaccuracies in divorce statistics

since the number of divorces in a given year are not the result of marriages in that year, but of marriages in all preceding years. Depending upon the (1) age groupings of the population, (2) earlier marriage patterns, (3) the propensity to seek divorce, and (4) the number of marriages in a given year, the number of divorces from the past (as a proportion of present marriages) can vary enormously and distort divorce rates in America.

Distortions of divorce statistics

To avoid some of the statistical pitfalls of reporting divorce data, the most accurate, but still incomplete, way to report divorce rates is to report the number of divorces in a year as a proportion of the en-

SOCIOLOGICAL INSIGHTS

ARE YOUR CHANCES FOR MARITAL SUCCESS DECREASING?

Almost every year the media reports a statistic that one in three or one in two marriages ends in divorce. Such statistics could certainly lead some, especially those holding traditional beliefs about family and divorce, to decry the "crumbling of the basic cornerstone of the society." Others may have their faith in romantic love lessened. Such feelings, however, are based upon illusionary statistics about divorces per 100 marriages. Typically, these illusionary statistics show the trend summarized below:

Year	Divorces per 100 marriages
1920	13.4
1930	17.0
1940	16.9
1946	26.6
1950	23.1
1960	25.8
1970	32.8
1973	40.6

These numbers are all too easily read as percentages, that is, 40 percent of all marriages end in divorce. The data do not say this. They do not indicate what your present chances for marital success are. They simply, and arbitrarily, compare divorces from *all* previous years of marriage to marriages in *one given year*. Perhaps your chances of success are only 60 percent, maybe they are 10 percent, five percent, or 40 percent. These data do not say, but the media and the public think that they do. And perhaps it is here that the "social problem" resides.

Table 3.2 **Divorces per 1,000 Married Women, 15 and Over, for Selected Years**

Year	Divorces per 1,000 Married Women
1920	8.0
1930	7.5
1940	8.7
1946	17.8
1950	10.3
1960	9.2
1970	14.9
1971	15.8

SOURCE: National Center for Health Statistics, Department of Health, Education, and Welfare, "Summary Report: Final Divorce Statistics," 1974.

tire married population, fifteen years or older. Most typically (because of the way the government collects the data), only females are in these comparisons so that the data will reveal the number of women who get a divorce in a given year as a proportion of the number of married women, fifteen years or older. These data do not, of course, say anything about the chances of a successful marriage; no data currently collected by the government can do this. But using this procedure enables us to examine divorce trends as far back as 1920. This trend is reported in Table 3.2.

As can be seen in Table 3.2, divorce appears to have fluctuated. It remained low until the post–World War II period, when so many hastily conceived marriages ended in divorce. Divorce rates declined until the 1970s, then rose sharply. The current trend continues, divorce rates will soon rival those of the post–World War II period. The data reveal that the divorce rate has increased, but it is not, however, at an all-time high. And to argue that these divorce rates signal a "pathology" in the family is premature, for we must assess additional information.

Patterns of Divorce. One important piece of needed information is: How long have those who seek a divorce been married? If long-standing marriages where children are involved end in divorce, this fact would have different implications for questions about the American family than if divorces occurred only among the newly married. The data reveal that most marriages, if they are going to be dissolved at all, end before the seventh year. But most divorces occur in the second year which, because of the time lag involved in getting a divorce, indicates that most marriages really end in the first year. Apparently the realities of marriage simply do not correspond to the expectations of "romantic love," and when conflicts over other family beliefs surface, the tension leads the newly married to seek a divorce.

What about children and divorce? While the research on the impact of divorce on children is far from complete, the available evidence indicates that children are not as negatively influenced by divorce as public opinion argues (Landis, 1960). Moreover, many youthful marriages that end within the first year are childless, and many late-in-life marriages are also childless. From 1920 to 1950 about 65 percent of all divorces involved no children, but over the last twenty-five years, this figure has shrunk to about 40 percent (K. Davis, 1972). To some extent, this increase in divorces involving children reflects the post–World War II "baby boom" that had subsided by 1965 and now appears to have vanished as birth rates have dropped dramatically. With a decline in the birth rate, the percentage of childless divorces in the future should increase. Thus, while children have increasingly been involved in divorce, it is not as harmful for them psychologically as was once believed. Moreover, there is good reason to believe that fewer children will be a party to divorce in the future.

Children and divorce

What happens to divorced parents? If people do not remarry, then this fact might signal a decline in the institution of marriage and family. But if they do remarry, this would indicate strength and vitality in the family. The evidence clearly argues for the attractiveness of marriage and family since divorced partners, probably still in accordance with "romantic love" beliefs, seek new marriage partners. As the demographer Kingsley Davis (1972) summarized: "At such rates . . . [remarriage] . . . the divorced population would soon be consumed if it were not constantly fed by newly divorced recruits." Thus, while people are more likely to seek a divorce, they are also more prone than ever to desire remarriage and the reestablishment of the family unit.

Divorce and remarriage

Reasons for Increasing Divorce Rates. Understanding which social groups and categories seek divorce can help us find an explanation for increasing divorce (and remarriage) in America. One of the most important factors in predicting divorce is the age of the partners at the time of their marriage. The evidence is clear that the younger the age at which partners are married, especially if they are under 20, the higher the incidence of divorce (Hetzel and Cappetta, 1973). The eco-

Age, economics, and divorce

nomic situation of a family also influences divorce patterns: the lower the income, the higher the divorce rate, regardless of age. Similar findings can be found for the prestige of the male's occupation (which, of course, is correlated with income): the higher the prestige and status associated with an occupation, the lower the divorce rate (Census Bureau, 1974). A final category concerns the issue of previous marriage: If marriage partners have been previously married and divorced, then the new marriage is more likely to end in divorce, although the data on this matter are incomplete and sketchy, and should thus be interpreted carefully (Carter and Glick, 1970).

Previous marriage and divorce

These data can perhaps offer some clues as to why the divorce rate appears to have increased. For the young married couple who are most likely to hold "romantic love" beliefs, the realities of family life, especially as they are exacerbated by conflicting beliefs about male and female roles, can generate such frustration and tension that the partners immediately seek family dissolution. For the less affluent, financial problems can present additional tensions with which marriage partners have difficulty coping. Such tensions can be aggravated with the working wife whose income may lessen the financial burdens of the family, but whose *combined* work and household burdens create other sources of tension between spouses. Since the working wife is most likely, in lower income families where husbands most typically hold traditional beliefs about male–female roles and authority, the working class wife is subjected to enormous pressure to perform both a full-fledged economic role and the wife-homemaker role. Under these conditions, maintaining a tension-free household apparently proves difficult.

The working wife and divorce

The sketchy data on divorce and remarriage would indicate that people do not necessarily learn from their mistakes. Apparently, divorced people seek remarriage in accordance with romantic love beliefs, but they also fail to alter other beliefs, or at least fail to recognize them as a potential source of marital discord. Thus, many of the role and authority conflicts are repeated in second marriages, and when aggravated by economic circumstances, another divorce becomes increasingly likely.

In response to the inevitability of divorce in a society where unrealistic romantic love beliefs, coupled with ambiguous and conflicting beliefs over male–female family roles, divorce has increasingly been simplified. Until very recently divorce law and court procedures were complicated and usually involved adversary procedures where "damages" by one party had to be demonstrated in a court of law. Often a legal charade was necessary to "demonstrate" that one party—usually the husband—had done something "wrong." The husband, for example, might be required to go to a motel room with another woman and, in the presence of "witnesses," demonstrated "adultery" which could then become "legal grounds" for the divorce (which probably had little to do with adulterous activities). Each state has its own divorce laws, most of which, until very recently, discouraged divorce. But over the last decade states have been liberalizing their laws so that divorce is increasingly a "no fault" matter in which partners simply agree to dissolve the marriage. Thus slackening of rigid divorce laws has, no doubt, encouraged people to seek the divorce option in an unhappy marriage. And as beliefs have begun to shift toward a more tolerant view of divorce, the inevitable tensions of the small, conjugal unit can now, with little stigma attached and lessened legal obstacles, be resolved through divorce.

Liberalized divorce laws

In summary, then, it is clear that high divorce rates are inevitable in American society. Family beliefs are in great flux, creating severe problems of adjustment for Americans and increasing the likelihood that they will seek marital dissolution. Just whether increasing divorce is a problem, or the resolution of inevitable family problems, is a matter of definition—a definition that will reflect people's personal beliefs. High divorce rates are inevitable, but as the remarriage rates of those who have been divorced reveal, they do not indicate a weakening of people's interest in family life. Rather, they underscore Americans' desires to have the harmonious family life that their beliefs lead them to perceive as attainable. From one perspective, divorce does not represent the weakening of the family but its reaffirmation as couples seek new family ties.

PROBLEMS OF FAMILY RELATIONSHIPS

Even though divorced partners seek remarriage, high divorce rates reveal that considerable strain and tension is exerted on relations between husbands and wives, as well as on children, in the American family. In order to understand the root causes of divorce patterns and the dynamics of American kinship, it is critical to examine key sets of relationships, namely those between spouses and those between children and parents (relations with other kin are less critical because of the isolated nature of the American family). While the family is comparatively isolated from other kin, it is subject to situational pressures from the outside that influence relations among family members. The analysis of the internal dynamics of the family and the problems these reveal must, therefore, involve a search for the internal and external sources of pressure on key role relationships.

HUSBAND–WIFE ROLE RELATIONS

Relations between husbands and wives in the American family are greatly influenced by the cultural beliefs that they hold and the situational pressures that they must endure. In turn, the age or maturity (as well as affluence) of the partners affects, to some degree, their ability to reconcile these pressures. With maturity, people are more likely to perceive, talk out, and discuss their problems, and with affluence, they can "buy" counseling assistance and other services—such as household help—that can cut down on pressures. Some of the cultural and situational pressures on husbands and wives in the American family are diagrammed in Figure 2. Each arrow represents a potential source of pressure on spouses, and in turn, on their relationship. The variables of age and affluence are listed in order to emphasize the mitigating impact they can have on these sources of pressure. The figure is not exhaustive, however, since for any marriage there is a unique configuration of pressures. What is intended is that only general classes or types of pressures affecting all families be isolated for examination. For husbands, cultural expectations are, as we noted earlier, relatively unambiguous. There is some conflict between basic values such as equality and freedom on the one hand, and beliefs about male dominance and avoidance of domestic chores in the household on the other. This conflict, however, only becomes severe when the wife's beliefs deviate significantly from the wife-mother-homemaker profile. In contrast to males, it is clear that females are subject to multiple and conflicting cultural pressures. Three contrasting beliefs exist, and it is increasingly rare for wives to adhere to only one. Most are likely to "believe" in elements of all three—thus setting up pressures on the wife, and indirectly, creating ambiguities, frustrations, and tensions in the relationship between husband and wife. And to the extent that these conflicting beliefs are also perceived as violating the basic values of activism, achievement, individualism, freedom, and equality, additional pressures are brought to bear on the wife and relations with her husband.

There are two types of situational pressures compounding these cultural forces: those revolving around household obligations and those existing outside the household. These are represented at the bottom of Figure 2. For husbands, household pressures usually involve maintaining the car, yard, and structural aspects of the house (painting, repairing plumbing, etc.). With affluence, of course, these pressures are lessened as "help" is hired, and they are often turned over to the wife who becomes the overseer of hired household labor. Husbands are also obligated to spend time with their children in

Cultural pressures on husband-wife relations

Situational pressures on husband-wife relations

spontaneous encounters at night and on weekends and in organized recreational activities. Most of the day to day care, feeding, transporting, helping, and disciplining, however, is turned over to the wife. Outside of the household the husband's major role is that of "breadwinner" on the job. He may also have recreational "roles" (golf, bowling, etc.) which are relaxing in themselves, but which can represent sources of pressure on relations with a resentful wife who is left to "hold the fort." Husbands may also have community service roles, such as civic clubs and organizations, that can exert the same kinds of pressures on the marital relationship. On the wife's side, the household chores of cleaning, laundry, meals, and dishes represent a drain on her time and emotions, especially if she must also perform work roles. Monitoring of children represents an additional burden, as does the time spent "talking" with the children. When community service and recreational roles also exist, they can create additional

Figure 2 **Pressures on Parental Relations**

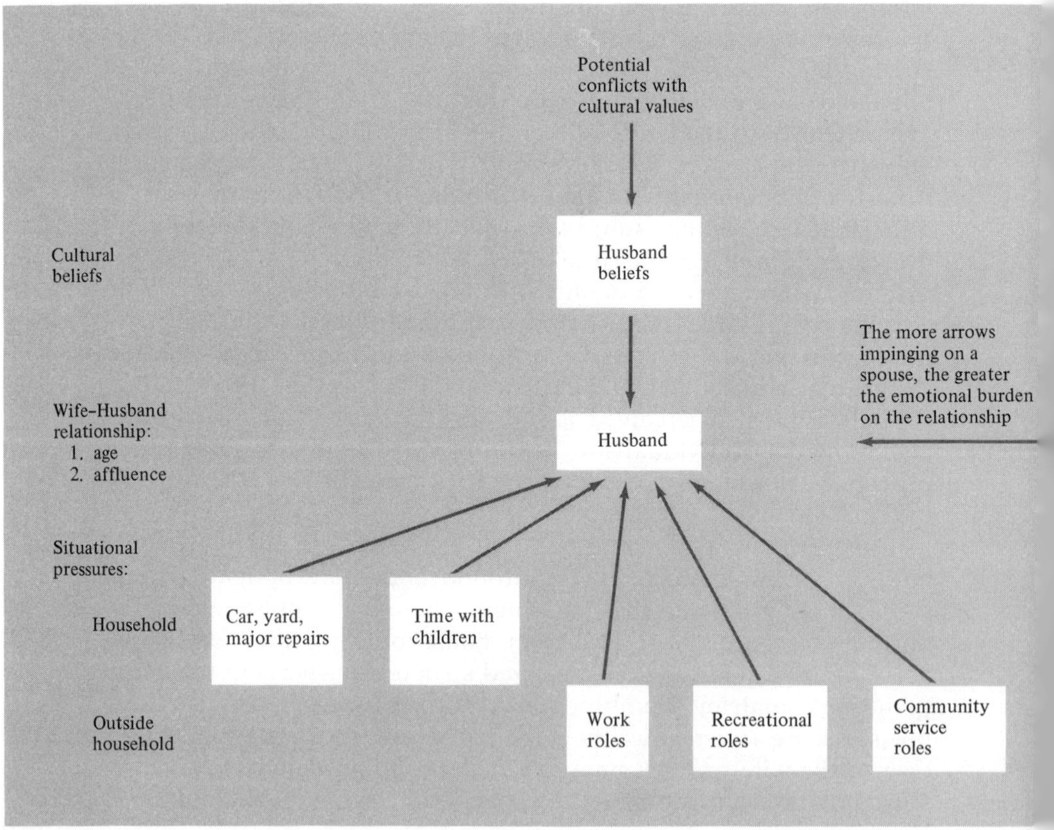

time pressures on the wife. The extent of such pressures depends upon whether or not she must work and whether she has the affluence to relieve herself of many time-consuming tiring household chores.

In looking at Figure 2, then, it is clear that the female partner is potentially subjected to considerably more pressure than the husband, particularly when she must work. These situational pressures can be compounded if she holds contradictory beliefs. Thus, by simply counting the number of relevant arrows for a particular partner, a rough indication of the pressures on that partner and on the relationship can be assessed. For those marriages where the number is high, and affluence and age are low, we can predict higher tensions leading, perhaps, to marital dissolution. It is in this sense that we can visualize family problems as built into the structure and culture of the American family.

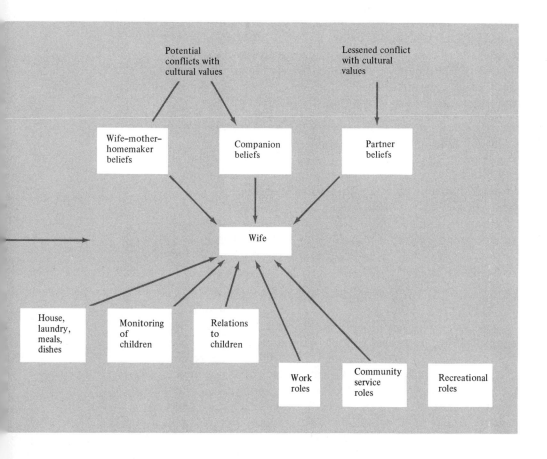

PARENT–CHILDREN ROLE RELATIONS

In an extended kinship system, where other relatives live with or close to a family, much of the children's family interaction is with adults other than their parents—grandparents, aunts, and uncles being the most immediate kin. But as the family has lost many of its functions and shrunk in size and composition, parents represent the sole emotional support objects for young children. And even as children grow and increasingly participate in the broader society, parents and the family unit still remain the vital center of social support. This structural situation, coupled with beliefs that parents should be loving and devoted to their children, places a heavy burden on husbands and wives. As the principal love objects of children, they must maintain individually warm relations with their children, even when under stress. Numerous studies have revealed, and as parents implicitly recognize, the nature of the relationship between parents has profound implications for their children's emotional well being. As we have seen, however, maintaining a tension free relationship between parents is often difficult. Moreover, the demands placed upon parents by constantly maturing children who also spend increasing amounts of time outside the home makes harmonious relations with children difficult while frequently placing strains on the marital bond. Thus, the problems of relationships between parents and children inhere in a set of inevitable structural relations:

Structural pressures on parent-child relations

1. There are few adults other than parents in the American family with whom children can relate emotionally.
2. Parents are under enormous pressure to be "good and loving" to their children, and yet, the husband-wife relationship has potential sources of strain that can make this difficult.
3. The young move quickly, within fifteen years, from highly dependent children to biologically mature, but emotionally and financially dependent "adults" or adolescents, who participate in peer groupings and organizations that are often ill-understood by their parents.

Each of these structural forces requires some elaboration. First, the reliance of children for emotional support is great since most interaction contexts outside the home, including many peer relationships, are more neutral. Clubs, schools, competitive play with friends, and the various organizations—Scouts, baseball, football, dance, recreation centers, and the like—put much emphasis on performance, creating the tensions that must be relieved in the more relaxed and supportive home environment. As numerous studies have indicated, basic personality traits such as self-esteem, achievement motives, aspirations, and emotional security are acquired in interactions with parents in an emotionally secure home environment. This state of dependency, and its importance for basic characteristics of children, is recognized by parents who, as we noted above, experience a great deal of strain over how to be "good" parents.

This brings us to the second point listed: Parents have many sources of strain and tension (as outlined in Figure 2) that can make it difficult to provide a warm, loving, and supportive environment. Moreover, norms of child-rearing in America are unclear; parents are somehow supposed to instinctively know how to raise children. But in reality, parents usually must grope and experiment in how to relate to and raise their children, a situation that can create the inconsistent and ambivalent responses from parents that can undermine the security and supportiveness of the home environment. Or, parents can disagree over how to treat children, compounding the problem. And when such ambiguities and outright disagreements are accompanied by marital tensions, then strained relations between children and their parents will create even further tensions which, in turn, compound existing tensions in an escalating cycle. The end result is for the marriage bond to be subjected to additional strain and for children to endure the harmful consequences of a stressful home environment.

The third structural problem listed revolves around the simple fact that children grow up. As they grow, parents must adjust their responses to a changing being, but this can often prove difficult when tensions already exist between husband and wife, between parents and children, or both. As adolescence approaches, this adjustment process can prove difficult even when harmonious relations have previously existed because now the children are biological adults with many out-of-the-home activities, and yet, they remain emotionally and financially dependent on their parents. Parents often have difficulty understanding the adolescent youth culture—dress, music, language, and the like—and the independence-dependence conflicts of their children for freedom from parental domination and for love and emotional support. Adolescents, on the other hand, have difficulty recognizing the problems that their parents have in visualizing the transition of their "children" into "young adults." This dependence-independence process, and all its accompanying confusion, is protracted in American society because of the extensive "credentialing" activities performed by schools. While prolonged involvement in educational structures is often unnecessary in terms of actual job requirements, parents, children, and employers believe that education is necessary, and thus, children are often required to remain financially tied to parents well beyond their adolescent needs to be emotionally supported by parents. Thus, the "need" for education can often create additional problems of adjustment for parents and children as they leave an already long adolescence and enter adulthood—an adulthood which can still involve independence-dependence conflicts with parents.

In viewing the relations between parents and children, it is clear that the potential for strain in these relationships is great. The small, conjugal unit is expected to absorb an enormous tension management load in a society where most nonfamilial contexts are either neutral or competitive. This load is made even more difficult because parents are given few cultural guidelines as to how they are to be "good" parents. For both parents and their maturing children, these built-in sources of strain can become highly problematic, especially as children mature, making a constant readjustment of children-parent relations necessary. At times these pressures and needs for readjustments harm both parents and children, emphasizing again the extent to which parent-child problems inhere in the structure of American kinship.

Parent-child problems inhere in our culture

PROBLEMS OF THE AGED IN THE AMERICAN KINSHIP SYSTEM

Perhaps the problems of the old do not seem related to kinship, but in societies revealing an extended lineage system, with elders living in the household unit (or with the young family living in the elders' house), "old age" is not a problem. In fact, it is often a venerated position that has many important functions, such as keeper of lore and religion, owner of family property, political leader of family units connected by lineage, and caretaker-teacher of grandchildren. The early American family often included the elderly who could assist with household chores and child-rearing, while providing a knowledge resource for both the husband and wife in their economic and household roles. With the creation of the small, mobile, conjugal family, however, kinfolk were excluded, including parents and grandparents, and it is this change in the structure of the family that has contributed to the problem of being old in America.

Exclusion of the aged

Many elderly must endure loneliness, a sense of worthlessness, low prestige, poor health, and poverty without either the support of kinship or government. While the forces of change have radically altered the kinship system, these same forces have yet to resolve one of the problems of this alteration: a place for the elderly in a society of isolated, conjugal family units. And the problem has assumed major proportions. There are now over 20 million elderly (over 65 years)

Increasing numbers of aged

The loneliness, despair, and poverty of the aged is a pervasive condition in American society.

who constitute 10 percent of the population, and by the year 2000, they will represent over 12 percent of the population. To put these figures in historical perspective, the population of the United States has experienced a 100 percent increase since 1900, but the number of people over 65 years of age has increased by 500 percent. The reasons for this shift in the age composition of the population are varied, but are related to the fact that the life expectancy of the average American has increased, while the massive immigration of the young from Europe has ceased.

Large proportions of elderly in a society do not constitute a problem per se. They become a problem when they are subject to negative stereotypes, are excluded from participation in society's institutions, and are forced to endure loneliness and poverty. The very industrialization and bureaucratization of the economy which created the conjugal unit that excludes the elderly has also forced the elderly out of the economy at age 65. The nature of jobs in the economy changes so fast that experience in work is less critical than "recent training," with the result that the older employees of a company can become a liability. Many companies will not hire those over fifty; they often encourage their employees to take early retirement; and most force their 65-year-old workers to retire.

In excluding the elderly from the economy, they can become the victims of negative beliefs that portray them as nonproductive, mentally slow, physically feeble, and a burden on their families and society. Such beliefs are perhaps inevitable applications of basic values to a population forced by economic policies to be "nonactive," "nonachievement oriented," and because of its stage in life, "incapable of progressing." Thus, the old are excluded from meaningful work roles which, in turn, makes them vulnerable to the harsh application of dominant American values. Such treatment is particularly severe in a society where the elderly are denied access to kinship ties that could make their exclusion from the economy more bearable. It is, therefore, in this context that their problems must be understood.

Values and the
stigma of being old

PROBLEMS OF STATUS

In America, status and prestige are usually reflections of work roles. Those who do not work are subject to negative stereotypes—whether they be welfare mother or a retiree—and the amount of prestige one can receive is usually tied to their occupation and in-

Some elderly can find companionship, happiness, and intimacy in their old age, but for many this is only a distant memory or a dream.

come. Since the elderly cannot work and are likely to have low, fixed incomes, they are denied the most typical sources of status and prestige in American society. Because they are likely to have always accepted these criteria as "right and proper," they now find themselves in the ironic position of having to use them to define their own situations of nonwork and low income. While many elderly have few problems in this area, many others find it difficult to maintain their esteem in a society that uses occupation and income as criteria for bestowing prestige.

POVERTY

Very large proportions of the elderly live in poverty, and many must seek welfare—an act that further lowers their self-esteem. Many retirement programs, including social security, are inadequate, especially in inflationary times. Often the elderly have been deceived and cheated out of, or simply been ignorant of, the "benefits" of their company and union retirement programs. The result has been for many elderly to have inadequate income to support themselves, with the outcome that they must appeal to charity and welfare—something that those holding values of activism, achievement, and individualism inevitably find degrading.

HEALTH

Problems of poverty are compounded by the declining health of the elderly because, at some point, all elderly will experience health problems which will require extensive medical care. While the federal Medicare program has helped many elderly poor, and while proposed national health insurance programs could prove even more beneficial, prolonged illness still represents a serious financial burden. Most private health insurance policies and government programs do not provide full extended-care coverage, a situation that can have many negative consequences: It can force the elderly to spend their savings; it can require the elderly to endure poor health and inadequate health care; and it can make the elderly "wards of the state" where they must endure the abuses and hardships of "convalescent hospitals."

LONELINESS AND MEANING

While the vast majority of the aged report a close relationship with their children, this relationship is often maintained at some distance since the mobile, conjugal unit often lives in another community or state. Coupled with the lack of a work role, or a child-rearing role for females, a considerable amount of isolation from kinship and community can occur. Older people who for most of their adult lives performed one of these roles, can frequently suffer from a decline in the "meaning"—a sense of involvement, pride, accomplishment—of what they do. Leisure roles are not always an adequate substitute for people who have defined their lives in terms of work and household roles.

The problem of meaning can be compounded by loneliness, especially when a spouse has died. Needs for companionship and sexual gratification remain, yet, few acknowledge the elderly's need for sex—preferring to define it as ludicrous, if not lurid. There is some recognition by government and family of the companionship needs of the elderly, but few conjugal families are disposed to disrupt their already overloaded relations to meet the day to day needs of older parents. Government has also failed to provide widespread opportunities for the elderly (especially the less affluent) to share friends or to acquire new sexual and marital companions.

When living a lonely and less meaningful life, the elderly are more likely to suffer ill health and drift into senility. As numerous studies have revealed, the physical health and alertness of the old is highly related to their ability to be involved in meaningful tasks and close emotional relationships. In traditional kinship systems family ties provided a natural setting for realizing this goal, but with the growing isolation of the elderly from the daily activities of their offsprings' families, the problems of meaning and loneliness are built into the structure of American kinship.

SUMMARY

This chapter reviewed the problems of divorce, conflicts in the family, and the plight of the elderly. These problems are the result of (1) changes in the structure of the family into an isolated, conjugal unit, (2) the false expectations generated by romantic love beliefs, (3) the ambiguity of beliefs about the proper family roles of husbands and wives, especially wives, and (4) beliefs about the elderly as being nonactive, nonsexual, and useless.

Many of the problems of the family are probably inevitable, especially since beliefs do not always correspond to dominant values or structural arrangements and since they are in a state of rapid change. Moreover, the increased social support functions of the family in a modern, industrial, and impersonal world are unlikely to recede, thereby placing a heavy emotional burden on an already burdened structure. However, these increased social support functions exclude the elderly and leave them alone to cope with their problems.

REVIEW QUESTIONS

1. Describe the changes in the American family over the last 150 years with respect to the following matters:
   > descent
   > residence
   > division of labor
   > authority
   > marriage and divorce
   > socialization
   > economics
   > maintenance and social support functions
2. List the tenets of the romantic love belief system.
3. What are the tenets of beliefs about the husband's role as well as the conflicting tenets of beliefs about the wife-mother-homemaker's role?
4. What are the problems with divorce statistics?
5. Summarize why high divorce rates are inevitable in America.
6. Discuss the multiple sources of tension in internal family relationships?
7. How is the situation of the elderly a result of changes in the kinship structure in America?

GLOSSARY

biological support functions the processes in which the adult members of the family do what is necessary to maintain the health and well being of children

conjugal family unit a family unit composed of parents and their offspring but which excludes other kindred from its daily life

descent (lineage) norms the norms indicating which side of the family, if any, is to be considered more important by a married couple

division of labor norms indicating how the male and female tasks and duties in the household are to be divided

divorce the process of dissolving the marriage relationship

economic support functions the process whereby some members of the family participate in the economy to provide for the sustenance and consumption needs of the family unit

husband-wife role beliefs beliefs that specify the appropriate activity for husband and wife in the family. Husband beliefs reveal a consistency while wife beliefs evidence considerable conflict and variability

marriage the institution whereby a man and woman are joined in a social and legal dependence for the purpose of founding and maintaining a family

romantic love beliefs cultural beliefs that marriage partners should be selected for reasons of attractiveness, personality, interpersonal compatibility, and other individual attributes which will lead to sexual and emotional fulfillment in marriage

socialization functions those processes in which one acquires the attributes that will determine one's ability to participate in society

social support functions the process of providing a supportive environment of warm, affectionate relations where frustrations and other personal feelings can be vented

PROLOGUE 4: CONTROVERSY AND CONCERN ABOUT THE SCHOOLS

In rural towns and counties of West Virginia in 1975, parents were angry. They had organized a boycott of schools and had packed school board meetings to protest books that they felt were threatening to their way of life. A giant bonfire was built and a huge pile of books from the pens of "progressive" and "immoral" writers were burned.

Boston, 1975: The beginning of school brought busing to South Roxy. It also brought 500 police and considerable violence. White students boycotted; their parents protested and bombed the offices of the NAACP. A judge was forced to take over the school, further inflaming the people's beliefs that outsiders had taken away their school.

Less than a decade earlier these same people and millions like them saw, with disgust and hatred, college students doing much the same thing: protesting against a world that was out of their control and yet influencing their lives. Many of these same people may have been the very ones who beat up college students protesting the war in Vietnam and the "oppression" of the university environment. Today, the reverse is true. College graduates of the Vietnam era perhaps feel the same emotions against others that were at one time expressed against them.

Sara Miles is a college graduate from a branch of the University of California. She is a low-ranking clerk in a Penneys' department store, still wondering where all the great opportunities for college graduates are. John Silva, a Ph.D. in history, asks the same thing as he drives a yellow cab around Milwaukee.

A morning newspaper in 1976 brings a front page story repeated several times over the last years: "Johnny cannot read or write." Neither can Alice, Susan, or many other students, if national tests mean anything. Year after year, for the last decade, national reading and math test scores have been going down and no one can figure it out. Many parents feel that it is the progressive pablum offered in the schools; teachers think it is the failure of parents to encourage their kids to read and stay away from the television; and, school administrators worry as they take the "heat" from irate citizens about the failure of schools to teach their children anything.

These events are real. They are what make education in America a problem. People are always unhappy about some aspect of our educational system, at all its levels. "Why don't the schools educate?" they ask. "Why can't college graduates get jobs?" "Why are outsiders meddling in our local schools?" These are the questions of the day and they are the social problems of the schools. In Chapter 4 we will examine the culture and structure of American lower and higher education, that is, our elementary and high schools as well as our colleges and universities. We will seek to determine how the beliefs of people dictate concerns over certain issues and how the structure of education perpetuates the events that many define as problematic. We will see that education in America presents a series of perplexing dilemmas which, because people hold different beliefs about what should be done, make their resolution difficult.

4

PROBLEMS OF EDUCATION

In modern societies, education becomes a dominant institution performing what are defined as "vital functions" for the society. One function is socialization of the young—the imparting of the culture as well as the basic skills for participation in the society as adults. Another related function is social placement—a process in which, depending upon the amount of education received, people are placed into different occupations. An institution so involved in these tasks inevitably must become a center of controversy. For the transmission of a society's culture from one generation to another and the placing of people into different social classes is at stake. Any organized structure so central to these tasks will, for some segment of the population, reveal profound problems.

Functions of education

For convenience of analysis, the educational system can be separated into a lower educational system of primary and secondary schools and a higher educational system of colleges and universities. The functions, culture, and structure of these two systems are somewhat different and, thus, we should examine them separately, while not losing sight of the fact that they are interrelated.

Lower education

At the lower educational level the American system has, from one perspective, been successful. Virtually every child in America receives a high school education, with close to one-half of these going on to some form of college. It is perhaps only in the context of such success that dilemmas become markedly evident in American lower education: (1) Despite the fact that American schools have "acculturated" several generations of immigrants and provided opportunities for millions, they still appear to exacerbate general problems of social class, ethnic, and racial discrimination, while posing dilemmas of how to deal with eliminating this discrimination; and (2) Despite the success of schools in reaching nearly all Americans, the dilemma of how best to educate is still present, particularly now that scores on standardized reading and mathematics tests have shown a steady decline over the last decade.

At the higher educational level, the turmoil of the late 1960s and early 1970s placed into bold relief some of the dilemmas facing colleges and universities. Again, many of these problems seem significant only because so many receive college instruction, but nevertheless, the functions of colleges and universities have been increasingly called into question: Should higher education educate the masses or the few? How should students be educated? What is the research function of universities to be? How independent of government, military, economic, and domestic interests should the universities be? And most recently, as some of these issues have become less manifest with campus tranquility, are the universities supposed to provide their graduates with training that will assure them jobs? Should and can the universities and colleges be a place where middle-class affluence is maintained?

Higher education

These are the current problems of education in America. They are defined as problems because people hold beliefs, hopes, and expectations about what education should be. That is, the culture of education in America defines and gives intensity to perceptions of educational problems. Moreover, as we will come to see, these beliefs are involved in the substance of problems inhering in the structure of education. People's beliefs can both legitimize current structural arrangements and provide the impetus behind tension and change in these arrangements. As we approach the study of educational problems in America, we must first outline the profile of certain important cultural beliefs; then, we can shift attention to the structural dilemmas of education and visualize how these dilemmas are compounded by cultural symbols.

THE CULTURE OF EDUCATION IN AMERICA

Much of the intensity of feeling and emotion surrounding the educational process in America stems from strongly held beliefs about what schools should be and what they should do. Following are some of the dominant beliefs about the educational system in America.

1. EQUALITY OF OPPORTUNITY BELIEFS

From the early years of mass inculcation of European immigrants, values of equality and freedom have been codified into beliefs about equality through education. From the perspective of these beliefs, a free and universal system of education is to provide opportunities for all to raise their stations in life. Accordingly, social mobility for the deprived is to occur through their "active" efforts to "achieve" in the educational system. This is considered the most "humane" way to make opportunities available to the less fortunate.

However, values emphasizing activism and individualism stress the importance of betterment through individual efforts. The school is to provide the opportunity, but the individual must seize these opportunities. There are limitations on how much the schools can do to compensate for people's failure to take advantage of opportunities presented to them.

Much of the controversy surrounding education in America concerns the issue of equality. While no direct data bear on the question, it is likely that close to a majority of Americans believe that the schools do, on the whole, provide equal opportunities. On the other side, many liberals and social scientists view the schools as highly discriminatory. Whether the issue is busing, affirmative action, or special programs in the schools, a considerable amount of commentary, debate, and civil disorder has ensued as different segments of the population seek to impose their beliefs about equality of opportunity.

Values and equality of opportunity beliefs

2. BELIEFS IN LOCAL CONTROL AND AUTONOMY

At the lower educational level, Americans strongly believe that local communities should control the administration of their schools. Such beliefs reflect values of freedom and individualism as applied to communities which are to be free from external constraints and which are to be allowed to pursue their own destiny. While racial prejudice is an important factor, much of the negative and violent reaction to "forced busing" to achieve racial integration is intensified by the belief that neighborhoods are losing control of their schools. And the recent controversy over textbook content is a similar reaction by parents who believe that "outside" educators are teaching their children alien and immoral percepts.

Values and local control beliefs

3. THE THREE R's VERSUS PROGRESSIVE BELIEFS

A considerable dissensus over what and how the schools should teach is evident in the general population. For many the value confor-

The early frontier school personified the belief that the local community would control the nature of education. It was the community, it was felt, that could best determine the needs of its students.

The early public school was used to assimilate generations of immigrants into "the American way of life." It was a rigidly structured school with an emphasis on "the three R's."

mity dictates that children should learn a standardized and basic curriculum of "reading, 'riting, and 'rithmetic," while for others the values of freedom, individualism, and progress require a more diverse, flexible, and issue-oriented approach to education. Again, while data have not been collected on the issue, it is likely that educators tend to take the latter position, while a large proportion of the population would prefer the three R's approach to education—again underscoring the cultural conflicts surrounding lower education.

Values and progressive beliefs

At the higher educational level, this cultural conflict manifests itself in the vocational versus liberal arts beliefs. As long as higher education remained elitist, the liberal arts view of the well-rounded student prevailed, but with the advent of mass higher education over the last three decades, beliefs in the "no nonsense" and "relevant" education—that is, a vocationally oriented education—have become prominent.

In sum, these beliefs define some of the parameters of the problems inhering in the structure of education. Beliefs do more than merely define areas of cultural conflict, however. Beliefs are rooted in core values and they influence the actual operation of the educational process in America. In so doing, they have affected the way education has become structured.

PROBLEMS IN THE STRUCTURE OF
LOWER EDUCATION

The questioning of the educational process in primary and secondary schools represents a reaction to the present system. Several features of this system should be highlighted:

First, in accordance with beliefs about equal opportunity, American lower education is "massified," providing education for all school-age children. The very size and scope of this task inevitably leads to a bureaucratization of public school structures that can, at times create a "bureaucratic ethic" revolving around the processing of students and the maintenance of control and efficiency. In so doing, the educational system realizes values of conformity, but at the same time this orientation, as it is translated into a myriad of concrete educational practices, can cause problems of how to realize the value of "freedom." How, for example, are flexibility, humaneness, and innovativeness to be taught students within a structure emphasizing control, order, and efficiency?

"Massification" and education

Second, compared to other modern societies and in accordance with beliefs in local control, American education is highly decentralized; it is financed and administered primarily at the state and local community levels. The United States is without any clear *national* education policy, system of financing, or administration. Although supplemented by federal funds flowing from an array of agencies, lower public education is financed principally by state and local taxes and administered primarily by local school officials. Such financial and administrative decentralization has often resulted in enormous discrepancies in the quality of education in different school districts, cities, states, and regions, thus violating the value of equality. Furthermore, dependency on local property taxes, as well as local administrative control, can subject schools to social and political pressures within the local community, creating problems concerning how the schools should be run and by whom. Moreover, the financing of schools through local property taxes aggravates the inequity of the tax system since property taxes are less progressive than income taxes.

Third, because schools are decentralized and are administered locally, teaching techniques and approaches vary. Such a situation gives the school system some flexibility to deal with local variations in the educational problems of students, but it has also created a situation where many unproven, ineffective, and harmful educational approaches are carried out without adequate controls or evaluative procedures. The fact that reading, writing, and arithmetic scores have been dropping each year for over a decade might suggest that many of the new techniques have failed in at least this sense, yet, they are still employed. While perhaps the drop in scores is attributable to testing errors, the trend has rekindled the three R's beliefs that argue for a more standardized and structured curriculum. More progressive educators contend, on the other hand, that reducing innovation and experimentation would impose a rigidity and structure no longer appropriate for our fluid, change-oriented society. At the very least, local variations and experimentations now pose a dilemma as advocates of three R's and progressive beliefs begin to do battle over what's "right" for America's schools.

Fourth, it has been noted by many that public schools are dominated by values emphasizing activism and achievement. While such an emphasis can encourage high levels of performance for some, it can also be discriminatory against those students who do not learn well under conditions of competition and constant evaluation for achievement. To the extent that educational attainment determines one's social status as an adult, this situation increases the likelihood that those from the middle classes, where competition and achievement are most likely to be emphasized (B. Rosen, 1956), will have a competitive advantage in schools and later in the job market over those from different class and cultural backgrounds where other val-

Decentralization, local administration, and financing

Teaching technique variations

Emphasis on competition and individual achievement

ues may be emphasized. Such a situation can perpetuate inequalities in American society.

The myriad of social problems that these four basic features of the primary and secondary schools can generate for some segment of the population can be, for our purposes, reduced to three basic educational dilemmas: (1) control versus freedom of students in the schools; (2) decentralized versus centralized administration; and (3) equality of education.

CONTROL VERSUS FREEDOM OF STUDENTS

Americans value conformity to authority and accepted practices as well as individual creativity and innovativeness (Williams, 1970:433–499). This conflict of values is reflected in educational ideology and practice since the schools are charged with imparting both the capacity to conform and innovate. At present, despite many people's belief that schools are too permissive, values of conformity appear to dominate in American schools. One reason for this apparent domination may reside in the fact that American schools were often expanded in the late 1800s to assimilate masses of diverse immigrants into "the American way of life." Another reason lies in the nature of the job market for which schools prepare students—a market dominated by routinized, standardized, and bureaucratized jobs requiring considerable control of worker activity. Even aside from these two forces, the very fact that America seeks to educate all its young requires a *mass* educational program which, in turn, creates extensive school bureaucracies—and bureaucratization tends to generate its own imperatives for conformity, control, and regularity.

The goals of mass assimilation and vocational preparation have, overtime, become bureaucratically institutionalized. Given a commitment to mass education, bureaucratization is perhaps inevitable; and given an emphasis on vocationalism, this bureaucracy, as it evolves its own structure in thousands of local communities, would be expected to be concerned with efficiency in imparting basic skills directly relevant to a job or college; and because educational bureaucracies are presently dependent on the goodwill of the local community for financing, they naturally have an interest in demonstrating their efficiency to the general public. One way to demonstrate efficiency is to maintain an orderly, serene, and controlled school environment.

Bureaucratization of schools

In one study, Jonathan Kozol (1967) found an unusual degree of emphasis on cultural uniformity and order explicitly stated in the teacher's manual at a Boston public school:

Character traits to be developed: Obedience to duty [and] constituted authority, . . . self-control, . . . responsibility, . . . gratitude, . . . kindness, . . . good workmanship and perseverance, . . . loyalty, . . . teamwork. . . .

Educators with a clear "progressive" bias have argued that schools operate in many subtle ways to induce order and conformity (Silberman, 1970:113–157; Friedenberg, 1963:155–188). For example, in most American schools there is considerable emphasis on the clock, time, and the schedule. School can at times, progressives argue, become a place where the clock and the schedule, rather than the needs and desires of students or teachers, determine what should occur. For these scholars, such scheduling can be exacerbated by the lesson plans used by most schools to implement a standardized curriculum. Further, administrative rules can, in some schools, emphasize silence, with a sign of "good teaching" and "efficiency" being a quiet and orderly classroom. Compounding the concern for silence, they note, is the restriction of free movement within the school. By governing movement, much like that on an assemblyline, the appearance of efficiency and order is again maintained. The grading system in most American schools, with its emphasis on competitive evaluation, further orders and constrains school activity. Moreover, critics emphasize, the use of standardized IQ and achievement tests, as well as the daily evaluations of teachers and the term grading system of schools, have allowed some schools prematurely to sort out students on the basis of their "ability" as established by tests and to direct them into "learning" or "achievement" tracks from which it can be difficult to escape.

Progressives critique of "the system"

From the perspective of progressives, the restrictive atmosphere of schools can become so institutionalized that teaching innovations (team teaching, televised instruction, "new" types of lesson plans, ungraded learning, and achievement rather than age groupings of students) are rendered less effective in realizing goals of individual creativity and innovativeness because of the bureaucratic imperative to appear efficient. Their charges have been partially supported by at least one study: John Goodlad (1969), for example, in summarizing the findings from a study of 100 kindergarten and first grade classrooms in 13 states, found little evidence that the reform movement of the 1950s and 1960s had made a significant impact on the way schools were administered. He and his researchers found that a single teacher tended to lead all instruction, with students passively responding, usually one by one, in a controlled classroom; pupils rarely did individual, self-sustaining work; standard textbooks were the most conspicuous learning instruments; small groups of students in the pursuit of knowledge were rarely found.

Thus, this one study contradicts the impression of many Americans that the schools are engaged in loosely structured programs. The emphasis on control and conformity, however, does appear to support the schools' desires for order and control. For example, a Louis Harris poll on parental attitudes conducted for a national magazine, notes that two-thirds of high school parents believe that "maintaining discipline is more important than student self-inquiry." Are the "failings" of the schools—that is, lower achievement scores on reading, writing, and math—a result of parents getting what they want? Or, are unproven experiments in each school disrupting the structured and formalized educational process. At present, no definitive answer to these questions exists.

The dilemma for American society becomes one of how to realize the value of conformity as well as the values of freedom and individualism. At the school level, this dilemma becomes one of implementing control and innovativeness within a formal, bureaucratic structure.

SOCIOLOGICAL INSIGHTS

FREE SCHOOLS AS AN ALTERNATIVE OR A PERMISSIVE NIGHTMARE?

In recent years the "free school" or "new school" alternative to current schools structures has been advocated and implemented. What are the principles of free schools? The ideology of free schools is summarized here as means of highlighting the conflict in America over "how to educate."

In the new schools of American lower education, the administration must actively seek to find ways to promote freedom of movement, contact, and discussion among students and, most of all, it must abandon the mania for the clock and the crushing routine typical of both elementary and secondary schools. Additionally, the social partitioning of students by age levels, as well as the partitioning of the school's physical plant, must be abandoned. Age stratification can be one of the most destructuve forces in education because it circumscribes the number of contacts and relationships possible among students, while imparting a compartmentalized view of the world. By making the physical plant more open and by eliminating, at least some of the time, age, grade, and sex restrictions on the use of facilities, more creative use of the school's plant will ensue.

The current system of grading in American schools must cease to be an end in itself and, instead, must become a diagnostic tool indicating a child's weaknesses and strengths. Coupled with changes in the grading system, state and national math, reading, and IQ tests must be used to evaluate school and teacher performance, not to categorize and stratify students prematurely into ability groupings.

The new school classroom can be a place where students talk, discuss, argue, and get involved in what they are doing. In such an environment, the teacher is the facilitator of learning that can involve both gentle prodding and drill. The new classroom will be noisier (and appear more chaotic), but the noise will reflect the excitement that comes with learning. If the classroom is to meet the intellectual and human potential of its students, it must become a relaxed, informal, comfortable place filled with interesting things to do.

The new school should have a curriculum because there are certain things that all students must know, but informal classrooms do not necessarily imply a "flabby" educational process. Elementary school students must be made aware that they are expected to learn certain materials, but the *manner* in which this awareness is generated does not have to be formally stated. Informal prodding, drilling, and even testing can communicate the teacher's expectation without imposing a rigid lesson plan and regular graded examinations.

An enormous burden falls upon the teacher in the informal system of new schools. The teacher must be more alert and constantly ready to respond to a student, while not being able to fall back on the lesson plan or school routine. What is commonly misunderstood about informal teaching is that teachers do not abandon their authority. Teachers enforce rules concerning good conduct; but in an informal system, they can enforce rules more effectively because authority is based on respect. Another misunderstanding about the teacher's role revolves around the belief that teachers abdicate teaching and instructing to the students. This is not the case because certain subjects—reading at the elementary level and some complex subjects at the secondary level—cannot be acquired without some direct teacher-to-student instruction. The manner of this instruction should deemphasize the "chalk talk" at the front of the room, however, with students sitting quietly and passively. The teacher must be willing to engage smaller groups of students informally—cajoling them, reacting to their inquiries, and yet imparting necessary substance. Another mistaken assumption about informal teaching is that it takes an exceptional teacher to be effective. But it can be argued that it is in the formal educational approach, with all its emphases on order, control, routine, silence, and scheduling, that teachers must be exceptional to ever reach the students.

Such is the ideology of free schools. Can it be implemented? In light of current public opinion about order and control in the schools and a return to the basic three[1] Rs, it would seem unlikely. Perhaps the free school will have to exist outside the public schools, posing a private alternative to public education in America.

CENTRALIZATION VERSUS DECENTRALIZATION

In America, as in no other modern industrial nation, education is decentralized. The task of financing and administering lower education has been given to the states, and they in turn delegate much to the local communities. While some funds flow into the states and communities from various federal agencies, state income and sales taxes, plus local community property taxes, provide the resources to support most lower public education. The consequences of such decentralization are far-reaching.

1. Decentralization can generate inequality in school facilities from state to state, as well as within any state or local community. With the financing of schools tied to state and community taxes, poor states and communities are less able to afford the same physical facilities or quality of teachers as can more affluent areas. The frequent result is that those who are most in need of educational opportunities, the poor and disadvantaged, are the least likely to get them. In 1971 the California Supreme Court ruled that the use of local property taxes to finance education "discriminates against the poor . . . [and] makes the quality of the child's education a function of the wealth of his parents and neighbors." If this landmark decision is upheld by the U.S. Supreme Court, statewide financing of education would become more equitable.

Consequences of decentralization

2. The decentralized profile of American lower education reduces the ability of the federal government to implement nationwide policies, such as school integration. Since schools are more financially dependent on local than federal funds, they are more responsive to local public sentiment. While the federal government has some financial leverage, it does not have as much as the states and communities. Equally important, the federal government has no centralized and clearly articulated administrative linkage with the states and local communities, except through the Office of Education, a subdivision within the Department of Health, Education, and Welfare which has only vague and shifting administrative and fiscal responsibilities.

3. With unclear fiscal or administrative linkages to the states and local schools, federal funds flow into the schools from many diverse agencies. While the Office of Education does coordinate these expenditures to a limited extent, much financial and administrative duplication occurs, sometimes resulting in the inefficient use of federal tax dollars.

4. Financing schools from local property taxes and state revenues has created a financial crisis in the schools. It is increasingly difficult to finance lower education from property taxes or limited state revenues. To do so has raised property taxes to such an extent that taxpayers are now consistently rejecting school bonds and tax override elections in even the more affluent suburban districts. In many large cities that already have severe financial problems, the lack of revenue has caused a decline in the quality of educational facilities—a fact that may help explain the drop in student achievement scores.

5. Finally, administrative and fiscal decentralization exposes the schools to the fads of public opinion and political manipulation in a community. In many local communities in America, education is a political issue, with the result that schools can become centers for political battles, only some of which concern the quality of education.

Centralization of education initially might seem like the easy solution to most of these problems. The schools could be administratively centralized into a cabinet-level department of education and financed by increased federal income taxes. Correspondingly, increases in federal taxes would be countered by a lowering of state income and local property taxes. Transforming American education in this way would give it a centralized profile similar to that in other modern nations; however, whether such a change is desirable is unclear. While partially resolving one set of problems, it may create new problems. The centralized school systems in large cities such as New York can offer some clue as to the dangers involved in centralization (Rogers, 1968).

First, centralization establishes a long chain of command and authority that can make teachers and administrators upward

Problems with centralization

oriented rather than student oriented. Level upon level of subordinates could, under some circumstances, make educators just as "politicized" as they sometimes become under pressure from the local community.

Second, large bureaucracies usually tend to evidence fragmentation of administrative units from one another, resulting in much duplication of effort. Whether such waste would be less than that in the current system cannot be known, but if previous experience with large federal agencies can serve as a guide, considerable fragmentation, isolation, and duplication might well be expected.

Third, fragmentation and isolation of administrative units creates a situation in which individual units spend most of their energies attempting to consolidate their power with respect to other units. In turn, strong informal norms emphasizing self-preservation are likely to emerge within administrative units, deflecting further attention away from organizational goals (such as educating students). These processes result in the bureaucracy's increasing insulation from, and ignorance of, its clients; and internal politics and personal career ambitions of bureaucrats could conceivably begin to take precedence over the goals of education and service to the children of a community.

As David Rogers (1968) points out, teacher professionalism and

With growing unionization of school systems, the teacher strike has become a common occurence. Here Chicago teachers have just voted to strike, shutting down over 650 city schools.

unionization, which are typical of highly centralized systems, can compound the trend toward bureaucratic isolation. While professionalism keeps competence high, it can isolate teachers and administrators from students; and as the national profession assumes prominence, the implementation of its latest fads, techniques, and formulas can take precedence over the unique needs of diverse groups of students. Similarly, unionism can give teachers needed wage increases, but at the same time it can enslave teachers in one more bureaucracy (the union) and thereby limit choices in dealing with their clients, the students. Thus, while centralization can perhaps reduce educational inequalities, resolve the current fiscal crisis, allow for more implementation of national policy through the schools, and make educators less vulnerable to local political pressures, it can potentially result in a waste of resources, isolation from students, and bureaucratic rigidity. The pros and cons of this issue make centralization versus decentralization an enduring dilemma in American education.

QUESTIONS OF EDUCATIONAL EQUALITY

Mass education in America was to become a democratizing influence, increasing the capacities for mobility among people who lived in and migrated to America. Public schools, in Thomas Jefferson's words, were to " . . . bring into action that mass of talents which lies buried in poverty in every country for want of means of development. . . ." To some extent mass public education has increased the overall abilities and talents of many Americans, but it does not do so equally.

This situation is of great importance in modern America, for the United States is now a credentialed society. One's chances for money and prestige in the occupational sphere are directly related to educational credentials and only indirectly to desire, ability, and performance on the job. While credentialing is a convenient and perhaps necessary way to assess qualifications of masses of potential workers, it grants the educational system the power to be society's gatekeeper. Those who conform to the system get the appropriate diplomas; those who cannot conform, for various personal, cultural, and socioeconomic reasons, are more likely to be placed at the bottom of the labor pool.

Education as society's gatekeeper

American education, thus, reinforces as much as it breaks down social class boundaries. While supposedly established to help the disadvantaged, public schools were not an important path to upward mobility among early immigrant generations—a situation that contradicted equality of opportunity beliefs. More frequently, mobility was achieved by forcing children into the work force so that they

*The current system of financing schools from local property taxes
(with some state and federal aid) creates an enormous inequality in
school facilities. Poor school districts will have inadequate schools,
affluent districts will have good schools. How much equality of
opportunity exists for this student?*

could contribute to the family's total income, thereby sacrificing the
younger generation's education (Thernstrom, 1964). Today, despite
an expensive and conscientious effort in many areas, schools have not
promoted equality. For example, by most statistics the educational
gap between nonwhites and whites has remained roughly the same.
Absolute gains in years of schooling for blacks and other minority
groups have been paralleled by similar gains in the white population,
therefore, preserving the gap. In the credentialed society, such educational gaps translate into income differentials, thus maintaining the
American system of inequality. This failure of the schools to be an
equalizing force can be attributed to two forces: (1) the structure of
public education and (2) the traits that lower-class children, especially minority poor, bring with them to school.

1. Structural Discrimination in Public Schools. Some critics have
argued that, historically, public schools have had the consequence of
imparting to the lower classes the habits of "obedience and submis-
sion necessary for public peace, a docile labor force, and the protection of property" (Silberman, 1970:60). While such a charge is certainly an overstatement, it does appear that many of the bureaucratic

rigidities of schools have operated, usually in an unintentional way, against children from nonmiddle-class backgrounds. For even in the face of an educational ideology and well-intentioned programs emphasizing equality for the poor, the structure of the schools has built-in racial, ethnic, and social class biases.

First, the very formality of the school system, with its frequent emphasis on the clock, scheduling, routine, silence, and restriction of movement, can potentially discriminate against some children from lower-class cultures, where some studies show that physical aggressiveness, noise, and spontaneity are more likely to be valued (W. Miller, 1969). Forced to sit quietly and follow routines, lower-class children can sometimes become alienated from a school system dominated by values of order and control.

Second, the teachers of public schools tend to be from the middle class. While most have a sincere desire to reach lower-class students, studies have shown that subtle attitude or expectation that these students will have learning problems can set up a false prophecy that the teachers themselves fulfill. Potentially, by expecting so little of their lower-class students, they can at times impart to them their middle-class prejudice—not necessarily intentional or malicious—that their students will have trouble doing well (Rosenthal and Jacobson, 1968; Silberman, 1970:83–86). The effects of open prejudice by teachers are obvious, but more pervasive is the conveyance of an unconscious, subtle, middle-class attitude toward lower-class children that perpetuates the very learning problems that teachers consciously want to eliminate. This bias, and the self-fulfilling prophecy that it generates, is probably inevitable as long as a large proportion of teachers—regardless of their good intentions—come from middle-class backgrounds.

Third, the testing and grading system discriminates against students from the lower classes. Whether an IQ test, a national achievement exam, or an in-class quiz, the very fact that a competitive and timed test is being given favors students from middle-class homes, where the importance of test taking and verbal competition is more likely to be emphasized. Furthermore, although some changes have been made on standardized national examinations, tests remain verbal and written—again giving children from the middle class, where greater stress is placed on words, a competitive advantage. Also, national achievement and IQ exams frequently portray a middle-class world. For example, a typical question from a standardized IQ test reads (Havighurst and Neugarten, 1967:78–79):

> A symphony is to a composer as a book is to what?
> ( ) paper ( ) sculptor ( ) author ( ) musician ( ) man

Biases against nonmiddle-class students

Because symphonies, sculptors, authors, and musicians are more familiar to middle-class children, they are likely to do better than their counterparts from the lower classes. Doing well on tests is crucial in American schools, for it is on the basis of national achievement and IQ examinations as well as classroom grades that students are labeled, channeled, and counseled into college preparatory or vocational programs (Cicourel and Kitsuse, 1963). Furthermore, since it is test performance that determines success, one's educational self-concept as a good, bad, or mediocre student is internalized on the basis of these examinations. Since such self-concepts determine not only performance but also educational aspirations, the current system of test taking appears to discriminate against the poor by convincing them, at a very early age, that they cannot survive in the competitive world of the middle classes.

The biases of the schools operate against all lower-class children, especially those who evidence distinctive cultural patterns that deviate sharply from the middle-class cultural ambience of the schools. It is for this reason that most studies of school achievement find that family background and neighborhood have more influence on a student's test scores than the quality of school facilities or teacher qualifications (Coleman, 1966; Jencks, 1969, 1972). When researchers originally discovered this fact, they were surprised. They had expected to find that inequality in school facilities suppressed achievement and accounted for the learning problems of students from poor backgrounds. Instead, variations in family background appeared to explain why students did not achieve in school. It cannot be doubted, of course, that certain family characteristics, such as unemployed parents, marital instability, lack of parental education, and crushing family poverty, can impair learning and hence school achievement. These researchers (Coleman, 1966), however, may not have devoted sufficient attention to another fact: school environments, structured in ways that discriminate against lower-class cultural patterns, will inevitably force researchers to the conclusion that underachievement is caused by the family background and neighborhood of the student. In fact, it may be the school structure (not its physical facilities, but its social and cultural environment) that is deficient. Perhaps, as many critics argue, the imposition of a middle-class world on lower-class students should not be viewed as a failing of the lower-class family, but alternatively, as a failing on the part of the schools for not reaching lower-class students.

School structures may be deficient

This argument has some merit. It would be difficult, however, to contend that these researchers have not isolated a key force in retarding educational achievement—the family. Current assessment of the problems of lower-class students are probably accurate for many, and thus, it is necessary to understand in more detail how family and school interact to reduce educational attainment for lower-class children.

2. Backgrounds of Students. The traits that children bring with them to the schools will obviously affect their performance. The school rewards some traits and punishes others; and a school system dominated by a middle-class, mass culture will be more likely to reward the traits of students who display middle-class rather than lower-class attributes. However, such a portrayal is too simple. The fact remains that many lower-class homes and environments are not conducive to success in schools, even if schools were structured along ungraded and noncompetitive informal lines and were to have lower-class teachers and administrators.

Family and performance in schools

Although it is difficult to establish culturally free criteria, it is likely that lower-class backgrounds do not lead to the cultivation of certain motives (McClelland, 1961), attitudes and values (B. Rosen, 1956), language patterns, and cognitive styles (Silberman, 1970:80) that will facilitate learning in *any* type of school. Attribute deficiencies are perhaps not as great as many educators imply, but some preschool training may be necessary for children from *some* lower-

Some efforts at individualized instruction for minority students from deprived backgrounds have been undertaken in many schools.

class backgrounds. Yet, in accordance with values of conformity and in partial contradiction to values of freedom and individualism, most current preschool programs not only attempt to overcome these basic deficiencies, but also attempt to indoctrinate students into more general behavior styles that will help them survive in middle-class schools. Such a program places an enormous burden on the individual student rather than on the school. For indeed, if the value of progress in helping the disadvantaged is to be realized, it may be necessary for the school to become more flexible and adaptable to lower-class cultural patterns.

Charles Silberman (1970:98–112), in his research on several "successful" slum schools, documents some of the conditions necessary for such success: (1) A warm and sympathetic school environment, (2) a school staffed by ordinary teachers who *expect* their students to do well, (3) administrators who will not allow teachers to fail and will hold the teacher rather than the student accountable for failure, (4) schools that also educate the parents and expect the parents to help in their children's education. Changes allowing for the implementation of these general goals might help reduce educational inequality.

HIGHER EDUCATION IN AMERICA

THE DILEMMA OF SIZE AND SCOPE

By 1972 there were over 2500 institutions of higher education in America (H.E.W., 1972). And in this same year one survey reported that 6.4 million students were enrolled in four-year colleges, with another 1.7 million in two-year colleges. These figures are conservative, however, since they come only from institutions answering a survey questionnaire (Parker, 1973). Since World War II state-supported universities have grown most rapidly, culminating in extensive multiuniversity systems in many states. The growing size of college and universities is a reflection of how much America has become a credentialed society. In order to get a "good" job, formal education credentials are increasingly considered necessary, with the result that close to one-half of college age youth have entered the credentials race. This percentage is just about double that of fifteen years ago—underscoring the rapid growth of higher education. While college enrollments have begun to level off in recent years, the problems associated with size and growth still pose a number of dilemmas which have yet to be resolved.

Expanded enrollments have increased the size of many college and university campuses. In turn, increases in size have led to even more

Growth of higher education

Many students attempt to assert their individuality in the highly bureaucratized world of American higher education.

SOCIOLOGICAL
INSIGHTS

EDUCATION AS BIG BUSINESS?

With over 8 million students attending universities and colleges, it can be expected that education has become a big business involving the expenditure of billions of dollars each year. For example, the expenditures for the staff of universities and colleges is enormous: The 266,913 teachers listed by the American Association of College Professors (a voluntary organization) in only 1242 colleges receive salaries totaling $4.38 billion. Coupled with the remaining teachers and support staff, a considerable segment of the population works directly in higher education. And, of course, many work in the construction trades that build and expand the physical facilities of colleges and universities. Moreover, colleges and universities keep 8 million workers out of the job market in a given year, thus, increasing their impact upon the economy. Higher education is, therefore, intimately involved in economic processes and this involvement extends well beyond its function of training the young in various intellectual and vocational skills.

bureaucratization: the ever-escalating specialization, compartmentalization, and neutralization of college life. To process the masses of students entering American universities has resulted in a shortage of funds for faculty and hence larger classes, as well as an increased reliance on centralized records, advance registration, and other cost saving and efficient ways of processing students.

However, increases in the size of universities have also resulted in the development of large libraries, excellent laboratory facilities, and concentrations of highly skilled faculties. Just how to reconcile these advantages of large size with the impersonality of the accompanying bureaucratization thus represents a major dilemma for America's large state and private universities (Sewell, 1971).

To the extent that the university's most important goals are the introduction of students into the processes of higher learning, the instillation of a commitment to use reason in the resolution of problems, and the development of both technical competence and intellectual integrity, the current system of mass education is only partially successful. (Such goals, of course, go against beliefs in vocationalism.) And yet, it appears difficult to organize mass education on other than

Higher education's goals

a large university and multiuniversity format since the costs involved in building and maintaining smaller campuses are high—a fact of economic life which threatens the solvency of many small, private colleges. Such mass organization, however, involves high levels of bureaucratization and all the attendant problems for students and professors caught in the organizational restrictions of large bureaucracies.

THE DILEMMA OF THE JOB MARKET

Most colleges and universities are ideologically committed to introducing students to "the life of the mind," that is, their concern is with education for its own sake rather than education for specific jobs and careers. While professional graduate schools, such as law, medicine, social work, and business, are structured along vocational lines, the undergraduate curriculum at most colleges and universities tends to emphasize a more general and broad training.

All surveys reveal that most students enter colleges and universities in order to prepare themselves for a "good job" and to acquire the necessary credentials for jobs carrying relatively high prestige and income. Although a broad liberal arts education may facilitate job performance, the actual skills required for most jobs are not acquired as undergraduates. They are often learned on the job. Some careers require highly specific training—law, medicine, dentistry, engineering, or social work—but much of this training could be done within a much shorter period of time.

Liberal arts versus vocational education

This fact raises questions that students themselves often ask: How much training do they need for most jobs in the labor market? Do they want a broad liberal arts education? Is it really necessary from the standpoint of the technical skills required of most jobs to force students to go through the expense and work of a college education? While there are no data on the matter, many students want "a degree" that "certifies" them as eligible for certain types of jobs. For many jobs this degree does not mean that they are anymore qualified than someone without the degree, or with less education, but employers and students have come to believe that the degree is a *necessary* requisite despite the fact that much of the college experience has involved little training directly related to many jobs that "require" a college degree. Thus, one of the questions to be raised is: How many jobs really require the training received from a four-year college degree? How many students would not go to college if they could get the same job with a year of vocational training? Or, have students and employers become trapped in a credential mythology, with employers believing that the brightest employees will have degrees and stu-

Masses of students graduate each year, each filled with hope and expectation of the good life to come. Increasingly, however, many of these graduates will have trouble finding jobs.

dents believing that degrees are necessary to document their brightness?

The swelling of college enrollments reflects students' beliefs that to make it in America they must have a college education. One result of this fact is that college degrees "mean less" because now many more people have them. At one time a college education provided a significant advantage in the job market, but ironically, with so many seeking degrees under the assumption that it represents an advantage, the advantages decrease. Hence, it is not difficult to document many cases of college-educated students taking "lesser" jobs that they could have taken with only a couple of years of college or none at all. While all statistics indicate that a college degree still "means something on the job market," it may mean less in the future.

This situation poses a dilemma for higher education: Is its function to encourage a credentials race among greater numbers of students who will be less and less marketable in a job market increasingly filled with college-educated workers? In many ways, an answer to this question must come from outside colleges and universities. Employers will probably have to decide that the college degree no longer assures them of the best employees and that other measures of ability and motivation are more important than college credentials. Such a transformation appears a long way off, but as students with degrees increasingly have trouble finding jobs, especially during economic recessions, then pressures for change may be generated. This situation will eventually pose a dilemma for colleges and universities as well as students who make the sacrifices to attend them.

THE DILEMMA OF RESEARCH VERSUS TEACHING

In all large universities the dilemma of teaching versus research prevails. This dilemma is a reflection of the dual functions performed by universities: to impart knowledge to students, especially knowledge related to a vocation, and to expand the existing body of knowledge in society through research. Both are necessary functions of the university, and yet to emphasize one appears to require a deemphasis of the other. To promote research requires the diversion of university funds into research facilities, a large pool of graduate students to perform research legwork, and time off from undergraduate teaching for professors. To concentrate on undergraduate education requires more teaching time from professors, less subsidy of graduate students, and large amounts of university funds for a wide variety of programs.

Part of the trouble in reconciling these two functions stems from the expectation that the same people—professors—must perform both functions: teaching and research. Too often students and professors have been led to believe that a good researcher is likely to be a good teacher because research keeps one up-to-date in their field. In reality, given the high degree of specialization within academic disciplines, it is more likely that researchers are behind in all areas except their narrow fields of interest. Furthermore, in addition to a breadth of knowledge, good teaching requires that professors spend time with

Research versus
teaching conflicts

students outside the classroom. Thus, except in rare instances, the same person cannot be both an excellent teacher and researcher. Excellent researchers can often be exceptional lecturers, but rarely do they have out-of-class time to spend with large numbers of students. Conversely, teachers who must keep up in their fields, prepare lectures, and spend time with students cannot become overly involved in time-consuming research activity.

In the abstract, the solution to the dilemma is obvious: Strike a division of labor between research and teaching. Some professors could be primarily teachers; others could concentrate on research, giving occasional lectures. Maintaining such a division of labor has proven difficult for several reasons:

1. Research productivity is more easily measured than is quality of teaching. Since all bureaucracies, especially large universities, require evidence of efficiency and performance, research is more likely to be rewarded than teaching.
2. The reputations of professors outside the local bureaucracy determines their mobility from university to university. A reputation as an excellent teacher rarely goes beyond the local campus, and it rarely extends even beyond the classroom. For professors to establish reputations, therefore, requires them to publish articles in trade journals. Professional prestige stems from the quantity and quality of these publications. Even within academic departments, prestige is established by one's nonteaching activities: research, publishing, and consulting.
3. Similarly, a university's prestige relative to other colleges is established not by the quality of its teachers as teachers, but by the quality of its teachers as researchers. Most administrators of universities, as well as most students and their parents, are concerned about reputation and prestige—thus unwittingly encouraging the very faculty research that can dilute an undergraduate teaching program.

The rewarding of research over teaching aggravates trends evident with bureaucratization: increasing distance between professors and students, large classes, and general lack of intellectual community. Yet, just how to transform the reward system in universities so as to encourage good teaching in addition to quality research is difficult. Some professors are unwilling to give up their mobility or suffer the interpersonal sting of their colleagues. Few administrators, parents, and students wish to allow a school's national reputation to decline in the name of good teaching, especially in a credentialed society where the reputation of the school from which one gets a degree is initially more important than one's actual capabilities. And for these reasons, the dilemma of teaching versus research will be one of the enduring problems of structure in American higher education.

THE DILEMMA OF INSTITUTIONAL COOPTATION

Since World War II the federal government has increasingly funded university research. Such funding has proven financially beneficial to America's large universities: Research funds have allowed them to increase their graduate student populations, to assemble excellent faculties, to construct large-scale and expensive research facilities and, by taking as much as 40 to 50 percent of research grants to pay for overhead costs (accounting, providing offices, etc.), they add to their general funds. In fact, to maintain the elaborate research facilities of most large universities, and a growing number of smaller campuses, now requires a constant flow of federal research funds and contracts. Most large research projects involving elaborate equipment and extensive personnel could not be conducted without federal funding—making the research enterprise, as well as much graduate and undergraduate education, dependent on federal monies. There are a number of dangers involved in such a financial liaison, however (Maccoby, 1964; Orlans, 1962; Lapp, 1962):

The dangers of financial liaisons

1. Government-financed research can become narrow and confined to the specific purposes of federal agencies. Fiscally confining the purview of university research violates one of the purposes of such research within the university: to expand knowledge in all spheres of human endeavor.
2. Large-scale, government-financed research tends to be bureaucratized, increasing the potential for a conservative, rigid, and efficiency oriented administrative apparatus that could, at times, stifle creative research. In fact, bureaucratized research can become banal because incumbents within both the federal and the university research bureaucracies can potentially seek to avoid controversy (Maccoby, 1964). Bureaucratic preferences for safe, predictable, and noncontroversial findings can, of course, run counter to basic university goals revolving around the free expansion of knowledge. Furthermore, bureaucratized research tends to be atheoretical since theoretical work cannot be easily measured and recorded by bureaucrats concerned with demonstrating output ("efficiency") for each research dollar. Routine, atheoretical, and applied experiments are highly functional for research bureaucracies, but often less useful from the standpoint of developing science.
3. In accepting money from the federal government, the university

accepts and supports the current ranking of national priorities. The university as a place of free inquiry where assumptions of all kinds are to be questioned can thus be put in a position of implicitly supporting the very societal conditions that it must, ideally at least, skeptically analyze. Under these conditions some researchers might be reluctant to speak out on issues, even when they have considerable expertise, because they fear losing lucrative and prestigeful research contracts or because of their inability to see, through the bureaucratic maze, the potential dangers of their work. As Robert Lapp (1962:21) notes, for researchers involved in work on "gyromechanisms, or miniaturized electronics, on plasma physics . . . [it is] easy to forget the monstrous machines of destruction to which their work is contributing."

4. Research funded to meet current national priorities indirectly shapes the programs and structure of the university with respect to "the kind of staff it hires, the types of buildings and laboratories it builds, the space it assigns to different activities, the types of academic programs it permits to grow fastest, the distribution of its faculty efforts between research and teaching, and the attention its faculty gives to university affairs" (Sewell, 1971:115). While the dangers of open political manipulation are obvious, these kinds of subtle alterations of the university's direction by the lure of the federal dollar could potentially pose a danger to academic freedom and inquiry.

In addition to direct federal funding of research, the university maintains many other ties to its institutional environment: Universities own stock in corporations, many of which are primarily defense contractors; universities are often large landholders and, in some instances, slum lords; they compete for lucrative research contracts, much like business corporations; their faculty members often act as consultants for both government and business; and members of their boards of trustees are usually prominent businessmen, frequently from the companies with whom the universities do business (Ridgeway, 1968). Many of these connections are desirable and necessary in order to keep in contact with the broader community and to maintain the solvency of the university. To sever them completely would require a drastic increase in tuition at private universities and an increase in taxes at state campuses.

This financial dependency of the university on its institutional environment—from government research to stockholdings—presents a perplexing dilemma: What kinds of institutional connections should universities have, and which ones can it sever without biting the hand that feeds it? To cut itself off completely from the government and business would transform universities and colleges.

No permanent solution to this dilemma is possible. However, the university community will probably have to accept a *continual* conflict and dialogue over the issue of its affiliations. This dialogue has become institutionalized in recent years so that it takes the form of dialogue and compromise among conflicting factions rather than the confrontation politics so evident in the 1960s.

SOCIOLOGICAL
INSIGHTS

WHY DID STUDENTS REVOLT?

In the 1960s, and briefly in the early 1970s, college and university campuses were often scenes of confrontation and violence between students and forces of social control. Why did this revolt occur? Many scholars have sought to answer this question.

The complaints of students in the 1960s were well known: Universities are too impersonal; they emphasize narrow specialization; they underemphasize undergraduate education in favor of graduate education and research; they interfere in students' private and personal lives; they have been coopted by government and industry while remaining indifferent to major social problems; and, they have actually contributed to these problems in their admission, personnel, and financial policies (Sewell, 1971). Since these conditions existed for decades, it was not just the dilemmas of university structure that caused the revolt. Rather, a new kind of student entered this structure in the late 1960s, and these students were less tolerant of university and societal structure.

Most studies of student activists indicated that they come from affluent, middle-class backgrounds. Student leaders tended to come from families in which both parents were well-educated and in which moral and ethical issues were taken seriously. Activist leaders, then, were much like their parents: questioning, skeptical, and critical of the society in which they lived (Flacks, 1970a, 1970b, 1967; Keniston, 1970, 1969a, 1969b, 1968).

Youths from affluent, liberal backgrounds where middle-class values and life-styles were questioned eventually confronted the realities of the broader society. Their values and occupational aspirations were deviant and had little place for expression and realization. There were few notches in either the economy or government bureaucracy for such youths; almost all job alternatives were visualized as too authoritarian, too constraining on self-expression and human dignity, and too irrelevant to, if not supportive of, societywide problems of injustice, discrimination, and inequality. Events of the 1960s made students even more aware of how few alternatives they had. Because of the war in Vietnam, male students had to choose among fighting, leaving the country, going to jail, or hiding in the impersonal university structure.

Aggravating this situation was the status of students as a minority caught at the juncture of postadolescence and preadulthood (Horowitz and Friedland, 1970:118–148). Physically, intellectually, and psychologically students are adults, yet they are dependent for resources on their "more-adult" parents. Students, thus, remained disconnected from the broader society while being concentrated in what were often exploitive student housing ghettos and impersonal university structures that often operated as heavy-handed *in locus parentis* institutions.

The modern university increasingly approximates, to use a polemical phrase, a "knowledge factory" (Horowitz and Friedland, 1970). It is heavily bureaucratized and often appears, from a student's perspective, concerned as much with the efficient processing of students as with their education. For students committed to values emphasizing humaneness and freedom of self-expression, the rigidities of the university bureaucracy were difficult to tolerate.

Students have always grumbled about the impersonality of large, bureaucratized universities. But for the sons and daughters of educated, affluent professionals who have instilled an ethic of education for its own sake, the factory-like university system, stamping out properly credentialed "cogs" to be fed into a bureaucratized society became, for some, the symbol of the mass society and culture they deplored; for some it became a part of the "corrupt" society that must be either changed or destroyed. The latter sentiment was especially likely in large, research-oriented universities where the connections among the university, government, and industry were so extensive as to give the appearance of one large "establishment."

> Three conditions interacted to generate student unrest in the 1960s: the perceived incongruity between what affluent students thought should be and what was; the situation of being an exploited minority; and the bureaucratized, factorylike university. Why they interacted as they did is not fully understood. These same conditions no longer appear to generate violent protest, and yet their persistence poses an interesting question: Could a revolt occur again?

THE DILEMMA OF PRIORITIES

Universities have five principal functions:

Functions of the university

1. They are charged with the socialization of general skills and knowledge.
2. In doing so, especially in a credentialed society, they place and allocate people in the broader society.
3. They store and preserve the culture of a society—its history, lore, technology, and general fund of knowledge.
4. They expand the cultural storehouse in a society through research in a wide variety of fields.
5. They are involved in transforming the society on a broad front, whether through research innovations, criticism of existing governmental policies and priorities, or special educational programs.

All of these are proper functions for universities and colleges. However, which ones should have priority is in dispute and is at the core of most problems confronting higher education in America. The dilemmas of teaching versus research, of university involvement with government and industry, of student dissatisfaction with the academic bureaucracy, of the failure of universities to address many social problems, and of the creation of a credentialed society are all a reflection of the conflict inherent in meeting simultaneously these priorities.

In making the hard choices in the coming decades, a number of critical questions will need to be addressed: First, can the university educate a near majority of the population? The education ethic has created a situation where all youths and their parents feel they *must* go to college. Compounding this compulsion is the fact that employers so often require college credentials as a condition of employment.

Resolving conflicts of priorities

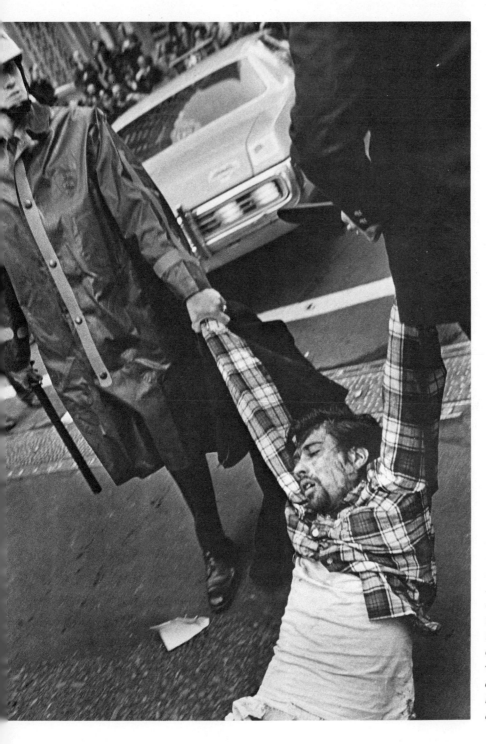

The questioning by students of the priorities in America's colleges and universities in the 1960s often led to violent confrontations between police and students.

Should both the education ethic and the concern with credentials be deemphasized, and should the university cease being society's gate-keeper? For indeed, is a college education critical for most jobs in the American economy?

Second, should the university continue to engage in basic research while cutting back on some of the applied research it currently undertakes? As long as the university is dependent on applied research funds, does it run the danger of being coopted by those agencies and enterprises that pay its bills?

Third, can the university transform society? Or, can problems of poverty, racism, urban decay, and inequality only be resolved by changes in the broader society? Do university personnel have an obligation to speak out on these issues, to address them in the classroom, and to consult with and criticize policymakers? But, then, can universities be staging areas for political protest?

While universities appear tranquil in the mid-1970s, they must operate under difficult financial problems. These financial problems will make questions of priorities and function even more important as colleges and universities begin to adjust to leveling student enrollments, severe economic difficulties, and graduates unable to find jobs.

SUMMARY

This chapter reviewed the problems of lower and higher education within their broader cultural and structural contexts. Specifically, cultural beliefs in equality of opportunity, local control and autonomy, and the three R's versus progressivism influence the definition and substance of America's educational problems. At the lower educational level, three problems currently pose dilemmas for Americans: (1) control versus freedom, (2) centralization versus decentralization, and (3) equality versus inequality. In turn, these educational problems are influenced by cultural beliefs as they have become incorporated into, and now legitimize, key structural arrangements: massification and bureaucratization, local financial and administrative control, local experimentation, and concern with individual achievement and activism.

At the higher educational level, the problems of size and scope of universities, of finding jobs for the educated, of trading off research and teaching, and of institutional cooptation are presently evident. These problems are the result of the cultural and structural conflicts over the priorities of universities in American society—that is, what they are supposed to do for students and society.

REVIEW QUESTIONS

1. List and summarize three dominant cultural beliefs about education.
2. Distinguish between lower and higher education.
3. Name four prominent features of lower education in America.
4. How is the conflict of control versus freedom manifested in lower educational structures?
5. What are the problems and prospects of educational centralization in America?
6. Indicate how inequality is built into the structure of lower education.
7. What are the priorities of higher education?
8. Discuss how conflicts among these reflect educational dilemmas built into the culture and structure of American education.

GLOSSARY

centralization the process of consolidating decision making and financing power in school systems in increasingly higher bodies of government. In the context of education, centralization means transferring financing and much decision-making power from the local communities to the state and federal governments

educational equality the question of whether or not the schools, in their structure, programs, and personnel, discriminate against certain groups of students and thus deny them the opportunity for an education equal to other students

higher education the term used to describe all educational institutions that educate high-school graduates

liberal arts education a college education stressing the importance of acquiring a broad knowledge base in all fields of human intellectual and creative endeavor as opposed to a highly specialized and technical education

lower education the term encompassing the elementary, junior high, and high school systems; those structures involved in precollege education in America

progressivism an educational philosophy which stresses the importance of school experiences facilitating adjustment to the broader world as opposed to rote learning of reading, writing, and arithmetic

the three R's an educational philosophy stressing the structured learning of reading, writing, and arithmetic as the most important and critical goal of education

PROLOGUE 5: POLITICAL PATTER

A few years ago, sitting on the lawn outside the student union at the University of California at Riverside was an emotional experience: One by one speakers would parade to a podium and denounce the priorities of government, its lust for war, its desire to kill the young, and its neglect of internal problems. Today, sitting in the same spot that I once cornered, I could hear students talking in much lower voices about somewhat different issues: "Why can't government provide jobs for people?" Why don't we have leadership?" "There is not much that can be done about government, it's too big to be responsive."

In the years between the turmoil of Vietnam and the present mood of quiet discontent, some important events in government occurred: A vice-president was shown, although not officially, to be guilty of crimes. An attorney general was convicted of a lesser crime after successful plea bargaining. A president was exposed after having openly lied to Americans and was forced from office. The once revered J. Edgar Hoover was shown to have blackmailed and intimidated citizens and politicians alike. And in the aftermath of Watergate, federal agencies were found to have abused citizens' rights.

Much has transpired in just five years. People once believed that "if he didn't know what he was doing, he wouldn't be in Washington." One would be hard pressed to find people who believed this today. But despite all the dissatisfaction and distrust of government, the anger and protest that typified the 1960s has given way to what appears to be a quiet resignation about government in America. I heard a conversation between two retired men on a park bench recently, and one said to the other, "government is just one of those necessary evils." The other nodded and that seemed to end their discussion about government.

Americans appear troubled by government. They are frustrated by its inability to deal with their particular problems, but they seem resigned in their frustration. They recognize that government is too big, too powerful, too removed from them for their desires and wishes to be heard, much less acted upon. Politicians still seek their vote, still make promises, and people still listen. But not with the same naivete, nor the same conviction that once typified their political activity.

The reactions of the public are expressions of people who are aware of the power of social structure to control and circumscribe their lives. The inability of government to help them is a result of forces built into the structure of government. It is this structure, and the culture surrounding it, that must be examined if we are to understand "what ails government" in America.

5

PROBLEMS OF GOVERNMENT

As American society celebrated its bicentennial, dissatisfaction, distrust, and disillusionment with government were evident. The aftermath of the Vietnam War, the Watergate scandals, and the exposure of abuses by the CIA, FBI, IRS, and other agencies has created, if only temporarily, a new examination of government in America. Moreover, the ideological conflict over how much government can and should do for its people has become an issue about which Americans are clearly divided. Thus, while Americans still support and believe in the form of government, it is viewed as an arena fraught with its own internal problems. These internal problems, however, have implications for other social problems. As the seat of power in a society, the actions of government influence the profile of problems in other social contexts—in education, in the family, in the economy, in the community, and in the distribution of scarce resources.

Social problems in America are intimately connected to political processes. Many have their roots in these processes, and all problems can be resolved only with the political will to confront and eliminate their causes. When government does not adequately address social problems, it can be said to have its own "problems of structure."

As we approach the study of political problems, however, we should remember that the problems of governance are not just the result of corrupt and evil politicians and power-hungry civil servants. Rather, corrupt politicians and violations of the law by federal agencies can exist in a system that is structured in ways that allow

Structure and political problems

123

SOCIOLOGICAL
INSIGHTS

**DOES THE PUBLIC TRUST
THE GOVERNMENT?**

The events of the last decade—Vietnam, Watergate, abuses of power by the CIA, FBI, and IRS—have caused rather dramatic changes in American's "trust," that is, their faith in government to "do what's right."

The following question and its results were taken from a national poll conducted by Market-Opinion Research Co. in 1964 and again in 1974:

Q. How much of the time do you think you can trust the government in Washington to do what is right?

	1964	1974
Always	14%	2%
Most of the time	62%	30%
Some of the time	22%	64%
Don't know	2%	4%

Source: Newsweek, December 15, 1975, p. 44.

and even reward political abuses. We must remember that it is not the individuals that must be examined; they simply enact roles from a script written by the structure of government.

While the individual incumbents in Congress, the judiciary, and the presidency obviously make some difference in what social problems are considered sufficiently grave to address and in determining what solutions are considered appropriate, the problems inhere in the structure and culture within which individuals operate. It is these problems of structure that we will analyze in this chapter because, in the long run, social problems in America will not be abolished by any politician until some of the cultural and structural dilemmas in government itself are overcome.

THE CULTURE OF AMERICAN GOVERNMENT

To understand the problems of American government requires an examination of some of the values and beliefs that legitimize and make political processes seem "right and proper." For while many Americans deplore some facet of politics in America, they simultaneously hold beliefs and values that sustain the very structures gen-

Americans believe strongly in the election of officials, even officials of questionable quality.

erating the problems that people perceive to exist. As with all enduring structures, they are not maintained only by deceit and fraud, or by raw power; rather, they are also believed to be "the correct" manifestation of strongly held values and beliefs. And recently, when government actions appear to some to violate the tenets of their political beliefs, a "problem" becomes evident.

Four dominant beliefs legitimize the key structural features of government in America and serve as a basis for the definition of social problems in government. For convenience, we label these (1) beliefs in local autonomy, (2) beliefs in big government, (3) beliefs in the balance of power, and (4) beliefs in the candidate democracy. In turn, as with all strongly held beliefs, they are rooted in the core values of American culture.

Dominant beliefs legitimize problems of government

Local governmental ceremonies still symbolize that American ideal of how government should be responsive to the needs of individual citizens.

BELIEFS IN LOCAL AUTONOMY

America was initially established as a federalist system in which a considerable amount of power and decision making was to occur at the state, county, and township levels. In accordance with dominant values of activism, individualism, and freedom, each state and local community was to be allowed freedom and autonomy to actively pursue their own individual interests. Such a situation was to represent the pinnacle of representative democracy as individuals within their local communities participated in those critical decisions affecting their daily lives. While the federal government now intervenes into most affairs of state, county, and local governments, this intervention goes against many strongly held beliefs about "big brother" and "big government as bad government." The phrases "states rights," "power to the people," and "local community con-

Local autonomy decreases

trol" have, at various times, mobilized the sentiments of a significant segment of the population to resist incursions on their autonomy, freedom, and right to actively pursue what they perceive to be their individual interests.

One of the consequences of these beliefs, as we will come to understand in more detail shortly, is that they encourage a federalist governmental system in which overlapping and conflicting roles among city, county, state, and federal governments are common. As a result, administration of national policies is difficult, inefficient, and involves many jurisdictional disputes among different levels of government.

BELIEFS IN BIG GOVERNMENT

While Americans believe in local autonomy and control, they also believe that the federal government "should do something about" and "provide solutions for" pressing issues such as poverty, unemployment, recessions, pollution, inflation, health care and education. Such beliefs do not just eminate from the "average" person, large corporations also want the government to "do something" about such matters as foreign competition, foreign cartels, international trade, domestic inflation, domestic competition, and regulation of domestic activities. For example, one survey by the U.S. Commerce Department revealed that even with high levels of dissatisfaction with government, 56 percent of the public still believe that some government regulation of economic activities is necessary.

Values like activism, egalitarianism, and humanitarianism stress the importance of government helping the individual, especially the average person and the deprived. The values of activism, progress, and achievement emphasize government involvement in fiscal, educational, and environmental issues, and these same values operate to legitimize the regulation of and subsidies to corporations and the problems they face in both the domestic and international markets.

Big government increases

Americans want local control and autonomy but at the same time they believe the federal government should intervene, regulate, control, and subsidize. Americans, therefore, hold contradictory beliefs—derived from the same values—about what government should do. It should stay out of people's lives yet help people; it should allow market competition yet not let such competition go to its logical extreme; it should let communities govern themselves yet it should help them with resources. At the same time Americans distrust big government and believe in the necessity of big government. These contradictions reflect structural conditions. Because of these conflicts, government action (or inaction) over some issue will thus be defined as a "problem" by some segment of the population.

BELIEFS IN THE BALANCE OF POWER

American government was founded on beliefs about the undesirability of unchecked concentrations of power. Basic values of equality dictated that the major decision-making bodies (the executive, legislative, and judicial) were to "check and balance" each other. Beliefs in controlling concentrated power are deeply held by most Americans who are distrustful of "dictatorships" and "power elites."

Yet, some degree of concentration of power has proved necessary; as we have come to see, the executive branch of government has become highly dominant and it alone is subject to fewer checks by the other branches than one hundred years ago. Such concentration of power—even in the wake of a deposed president—violates basic beliefs in the balance of power, while supporting beliefs in big government. But when clear balances are evident, as is the case over some issues, decision making at the federal level has, at times, become stymied. One consequence of the dilemma over centralized versus decentralized power has been the surreptitious taking of power by the executive branch. In this way, power becomes concentrated but does not violate the public's beliefs in the balance of power since much of the concentration is hidden and secret. Thus, in a curious way, balance of power beliefs often operate to encourage more covert concentrations of power in American government since overt concentrations would come into clear conflict with dominant beliefs. Rather than encouraging and dictating the limits of what are necessary concentrations of power in modern, industrialized society, however, traditional balance of power beliefs have sometimes encouraged hidden imbalances of power.

The balance of power ceases

BELIEFS IN THE CANDIDATE DEMOCRACY

Values of activism, achievement, and individualism dictate that political candidates be "their own men." The values of freedom and equality require that the political process be free and open to all who seek to represent the needs and wishes of the people. One result of the application of these values to political processes has been the codification of beliefs in the "candidate democracy." Americans distrust tightly organized political parties and are usually proud to proclaim that they "vote for the man and not the party." Actual voting data reveal that they more often vote for parties than candidates, but in most elections there is a sizeable swing vote that switches party affiliation and votes for the candidate. It is for this reason that candidates are often more important than the party, and in fact, parties usually hunt for the candidate who will "win over the people." Thus,

Americans emphasize the qualities and charisma of the individual candidate over party organization. It is the candidate, rather than the party, that is to win the election and this fact rings true at all levels of government.

political party organization is loose compared to other political democracies and socialist countries. Americans prefer to believe that they vote for the person who best represents their interests, and in this way they presume that a more representative political democracy exists.

In some ways, as we will analyze shortly, beliefs in the candidate democracy encourage a situation where the general populace achieves less representation than well organized and financed interests. In order to win an election candidates must often finance expensive primaries, and if they win these, they must finance a general election. Because party organization is loose and because selection of party candidates often occurs outside the party organization, candidates must seek financial backing independently from the party, especially during primary campaigns. Monies are most easily procured from large organized interest groups whose goals may not coincide with the general public. These monies are then used to finance media campaigns designed to convince the public of the candidates "qualities." Thus, at times, beliefs in the candidate democracy produce highly unrepresentative government as well-financed candidates are more likely to win elective office than those who avoid monies from large interests. In contrast, when party organization is tightly knit and its goals clear, candidates are chosen from the party hierarchy and represent more honestly and unambiguously the position and goals of the party. But in American society, party goals and positions remain vague and ill-defined as parties seek candidates who, because of their vote-getting and money-getting qualities, can win elections.

Candidate "democracy" is dependent on finances

These four beliefs are now an intimate part of the political processes in America, and they will help us understand why American government is structured the way it is. It is the combination of structure and legitimizing beliefs that create America's problems of government. In analyzing these problems we will focus our discussion around the three dilemmas which, by recent polls, concern Americans the most: (1) the dilemma of centralization and decentralization, (2) the dilemma over the balance of power among branches of government, and (3) the dilemmas of how to prevent the abuse of power by government.

PROBLEMS OF GOVERNMENT STRUCTURE: CENTRALIZATION VERSUS DECENTRALIZATION

Government in America reveals an inherent dilemma: First, in accordance with beliefs in local autonomy, it is a decentralized, federalist system with 50 individual states and thousands of local communities

Original concept of government

supposedly determining much of their own destiny. Such a decentralized system represents the original concept of the federal government as one that will perform best when its duties are restricted to "housekeeping" chores: defense and security, coinage of money, and regulation of trade. Complementing this concept are beliefs in the desirability of local control and autonomy. Moreover, laissez faire beliefs stressing that the free enterprise system of conpetitive markets and privately owned corporations is necessary for prosperity and progress further buttress this concept of "good" government. In contradiction to federalism and beliefs in local autonomy and laissez faire, however, is a second feature of American government: the trend toward centralization. Increasingly, decision-making power is passing from states and local communities to the federal government, and within the federal government, into the hands of the president and away from Congress and the juciciary.

In all federalist systems, problems of planning and arranging national priorities are a reflection of the contradictions in federalism and beliefs in local control on the one hand, and a large, centralized government on the other. A decentralized federalist system is attuned to local, rather than national interests, with the result that efforts by Congress to create national programs are likely to encounter resistance by coalitions of local interests. Furthermore, when national programs are enacted, the federalist structure of government can potentially neutralize them. In an attempt to work through local governments and utilize the private sector of the economy (in accordance with laissez faire beliefs), many federal programs can be rendered less effective by waste, inefficiency, graft, and corruption at the local level. Thus, national planning, coordination, and control are inherently difficult in a political system that values competition among different levels of government.

Centralization of government into the hands of federal agencies has been one response to this problem. While resolving a set of problems, national centralization creates other difficulties. First, large bureaucracies can often be inefficient themselves. Once created, it is difficult to dismantle them, even if their effectiveness is questionable. Second, large centralized bureaucracies can become less sensitive to local needs and interests while remaining attuned to their internal bureaucratic traditions and the dictates of their central authority structure. Third, in large, centralized bureaucracies the potential for the abuse of power is greater than in smaller, decentralized systems, since it is more difficult to oversee and regulate a large and powerful bureaucracy's activities.

A fourth problem with centralization concerns the issue of national priorities. Once large bureaucratic establishments are created,

Problems of
decentralization

Problems of
centralization

changing national priorities becomes more difficult since large bureaucratic agencies have considerably greater political power to lobby for their own interests than the disorganized public. In the recent American experience, the military establishment—Pentagon, NASA, and related agencies—poses constant problems over military versus domestic priorities. While the creation of a centralized federal government during the 1930s revolved around domestic programs (social security, housing, and welfare), the post–Korean War period has seen domestic programs consume a smaller proportion of the budget, although they still represent a slight majority of expenditures. Meanwhile, the military budget has risen to support levels equivalent to that during the Korean mobilization (Lieberson, 1971). This conflict will continue to pose a dilemma as to what ends or goals centralization should be directed.

The centralization versus decentralization conflict, thus, is rooted in America's cultural beliefs. The system that has evolved reveals many of the problems of both a decentralized federalist system and a centralized form of governmental decision making. Many of the problems of this situation are endemic to both centralized and decentralized forms of government, but these endemic and inevitable problems have been compounded by the problem of how to maintain balances of power as government centralizes.

PROBLEMS OF GOVERNMENT STRUCTURE: MAINTAINING THE BALANCE OF POWER

THE EXECUTIVE BRANCH

The Growing Power of the President. The U.S. Constitution originally defined the powers of the presidency rather ambiguously. But over time, in response to a long series of national crises ranging from war to economic depression, this ambiguity has become translated into far-reaching power: to appoint and remove administrators from office, to direct administrative agencies, to initiate most legislation for Congress, to direct and control the military, to make war, to regulate the budget by selectively administering funds granted by Congress, and to appoint and direct cabinet officers and the administrative bureaucracy under them.

This centralization of power has occurred in the face of strong beliefs about local autonomy and control and about balances of power. To have overcome these traditions indicates that powerful forces had been operating to create a centralized political system. One of these has been the sheer growth in the size of the nation from a small,

Reasons for increasing presidential power

Whether the massive war mobilizations of earlier years (top) *or the more recent guerrilla war fought in Asia, war has been a force in the centralization of government.*

agrarian population to an industrial, urban populace of over 200 million. Large urban and industrial societies probably cannot be governed by local government because the proliferation of nationwide problems makes decentralization most difficult. A second force leading to government intervention has been the potential destruction of a capitalist economy through monopolization by a few corporations. The "boom and bust" cycles of the economy, culminating in the Great Depression, have also necessitated further control and regulation of the economy. Still more pressure for centralization has come from the redefinition of citizenship and civil rights for formerly disfranchised groups who have demanded federal intervention in the social and economic spheres.

Another source of pressure for centralization has come from war. For example, from 1776 to 1900 American army units participated in an estimated 9000 battles and skirmishes, and naval units engaged in 1100 missions involving violent conflict. These figures average about 90 violent conflicts per year for the first 125 years of American government (Wright, 1942; Dentler, 1967:57). When twentieth-century conflicts are added to this inventory, the military involvement of American government becomes clear: Aside from World Wars I and II, the United States, in recent decades, has engaged in military actions in Korea (1950–1953), Indochina (1951–1953), Guatemala (1954), the Congo (1960), Cuba (1961), Laos (1961), Vietnam (1962), the Dominican Republic (1965), Cambodia (1970), and Laos (1971).

SOCIOLOGICAL INSIGHTS

THE SCOPE AND BASES OF PENTAGON POWER

The military establishment, or "military-industrial complex" as President Eisenhower once described it, is the most powerful agency in Washington. What are the bases of its power? Below is a partial list:

1. There is a real need for a strong military in the face of world political realities, and hence, the majority of Americans are willing to support its activities.
2. Many important corporations—General Dynamics, Lockheed, Boeing, North American Rockwell, Ling-Temco-Vought—are highly dependent upon military contracts, thus making their management and workers willing lobbyists for the Pentagon.
3. The military has extensive resources to lobby for its interests and to influence Congress to grant further appropriations.
4. The military can mobilize certain beliefs held by Americans to support its interests: (a) without a strong military, there would be no ability to deter others from attacking America, and thus, it is constantly necessary to increase America's deterrence capacity; (b) work for the military increases the level of technology in nonmilitary areas of concern to Americans; (c) military production is necessary for economic prosperity; and, (d) the United States can afford both "guns and butter"—that is, both extensive military and domestic expenditures. As with all beliefs supporting a particular interest, they are self-serving and not necessarily based upon fact.

Whether a full-scale or limited involvement, war activities encourage centralization of government since people and resources are mobilized on a national scale. War activities create both social problems (protests, hardships, veterans' benefits, etc.) and economic problems (inflation, for example), thus furthering the need for even more centralized power. And once a large military establishment is created, economic, social, monetary, and political policies become interwoven with this establishment. Such interconnectedness with the military not only furthers the power of the president as commander-in-chief, and the Pentagon, it also makes the redirection of national priorities toward domestic issues by the executive branch of government a divisive issue for Americans.

THE LEGISLATIVE BRANCH

The Decline of Congressional Power. In the system of checks and balances, Congress is to mitigate the powers of the president. Under the provisions in the Constitution, Congress was empowered to initiate most legislation, to establish national priorities, to set up and regulate executive agencies, and to determine the structure of federal courts. Since Congress was set up as a representative body, the will of the populace was to guide the form and direction of the federal government. Despite beliefs about balances of power and distrusts of big government, Congress has abdicated much of its power to the executive branch. Now the president and executive agencies, such as the Departments of Defense and Health, Education, and Welfare, establish national priorities and initiate the most important legislation.

SOCIOLOGICAL INSIGHTS

DID THE SYSTEM WORK?

In many ways, the abuses of Watergate and the presidential coverup activities were the result of the growing perception by the Nixon administration of their power. Many commentators have noted that the "system worked," for indeed, the abuses were uncovered, a president was forced to resign under threat of impeachment, and key figures in the Nixon administration were prosecuted.

But other commentators have noted that the system did not work. They ask a simple question: What if there had been no White House tapes? Would Watergate coverup activities have been exposed? Would the President have been forced to resign in order to avoid impeachment in the

House and prosecution in the Senate? And would key Nixon administration figures have been successfully prosecuted? Would, in fact, the public know much about the abuses of power by the executive branch of government. It may be that the system worked rather badly since the impeachment process was never completed, and it would never have been initiated without the tapes.

No president is likely to tape himself again, and thus, it can be asked: Can abuses of power be uncovered again? And can the impeachment processes ever be an effective check on presidential power? Or, is there something about the structure of government in America that bestows enormous power to the president? Or, is it possible for Congress to regain much of its lost power?

These are the questions that a structural analysis can help answer.

Yet, Congress has retained some of its power in that it can still fail to pass programs initiated by the President, refuse to confirm his appointments, block attempts at reorganization of departments, and most importantly, withdraw funding of most any government program or agency, and of course, impeach and convict the president. But even in the post-Watergate era, when Congress was to regain much of its lost power, it has remained more of a *reactive* than an active force in determining the direction of the nation. The Senate and House are more likely, though not always, to check rather than initiate national policies and priorities. Furthermore, despite changes in campaign spending laws, congressional action, or reaction, tends to reflect the power of well-financed and well-organized interests rather than the will of the poorly organized general public. As such, Congress has often been a conservative force preserving the status quo.

Congress as a reactive force

Problems of Decision Making in Congress. The fact that Congress is an elected body would seemingly assure representative democracy in America. Two features of representation, however, have tended to skew congressional decision making in a less representative direction.

1. It costs money to be elected in a media-dominated society. Candidates for either the House or Senate inevitably become indebted to those well-financed interests that provide major financial backing. In

Key House chairs are often from rural, southern backgrounds. Only under extraordinary circumstances, such as those surrounding Wilber Mills of Arkansas, can chairpersons be forced or induced to relinquish their power. Until his acts of public drunkenness and questionable emotional stability became public, Chairman Mills headed the most powerful committee in the House for close to two decades.

a society where beliefs in a candidate democracy are strong and, hence, enormous emphasis is placed upon candidates demonstrating their uniqueness, it is inevitable that campaigning will be expensive and therefore open to influence by big-monied interests. The effect of the new campaign spending laws and their reinterpretation in 1976 by the Supreme Court has yet to be determined. Some state laws and the increasingly suspicious public may have some impact in reducing the influence of monied interests, but it is presently difficult to determine if any significant changes in campaign financing have occurred.

Influence of campaign contributors

2. The House of Representatives has a definite rural bias. Despite Supreme Court decisions requiring that representation in the House reflect the distribution of the population, reapportionment has not eliminated overrepresentation of congressmen from rural areas. The fact that these congressmen are frequently the chairs of important committees makes the rural bias in Congress even more pronounced. In a society that is highly urbanized, the overrepresentation of rural populations can at times pose a roadblock to needed urban-oriented legislation. For example, the respective power, influence, and current

Disproportionate rural representation

level of funding in the Department of Agriculture and the Department of Housing and Urban Development is a reflection of the anti-urban profile of the House, since the Agriculture Department's budget is many times that of HUD.

Within Congress, legislation on a national level (except on defense and "safe" issues such as social security) is at times rendered less effective by local interests. To get to the floor of either the House or Senate, legislation must pass through the appropriate committee. Committees have virtually complete control over the fate of legislation in that they can pigeonhole, rewrite, stall, or kill any bill. Committee chairs, usually selected on the basis of seniority, have enormous power to prevent legislation from getting through their committees, and they can delay committee hearings and prevent legislation from coming to a vote. Because seniority rather than competence is the most frequent basis for selecting committee chairs, senators and representatives from states and districts where the constituency and interests are stable (i.e., conservative) will be most likely to chair important committees. Since rural areas tend to be the most stable, committee chairs in the House will tend to evidence a rural bias. In the Senate, committee chairs will most likely come from small states with comparatively homogeneous constituencies and stable interest groupings, as is evidenced by the large number of Senate committee chairs from the South. In a nation that is highly urbanized, constantly changing, and rife with diversity, the overrep-representation of crucial committee chairs by representatives from rural, conservative, homogeneous, and stable areas renders decision making on the critical issues of the time more difficult.

Influence of local interests

SOCIOLOGICAL INSIGHTS

SIGNS OF CONGRESSIONAL REFORM?

In January of 1975 a reform movement swept the House of Representatives—perhaps signaling the beginnings of change in congressional decision making. Three of the oldest and most powerful committee chairs met their downfall: The Democratic caucus in the House voted to unseat the chairs of the Armed Services Committee, the Agriculture Committee, and the Banking and Currency Committee. Coupled with the forced resignation of the Chair of the House Ways and Means Committee, the seniority system which has for years prevented the enactment of comprehensive and change-oriented legislation began to break down. The downfall of these committee chairs may indeed be followed by further changes, and at the very least, other chairs will be less arbitrary and dictatorial in their actions.

The replacements on the Agriculture, Banking, and Ways and Means Committees are more urban and change-oriented than their predecessors, and thus, they more accurately reflect the needs and priorities of the nation. The new Chair of the Armed Services Committee, which rules over the Pentagon budget, differs little from his predecessors, although there is some indication that he is more sympathetic to domestic programs.

Thus, the rigid seniority system is no longer intact. These recent changes perhaps signal the beginnings of congressional reform that can make Congress a more active, as opposed to reactive, force in American government.

When a piece of legislation does get to the House or Senate floor, it faces another challenge, particularly if the legislation involves national planning for change, because now it must confront a multitude of local and national interest groupings that have all helped finance campaigns. Legislation that proposes change on a national level will usually go against a coalition of some of these interest groups which, because of their contributions, have influence with the senators and representatives.

Interest Groups and Lobbying. In any large and complex society there will be many diverse groups pursuing different goals. Many of these groups are highly organized to exert political influence and can, therefore, be labeled *interests*. These interests often maintain elaborate offices in Washington, staffed with paid professionals. Frequently, former employees of legislators are kept on a staff to provide a particular interest with the necessary informal contacts to exert influence.

Traditionally, the most intense lobbying activities have come from organizations in the private sector. However, over the last 20 years executive branch agencies, most notably the Pentagon, have become conspicuous lobbies on Capitol Hill. For example, the yearly lobbying expenditures of the Pentagon in Washington alone probably approach many millions of tax dollars. The fact that executive branches of government have become some of the most well-financed lobbies, exerting the most influence, is perhaps another indicator of the centralization of power into the executive branch of government.

Executive agencies are active lobbyists

Defense Secretary Donald Rumsfeld of the Ford Administration lobbies with friendly chair of the Senate Armed Services Committee, Senator John Stennis (another rural, southern chair of a major committee). Lobbying by the executive branch of government has become a big business.

In the abstract the principle of effective lobbying sounds democratic: it enables diverse segments of society to have the ear of legislators. However, access to legislators can, too often, depend on wealth and degree of organization. This indicates that well-financed and well-organized groups are likely to have more influence on the legislative processes than the poorly organized public. As long as this situation persists, national planning will be more difficult since change-oriented, national legislation will often run up against the resistance of some de facto coalition of interests that may have little in common except their opposition, perhaps even for different reasons, to a comprehensive piece of legislation.

In light of this situation, the only recourse for the public has been to become organized. For the poor, the black, the victims of industrial pollution, and even for middle America, organization may increasingly become a last recourse, and the beginnings of a movement toward such organization are currently evident. For example, the National Welfare Rights Organization, the Consumer's Union, Common Cause, and the Sierra Club all reflect a newfound awareness of the only alternative available to a public which is becoming increasingly aware of, and dissatisfied with, the disproportionate influence of interest groups on national priorities and change-oriented legislation. Just how effective these new public lobbies can be in the face of the well-entrenched Pentagon, Department of Agriculture, big business, industry, and affluent labor is unknown. But until these newly emerging people's lobbies display more organization, broad-based support, and increased financial resources, national planning and reordering of priorities will be, at best, very gradual. This prospect underscores the extent to which these will remain dilemmas inherent in the present culture and structure of American government.

THE JUDICIAL BRANCH

Probably one of the most effective forces for social change in America is the federal court system, culminating in the Supreme Court. The list of reforms by the Court, from school desegregation and protection of civil liberties in criminal cases to draft reform and reapportionment, is impressive—coming close to equaling those of both Congress and the presidency. In passing on the constitutionality of various laws and practices, the Supreme Court has been able to legislate new, reform-oriented laws. Contrary to the Court's detractors, this legislative function of the Court is not an abuse of its power, but rather, an obligation imposed by the Constitution. For disfranchised, poorly financed and organized segments of the population, the sympathy of the Supreme Court has represented one of the few legitimate channels for addressing grievances. With comparatively few resources and only a small organization, groups can initiate test cases to challenge unfair laws and practices. In many ways, the court system has represented a counterforce for the public and small interests against the well-financed and organized interests exerting a disproportionate influence on Congress. Further, the Court has forced consideration of issues such as civil rights—an issue Congress might prove incapable of resolving in a clear and forthright manner.

Functions of the Supreme Court

Naturally, there are limitations on the Supreme Court's capacity to initiate change and reform in American society. First, the Court rules on the constitutionality of practices, but it cannot administer in detail the required action. The courts are not regulatory agencies and, in fact, they must often await a law suit to determine if rulings are being carried out properly. Thus, the courts can set general policies, but they cannot dictate just how these policies are to be implemented. The result of this fact has, at times, been inefficient, reluctant, and even subversive administrations of court rulings. Probably the best example of the problems of governmental administration of unpopular court decisions is in the area of school integration; some twenty years after *Brown* v. *The School Board* integration is still resisted, often with considerable violence by the public. And as long as public resistance is high, representative bodies at all levels of government will be reluctant to enact clear administrative guidelines and to enforce those established by lower federal courts.

Limitations on the Supreme Court

Second, the Court rules on *specific* issues brought before it; it cannot always establish comprehensive policies that take related issues into consideration. Such comprehensive policies are best established through legislative action by Congress, but as we have discovered, the structure of government presents a number of roadblocks for change-oriented, national, and comprehensive legislation that might reorder national priorities.

Third, the composition of the Supreme Court determines, to a great extent, just how change-oriented decisions will be. The Supreme Court is ultimately a political body that can evidence a liberal, moderate, or conservative profile. Over the last twenty years the Court has evidenced a liberal profile, but in recent years its composition appears to have shifted toward a more moderate profile. While decisions on specific cases can still be labeled "liberal" or "conservative," the cumulative impact of many decisions appears to have shifted judicial policies toward a more moderate and less change-oriented profile.

These limitations suggest that the court system is inherently less capable of generating national planning and reordering national priorities than either the executive or legislative branches of government. It is only in the face of the growing power of the executive

SOCIOLOGICAL
INSIGHTS

TESTIMONY AND COMMENTARY BEFORE THE SENATE BY ALVIN TOFFLER, AUTHOR OF "FUTURE SHOCK"

AMERICA'S FUTURE

"Some people plan, others are planned upon. Some governments plan, others are planned upon.

"The American future is being stolen, dribbled, and bumbled away by a government that does not plan for the long range, does not know how to plan, is afraid to talk about the need for long-range planning, and is, therefore, outplanned at every step by major corporations who are staking out pieces of the future for themselves, as well as by foreign nations who are doing the same on a global scale.

"Failure to look at America's current economic and political crisis in terms of the next 25–50 years is costing us unmeasurable billions of dollars in lost economic and social opportunities and is leading us toward technological and

military policies that threaten the survival of the entire
planet.

"The United States, in order to avoid bloodshed over
the next few decades, must begin now to develop very long-
range strategies—and must invent wholly new forms of
planning that involve not merely a handful of technocratic
experts, but millions of ordinary citizens. We must become
an anticipatory democracy. . . .

". . . Anticipatory democracy is the only kind of democracy possible in a period of high-speed social, technological, and political change. Failure to anticipate will
lead to tragedy in America. By the same token, long-range
thinking that is unconnected to the ideas, energy and imagi-
nation of our whole population, long-range thinking that is
merely top-down, and not equally bottom-up, could also produce the end of democracy. It is only by combining long-
range strategies for tomorrow with the involvement of millions in formulating goals that we can assure ourselves
that there will be an America 2000."

Testimony before the U.S. Senate Subcommittee on Environmental Pollution, December 15, 1975.

branch, coupled with the structural impediments to congressional
consensus and concerted action, that a reliance on the courts has
been so necessary for those who desire to change national policies.
But the appropriate limitations on the power of the courts simply
dramatize the current problems of structure in American government.

PROBLEMS OF GOVERNMENT STRUCTURE:
PREVENTING THE ABUSE OF POWER

During the early years of this decade, a number of illegal activities by
agencies of the federal government were exposed: The FBI was found
to have attempted character assassinations of Dr. Martin Luther
King, while keeping files on politicians in order to blackmail them for
their support. The CIA, contrary to its charter, was discovered to have
engaged in domestic spying, while maintaining extensive files on citizens. The Pentagon was revealed to have a file on those who, in exer-
cising their constitutional rights, had protested the Vietnam War.

J. Edgar Hoover directed the FBI for most of its existence. The abuses of such a concentration of power in the hands of one man have only recently been exposed: illegal wire tapping, blackmail of members of Congress and perhaps the presidency itself, inciting riots, and efforts to discredit public figures, such as the late Martin Luther King.

The IRS was found to have audited people's income tax returns at the request of politicians, while giving favorable treatment to key political figures. A president was exposed as having condoned illegal staff activities against "enemies" of his administration, while lying to the American people about his involvement.

These activities clearly violated people's beliefs about what government should be and they confirmed for many the dangers of "big government" and "big brother." Initial shock, surprise, and dismay have now, in many quarters, become transformed into apathy about these illegal activities. But the abuse of power that these activities represent will remain an enduring problem of culture and structure in America.

Most of these abuses of power revolve around activities to get and store information on citizens in order to neutralize their resistance to the use of power—activities that go against basic values of individualism and freedom, but the centralization of power makes inevitable the desire to preserve power. Power is best exercised when resistance can be overcome, thus, agencies of the government have an interest in knowing the potential areas and sources of resistance to their policies. The Pentagon, FBI, CIA, and other agencies given the necessary

Information gathering and storing abuses

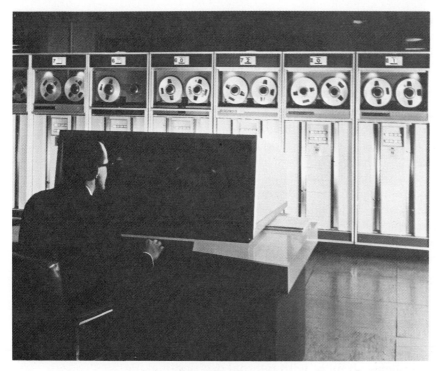

Government agencies have, for some time, been storing information about Americans. How much information should be kept in a free society? What does the government have a right to know, and who is to operate as a check on government agencies?

power will, unless constantly checked and monitored, seek the information that will allow them to use and expand their power.

With new technologies such as electronic equipment and computer data banks, it becomes possible to acquire, process, store, and retrieve information with much greater efficiency, speed, and accuracy than ever before. Thus, the temptation for illegal surveillance and data banks is much greater than previously. Moreover, these new technologies allow for greater secrecy and freedom from detection from outside investigators than was at one time possible.

Why are people in agencies willing to engage in illegal covert activities in a society valuing individual freedom? The answer to such a question is manifold: (1) those engaged in these activities often do not view them as illegal or immoral, but as necessary and proper; (2) the organizations where such activities are most likely to occur are often charged with the tasks of defense and security of the nation, hence, it is often easy to justify questionable activities in the name of this higher goal; (3) Congress and the American people have tradi-

Illegal actions by government agencies

tionally held in high esteem those organizations that have engaged in illegal activities, and thus, monitoring and supervision have been minimal; and, (4) these agencies have been given considerable power, and power often becomes its own goal; that is, power begets efforts to increase power.

As reprehensible as illegal activities by government may appear to some, we should not lose sight of the basic dilemma through moralizing. The dilemma revolves around the question of how much power should be bestowed on any agency and on what amount of information is necessary for that agency to perform its function. In a modern society with a myriad of programs and agencies charged with their administration, a considerable amount of information is necessary if the agency is to do its job. But how much information? And what kind is necessary? And who is to decide what is and what is not necessary?

There are no easy answers to these questions. People appear to desire the protection and services of federal agencies despite their beliefs about big government and about local control and autonomy. They want the services that centralized, concentrated power allows, but they want to preserve individualism and freedom. Thus, most seek to control and monitor agencies that, in all likelihood, would create another centralized agency with considerable power. Moreover, in the face of a Congress fraught with internal decision-making problems, and subject to lobbying pressures from the very federal agencies it seeks to regulate, it may prove difficult to establish effective or permanent congressional oversights of federal agencies; and therein lies one of America's more enduring problems of structure.

SUMMARY

We have examined three basic problems of government: (1) centralization versus decentralization, (2) maintaining the balance of powers, and (3) preventing the abuses of power. Inherent in these larger problems are the specific problems of individual citizens, including the unresponsiveness of government, the use of resources for purposes that are defined as less important, the inability to deal with problems, and actions of government *against*, instead of for, its citizens. These problems are intimately connected to several important cultural beliefs: (1) beliefs in local autonomy, (2) beliefs in big government, (3) beliefs in the balance of power, and (4) beliefs in the candidate democracy. These beliefs define, for many, the problems in government, while often legitimizing the structural arrangements giving rise to these problems.

REVIEW QUESTIONS

1. Indicate some of the ways that America's culture of politics and government defines, for various segments of the population, certain problems of government.
2. How are structural conflicts in American government reflected in cultural beliefs?
3. How are abuses of power in government a result of increasing centralization in the federal government?
4. How are the problems of societal planning and the reordering national priorities inherent in our federalist system and in the balance of powers within the federal government?
5. Why has government centralized? What forces operate to check centralization?

GLOSSARY

balance of power the concept in American government referring to the way the three branches of government—the executive, legislative, and judicial—supposedly check the power of each other.

federal agencies offices and organizations operating within the federal government; "agencies" are usually attached to the executive branch of government

lobbying the process in which various groups and organizations attempt to exert influence on political decision makers

national planning the process in which nationwide plans are drawn up as a means for realizing ends or goals

national priorities selecting and determining the importance of goals or ends toward which resources in the society are to be allocated

Pentagon Department of Defense and its sphere of administrative control

power the capacity to realize ends and goals even in the face of resistance

PROLOGUE 6: ON ANY DAY IN AMERICA

On almost any day in America, these events can be observed:

· In Camden, New Jersey, a lady enters a supermarket and discovers that most prices, especially those for protein rich-foods, have risen by a few cents. Her husband brings home a larger paycheck than ever, but it seems to cover no more than when he earned less.

· In Detroit, a young black has spent two days looking, once again, for a job. He is young and eager, but undereducated. He wonders why even an unskilled, lousy paying job is unavailable.

· A man in his middle forties who has worked for a large steel company in Ontario, California, for thirteen years is laid off. Production has been cut back and, despite his years of service, his job is not protected.

· Four large oil companies announce price increases for gasoline. Two public utilities appeal to state and federal agencies for price increases for electricity.

• In Los Angeles, two elevator operators jobs for the county have 900 applicants

• The Federal Trade Commission in Washington announces that company X has signed a consent order and will stop deceptive and misleading advertising.

· In Freemont, California, a worker decides to drop a car from his fork lift. He will claim error in judgement, but in reality he is simply frustrated at the boredom of his work. The company will accept this and other expressions of frustration as regrettable, but nonetheless inevitable.

· A radical college professor will decry the evils and internal contradictions of capitalism and extoll otherwise bored students to change the economic system.

All these events occurred. They are not unusual, but common. They are but a few of the many ways the economy affects people's lives. They are but one indicator that people are troubled by a system of economic arrangements that is beyond their control or comprehension. There is a common thread to the events listed above. This thread is composed of the cultural ideas and concrete structural arrangements of our industrial economy. We could not connect these events or see beyond their specific implications unless we were willing to examine the overall structure and culture of the economy. Ultimately, people's personal worries and the actions of government and corporations stem from forces built into economic processes. Our task in Chapter 6 will be to present a profile of the culture and structure of the American economy, and to view specific problems as outgrowths of this profile. In this way our own personal experiences and knowledge of fast-moving daily events can be placed into a context that will allow for more enduring insight.

6

PROBLEMS OF
THE ECONOMY

The economy involves certain critical social processes: (1) the gathering of natural resouces from the environment, (2) the production of goods and services, and (3) the distribution of these goods and services to the population. These processes are vital to the perpetuation of society, thus, the economy of a society is likely to be a topic of great concern to people coping with the economy in their daily lives.

Each society has a somewhat different pattern of economic organization. American society has what is termed a *capitalistic* form of economic organization in which important economic units are privately owned and where attempts are made to use a relatively free and unregulated market to distribute goods and services. Our economy is the most productive in the world. The nature and size of the American economy has produced many problems which concern at least some segments of the population. For example, rapid inflation, widespread unemployment, recession, the vulnerability of the economy to whims of foreign governments, the size of conglomerates and multinational corporations, the apparent increase in consumer fraud, the disproportionate influence of corporations on political processes, the perceived failure of federal regulatory agencies to work for the public, instances of price fixing and monopolistic practices among large corporations, the waste and pollution created by many economic activities, the existence of a poverty class, and the frustrations and alienation of many workers all amply document that numerous problems are perceived to exist within the American economy.

Functions of economy

In approaching such a long list of problems, we must acquire some background. Our purpose in this chapter will be threefold: (1) to review the cultural beliefs surrounding economic organization, for it is in these beliefs that the definition and substances of many problems reside; (2) to outline the prominent structural features and trends of the American economy; and, (3) to draw upon our cultural and structural discussion in an effort to better understand social problems associated with the economy.

THE CULTURE OF THE AMERICAN ECONOMIC SYSTEM

To understand the American economic system we must visualize its operation in the context of beliefs about "American capitalism." These beliefs maintain that certain types of economic arrangements are more desirable than others and that we should seek to maintain these arrangements. As we will come to see, however, there are certain tendencies within the actual operation of the economy that often make these beliefs difficult to realize, yet, they remain a powerful ideological force in America. Some people feel America has not maintained adherence to these beliefs, and this is the "problem" with the economy. Others feel these beliefs are outmoded and that the problem with the economy is a failure to abandon these beliefs and the economic arrangements they support.

The beliefs regarding the economic system answer such basic questions as: (1) Who is to own and control the productive machinery of the economy—individuals, corporations, or the government? (2) How much *capital*—wealth that is used to buy and organize economic production—should be allowed to become concentrated in the hands of individuals, corporations, or government? In other words, how big should corporations or government become, and how wealthy should individuals who own corporations become? (3) Should corporations always be profit making? If so, how great should their profits be? Should there be some regulations and limits on profits? (4) Should the *market*—the place and process of selling and buying labor, goods, and services—be free of regulation? Should corporations and individuals be completely free to pursue their profit-making interests? Or, should there be constraints and limitations?

Current beliefs about American capitalism can be labeled either conservative or liberal, depending on how each of the above questions is answered. A list of dominant beliefs and the points of disagreement between conservatives and liberals would include:[1] (1) Capital—wealth or any asset that can be converted into money— should be concentrated in the hands of private individuals to invest as

Beliefs in American capitalism

Liberal and conservative beliefs

they see proper. The disagreement over conservatives and liberals is not over private property (or private capital), but over how much capital should be held by government and whether government has any right to regulate capital accumulations among private citizens. (2) The accumulation of capital should be encouraged since large sums of capital can be invested in economic enterprises, thereby encouraging increased productivity which creates jobs and income and thereby promotes the general welfare of all citizens. Liberals and conservatives disagree, however, over how far capital accumulation by one corporation or individual should be allowed to go. (3) The most efficient means for accumulating and using capital for the production of goods and services in the corporation should be used. This allows for the pooling of capital, the organization of labor, the development of technology, and the use of natural resources to produce and distribute goods and services to the people. Conservatives and liberals will disagree, however, over the extent to which government should control and regulate corporate activities. (4) Corporations must be profit-making units if investors are to be encouraged to risk their money or capital in various economic enterprises. But conservatives and liberals will usually fail to agree over the extent to which profits should be regulated. (5) The market—the place and process where people exchange their money for goods and services produced by individuals and corporations—is an efficient way to allocate the resources of a society since the demands for goods and services will lead profit-making individuals and corporations to invest capital in those activities for which people's demand, as expressed in their willingness to spend their money, is high. In this way the economy can best meet the needs of the citizenry. Conservatives and liberals do not agree, however, on whether or not supply and demand in the market should be the only way to allocate resources. (6) A "free" market where individuals and corporations, all guided by a profit motive, can compete with each other is the best way to induce economic units to keep their costs down, and hence, their prices low. Conservatives and liberals often disagree, however, on whether or not free competition will always occur, whether it will always lead to efficiency and low prices, and whether it is desirable in all sectors of the economy.

At the level of beliefs, then, capitalism can be defined as a "desirable" mode of economic organization which is presumed to provide an efficient way to organize capital (wealth), labor, technology, and natural resources so that low-cost goods and services can be produced to meet the needs and desires of people as expressed by their purchases in the free marketplace. There is, however, considerable disagreement over how free and unregulated economic activity should be, as is summarized in Table 6.1.

Table 6.1 **Conflicting Cultural Beliefs**

Conservative Capitalist Beliefs	Liberal Capitalist Beliefs
All capital should be in the hands of private citizens.	Some capital should belong to government.
A free market will automatically lead to the optimal allocation of resources in society.	Some control of demand and supply in the market is necessary to meet societal goals.
The laws of supply and demand should be free to operate in the market.	Free markets represent the best allocative mechanism in some sectors; regulation is necessary in other sectors.
The *profit motive* is what brings capital to certain enterprises; as long as markets are free and allow for profit, then desired economic activities will be performed.	There is a tendency for corporations to begin to monopolize markets and, hence, raise prices. Corporations will often fix prices and engage in other collusionary practices. Government must, therefore, prevent such domination in order to foster the competition that keeps costs and prices low.
A free competitive market guided by a profit motive keeps costs and prices down, since corporations must compete with each other.	Government must regulate profits in some key industries; it must also prevent practices which allow corporations to make excessive profits; however, by allowing subsidy profits in certain economic sectors, the government can encourage investment in that sector.
Profits can be defended as rewards for those with capital taking risks in the market.	Because of the size of key corporations and the interlocking nature of economic activity, government must not allow vital industry to fail; profits must, at times, be maintained through subsidies.

As only a cursory review of liberal capitalist beliefs reveals, they are the most consonant with core values in American culture. The values of activism, freedom, achievement, and materialism make an economic system in which individuals are free to pursue profit and material wealth through their activities seem proper and necessary for the continued progress of the society. American values emphasize that individuals should be free to express their needs and desires in the marketplace, and others should be free to actively seek to organize capital, labor, and technology in an effort to provide for these needs. In so doing, it is believed, these entrepreneurs should be allowed to enjoy the material benefits of their achievements. It is only when economic practices such as monopolization and price fixing, and when undue hardship become prevalent that government must step in to preserve freedom and individualism, while implementing the value of humanitarianism for those who are suffering from ex-

Values and the economic system

isting economic arrangements. It is in this sense, then, that liberal capitalist beliefs are more concrete representations of dominant American values, and it is this fact that makes existing economic arrangements seem proper to the vast majority of Americans.

Liberal capitalist beliefs not only correspond closest to core American values, but they also describe, to some degree, actual structural arrangements within the economy itself. In reconciling general values to concrete economic arrangements, liberal capitalist beliefs represent a powerful source of legitimization for the American economy (Williams, 1970:166); that is, these beliefs make the structure and operation of the economy seem "right and proper" to most Americans. Yet, despite the effectiveness of this belief system in legitimizing current economic arrangements, there are certain inherent trends in the structure of capitalist systems that often make these beliefs difficult to realize.

STRUCTURAL TRENDS IN THE AMERICAN ECONOMY[2]

We will now analyze prominent trends in the economy and how these can contradict dominant beliefs. Our long-range goal, however, is to visualize these trends, and the cultural tensions that they create, as the source of specific social problems. We could not, for example, understand unemployment, inflation, price fixing, consumer fraud, or worker alienation without understanding the broader structural forces in the economy. We will examine five major trends: (1) monopoly and oligopoly, (2) patterns of intercorporate control, (3) multinationalization, (4) unionization, and (5) the growth of big government.

MONOPOLY AND OLIGOPOLY

The basic assumption of the conservative capitalist belief system is that open competition in a free market is the best form of economic organization. In fact, many of America's basic core values arose as a means to justify and legitimize early forms of capitalism. However, as became evident during the last century, if left unregulated such a system soon becomes dominated by monopolistic practices which, in turn, cut down on competition and freedom and which violate the very values created by early capitalism. As some corporations become profitable and as they grow in size and power, they acquire the power to cut prices, absorb temporary losses, and thereby drive other less-solvent units out of the market. Or, by threatening to do so, they can begin to indirectly regulate the activities of other economic units, and once economic organizations possess this kind of "overlord"

Monopolies

power, not only can they dictate how competitors are to operate, but they can also control smaller units which depend upon powerful monopolies for their business. For example, at one time in America the John D. Rockefeller family so dominated the oil industry that it could suppress or control all competitors, all small suppliers, and all buyers of oil. Once this kind of control of the market occurs, economic units are not free, competition is suspended, and goods are no longer allocated in accordance with the laws of supply and demand. Such a situation clearly violates basic American values of individualism, freedom, and achievement since individuals and corporations are no longer free from external constraint and they no longer have an equal opportunity to achieve success in the market.

It is this inherent dilemma of capitalist forms of economic organization that has caused governmental regulation of economic organizations. Yet, increasing concentrations of capital and the growth of "successful" corporations are inevitable in capitalist systems, despite efforts to maintain competition (Sherman, 1968) and despite the fact that such a situation violates basic values and beliefs. Several forces work against governmental efforts to maintain the market mechanism for allocating resources: First, the profit motive mandates that economic units are to increase their profits by expanding and growing. Second, certain economic activities in modern societies (transportation, communications, utilities) can probably be more efficiently performed by large organizations controlling most of the market. Third, large and successful corporations which employ large numbers of workers can exert enormous political influence and thereby mitigate governmental efforts at regulation. And fourth, some forms of economic activity require substantial concentrations of capital, making it more profitable for corporations to be large and, hence, achieve the "economies of scale" that come with size, and coincidentally, market domination.

The result of these inherent forces in America is for large sectors of critical resource markets to be controlled by a relatively few corporations which are subjected to only some governmental regulation. As opposed to *monopoly*, where one corporation dominates the market, the situation of a few large corporations controlling the market is termed *oligopoly*. Competition is usually quite intense among smaller corporations in less central markets, but, with few exceptions, in markets where there is high consumer demand and when large quantities of scarce resources are utilized, the oligopolistic tendencies of liberal capitalism are most evident. In Table 6.2 an attempt is made to document the high degree of capital concentration in the American economy. Table 6.2 reports the percentage of manufacturing assets held by the largest 100 firms in America. As can be seen, these firms

Oligopolies

Table 6.2 **Percent of Manufacturing Assets Held by the 100 Largest Firms**

Year	Percent Held by 100 Largest Firms
1925	35.1
1931	42.3
1939	42.4
1948	40.1
1955	43.8
1960	46.0
1965	47.6
1971	48.9

SOURCE: *Studies by the Staff of the Cabinet Committee on Price Stability,* Washington, D.C.: Government Printing Office, 1969, pp. 45, 92; *Statistical Abstract of the United States, 1973,* Washington, D.C.: GPO, 1974, p. 483.

now control about one-half of the total economic assets—a rather high percentage when it is remembered that there are over 150,000 manufacturing firms in America. Supplementing the data in Table 6.2 is an unpublished report by Professor Willard Mueller of the University of Wisconsin that documents the fact that the 200 largest corporations (as opposed to the 100 largest reported in Table 6.2) now control two-thirds of all manufacturing assets. The significance of this figure lies in the oligopolistic trend it underscores: In 1941, the 1000 largest manufacturing corporations did not control this great a share of the manufacturing assets. Buttressing these data, and supplementing those in Table 6.2, is the report by William Shepard of the University of Michigan that industries in which four firms or less control 50 percent or more of the sales now account for 64 percent of all manufacturing sales—indicating again the increasing oligopolistic control of the American economy.

Table 6.3, the percent of profits earned by corporations of varying

Table 6.3 **Concentration of Assets and Profits in Manufacturing, First Quarter, 1968**

Corporations Having Assets of:	Number of Companies	Percent of Companies	Percent of Manufacturing Assets	Percent of Manufacturing Profits
$1 billion or more	78	0.04%	43%	49%
$250 million to $1 billion	194	0.1	21	20
$10 million to $250 million	2,165	1.2	22	19
Under $10 million	185,000*	98.7%	14%	12%
Total	187,437	100.0%	100%	100%

SOURCE: *Studies by the Staff of the Cabinet Committee on Price Stability,* 1969, p. 92.
* Estimate.

Table 6.4 **Monopoly Power in Selected Industries, 1963**

Industry	Percent of Sales Made by Four Largest Firms
Automobiles	99%
Aluminum	96
Flat glass	94
Steam enignes and turbines	93
Light bulbs	92
Cigarettes	80
Copper	78
Metal cans	74
Soap and detergents	72
Tires and inner tubes	70
Blast furnaces and steel mills	50%

degrees of capital (asset) formation, offers another way to visualize the degree to which all economic activity is controlled by a few large corporations. And in Table 6.4, the percentage of total sales made by the four largest firms in such key market areas as automobiles, aluminum, glass, tires, and steel is reported to provide another indication of large corporate domination of the American economy.

SOCIOLOGICAL INSIGHTS

WHO OWNS THE LARGE CORPORATIONS?

Tables 6.1, 6.2, and 6.3 reveal the extent to which large corporations dominate the market. But who owns these large corporations? In other words, who owns the stock? And how concentrated is the stock in the hands of the rich? Can the "little guy" also share in ownership? Using data from Internal Revenue Service files, three researchers from the University of Pennsylvania have just completed a study of stock ownership of American corporations for the year 1971. Results: 1 percent of the nation's families—that is, those with incomes over $50,000 in 1971—own 51 percent of the stock and collect 47 percent of the dividends. The 53 percent of American families with incomes of less than $10,000 in 1971 owned less than 10 percent of the stock and collected about 11 percent of the dividends.

Source: Newsweek, December 18, 1974.

MULTINATIONALIZATION

Capitalist corporations are regulated by profit considerations, so they inevitably seek resources in their cheapest form. Coupled with the enormous capital of America's large corporations, this search for cheap resources—whether natural or human resources—has led to an extensive international involvement of America's largest corporations. In fact, it is now clear that most large corporations are *multinational*—having extensive holdings and projects in several countries. In the energy crisis of 1974, for example, attention was dramatically drawn to the multinational profile of oil companies, but virtually all

American corporations are now multinational in profile, making their domestic regulation difficult.

large corporations in every sector of the American economy have considerable capital invested in other nations.

Multinationalization is perhaps an inevitable result of the logic of capitalistic economic organization: First, as raw materials become scarce under the impact of massive domestic extraction, corporations inevitably seek new sources that can be extracted at lower costs. Second, in both extractive and manufacturing industries, labor in less-modernized societies is considerably cheaper, allowing for lower labor costs and higher profit margins. Third, the very great manufacturing capacity of large corporations often allows for the production of goods in excess of domestic demand, the result being that corporations seek markets for their goods and services in other societies. And fourth, world markets still remain comparatively unregulated when compared to the domestic market, thus, corporations will often seek a foreign market where a government cannot (or will not) regulate prices and profits, especially in those markets where the demand is high and supply is short.

As the data presented earlier document, the assets and manufacturing capacities of the American economy are not only controlled by a few hundred large corporations, but these same corporations also serve other nations and have extensive holdings in other societies. The result of this situation is to make government regulation of America's large corporations less effective since they can produce and distribute goods and services in the international market whenever government policies become too restrictive. Such a situation will, as is most dramatically evident for oil and other raw materials, make the American market increasingly influenced by supply and demand forces in the comparatively unregulated international market. And with modernization of the Third World, the international demand for all goods and services enjoyed by Americans will increase as other countries seek to raise their material standards of living.

UNIONIZATION

Workers in capitalistic economies become a type of "commodity" in a labor market. Whether such a dehumanizing situation is regarded as "good," "necessary," or "evil" cannot be determined here, but it is clear that labor costs are like other costs to a corporation seeking to make a profit. And thus, corporations will typically attempt to keep labor costs low and hence realize greater profits. During early capitalism, the labor market works in favor of the corporation since workers must often endure very low wages, poor working conditions, or lose a source of income. Eventually, as workers become concentrated, as dissatisfaction increases, and as industries

Reasons for
multinationalization

The union movement in America has often been violent. Here Teamster and rival union heads do battle at O'Hare Airport, Chicago.

become large and in need of steady labor so as not to idle massive factories, labor succeeds in forming effective unions that become the bargaining agents of workers in the labor market.

The history of union organization in the United States is torn by violence, but by the 1930s unions overcame the resistance of large-scale industry and began to bargain collectively with individual corporations and with groups of corporations comprising entire industries. Thus, union organization in America tends to be industrywide as is the case with autos, steel, and mining; and if not industrywide, smaller unions are organized into large umbrella unions such as the Teamsters or large confederations like the AFL–CIO. Such large-scale union organization is a direct response to the prominence of large corporations. It is an inevitable force in capitalist economies because (1) workers need to protect themselves from abuses in the name of corporate profit motives; (2) workers need to have some security from the recurring economic cycles typifying capitalistic markets; (3) the

Unionization in response to corporations

industry itself begins to seek stabilized relations with the large working labor pool that can easily disrupt and shut down the massive capital investments of a large-scale industry; and (4) government itself has an interest in avoiding conflict between economic elites and the working masses of population. Under these pressures, then, unions have become an integral part of mature capitalist economies.

Unions restrict open competition not only in the labor market but in other markets as well; now, another type of large-scale organization controls one of the key resources of any economy, labor. Such control has been undoubtedly necessary in terms of humanitarian values, but it creates one more rigidity in market: wages do not respond to supply and demand—that is, they rarely go down when the need for labor is less—thus, there is a constant pressure for prices to increase as corporations seek to maintain and increase their profits in the face of rising labor costs. Further, the wage-price spiral of one sector extends to others since labor in all sectors of the economy is organized to support the activities of labor in any other. There is no necessarily "good" or "bad" in this situation—it is an inevitable dynamic of capitalism. As capital becomes concentrated, labor becomes organized, with the result that individual workers' lives become increasingly controlled, not just by the corporation but also by the union.

BIG GOVERNMENT

Partly as a result of these pressures toward monopolization, multinationalization, and unionization, government has been inexorably drawn into economic affairs in America. Such interference has clearly violated the conservative capitalist belief system, but so do all the forces that disrupt the operation of the laws of supply and demand. This involvement has been justified by the liberal capitalist beliefs that recognize those inherent processes of capitalism which, if left unchecked, would suspend completely the free and competitive market, while violating other core American values.

Much governmental intervention in the economy has occurred as the goals of government have grown. Whether military or social in nature, the federal government has sought to regulate market processes to meet national goals. In this effort, the *pattern* of government intervention in the economy has been greatly influenced by the power of large corporations, the international politics of resource distribution, and the power of organized labor. A pattern of involvement reflecting such multiple influences will, of necessity, be highly complex. In general, however, government has used a variety of mechanisms to achieve some degree of control over market processes: (1)

Government intervention in economy

cash subsidies to selected industries, as has been the case for airlines, railroads, and various public utilities; (2) massive purchases of goods and services in the market, including airplanes, warships, agricultural goods, and war-related technologies; (3) regulation of money flows through the tax and Federal Reserve systems, for example, when taxes are raised or lowered and when government forces interest rates to climb by restricting money available; (4) export–import policies affecting the export and import of goods to and from selected nations, such as the import taxes levied on imported automobiles; (5) direct "control" through regulatory agencies and licensing policies, such as interstate commerce and air travel; and (6) direct control of prices and wages in selected industries, and at times, in all or most industries, as was the case in the early 1970s when wage and price controls were implemented.

Just how these various types of regulation are used will wait an analysis of specific economic problems. For the present, it should be noted that government regulation has, in accordance with liberal capitalist beliefs, sought to maintain competitive markets when possible. At the same time, however, the government has allowed and even encouraged those very processes that can cut down on the amount of competition in the market. Namely, the federal government has tolerated the growth of large corporations that seek to suspend competition; it has also encouraged large unions and noncompetitive relations between labor and management; and, it has regulated monetary, military, and export–import policies to protect big corporations and unions from foreign competition. There are many contradictions in these governmental efforts, perhaps underscoring the structural dilemma of mature capitalism.

It is in the context of these trends and structural dilemmas that current economic problems must be viewed. Indeed, in light of these basic dilemmas many economic problems are inevitable. Equally important, solutions to one set of problems can often aggravate other economic problems. It is these facts that make the resolution of specific economic problems very difficult.

PRESENT ECONOMIC PROBLEMS IN AMERICA

INFLATION

For several years, the American economy, as well as those in other capitalist societies, has seen steady increases in the prices of goods and services. Inflationary periods, or episodes, are inherent in capitalistic forms of economic organization, but equally important, infla-

SOCIOLOGICAL
INSIGHTS

THE SHRINKING DOLLAR

The following chart reports the cost of key items over the last thirty years. Naturally, incomes for Americans have increased as prices have escalated, underscoring the inflationary trends in the American economy. This chart reflects the purchasing power of the dollar from October 1944 to October 1974.

Year	Round Steak (1 lb)	Sugar (5 lb)	Bread (1 loaf)	Coffee (1 lb)	Eggs (1 doz)	Milk (Half gallon)	Lettuce (1 head)	Butter (1 lb)	Stamp (First-class mail)	Gasoline (1 gallon)
1944	$0.45	$0.34	$0.09	$0.30	$0.64	$0.29	$0.12	$0.50	$0.03	$0.21
1954	0.92	0.52	0.17	1.10	0.60	0.45	0.19	0.72	0.03	0.29
1964	1.07	0.59	0.21	0.82	0.57	0.48	0.25	0.76	0.05	0.30
1974	$1.78	$2.08	$0.36	$1.31	$0.84	$0.78	$0.43	$0.95	$0.10	$0.53

SOURCE: U.S. Bureau of Labor Statistics, Consumer Division, 1975.

tion may increasingly become a world problem that could prove difficult to resolve.

While inflation is a complex process, the result of inflation is easily comprehended by the average American: higher prices. What causes prices to periodically escalate? The answer to this often asked question resides in the structural dilemmas of liberal capitalism. One force causing higher prices is the size of corporations that no longer need be completely responsive to competition. For example, U.S. Steel, General Motors, and Exxon are capable of dominating their respective markets to the extent that it is not always necessary for them to lower prices in the face of slackening demand. In light of their partial immunity to effective competition, they are likely to *raise* prices to make up for decreasing sales and hence maintain their profits. Other "competitive" corporations must be careful of undercutting such corporate giants because in an all-out price war smaller competitors could not survive. Thus, there are pressures for smaller companies to follow the leads of the larger; and if larger companies raise prices, others will faithfully follow—thus raising prices across the entire market sector.

Competition and inflation

Once one sector of the economy raises prices, the price increases become higher costs for those companies using the goods and services in their manufacturing operations. Thus, should U.S. Steel raise prices, General Motors' costs increase, and it too is likely to raise the price of its cars. Price increases by resource and basic commodity in-dustries reverberate throughout the economy, setting off waves of price increases by all the companies comprising the complex web of interconnections in a modern economy.

Labor and inflation

Another inflationary pressure comes from organized labor. Capitalistic economies are built around growth and expansion, creating a highly affluent standard of living for the majority of the population. Accordingly, labor becomes accustomed to a constantly escalating standard of living (made possible by successful wage increases) and seeks to buy the myriad of goods and services provided by mature capitalism. Unions constantly work for increased wages and other benefits which, from the corporation's viewpoint, represent higher costs. Unless savings can be made in other cost areas, or unless corporations are willing to decrease their profits, prices will continue to increase. At times these cyclical processes escalate so rapidly as to create a *wage-price spiral* like that of the late 1960s and 1970s—in trying to keep up with higher prices labor seeks higher wages, thus

Recent years have seen such rapid inflation that the public—usually distinguished for its apathy—has begun to protest.

assuring higher prices. Such wage-price cycles would be less likely *if* Americans were not accustomed to ever-increasing levels of material well-being; *if* corporations were not oriented toward ever-increasing profits, and *if* a few corporations could not dominate markets. But as long as workers and corporations think in terms of *short-range* profits and wages, wage-price spirals are easily initiated in advanced capitalistic economies.

Such spirals are difficult to control by governmental regulation because government is not geared to establish and implement a national economic policy. First, the nature of political democracy in a society as diverse as that in America makes it difficult to agree on any unified national policy, especially in the economic sphere where there are so many inherent conflicts of interest. Second, even if agreement over a policy could be established by Congress and the president, implementation is difficult because of the nature of governmental intervention in the economy. For much intervention has been *indirect,* using the free market mechanism to stimulate demand or to decrease demand. For example, rather than directly establish wages, prices, and supply levels of goods and services, government has sought to influence all of these through tax policies, Federal Reserve actions, import–export policies, and government purchases. Thus, government in America is not set up to *directly* control supplies, prices, and wages. For indeed, the government does not "own" the capital of the economy.

A final inflationary force is the international involvement of the American economy. Basic resources are now in shorter supply because of growing international demand, coupled with less accessible supplies in the United States. Americans must now compete with other nations for many essential resources that were formerly purchased at lost costs in Third World countries. As these countries have become aware of the growing dependence of the "modern" world upon their resources, they have begun to organize and exert monetary and political influence. The Arab oil cartel is but the first, and still the most conspicuous, example of a phenomenon that will become increasingly prevalent in the world market. Just as giant, monopolistic corporations can begin to dictate prices in a domestic market, countries with large quantities of needed resources can begin to dictate prices in the international market. Such *monolistic* practices are inherently inflationary since Third World countries are likely to raise prices in order to increase their world power and to develop their own countries.

Inflation and the world market

Inflation, then, is likely to be a periodic, if not chronic, problem in America. As long as the Third World countries "sold" their resources cheaply, as long as American corporations were small, as long as corporations were national in character, as long as labor was less accustomed to ever-increasing wages, and as long as Americans were used to shortages, then government market policies could influence inflation. The very "success" of American corporations and labor unions, plus the new consciousness of the Third World, has made domestic inflation much more difficult for government to control.

ECONOMIC CYCLES AND STAGFLATION

Capitalist forms of economic organization are subject to what is now called the *business cycle* in which periods of economic prosperity (high profits, full employment, and higher wages) are followed by recessions and depressions (declining profits, high unemployment, and

Economic cycles have often been severe. Here unemployed men desperately scan the employment bulletin during the Great Depression of the 1930s.

lower wages). The American economy has been subject to many such vacillating cycles, but despite their inevitability and methodical frequency, economists still debate their causes.[3]

Since the 1930s governmental policies have been directed at mitigating the consequences of the business cycle. Various programs sought to assist unemployed workers and government policies have been designed to keep demand for goods high enough to prevent a severe cutback in production. Recently, recession has been accompanied by inflation. In previous recessions, unemployment and decreased production caused prices to go down because individuals and corporations did not have money to spend, hence the demand for goods and services decreased. But because of the built-in pressures for inflation discussed in the previous section, recent recessions have not lowered prices. The result is *stagflation*—an economy where production is down, unemployment remains high, and prices are rising.

Stagflation

This situation is perhaps inevitable in economies where (1) unions are able to keep wages high even in the face of unemployment, (2) where large oligopolies and multinationals can control domestic and world markets and, thus, not need to lower prices even with less de-

During severe recessions some people must scratch for survival. Shanty dwellings like these used to be—and still are—common in many cities.

mand for their goods (in fact they may raise prices to recoup their falling profits), and (3) where government is not structured for directly controlling wages, prices, and employment.

WASTE AND POLLUTION

In an economic system guided by profit considerations, efforts are directed at keeping costs low in relation to prices, thereby increasing profits. Such considerations may at times allow organizations to achieve a considerable degree of efficiency in their internal operation, but this is likely to lead to wasteful and polluting manufacturing processes. Pollution control and abatement equipment is expensive and it is unlikely that economic organizations will make purchases that drive up their costs. Further, it is often cheaper to extract resources and manufacture goods by letting much valuable material go to waste, only because to use all materials or to recycle other resources is more costly than wasteful extraction and manufacturing. Only when it is less expensive to conserve and recycle can there be any strong incentive for profit-oriented corporations to use the least wasteful forms of manufacturing. And only when pollution becomes "costly" in terms of profit considerations are organizations likely to be concerned with ecological questions.

The basic question in dealing with waste and pollution is: Without direct government controls over economic processes, how is the government to induce or coerce corporations to employ less wasteful and less polluting forms of extraction and production? Problems of overcoming corporate and union political influence, of effective monitoring of pollutants and wastes, and of assessing taxes or fines make it extremely difficult for government in an economy dominated by large, private corporations and large unions to impose rules and regulations that might cut into profits, lower productivity, or cost workers jobs. (See Chapter 13 for a fuller discussion of pollution problems and solutions.)

Waste and pollution in capitalist economies

CONSUMER DECEPTION AND MANIPULATION

In recent years, a considerable amount of consumer deception has been exposed. A high degree of consumer manipulation, deception, and outright fraud is probably inevitable in an economic system structured for profit in a quasicompetitive market. Competitive markets encourage extensive advertising to induce consumers to purchase goods and services, but the drive for profits can sometimes lead corporations to deceive consumers about the nature of various products. Advertising is also necessary to encourage the growth so essential to maintain capitalist economic systems. Thus, corporations seek to expand demand for goods by creating "needs" in consumers for even more goods. Instilling new needs for the "latest" model and a plethora of "new and improved" goods constitutes a form of corporate manipulation which, at times, extends into deception about the true nature of a product.

As the economy becomes dominated by large corporations, advertising assumes a new function: to convince the public that giant corporations are in the public's best interest. For example, oil company advertising has often assumed a "public information" format, seeking to convince consumers that oil cartel control of the world market is necessary and desirable to meet "America's energy needs." Thus, as competition among giant corporations recedes, advertising becomes much more deliberately manipulative and seeks to persuade the public that the current state of economic affairs is desirable. Moreover, advertising costs enormous sums of money and adds nothing to consumer knowledge and product superiority. The result of this situation is for consumers to pay more for goods whose prices are inflated by advertising costs.

Regulating small and large companies in a quasicompetitive market has proven difficult. Many of the regulatory problems are endemic to capitalist forms of economic organization: First, the large number of manufacturing corporations producing millions of goods makes it extremely difficult to monitor advertising integrity, product safety, and various fradulent activities. Second, there is a tendency for regulatory agencies to become coopted by the larger organizations they are set up to regulate because day-to-day contact is not with consumers but with corporate officials. Third, the political power of corporations has often worked to weaken regulatory laws and thus make government agencies impotent, hence, easily coopted. As a result of these forces, a considerable amount of abuse, deception, and manipulation of consumers occurs. And without consistently effective regulation by such agencies as the Food and Drug Administration, the Civil Aeronautics Board, the Interstate Commerce Commission, Public Utilities Commissions, the Department of Agriculture, the Department of Interior, the Department of Justice, and the many other agencies with regulatory responsibilities, it would be impossible to prevent consumer abuse.

Problems of corporate regulation

The failure of government to effectively protect their clients, the public, has forced nongovernmental organizations (such as consumers unions and the Ralph Nader organization) to investigate and bring suits against both corporations and government for initiating and tolerating consumer abuse. This conflict between nongovernmental organizations and corporations is probably inevitable in capitalist systems where large corporations, unions, and government agencies can, at times, work against as much as for consumers' interests.

WORKER FRUSTRATION AND ALIENATION

Early capitalism tends to be highly exploitive of unorganized labor, since individual workers are not in a position to bargain with corporate management over salary and working conditions. But as labor becomes organized, it acquires considerable bargaining power,

As work has become "nationalized" in large corporations, it soon becomes routine, repetitive, and psychologically unfulfilling. Under the conditions depicted above, workers experience considerable frustration, alienation, and, sometimes, anger.

especially in industries with heavy capital investments where a shutdown becomes enormously costly. Under these conditions, organized labor is able to improve wages, working conditions, and fringe benefits.

Large and effective labor unions, then, are a response to titanic corporations which, as they become large, are vulnerable to strikes and shutdowns. In organizing, however, industrial workers place themselves between two bureaucracies: the corporation and the union. Work within the corporation tends to be monotonous, highly regulated, uncreative, and ungratifying, while union membership imposes restrictions on occupational mobility, job classification, and take-home pay. As industrial workers have become somewhat affluent and secure in their work, it appears that they also become more attuned to their dependent situation. Such awareness has created what has become known as the "blue-collar blues" in which the lack of individual freedom and incessant monotony of work in large industries has stimulated a search for more meaning and satisfaction in work.

This problem is endemic to corporate desires for profits using the most efficient and least expensive production process in which machine and human labor are made highly standardized. However, as blue-collar blues—resulting in poor job performance, high absenteeism, and high worker turnover—have become costly, alternative work settings have been sought by industry, but it is not yet clear that large, profit-oriented corporations can implement work settings with less supervision and monotony on a wide scale. Blue-collar dissatisfaction and corporate-union efforts to create more meaningful work is thus likely to be one of the basic problems of mature capitalism in America.

Much of the work force, however, does not belong to a union. As will be emphasized in the chapters on inequality and poverty, many workers are subject to hardships generated by the business cycle, and the low wages stemming from intense competition in the unskilled labor market. Such workers experience enormous dissatisfaction and frustration with an economic system incapable of providing them with meaningful and well-paying work. The racial riots of the 1960s were, in large part, an expression of such frustration to participate in the mainstream of the economy. Whites also experience these same impediments, and during times of deep recession, this marginal labor force can pose a threat to civil order.

Without union organization, these marginal workers must rely on government to protect and assist them; yet, only during a deep recession or outright depression has government been willing to provide an extensive system of public service jobs. But even these jobs are de-

Corporations, unions, and the blue-collar blues

Frustrations in the nonunion work force

fined as "temporary measures" to take up the "slack" in the employment picture of the economy. The unskilled, nonunion worker must endure constant employment uncertainty in a cyclical economy that is only partially regulated by government, thus, heightening frustration and, at times, rage against both the economic institutions and the entire society.

COORDINATION, CONTROL, AND NATIONAL PRIORITIES

Like most capitalist systems, the American economy is a "mixed economy" with the free market mechanism operating in some sectors and government regulation in other sectors. Any large economy presents problems of coordination and control in meeting politically established goals. In capitalist systems growth and profits are the primary goals of economic units, while high wages, security, and meaningful employment are the major goals of workers. To some extent these goals correspond with national priorities, but in some instances they do not. Goals such as racial equality, ecological preservation, international humanitarianism, national self-sufficiency in energy, consumer protection, community planning, and many other national goals come into conflict with the priorities of corporations and unionized workers.

Coupled with the economic and political problems associated with the business cycle and inflation/stagflation, government inevitably intervenes in the market mechanisms and seeks to allocate human and material resources to meet *political* goals. In so doing, government usually attempts to utilize the market mechanism as much as is possible, resulting in a system of market incentives and subsidies for economic organizations conducting certain types of economic activity. Tax credits for manufacturers, cash subsidies to farmers and airlines, price supports for dairy products, depletion allowances for extraction corporations, accelerated depreciation for real estate activity, and a host of incentives and subsidies usually operate to leave some semblance of the market mechanism. Control and regulation is thus indirect and it is not always possible to coordinate precisely economic activity in pursuit of political goals.

With government increasingly concerned with the well being of citizens, it is inevitable that economic and political goals will come into conflict. Capitalist systems are simply unprepared to coordinate economic activity, not only because of the indirect nature of regulation through the market, but also because large corporations, large unions, large conglomerates, and foreign governments are able to exert an independent base of power in a political democracy. This

Government and the market

Conflicts of economic and political goals

power is disproportionate, but as long as government is designed to be receptive to influence by private citizens' interests, then it is inevitable that well-financed and organized interest will exert more influence on political decisions than individual citizens.

This conflict between citizens and economic organizations in establishing national priorities and allocating societal resources is inherent in the American economic system. As a result, coordination and control of economic activity in pursuit of political goals will, in all probability, pose a constant problem of structure in American society.

SUMMARY

We have explored the problems of inflation, economic cycles and stagflation, waste and pollution, consumer deception and manipulation, worker alienation and frustration, and control of the economy in the face of conflicting political priorities. These problems are not isolated from each other. They are interrelated and the result of certain forces and trends operating in America's capitalistic economy. These broader trends include monopoly and oligopoly, multinationalization, unionization, and the growth of government.

Cultural beliefs are intimately involved in America's economic problems. A belief in capitalism encourages trends which, if left unchecked, would suspend the free market and capitalism itself. Beliefs have, therefore, encouraged and legitimized those very trends that have created current economic problems. At the same time, these beliefs dictate, even in the face of trends to the contrary, that capitalism and the market must be preserved. Thus, a pattern of government intervention and regulation that presents additional problems of coordination and control has been legitimized by liberal capitalist beliefs. Beliefs have operated to define what is desirable and appropriate action in economic affairs, and it is in this sense that economic problems are the outgrowth of both cultural and structural forces.

NOTES

1. This section draws heavily from several useful references: Eric Roll (1942), Paul Sweezy (1942), Maurice Dobb (1946), Robin Williams (1970), and Neil J. Smelser (1963).

2. This analysis of problems draws heavily from Maurice Zeitlen (1970), Williams (1970), and Sherman (1972).

3. Two forces appear to set the business cycle into motion (Sherman, 1972:82–90): (1) Wages as a proportion of aggregate or total income actually *decline* during periods of prosperity, eventually translating into decreasing demand relative to productivity. In absolute dollars, of course, wages increase dramatically, but relative to escalating profits, the buying power of wages as a proportion of all income

(wages, profits, etc.) and production decreases. (2) During prosperity, the high demand for capital goods (machinery, factories, etc.) and basic resources (fuels and necessary minerals) increases their cost to manufacturers, with the result that profits per unit of production begin to decline. At some point the slackening demand resulting from the aggregate decline in wages, plus lower per unit profits, discourages further investment in capital expansion, setting into motion decreased production, unem-ployment, and lower wages. But traditionally during recessions, wages as a proportion of aggregate or total income have *increased*, creating greater demand which encourages renewed investment, that leads to fuller employment, higher wages, and even greater consumer demand. Eventually all of these processes create overproduction relative to demand from wage earners, and thus, the cycle is set into motion once again.

REVIEW QUESTIONS

1. What does an economy do for a society?
2. What are the basic features of a capitalist form of economic organization?
3. What are the crucial cultural beliefs about the most desirable form of economic organization in America?
4. List and discuss the basic structural trends of economic organization in America.
5. For each of the following problems, indicate how these trends create and maintain economic problems:

    inflation
    economic cycles and stagflation
    waste and pollution
    consumer deception and manipulation
    worker alienation and frustration
    political coordination and control

6. For each of the above-listed problems, discuss how cultural beliefs impose restrictions on what Americans would perceive as a desirable way of dealing with the problem.

GLOSSARY

business cycles the tendency in capitalistic economies for alternating periods of high production and employment followed by lowered production and unemployment; sometimes termed *economic cycles*

capitalism that form of economic organization where the assets are held by private individuals and where the market mechanism is used to allocate and distribute labor, goods, and services

inflation the economic stage when the prices of goods and services are rising, thus decreasing the purchasing power of money

monopoly a situation in capitalistic economies where one corporation controls virtually the entire market for a good or service

multinationalization when a corporation is engaged in extensive projects, or has extensive holdings, in several countries

oligopoly a situation in capitalist economies where several large corporations control a vast majority of the market for a good or service

stagflation the economic stage when prices are rising as production of goods and services and employment are decreasing

unionization the organization of labor in order to create a unified front in negotiating with the management of corporations and industries over salaries, working conditions, and fringe benefits

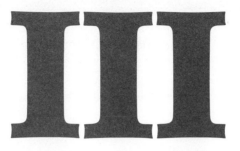

PROBLEMS IN
THE DISTRIBUTIVE
SYSTEM

The existence of inequality has been a fact of social life ever since human technology first allowed for the creation of a surplus above and beyond bare subsistence needs. Since a surplus was created, humans have competed and fought for a share (Lenski, 1966; Turner and Starnes, 1976). As a result, human affairs are now dominated by such protein questions as: Who gets how much of the surplus? Are there vast inequalities in its distribution? Can people improve their chances at getting more surplus in their lifetime?[1] Answers to such questions can reveal a great deal about the structure of a society. Inequality is the result of the structure of basic institutions. Thus, people's access to valued resources is determined by the structure of the basic institutions of economy, government, family, and education (Turner, 1972b). In analyzing the causes of inequality and its consequences for social problems, then, an understanding of how basic institutions operate to limit or open people's access to resources will be necessary.

Part III will be divided into four interrelated topics, all of which pose problems of structure for America: (1) the overall system of inequality, (2) the creation of a vast pocket of poverty from this system, (3) the maintenance of racial and ethnic discrimination by this system of inequality, and (4) sexual discrimination.

INEQUALITY

Various cultural and social forces have perpetuated a system of inequality in the United States, a system that has changed little over the last 25 years. While there is affluence among the large middle classes, the lowest ranks and those in minority categories are not, relative to the rest of the population, much better off than they were immediately after World War II. Thus, despite a war on poverty, the extension of welfare, and widely publicized ameliorative legislation, there has been little, if any, change in the pattern of inequality in the United States. Such stability in the resource distribution can either be viewed as a problem or seen as an index of the respective abilities of individuals. But, as will become evident in Chapter 7, inequality in resource distribtuion frequently has little to do with the "ability" and "merit" of individuals in American society. Rather, inequality often reflects powerful economic and political forces that are legitimized by dominant cultural beliefs that serve to maintain a consistent pattern of inequality.

POVERTY

One of the results of the current system of inequality is to create a vast pocket of poverty in the midst of the most affluent land in the world. Historically, poverty has periodically been rediscovered in America. In the 1960s, for example, one such rediscovery occurred and two contrasting conceptions of why people are poor emerged. These two concepts, in turn, dictated entirely different programs of how to eradicate widespread poverty in the midst of affluence (Skolnick and Currie, 1970:19–22).

One conception viewed poverty as a failure of certain segments of the population to become modernized. Poverty was seen as a separate and deviant culture, transmitted from generation to generation, that kept the poor from access to the mainstream of American life. From this veiwpoint, poverty could only be eradicated by a massive assault on the habits, life-styles, values, beliefs, and aspirations of the poor in order to "bring them into line" with those of the middle class. A second conception of poverty emerging in the 1960s held that the plight of the poor was not the result of their "cultural deficiencies," but of how the wealth was distributed in America. The poor were poor not because of their cultural shortcomings, but because of a well-institutionalized and established system of inequality that

consistently favored the wealthy and affluent. This controversy
will occupy much of our discussion of poverty.

RACIAL AND ETHNIC DISCRIMINATION

Inequality and poverty are compounded by a third dimension in
America: race and ethnicity. In addition to the conditions
maintaining the current system of inequality and
impoverishment of millions, there are a series of discriminatory
forces that operate against certain racial and ethnic groups. The
widespread poverty among racial and ethnic groups is, as will
become clear, not the result of "biological inferiority," nor is it
just a matter of "cultural deprivation"; rather, it is social
institutions (the economy, the law, the government, and the
educational system) which, by favoring the white majority,
discriminate against members of minority groups.

SEXUAL DISCRIMINATION

The final chapter in Part III will focus on the problems of
discrimination against women. We will view the inability of women
to assume work roles equal to those of men, and thus come to

realize how many dominant American values and cultural beliefs about women's "natures" legitimize patterns of discrimination in economic, educational, legal, political, and kinship institutions. Such discrimination denies many women access to such valued resources as money, prestige, and power; therefore, it is viewed as a problem of the distributive system.

PROLOGUE 7: MAKING IT IN AMERICA

Although most Americans live in large metropolitan areas, the best research on class and status in the United States has been limited to studies of "middletown" (Muncie, Ind.), Levittown, and other comparatively small communities. One notable exception is the work of urban sociologist Richard Coleman, who recently completed a major study of how adults in two major cities classify themselves—and each other—according to income, occupation, size of home, and other symbols of status and success.

Beginning in 1971 teams of housewives, under the direction of Dr. Coleman and sociologist Lee Rainwater, both of the Harvard and Massachusetts Institute of Technology Joint Center for Urban Studies, conducted in-depth interviews with 900 residents of the Kansas City and Boston metropolitan areas. The results, which will be published in a book next year, reveal how a wide range of urbanized Americans feel about "making it" in contemporary society. Coleman's seven categories are:

1. *The success elite* (minimum family income: $50,000). "These are the people who others feel have really made it," Coleman reports. Included in this elite are the "old rich," such as the Harrimans and Rockefellers, the "celebrity rich," such as famous actors and star athletes, the "anonymous rich," including surgeons who perform expensive operations, and the "run-of-the-mill rich," best typified by the doctor who can take every Wednesday off to play golf.

"This," says Coleman, "is what the average man considers upper class."

2. *People who are doing very well* (minimum income: $30,000). "To do well, you usually have to have a college education," Coleman notes. Thus, the people in this class tend to be graduates of professional schools—dentists, engineers, and business managers. They often live in eight-room houses, have two cars, travel abroad at company expense, belong to semielite country clubs and can afford to send their children to good state universities without strain.

3. *The middle-American dream* (minimum income: $19,000). "These people are not dabbling in luxuries, but they do have lots more than necessities," Coleman calculates. Typically, they live in a house with three bedrooms and a family room, and one of their two cars is a station wagon or camper. The parents usually eat out once a week and take a three-week family vacation in the United States every summer. Looking at them, says Coleman, a working man would muse: "If I were making that kind of dough, I'd be in fat city."

4. *The average-man comfortable existence* (minimum income: $15,000). "Families at this level can pay their bills on time with a modest saving to tide them over the rough spots," says Coleman. Home is a single-family house with six rooms which is owned, not rented, in a racially untroubled suburban neighborhood.

5. *The world of just getting along* (minimum income: $9,500). In these families, both husband and wife probably had to go to work right after high school. Now, he works in a factory or clerks in an office, she is a waitress or perhaps a telephone operator. They may rent either a small house with two bedrooms or perhaps five rooms on one floor of a multifamily building. They take good care of their six-year-old car, own two black-and-white TV sets and a clothes washer—but no drier or dishwasher. They enjoy bowling, eating at McDonald's and attending drive-in movies, which saves the price of a baby-sitter.

6. *Having a real hard time* (minimum income: $5,750). These families are just a step away from welfare and are proud to say they work. They rent a substandard flat in an old building owned by an absentee landlord. The man and his wife quit school at about the ninth grade and now work as, perhaps, a garbageman and a domestic. In their spare time these families enjoy picnics in the park and other diversions that are free. They watch a lot of TV and sandlot baseball; the only long trips they take are for funerals. "The Lions or Knights of Columbus wouldn't have us," is the way one hard-timer sums up his status.

7. *The poor* (income up to $4,500). Most families on this bottom rung

are on welfare. They rent tenements in the inner city or the ghetto, where the bathrooms are usually down the hall and there is no hot water. Rooms are "carpeted" in wall-to-wall cockroaches, recreation is watching TV, and transportation is strictly public. Significantly, Coleman's research on the poor is spotty and derivative. Most of the people who did the interviews for his book, he acknowledges, "flatly refused to work at all in lower-class neighborhoods—which is itself an illustration of how much middle Americans abhor and fear contact with these people."

As might be expected, the minimum income reported for each class level must be adjusted regionally—up for New York City, down for Nashville or Austin. Moreover, what families at each level can actually do with their income depends upon such variables as savings, how long they have been earning at that level, and how they balance one ambition—such as private education for their children—against other goals. "People at lower income levels usually fail to realize that ambitions rise with income so that at almost every level money always seems to dribble away," Coleman observes.

Despite these qualifications, Coleman believes that the vast majority of middle-class respondents show a surprisingly realistic grasp of the relationships between class, status, and current income distribution in the U.S. Thus, as measured by the latest 1974 census statistics, the 1.1 percent of American households that enjoy incomes of $50,000 or more do indeed represent a "success elite"; those reporting incomes of $30,000 or better are, comparatively speaking, "doing very well." In fact, the hard truth is that for eight out of ten U.S. families, and annual income of $19,000 remains what Coleman reports it to be—a middle American dream, not a reality.

From an article by Kenneth L. Woodward with Mary Lord (in Boston),
Newsweek, January 5, 1976, p. 67. Reprinted by permission.

CHAPTER

7

THE PROBLEM
OF INEQUALITY

The dynamics of any society are intimately connected to the distribution of money. Who controls the wealth? How much wealth is held by different groups? How is wealth used? These are not trivial questions because the distribution of money in a society influences people's access to such basic resources as power, prestige, and health. In other words, people's life-styles—their homes, leisure activities, clothes, food, medical care, and educational opportunities—are tied to their income. And while we are accustomed to visualizing income as simply a matter of people's jobs, we must also view income and jobs as part of a broader *system of distribution.*

The income associated with a job is influenced by how all monies are distributed in the society. If some jobs pay less, or more, than others, this fact is connected to a system of distribution. Furthermore, income that comes from a welfare check, a government subsidy, or a tax loophole is also a part of an overall system of resource distribution. Thus, in studying a society, we must be willing to look beyond our paycheck, the welfare recipient, the tax loophole, the guaranteed government loan, and other specific ways of distributing income and wealth. We must be prepared to visualize these and other means of distributing money as part of a larger set of structural arrangements and corresponding cultural beliefs that determine why and how some jobs receive more income than others, why and how welfare payments are allocated, as well as why and how other subsidies to individuals and industry are given. Only by examining these processes can we find

The broader
implications of
inequality

an answer to the fundamental questions: Who controls how much of the wealth? What consequences does this control have for society? An answer to these questions will offer much insight into a society and its people because if some control most of the wealth, others can sometimes suffer. And if the same people consistently maintain their privilege over several generations, while others live in perpetual poverty, a society is likely to reveal restrictive and discriminatory social patterns, while being vulnerable to disruptive social conflict. Not only does the distribution of wealth effect people's life-styles, but it also has implications for virtually all activity in the society. Indeed, the existence of poverty, the nature of racial and ethnic discrimination, the rates of crime, the administration of justice, the political process, the quality of education, the operation of the economy, the potential for conflict, and the profile of communities are all influenced by the degree of inequality in a society. It is for this reason that the profile of inequality presents many social problems.

In this chapter, our goal is threefold: (1) to review the available data on the nature and degree of inequality in America, (2) to examine the way inequality is structured into America's economic and political institutions, and (3) to understand how these structural arrangements are legitimized by dominant cultural beliefs and values.

THE PROFILE OF INEQUALITY

How much inequality exists in America? There are two types of statistical indicators of inequality that can give a tentative answer to this question: (1) income distribution and (2) asset or wealth distribution. *Income distribution* refers to how much of the total income in a given year different segments of the population command, while *asset distribution* concerns what proportion of all the valuable assets—money, cars, stocks, bonds, homes, and the like—are held by different segments of the population. More is known about income distribution than wealth distribution, primarily because the government has been collecting data on people's income through the Census Bureau and Internal Revenue Service. The government, however, has not collected recent data on how and where wealth has been accumulating, as a result, we are forced to rely upon data that are over a decade old.

In Table 7.1, the distribution of family income by income fifths for the last 25 years is reported.[1] To read the table it is necessary to know what an "income fifth" is. Basically, *income fifths* are statistical groupings and are constructed by rank ordering every family in America by its total income for a given year—from the highest to

Income and wealth distribution

Table 7.1 **Percentage of Total Income Received by**
Different Income Groups, 1947 to 1973

Year	Total Percentage	Income Rank					
		Lowest Fifth	Second Fifth	Third Fifth	Fourth Fifth	Highest Fifth	Top 5 Percent
1973	100.0	5.5%	11.9%	17.5%	24.0%	41.1%	15.5%
1972	100.0	5.4	11.9	17.5	23.9	41.4	15.9
1971	100.0	5.5	12.0	17.6	23.8	41.1	15.7
1970	100.0	5.4	12.2	17.6	23.8	40.9	15.6
1969	100.0	5.6	12.4	17.7	23.7	40.6	15.6
1968	100.0	5.6	12.4	17.7	23.7	40.5	15.6
1967	100.0	5.5	12.4	17.9	23.9	40.4	15.2
1966	100.0	5.6	12.4	17.8	23.8	40.5	15.6
1965	100.0	5.2	12.2	17.8	23.9	40.9	15.5
1964	100.0	5.1	12.0	17.7	24.0	41.2	15.9
1963	100.0	5.0	12.1	17.7	24.0	41.2	15.8
1962	100.0	5.0	12.1	17.6	24.0	41.3	15.7
1961	100.0	4.7	11.9	17.5	23.8	42.2	16.6
1960	100.0	4.8	12.2	17.8	24.0	41.3	15.9
1959	100.0	4.9	12.3	17.9	23.8	41.1	15.9
1958	100.0	5.1	12.4	17.8	23.7	41.0	15.8
1957	100.0	5.0	12.6	18.1	23.7	40.5	15.8
1956	100.0	4.9	12.4	17.9	23.6	41.1	16.4
1955	100.0	4.8	12.2	17.7	23.4	41.8	16.8
1954	100.0	4.5	12.0	17.6	24.0	41.9	16.4
1953	100.0	4.7	12.4	17.8	24.0	41.0	15.8
1952	100.0	4.9	12.2	17.1	23.5	42.2	17.7
1951	100.0	4.9	12.5	17.6	23.3	41.8	16.9
1950	100.0	4.5	11.9	17.4	23.6	42.7	17.3
1949	100.0	4.5	11.9	17.3	23.5	42.8	16.9
1948	100.0	5.0	12.1	17.2	23.2	42.5	17.1
1947	100.0	5.1%	11.8%	16.7%	23.2%	43.3%	17.5%

Source: J. H. Turner and C. E. Starnes, *Inequality: Privilege and Poverty in America*, Pacific Palisades, Cal.: Goodyear Publishing, 1976, p. 51.

lowest—and then dividing this rank-ordered list into five equal categories from the top to the bottom fifth. Each income fifth is equal in
size, and represents 20 percent of the population, but its proportion
of the total income in a given year will vary. In Table 7.1, by reading
down the columns for each income fifth, it is evident that the bottom
fifth of the population has derived only about 5 percent of the total income in a given year, while the top fifth has received about 40 percent. The second, third, and fourth income fifths have, respectively,
derived around 12 percent, 17–18 percent, and 23–24 percent of the
total income. Two features of these government figures are note-
worthy: First, income distribution has remained constant over the
last twenty-five years; there has been virtually no redistribution of
income in the United States. Second, over 40 percent of all income

Income fifths

Table 7.2 **Distribution of Wealth by Income Fifths, 1962**

Income Fifths	Percent of Total Wealth Held
Highest fifth	57.2%
Fourth fifth	15.6
Third fifth	11.4
Second fifth	8.6
Lowest fifth	7.2
Total	100.0%

SOURCE: Board of Governors of the Federal Reserve System, *Survey of Financial Characteristics of Consumers, 1962,* Washington, D.C.: Government Printing Office, 1962.

Table 7.3 **Distribution of Wealth by Wealth Fifths**

Wealth Fifths	Percentage of Total Wealth
Highest fifth	76.0%
Fourth fifth	15.5
Third fifth	6.2
Second fifth	2.1
Lowest fifth	.2
Total	100.0%

goes to only one-fifth of the population, signaling enormous inequality in income for families in America.

In Table 7.2, the amount of total wealth, that is, the sum of all assets, held in 1962 by income fifths is reported. By referring back to Table 7.1 for the year 1962, it is possible to compare the amount of the income earned in that year and the total wealth held for comparable statistical groupings. It is important to caution, however, that such a comparison does not reveal the degree of wealth inequality because wealth is computed for income fifths, and it is likely that some very wealthy families did not earn high incomes in a particular year.

This fact becomes immediately evident when *wealth fifths* are computed. Such fifths are computed in the same manner as income fifths, except this time it is wealth—a family's total assets—that is rank-ordered and grouped into five equal categories; wealth fifths are reported in Table 7.3. As can be seen, one-fifth of the families controlled about 76 percent of all the assets for the year 1962. Phrased differently, the bottom three-fifths, or 60 percent, of the population held less than 9 percent of all assets in 1962—that is, cars, houses, stocks, bonds, securities, money, or anything that can be converted into money. Such data, despite the fact that they are over a decade old, reveal considerable inequality in America. No comprehensive or systematic data on wealth inequality have been collected by the government since 1962, but it is evident from these data that considerable wealth is concentrated among a comparatively few families.

In Table 7.4 the percentage of total wealth held by the wealthiest 1 percent of the population is reported. These data span a greater period of time and have been collected up to 1969, giving a more comprehensive and complete picture of wealth concentration among the richest people in America. It should be cautioned, however, that these

Wealth fifths

Table 7.4 **Share of Wealth Held by Richest 1 Percent United States**

Year	Percent of Wealth Held	By 1 percent of:
1810	21.0	U.S. families
1860	24.0	U.S. families
1900	26–31.0	U.S. families
1922	31.6	U.S. adults
1929	36.3	U.S. adults
1933	28.3	U.S. adults
1939	30.6	U.S. adults
1945	23.3	U.S. adults
1949	20.8	U.S. adults
1953	27.5	U.S. adults
1956	26.0	U.S. adults
1958	26.9	U.S. adults
1962	27.4	U.S. adults
1965	29.2	U.S. adults
1969	24.9	U.S. adults

SOURCES: For 1810, 1860, and 1900, Robert E. Gallman, "Trends in the Size Distribution of Wealth in the Nineteenth Century," in Lee Soltow, ed., *Six Papers on the Size Distribution of Wealth and Income*, New York: National Bureau of Economic Research, 1969, p. 6.

For 1922, 1929, 1933, 1939, 1945, 1949, and 1956, Robert J. Lampman, *The Share of Top Wealth-Holders in National Wealth, 1922–1956*, New York: National Bureau of Economic Research, 1962, p. 204.

For 1953, 1958, 1962, 1965, and 1969, James D. Smith and Stephen D. Franklin, "The Concentration of Personal Wealth, 1922–1969," *American Economic Review* 64:2(May), 162–167, 1974.

Note: Smith and Franklin report that data for 1962, 1965, and 1969 were adjusted to achieve statistical comparability with the earlier 1953 and 1958 data. The result sacrifices their best estimates for the later years in the interest of consistency and, they note, produces a downward bias in their best estimates of wealth concentration. The bias is, itself, estimated to be 10–15%. Thus, the actual concentration of wealth in the years 1962, 1965, and 1969 could run as high as 27.8%, 29.6% and 25.3%, respectively.

data are not completely comparable from year to year (see note on table), but they do give a rough calculation (and only a very rough calculation is possible) of wealth concentrations at the very top. In general, it appears that about 25 percent of all assets in America have been held by 1 percent of the population—another indicator of the degree of inequality in America.

While the data are not complete, they do provide an approximate picture of inequality in America. There is considerable income inequality which has accumulated over time into vast wealth inequalities. The critical question now becomes: What social and cultural forces have caused, and now perpetuate, such a high degree of inequality? The remaining pages of this chapter are devoted to answering this question.

As we approach an answer to why high degrees of inequality exist in America, we must remain attuned to a potential danger: The assumption that inequality is either "good" or "bad." For some inequality is not only "good," it is necessary for economic growth and prosperity. For others, inequality is "bad" because it promotes privilege for the few, relegates others to poverty, and increases the potential for conflict. Our purpose in analyzing inequality is to determine its causes and suggest some of its consequences. Depending upon one's values and beliefs, these causes and consequences will be good, bad, or inevitable. For as we enter a topic so determinative of people's life-styles and sense of well-being, we inevitably confront deeply held values and beliefs—topics that also must be analyzed. The problemness of inequality, then, is a matter of individual definition. The good and bad of inequality is a moral matter—one that we cannot answer for the reader. Our task is to understand how inequality is created and maintained and why its consequences for many, but by no means all, people are regarded as problematic.

Inequality and social problems

THE ECONOMIC STRUCTURE OF INEQUALITY

As we discussed in Chapter 6, people's lives are profoundly influenced by their participation in the economy—as both workers and consumers. It is not surprising, therefore, that their access to scarce resources (most notably money, and all it can buy) is influenced by their place in the economy. People have different experiences and chances at different places within the economic scheme of things. One way to understand these differences is to ask: What forces operate on behalf of, and against, different types of workers? In this way we can visualize how economic arrangements can operate to the benefit and to the detriment of the poor (or the bottom income fifth), the more affluent worker (the three middle income fifths), and the more wealthy (the upper income and wealth fifth).

THE ECONOMY AND THE POOR

As we noted earlier, the American economy is subject to periods of recession and stagflation. It is during these periods that the economy can cause severe hardship for the unskilled, uneducated, and poorly paid worker. While most corporations and businesses do not like to lay off employees, recessions and stagflation place their operators in a cost-profit squeeze: costs must be cut in the face of falling profits. One solution is to lay off the least skilled and essential personnel. For these workers the only alternative available is welfare and temporary unemployment insurance, as is revealed by the fact that one-fifth of those on welfare in a given year are the heads of families who have been laid off because of economic cutbacks (Seligman, 1970). In making cutbacks, a bias against the nonunion, unskilled worker

The poor are first to be layed off

Workers like these are highly vulnerable. They make little money; they have few skills to offer; they usually do not belong to a union; and, they have no savings. And yet, they must compete desperately for jobs with little pay and no future.

exists. This is not a bias stemming from prejudice or bigotry against the poor, but one stemming from hard economic facts: someone has to be let go to reduce costs. In most instances, the unskilled are less essential than the skilled, and the unskilled are the least likely to be unionized. Without a union and the benefits it can provide, workers have no recourse but to turn to state unemployment insurance and welfare. The benefits of these programs are rarely equal to already low wages, hence, the worker is forced to live at an even more impoverished existence.

Naturally, if a recession becomes severe, as in the middle 1970s, then many employees are laid off, including unionized and professional white collar workers. But in contrast to the uneducated and nonunion poor, these workers have more financial resources, better types of unemployment compensation, and most important, better alternative job prospects.

The problems caused by these economic cycles are aggravated by a labor market that places the poor in intense competition with each other. In a modern economy in which automation can, at times, displace unskilled jobs, the uneducated can be thrust into severe competition for the few remaining menial opportunities left on the open job market. In a market economy, the existence of a surplus of unskilled labor, such as in farm, service, and other menial categories, tends to keep wages down and places workers in a situation of having to compete aggressively for low-paying jobs. Coupled with the fact that the labor market has been increasing at a rate of over 1.5 million persons per year, the low-income worker, who does not enjoy the increased protection that union membership or eduction can afford, is constantly faced with job insecurity.

Competition in a labor market subject to disruptive economic cycles has kept wages paid to the poor extremely low. Since the New Deal era, the federal government has encouraged collective bargaining between organized labor and management. This encouragement has kept the wages of skilled and semiskilled workers belonging to unions sufficiently high to provide a well-above-subsistence income. However, for the protection of unskilled workers for whom unionization is a long way off, only a federal minimum wage exists. This wage cannot provide even a subsistence living for the unskilled, nonunion worker who works 40 hours a week all year long. For example, maids, busboys, dishwashers, some farm laborers, many custodians, institutional laborers such as hospital orderlies and industrial handymen, waitresses, low clerical and sales workers, ambulance drivers, and many categories of nonunion, uneducated, and poorly paid workers cannot earn enough to support a family of four above government established subsistence levels. Many of these workers must seek welfare supplements, and others must hold two jobs. Government has been reluctant to maintain the minimum wage above subsistence levels because to do so would increase labor costs for business and industry, while raising prices for consumers. The dilemma, therefore, boils down to: Some workers cannot earn enough to support themselves; increasing their wages would raise costs and prices; and since the vast majority of Americans will resist increased prices, there is little the poor, who are a minority of the population, can do to alter their economic plight.

These are examples of how economic processes operate to maintain a situation where many workers and their families can earn, at best, only a subsistence living. These processes do not always work consciously, rather they are built into the structure of the economy. Few managers and owners of economic organizations want to lay off their workers or see people in poverty. Nor does a public

Job competition among the poor

SOCIOLOGICAL
INSIGHTS

**THE WAGE DILEMMA OF THE
UNSKILLED, NONUNION WORKER**

The most recent increase in the minimum wage to an average of $2.25 per hour in 1976 (the actual minimum varies somewhat in different occupations) was delayed for several years because in 1971, when an increase was first proposed, President Nixon declared that it was "inflationary" and that the increase should be gradual. In contrast, in the same year, auto workers, steel workers, and many other categories of industrial union workers negotiated substantial wage increases over the same three-year period—increases that were declared inflationary but that were tolerated nevertheless. Hence, unlike many of their skilled counterparts who belong to a union, many unskilled workers do not have assurance from a union contract or from the federal government that even if they work full time they can earn a sufficient living to stay off the welfare rolls.

already squeezed by price inflation enjoy a poverty sector. But the public and economic organizations are drawn by a market economy to seek, respectively, lower prices and costs, with the result that many workers are forced to live in poverty.

THE ECONOMICS OF AFFLUENCE

In times of inflation many union and white-collar workers have suffered a decrease in their standards of living, but middle income groups do enjoy more protection from economic vicissitudes than the poor. Unionized blue-collar workers and white-collar workers of large industries, for example, are more likely to be protected from economic cycles, intense competition in the labor market, and the resulting low wages. Unions provide some benefits for union workers during unemployment, but equally important, large unions have political power and can pressure government to assist industries where large numbers of union members work. Thus, when economic recession causes widespread unemployment in heavily unionized industries, pressure can be put upon government to directly subsidize the industry, to make large purchases in the relevant market, or to impose import–export restrictions in order to cut down competition

Protection for
union workers

*These workers, despite the differences in their jobs, have some
security. Education or union membership help them keep their jobs,
even during economic recessions. Moreover, they belong to
organizations lobbying with government to protect their interests.*

from other countries. For example, workers in the auto industry have received a number of subsidies in recent years, from devaluation of the dollar which acts to raise the prices of import autos to an outright import tax on some foreign cars. Such policies have made the prices of American cars competitive and thus kept production, employment, and wages at higher levels than they would be otherwise. The necessity for this kind of governmental action cannot be questioned, but the fact that governmental subsidy of the poor's income has not been so immediate attests to the comparative powerlessness of the poor to pressure the federal government to intervene in economic processes affecting them. Similar subsidies from the government exist for virtually all "essential industries" which have large numbers of unionized workers. For example, Congress voted and the president signed an income tax bill in March, 1975 which provided purchasers of newly constructed homes with up to a $2000 tax credit. This same bill provided substantial tax rebates for the poor and affluent, and this fact should be emphasized, but it directly sought to "stimulate" the housing industry and the union workers it employs, while at the same time subsidizing those who could afford to purchase a home.

White-collar workers also benefit from union pressures, but they are afforded additional protections: (1) Their skills usually make them less in supply, and hence, more in demand in the labor market; (2) they perform much of the "brainwork" of the wealthy who possess considerable political power to keep their investments prospering; and (3) the large organizations and professional associations of white-collar workers display considerable political power. Hence, government is more likely to be pressured by the wealthy and the large organizations and associations of the affluent to subsidize either directly or indirectly the jobs and income of certain classes of workers. For example, the $250 million loan guarantee to Lockheed Corporation was only unusual for its size, but it illustrates a general tendency of government to assist industries with high proportions of professional and managerial personnel. Whether through a " loan," a new government contract, or a tolerated "cost overrun," white-collar industries are often subsidized by the government, the result being that white-collar (and of course blue-collar) jobs are preserved and wages are maintained. The poor rarely have this type of intervention on their behalf.

Protection for white-collar workers

We should take care not to view this situation as being either good or bad. It is inevitable that those who fare better in the economic system will have the resources to pressure government to help them continue their affluence. Moreover, these political pressures are consistent with beliefs about the appropriateness of government remaining responsive to the needs of large segments of the population (see Chapter 5). However, one consequence of the capacity of middle income groups to generate political influence is for less successful workers to receive less assistance from government. The result is that the income gap between the poor and more affluent remains relatively constant.

THE ECONOMY AND THE WEALTHY

The very wealthy, or top 1 percent, own about one-quarter of all assets in America—stocks, bonds, real estate, and utilities (see Table 7.4). American corporations are under considerable control by wealthy investors who quite naturally have an interest in some government policies and not others. And they clearly have the assets to finance campaigns, to bribe officials, to lobby, and to exert other forms of political influence as individuals and as directors of the larger corporations. Their efforts benefit not only the workers of their

Protection for the wealthy

The wealthy rarely worry about economic recessions. They have the money and power to influence government in ways that protect their privileges.

corporations, but they also protect their investments and assure profits on these investments. By protecting profits, the wealthy can be assured of maintaining their high levels of income. For example, it is not surprising that the exposed campaign financing abuses in the Nixon administration came from large corporations, such as Gulf Oil and American Airlines, and trade associations that are subject to federal regulation and subsidy like the Milk Producers Advisory. Indeed the corporations themselves, and their wealthy stockholders, have a vested interest in maintaining profits and have thus been willing, at least in the past, to use some of this profit and wealth to exert political influence.

In looking at the poor, the affluent, and the rich in relation to economic processes, we must conclude that the affluent worker and wealthy investor are in a better position than the poor to pressure government into selective economic intervention. Such intervention has less impact for the uneducated and nonunion poor who are marginal participants in the economy and who do not have the wealth or collective organization to exercise political influence proportionate to their needs. It is these differences in the political power of different economic groupings that appear to have *structured* a political-economic system favoring the wealthy and affluent, while subjecting the poor to some of the unfortunate instabilities of the free enterprise system and a labor market that has less demand for their services than for those of the more affluent. Inequality is structured not just in the economy, but also in the political system.

GOVERNMENT AND INEQUALITY

In America, as in almost all other societies, economically advantaged segments of the society have a greater capacity than the less advantaged to exert the political influence that maintains their advantage. Once members of the society have some affluence and assets, it is in their interest to maintain their position, and since they have financial and organizational resources not always available to the less affluent, they are in a position to better realize their interests. Naturally, all segments of a society have some political power, but the critical questions in analyzing how power influences inequality are: How much power is held? And what type of power is held?

There are many problems in analyzing power; the concept and phenomena it denotes are most illusive. *Power* is usually defined as the capacity to realize one's goals, even in the face of resistance. But there are many different types of capacities, many diverse goals, and many different types and degrees of resistance. Also, many capacities

The concept of power

remain hidden and are not easily seen, as is the case, for example, when lobbyists informally, over a long period of time, convince legislators of the "rightness" of their cause. Further, goals are not always clearly articulated or understood, nor are they always uniform and without contradiction. Resistance, too, can take many forms including, for example, conflicts among interest groups, technical difficulties in achieving goals, lack of sympathy among political decision makers, and so on. Another problem in analyzing power is isolating power groups. While it is sometimes easy to visualize a discrete interest group, such as the American Medical Association, the Milk Advisory Board, General Motors, and the like, it is sometimes difficult to visualize the poor, affluent, or rich as a "group" because there is considerable diversity and oftentimes conflicts of interest among segments of these rather broad categories.

The analysis of political influence and inequality begins with these analytical problems. They are not easily resolved; and for our purposes, they are emphasized as points of qualification for what must be a somewhat over simplified portrayal of how different segments of the society exert different degrees of political power, and thereby, perpetuate the pattern of inequality outlined in Tables 7.1 to 7.4.

In previous discussions the poor (bottom income and wealth fifth), the affluent (middle three fifths), and the wealthy (top fifth, and at times, 1%) have been isolated as groupings in the American stratification system. These groupings are not "social classes" in the traditional sense of the term, that is, groups with common economic interests, basis, power, life-styles, and cultural symbols. Rather, as was emphasized in Tables 7.1 to 7.4, they are *statistical categories* that group families and individuals in terms of their share of the income and wealth in America. Yet, because they involve a rank ordering of families, they are a good indication of the relative degree of access to scarce resources possessed by Americans. And while the top of the bottom fifth in a given year may resemble the bottom of the fourth fifth in terms of economic interests, life-style, and culture, it may still be convenient for purposes of analysis to treat these statistical categories as real groupings, and perhaps, even as social classes. It is important, of course, to recognize that such treatment is a simplifying assumption, but for the purpose of understanding the overall pattern of inequality in America, this can be a useful assumption, as long as we recognize its limitations.

With these necessary qualifications, our attention is now drawn to Table 7.5, where estimates of the power of different groups are made. It should be emphasized, of course, that these are *estimates*, for indeed there is no way to measure accurately the power of the bottom income and wealth fifths, or that of any other statistical grouping.

The power of the poor, affluent, and wealthy

Table 7.5 **Economic Groups and Political Power**

	Poor	Affluent	Wealthy
(1) Size	Large	Very large	Small
(2) Distribution	Rural and urban; high concentrations in cores of large cities	Urban; large masses in suburbs	Rural, urban, suburban; much dispersion
(3) Degree of Organization	Low; few effective national organizations	High; unions, professional and trade associations; the corporations where they work	High; corporations they own and manage; trade associations of their corporations
(4) Nature of Organization	Fragmented; often in conflict; loose organization at national level	Highly centralized, tightly coordinated national confederations with clear goals	Highly organized; covert and overt confederations
(5) Financial Resources	Meager	Great	Vast
(6) Lobbying Tradition	Short	Long; at least 100 years; most effective since 1940	Long; over 100 years; always been effective
(7) Tradition of Influence	Little	Much, especially since 1940	Much, always been effective
Total of Power	Low	High	Very High

Table 7.5 provides only rough estimates of the relative degrees of power held by (1) the poor, (2) the more affluent blue- and white-collar workers, and (3) the highly paid professional worker and wealthy investor. It should be recognized that the large middle category—the affluent—embraces people such as auto workers, carpenters, sales clerks, and the like, who may not consider themselves well off, and the wealthy category includes people, such as lawyers, dentists, doctors, high-level college professors, high-ranking military officers, and the like who are usually defined as only "upper middle" class. But statistically, and in actual fact, these people enjoy a degree of affluence or wealth unequaled in any part of the world; and thus, while this categorization is certainly an oversimplification, it does reflect meaningful (in terms of relative access to resources) differences among segments of the population. The poor live very marginal lives, the affluent must sometimes scrape and save, but they are able to meet most or all of their material and many of their psychological needs, and the wealthy have little difficulty in meeting all needs.

Table 7.5 does not address inequality as a social class issue, nor does it focus on traditional class distinctions such as poverty, working, middle, and upper classes; but rather, it addresses the issue of who gets resources, leaving the question of how these resources are spent—whether on campers or large cars—to those who wish to distinguish, for example, working class culture and life-style from middle class life-styles. In terms of income and wealth, the middle and working classes overlap to such an extent that they can often be distinguished only by life-style and cultural variables. Such variables do not point to inequality but merely different preferences for how money is spent. Thus, the affluent in America constitute a rather diverse group whose family incomes range from $12,000 to $16,000 and whose values, beliefs, and life-styles vary. Those earning less are poor in terms of current standards of living in America, while those earning more are wealthy.

Seven dimensions affecting the respective ability of the poor, affluent, and wealthy to exert political power are listed in Table 7.5 (Turner and Starnes, 1976). In each column under the three income groups is listed the current situation of the poor (bottom fifth), affluent (middle three fifths), and wealthy (top fifth) for each of the seven dimensions. At the bottom, the cumulative amount of power of these three income groups is estimated (only a rough estimate is possible). As can be seen, the poor do not fare well on these seven dimensions of power, the affluent do much better, and the wealthy do very well.

From (1) and (2) on Table 7.5, it might initially seem that the poor's size and concentration in the cores of cities and in rural areas might help them consolidate power. However, the affluent represent an even larger group who are also concentrated in urban and suburban areas; and as dimensions (3), (4), (5), (6), and (7) reveal, it is the degree of political organization that can be decisive in influencing political decisions. The poor are not organized; they have few financial resources to support organizations; and they have never developed a lobbying tradition or effective channels of political influence. In contrast, the affluent are represented by many organizations such as unions, professional associations, and the corporations in which they work; the resources of these organizations are great; and they have a longer lobbying tradition as well as more developed influence channels. The wealthy reveal all of these characteristics and thus can exert enormous political influence.

It is not necessary to assume corruption in government to visualize just how the size, organization, and resources of different income groups creates a set of political pressures supporting the present profile of inequality. While illicit practices undoubtedly occur, reform legislation would not necessarily alter this present balance of power. The affluent represent a majority, and their organizations have effectively pursued their interests. Because of their ownership of key industries, the wealthy and governmental officials usually cooperate to

The consequences of power

assure the economic stability necessary for keeping the large affluent groupings content. While the wealthy's control of income and wealth deprives both the poor and affluent, the middle income group's short-run interests—economic stability, steady work, and an above-subsistence income—drive them to form an uneasy coalition with the wealthy. For indeed, people are not likely to seek change in a system that gives them at least some degree of comfort, especially when such change and the resulting disorder might temporarily threaten their affluence.

These political forces have resulted in different governmental policies affecting different segments of the population. Most of these policies are intended for the benefit of the total population, but they have had the consequence, in many instances, of creating vast inequalities. In turn, this pattern of inequality has caused many social problems, such as poverty and urban tensions, while aggravating many other social problems.

GOVERNMENT POLICIES AND THE POOR

The response to poverty in America has been the creation of the welfare system. While this system does provide aid to people in need, it also perpetuates the system of inequality in America. We will examine the operation of the welfare system in more detail in Chapter 8; our task here is to understand how the system operates to produce inequality.

The welfare system and poverty

Welfare payments are always kept low and provide only the most minimal form of subsistence. By keeping welfare payments low, people are often forced to take jobs that offer an income that is only slightly above welfare support levels, since even a small increase in income can represent the difference between subsistence and severe deprivation.

The wealthfare system of subsidies

This traditional feature of welfare keeps people in marginal economic conditions that perpetuate their poverty, but equally important, welfare sometimes operates as a subsidy for more affluent sectors of the population. By keeping welfare payments low, a labor pool is maintained for industries that need low-cost seasonal labor, or for individuals who need temporary or permanent "help." For example, upper-income groups are able to secure low-cost maids, gardeners, and handymen; all Americans enjoy inexpensive fruits and vegetables planted and harvested by the labors of migrant workers; and all people enjoy inexpensive meals at restaurants staffed by poorly paid workers. The situation of the marginally employed is justified by the recognition that they *can get welfare* when laid off; and even when they are working, some can have their in-

*Those who are poor must depend on the meager "government dole"
punctuated by the bureaucratic maze that they must
negotiate if they are to receive help when unemployed.*

comes supplemented by welfare payments and programs. Such justi-
fications only highlight the fact that welfare can become a form of
subsidy to the more affluent since they are getting goods and services
at costs considerably below what they would be if the poor were paid
an above-subsistence wage. Thus, government welfare enables the
poor to survive when not needed in the labor pool, but induces or
forces them to work for low wages in menial jobs without many
fringe benefits. Such a system is designed for the "poor's own good,"
but when viewed from the perspective of overall inequality, it also
works as a government subsidy for the affluent and wealthy who desire inexpensive labor. This form of government subsidy is but another reflection of the respective political power of different income
groups.

GOVERNMENT POLICIES AND THE AFFLUENT

While welfare can serve as a subtle subsidy to the more affluent,
there are more direct and clear-cut patterns of government subsidy
that promote inequalities. We should emphasize, of course, that sub-

sidies are not necessarily "bad" or "unnecessary"; on the contrary, they may be desirable and even necessary for economic stability and people's well being. What must be recognized, however, is that in contrast to welfare subsidies that promote poverty, other subsidies to the affluent and wealthy are considerably more generous than those to the poor. And since it is the middle-income groups who most often complain about the high cost of welfare and "welfare cheaters" (Feagan, 1972), we should, in fairness, discuss some of the ways that government spends billions in middle income benefits each year. This differential in the pattern of subsidy to different populations is, in large part, responsible for inequality in America.

Government subsidizes the well being of the affluent and wealthy in many ways, but in contrast to welfare payments to the poor, the subsidies are not so obvious, nor are they as carefully monitored. There are at least four basic forms of government subsidy: (1) government contracts, (2) government price supports, (3) government export–import programs, and most importantly, (4) federal tax expenditures.

1. When the government "lets out" a civilian or defense contract to industry, it is subsidizing the salaries of workers and the profits of owners. Much of this subsidy is necessary to provide vital products and services as well as to maintain economic stability, but these contracts are nevertheless a subsidy and can be considered a type of government "make work" for the affluent. The major difference between this make work and the forced labor of the welfare recipient is that the wages, fringe benefits, length of tenure, and working conditions of the job are considerably better than those in the work performed by the poor.

Government contracts as subsidies

2. Government controls the prices of many commodities in the market, as is the case, for example, with many agricultural and dairy products. While wage and price controls make regulation at times most explicit, it is the more subtle forms of regulation that have typified government market policies. The actual mechanisms for regulation are complex, but they involve (1) indirect attempts to manipulate supply and demand and, hence, prices in the open market or (2) direct efforts to set the price of goods and commodities. When indirect programs to manipulate supply and demand are employed, production is either encouraged or discouraged through taxation, massive government purchases, and export–import programs designed to regulate the flow of competitive goods in and out of the country. When prices are directly set by government, they can be established at above or below what their open market price would be. If the price is set artificially high, owners, managers, and workers receive a clear subsidy in the form of increased profits, heightened job security, and

higher wages. And if prices are kept low, then government usually (not always, of course) "makes up the difference" with a cash subsidy.

Government price regulation is designed to affect "basic" indus- *Price regulation* tries that tend to employ large numbers of unionized employees (with agriculture the most notable exception) and that tend to have heavy capital investment by the wealthy. Such price regulation is undoubtedly essential, but it tends to be selective: the industries of the affluent and wealthy are more likely to be subject to price regulation. Wages for more marginal workers outside big industry, such as those for maids, gardeners, dishwashers, seasonal agricultural workers, and other categories of poor, remain unaffected by price policies except, of course, to make these poor pay higher prices.

3. Export–import policies are designed to control the impact of exportation and importation of goods on prices in the domestic market. To allow excessive export of a commodity will lower its price since supply will increase relative to demand. By allowing some companies to export, and by protecting others from imports (through quotas and taxes), government keeps prices high and maintains the salaries of workers and the profits of owners. In a world economy clearly influenced by international politics, export–import regula- *Export–import* tion is critically necessary. But again, this regulation has a selective *subsidies* impact; the large industries owned by the wealthy and in which the more affluent work are the most likely to be affected. Lumber, steel, cars, chemicals, aerospace, computers, textiles, and many other basic industries are the most affected, and while in some of these industries poor workers benefit, the subsidy more typically assists the already affluent worker and the rich investor. It is in this way that export–import policies can be seen as a form of subsidy to the affluent.

4. Probably the most obvious form of subsidy is through the tax system. In America, federal income taxes are "progressive"—the more the net income, the higher the tax. On paper, individuals are supposed to pay from 0–70 percent of their net income in taxes, de- *Tax loophole* pending on how much they make. Corporate taxes on net profits are *subsidies* not progressive since, on paper, all net profits are to be taxed at a 48 percent rate. These tax rates are rarely maintained in practice because of conspicuous loopholes which undermine the progressivity of individual taxes, and which reduce the rate of corporate taxation. Loopholes represent a subsidy because they allow some people and corporations to avoid taxes and unpaid taxes represent revenue lost to government—revenue that could potentially be used to resolve America's many social problems. The extent of the revenue loss is enormous, and by conservative estimates it is over $60 billion a year. In contrast, the federal government spends less than $10 billion on

welfare for the poor each year (state and county governments, of course, spend considerably more than this figure).

There are five basic types of loopholes, all of which help the wealthy, some of which assist the affluent, and few of which benefit the poor: (1) exclusions from income, (2) deductions from income, (3) tax credits, (4) special tax rates, and (5) tax sheltering.

Exclusions. Much income does not count for tax purposes and is excluded from net income. Income from an expense account, income earned abroad, sick pay, welfare payments, exercise of stock options, employer contributions to medical insurance, the first $100 on stock dividends, the interest on life insurance savings, and the interest on local and state bonds are but conspicuous examples of a general practice to exclude certain forms of income from taxation. Some of these exclusions are helpful to the poor, such as welfare payments, but most favor the affluent and wealthy who own stocks, bonds, and large life insurance policies, and who work in jobs where expense accounts, medical insurance, and stock options are fringe benefits. While many of these tax policies are for "good" purposes, they violate the progressivity of the federal income tax structure because they prevent the fair and progressive taxation of income earned by the more affluent and wealthy sectors of the society. They are in reality, tax expenditures for the affluent and wealthy.

Deductions. Individuals and corporations are allowed to deduct their expenses. These deductions can be quite appropriate when the expenses are directly involved in earning an income since only net income—that is, income less the cost in earning it—is supposed to be taxed. But some individuals and all corporations are allowed to deduct much more than their actual expenses, thus signaling another form of tax expenditure or subsidy. The deduction of 50 percent of all capital gains income (the major source of income for the wealthy), the accelerated depreciation allowed for real estate, oil wells, cattle, or orchards, and the deduction of depletion allowances are conspicuous ways the wealthy and corporations protect income by amassing deductions that bear little relationship to costs incurred in making money. For the less affluent and poor, interest on home mortgages and other purchases can be deducted, as can state income, sales, and gasoline taxes. These are small subsidies when compared to those available to the highly affluent and wealthy.

Tax Credits. Some forms of income are given tax credits, that is, a percentage of their income from certain areas will not be taxed. For example, the elderly receive tax credits for retirement income, but more significantly, corporations receive tax credits of 10 percent of the cost of machinery. Such credits allow companies and individuals to avoid taxation, hence, keep their income. While credits give some benefits to small companies and poor individuals, they provide enormous benefits to the wealthy and larger corporations. It is this kind of credit that represents government subsidies for the companies of affluent workers and rich owners, thereby assuring their favored position.

Special Tax Rates. Some types of income are taxed at a special rate. The most conspicuous example of this practice is the capital gains tax which reaches a maximum rate equal to only one-half of the rate charged against other types of income (such as wages). It will be recalled that 50 percent of all capital gains income can be deducted (not counted) for tax purposes, and now, the remaining 50 percent is taxed at only one-half the ordinary rate (i.e., tax is paid on only 25% of total income). Some relevant figures reveal just who the recipients of these subsidies are: 65–70 percent of all capital gains income goes to those who make over $25,000 per year; and among those who make $1 million or more a year, 82 percent of this income is capital gains. Thus, the very affluent and wealthy have a special tax rate that costs the federal government more money in uncollected income than all federal expenditures for welfare to the poor in a given year.

Tax Sheltering. Various combinations of tax laws allow people and corporations to defer (sometimes almost forever) paying their taxes. By allowing massive paper deductions, credits, and exclusions from gross income, people and corporations can " shelter" their real income. For example, by using accelerated depreciation—that is, depreciating the entire amount of an item such as a piece of equipment in the first years of its purchase—plus tax credits for purchasing the equipment, a corporation can show a paper "loss" and pay no taxes, even though they may have earned huge profits. To take another example, rich investors who put their money in cattle ranches, orchards, and real estate can then take both accelerated depreciation (on items whose value is appreciating) and depletion allowances (on items that are not always depleting) and, thus, show a paper loss that can be deducted from income derived in totally unrelated areas. In these ways, the rich shelter and protect their incomes and avoid paying taxes. Allowing the rich to do this is but another form of government subsidy.

$10 billion for the poor, $60–$80 billion for the wealthy

How much do the subsidies for the poor, affluent, and wealthy cost the government? About $10 billion is spent by the federal govern-

SOCIOLOGICAL
INSIGHTS

A TAX EXPENDITURE BUDGET

If uncollected taxes were viewed as expenditures, a tax expenditure budget could be constructed. The Treasury Department has recently begun to draw up a tax expenditure budget. Some of the major items on this budget are listed below. This is where uncollected tax revenues were being "spent" in 1972. Note how many of these expenditures are likely to go to the highly affluent and wealthy. The items on the budget are listed under five headings: (1) individual consumers, (2) individual investors, (3) wage earners, (4) recipients of government welfare and assistance, and (5) expenditures on industry and corporations. This is the *most conservative* way to compute the budget:

1. Individual Consumers
   standard deduction
   support of philanthropy tax break
   home-ownership interest and tax deductions
   governmental tax (state and local) deductions
   medical deductions
   deductions of interest on purchases
   deductions for educational expenses
   deductions for causality losses
   deductions for home services
                             Total: $20.7 billion

2. Individual Investors
   exclusions on stock dividends
   exclusions of interest on bonds
   favorable capital gains treatment
   exclusions of interest on life insurance
   real estate capital gains treatment
   shelter investments
                             Total: $13 billion

3. Wage Earners
   exclusion of pensions, insurance, sick and unemployment benefits
   expense accounts
   exclusions for armed service employees
   workman's compensation exclusions
   exclusions for income earned abroad
   favorable employee stock option treatment
                             Total: $9.4 billion

4. Recipients of Welfare and Government Assistance
   provisions for the elderly
   exclusion of welfare assistance
   exemptions for the blind
   veteran's benefits

   Total: $4 billion

5. Expenditures on Industry and Corporations
   investment credits
   depreciation deductions
   capital gains treatment
   depletion allowances
   exemptions on bonds
   exclusions of foreign income

   Total: $15 billion

   Grand Total: $62.1 billion

Source: House Committee on Ways and Means, "Estimates of Federal Tax Expenditures," Wash., D.C.:GPO, June 1, 1973, pp. 8–12.

ment on welfare to the poor, while $60–$80 billion is spent on the affluent and wealthy. Some of this money goes to the less affluent, but most of it goes to the affluent and rich. We must recognize, of course, that the affluent and wealthy represent the vast majority, thus, they will receive proportionately more subsidy than a minority of the population. The problem with subsidies to the more affluent and wealthy, however, is that they are subtle and hidden. This fact obscures the amount and type of subsidy. Moreover, since the poor's welfare is constantly monitored, the affluent avoid the stigma of having their subsidies defined as charity. If all these uncollected taxes were collected in accordance with principles of progressivity, and then distributed in accordance with national priorities, then the public could see just how their tax monies are spent. As it stands now, the beneficiaries of tax subsidies remain hidden and obscured by the complexity of tax subsidies and by the indirectness of the payment. One meaningful way to visualize just who the beneficiaries of tax subsidies are is to compute the average tax expenditure on people in different income groups. This is done in Table 7.6 for the year 1972. People making a medium income of $11,000 receive a tax expenditure payment of about $400; those making over $500,000 get over

Subsidies to the affluent—like those that go to the millionaire owner of this "family farm"—are hidden and less obvious than "government doles" to the poor. And yet they, too, are costly to the taxpayer and might be termed "wealthfare."

Table 7.6 **Tax Subsidy Payments to Different Income Groupings in 1972**

Income in 1972	Average Tax Wealthfare Payment
Under $3,000	$ 15.00
$3,000–$5,000	143.00
$5,000–$10,000	286.00
$10,000–$15,000	411.00
$15,000–$20,000	600.00
$20,000–$25,000	871.00
$25,000–$50,000	1,729.00
$50,000–$100,000	5,896.00
$100,000–$500,000	29,503.00
$500,000–$1 million	216,751.00
$1 million and over	$726,198.00

$200,000; and those earning over $1 million are on the "government dole" for $726,000. And the poor get very little from these tax expenditures.[2]

In sum, the differences in the political power of different income groups have created a system of subsidy which is necessary in many other respects, but which maintains the profile of inequality in America. This profile reveals that a large number are kept poor, a majority maintain some degree of affluence, and a very few enjoy massive privilege. This system is tolerated since many subsidies are not easily seen because they are hidden and often indirect, whereas welfare subsidies to the poor are highly visible and direct. But no social pattern persists by invisibility alone; it usually must be justified by dominant cultural values and beliefs.

THE CULTURE OF INEQUALITY

Subsidies are legitimized by a series of cultural beliefs. Indeed, all societies have a set of cultural ideas that, on the one hand, guide concrete behavior and institutional arrangements and, on the other hand, are created and maintained by these arrangements. It would be difficult to document how inequality is woven into the fabric of a society without, at some point, examining some of the cultural beliefs used to justify and legitimize such inequality. Without these cultural beliefs, inequality in a society would persist only by the blatant use of force and coercion. Such legitimization in America occurs through two related processes: (1) Cultural beliefs make current inequality seem correct and proper, and (2) some of these beliefs divert the majority's attention away from the privilege of the rich and focus it on the poor, thereby giving indirect support for large sub-

The functions of cultural beliefs

sidies to the wealthy, while making the majority suspicious of welfare to the poor.

Four basic beliefs legitimizing the subsidy system appear to operate in America (Turner and Starnes, 1976): (1) national interest beliefs, (2) "trickle-down" beliefs, (3) the work ethic, and (4) the charity ethic. These beliefs should not be viewed as necessarily negative, for indeed many of the benefits enjoyed by Americans are partially the result of people's mobilization by such cultural orientations. Yet, despite the benefits ensuing from these four beliefs, they have the consequence of legitimizing vast inequality in America. It is this particular consequence that should presently occupy our interest.

Legitimizing beliefs

NATIONAL INTEREST BELIEFS

Tax expenditures and government subsidies in the economic marketplace are often termed as being in the "national interest" because they allow the society to pursue and meet its goals. For instance, cost overruns to defense contractors are defined as regrettable but necessary to maintain a strong military deterrent; tax expenditures on wealthy investors are deemed necessary to encourage investment in the economy and thereby achieve the goal of continued economic growth; and tax loopholes for corporations are seen as necessary to encourage certain economic activities that are seen as instrumental in meeting national goals. By reading a newspaper on any given day, subsidy programs are justified as in the national interest because they maintain vital industries, keep jobs open, reduce hardships, stimulate the economy, and maintain the national defense.

National interest beliefs are reconciled with core values by the assumption that the subsidies they legitimize will (1) allow people to be "active" (in a job) and to "achieve" material comfort; (2) encourage corporations to grow and "progress;" and (3) keep America strong and enable her to "compete" in the world economy and in world political affairs. Through such reconciliation with values, and through the simple fact that subsidies provide the majority of Americans with tangible benefits, most people regard the system of subsidy as just and proper. Few realize, however, that this system also promotes vast inequality and exacerbates all the tensions—racial, ethnic, and class—associated with inequality and with a large impoverished sector.[3]

"TRICKLE-DOWN" BELIEFS

There is a strongly held belief that tax expenditures and market subsidies "trickle-down" to all segments of the society, even the poor. While this belief implicitly acknowledges that subsidies are initially

Beliefs that distort reality

bestowed on the wealthy, it is argued that the money is ultimately invested, causing economic expansion, and creating jobs for all segments of the work force. To a limited extent, some money does trickle-down to the more affluent workers in large industries, but very little reaches the really poor and a great deal stays in the hands of the rich. And yet, a cursory reading of a newspaper will reveal the extent to which this belief is used to justify subsidies to the already affluent and wealthy.

Much as with national interest beliefs, trickle-down beliefs are reconciled with core values by the assumption that such subsidies enable people, corporations, and the nation to be active, to achieve, to expand materially, and to progress. The belief that the subsidies do indeed trickle down to the poor also satisfies the values of humanitarianism and equality, since it is assumed that the expansion of the economy through subsidies creates job opportunities for the poor which will give them an "equal opportunity" to be socially mobile and to achieve material comfort (assuming, of course, that they are "active" and hence worthy of the opportunities presented to them).

In sum, national interest and trickle-down beliefs legitimize subsidies to the more privileged sectors of the society. As will become evident, the work and charity ethics justify the current welfare system; and in so doing, they help perpetuate a system that can, at times, stigmatize the poor, while keeping them impoverished. Furthermore, unlike national interest and trickle-down beliefs, these two "ethics" bear little relationship to actual conditions, and in fact, they effectively divert the affluent majority's attention away from both the plight of the poor and subsidy abuses to the affluent and wealthy.

THE WORK ETHIC

One of the most pervasively held beliefs in America is that income should come from work and the job. Such beliefs are derived from basic values of activism, achievement, and materialism and represent the concrete application of these values to the work sphere. Americans fervently believe that material rewards (i.e., income) must come from people's activities and achievements in a job. This belief is partly responsible for the efficient and energetic work of labor in America's successful corporations, but it can also distort people's perceptions about the availability of decent work for the poor, while implicitly supporting the belief that the wealthy always "work" for their income. For the poor, good paying jobs with some security and fringe benefits are frequently not available. Yet, because they, too, hold to the "work ethic," their failure to secure work is often defined by them, as well as by the affluent, as their own fault. For indeed, the work ethic enables the affluent to view the poor's plight as the result of inadequate desires and motivations to work their way out of poverty—that is, their failure to be "active" and to "achieve." This condemnation of the poor by themselves and by the affluent majority ignores the fact that the pay and tenure of most jobs available to the poor will perpetuate their impoverishment.

THE CHARITY ETHIC

The work ethic makes the bestowing of welfare subsidies highly conditional: Subsidies should be given only when there is no work alternative. Thus, if someone is disabled, old, or *temporarily* out of work, then they should be assisted. Such a belief is consistent with

Little has "trickled-down" to this man, and "charity" does not seem to be forthcoming. In an economic system incapable of employing the entire work force, and with government policies geared to subsidize the affluent, many poor are reduced to poverty and degradation in the most affluent land in the world.

humanitarianism values. But beliefs dictate that people's ability to work, even at the most menial, low-paying, and ungratifying jobs, should be constantly monitored in order to force adherence to the work ethic, and to the dominant values from which this ethic is derived.

The work and charity ethics divert a considerable amount of public attention to the poor, especially those who receive welfare. Payments are kept low in order to induce or force the poor to work; recipient's life-styles and availability for work are constantly monitored; and, people are often subjected to abusive practices by welfare workers (see Chapter 8). Newspaper headlines will expose welfare cheaters and other welfare "abuses," and in so doing, they will occupy a considerable amount of public attention and foster false stereotypes about the character of the poor. These beliefs can then be used to justify low welfare payments and other practices which keep the poor poor. But they also divert attention away from the $60–$80 billion in tax expenditures and the many unknown billions in market subsidies given to the more affluent sectors of the society. Moreover, they not only divert attention away from the existence of subsidies to the nonpoor, but make many people less sensitive to the "abuses" of those receiving these subsidies.

SUMMARY

In this chapter we have reviewed the extent of income and wealth inequalities. We have focused on these issues because people's life-styles and their access to other valuable resources, such as power, prestige, and health, are highly correlated with their income and wealth. From our review we have noted the high degree of income inequality and the even greater degree of wealth inequality.

Inequality has been viewed as the result of the different degrees of influence among economic groups to exert political power. This disproportionate power has created a general system of subsidies that preserves the privilege of the wealthy, the affluence of the majority, and the poverty of the poor. This system is legitimized by at least four dominant cultural beliefs: national interest beliefs, trickle-down beliefs, the work ethic, and the charity ethic. Inequality in America is a problem of structure and culture because it is built into economic and political arrangements as well as into key cultural beliefs and values.

Many may not view inequality as a social problem, but for others, it is one of the things "wrong" with America. From this latter perspective, it is the high degree of inequality that is troublesome. Some degree of inequality is probably inevitable, but great inequalities are considered problematic because they create many tensions and conflicts. Moreover, high degrees of inequality aggravate many other problems. It gives comparatively few control over resources which from the perspective of those who see inequality as a problem, could be used to address problems in education, pollution, housing, transportation, crime, drug control, health care, and so on. Further, independent of depriving the government of needed revenues, the possession of vast wealth by individuals and corporations gives them a degree of political influence that, at times, prevents the reordering of national priorities so that many problems affecting the majority of the population can be addressed by government.

In the specific context of stratification, inequality directly aggravates several problems in America: (1) poverty, (2) racial and ethnic tensions, and (3) sexual discrimination. While inequality has consequences for all phases of social life, it has its most direct impact on the persistence of poverty in the most affluent society in the world, on enduring racial and ethnic tensions in the "melting pot" democracy, and on patterns of sexual discrimination against women. It is to these topics that an analysis of inequality in America must eventually turn.

NOTES

1. Numerous studies of income distribution include: Kolko, 1962; H. Miller, 1964, 1965, 1968; MacDonald, 1968; Lampman, 1965, 1967, 1969; Department of Labor, *Manpower Report to the President*, 1969; Department of Commerce, *Social and Economic Conditions of Negroes in the United States*, Current Population Reports, No. 24, 1967; Schaffer, Schaffer, Ahrenholz, and Prigmore, 1970:28–66; Solow, 1967; S. Goldsmith, 1967; and Turner and Starnes, 1976. For a defense of inequality and a critique of these studies, see I. Krostol, 1974.

2. For a more detailed analysis of taxes and tax expenditures, see Turner and Starnes, 1976; Stern 1974; and Surrey, 1973.

3. For an argument as to how these beliefs result in more net harm than good, and get in the way of achieving national goals, see Turner and Starnes, 1976.

REVIEW QUESTIONS

1. Describe the overall profile of income and wealth inequality in America.
2. Why has the government been unable to collect more recent data on wealth distribution?
3. How are the poor, affluent, and wealthy affected by economic and political arrangements?
4. What beliefs and values legitimize these arrangements?
5. Why is inequality a social problem for some?
6. Do you think that inequality is inevitable? How would you use the sociological perspective to buttress your answer?

GLOSSARY

the affluent people located in the middle three fifths of the income and wealth distribution categories

income distribution the share of total income in a given year received by various percentages of the population

income (and wealth) fifths the standard statistical category for determining shares of the wealth or income held by graded fifths of the population

the poor people located at the bottom of the income and wealth distribution category

the rich (wealthy) people located in the top income and wealth distribution category. The closer to the upper 1 percent of income and wealth fifths, the wealthier an individual or family

subsidy a process used by the government to bestow income and wealth, either directly or indirectly, overtly or covertly, upon individuals and corporations

tax expenditure a way of conceptualizing tax subsidies wherein all taxes that are uncollected because of "loopholes" in the tax codes are viewed as expenses and are itemized into the federal budget

wealth distribution the share of total wealth in a given year possessed by various percentages of the population

PROLOGUE 8: ON BEING POOR IN AMERICA

From the files of the Office of Economic Opportunity comes this self-report of a white woman in Tennessee, but she could be male, black, Mexican American, Cuban, Puerto Rican, or any one of the millions of poor in America:

"Here I am, dirty, smelly, with no proper underwear beneath this rotting dress. I don't know about you, but the stench of my teeth makes me half sick. They're decaying, but they'll never be fixed. That takes money.

"What is poverty? Poverty is getting up every morning from a dirty and illness-stained mattress—a hard, lumpy mattress. Sheets? There are no sheets. They have long since been used for diapers, for there are no real diapers here, either.

"That smell? That other smell? You know what it is—plus sour milk and spoiled food. Sometimes it's mixed with the stench of onions cooked too often. Onions are cheap.

"We're like dogs in that we live in a world of smells and we've learned to identify most of them without searching them out. There is the smell of young children who can't make it down that long path at night. There is the smell of the filthy mattress. There is the smell of food gone sour because the refrigerator doesn't work. I don't remember when the refrigerator did work. I only know it takes money to get it fixed. And there is the smell of garbage. I could bury it, but where do you get a shovel without money?

"Poverty is dirt. You may say, in your clean clothes and coming from your clean house, 'Anybody can be clean.' Let me explain house-keeping with no money. For breakfast, I give my children grits with no margarine, or cornbread made without eggs or oleo. For one thing, that kind of food doesn't use up many dishes. What dishes there are, I wash in cold water. No soap. Even the cheapest soap has to be saved for washing the old sheets I use for the baby's diapers.

"Look at these cracked red hands. Once I saved up for two months to buy a jar of Vaseline for my hands and for the baby's diaper rash. When I had the money and went to buy the Vaseline, the price had gone up two cents, and I didn't have another two cents.

"Poverty is asking for help. Have you ever had to swallow what pride you had left and ask for help, knowing your children will suffer more if you don't get it? Think about asking for a loan from a relative, if that's the only way you can really understand asking for help.

"I'll tell you how asking for help feels: You find out where the of-fice is, the one from which paupers are supposed to get help. When you find it, you circle that block four or five times trying to get up nerve enough to go in and beg. Finally, the thought of your children's need and suffering pushes you through the door. Everybody is very busy and official. After an eternity a woman comes out to you and you tell her you need help, and you force yourself to look at her.

"She isn't the one you need to see. The first one never is. She sends you to see someone else and, after spilling your poverty and shame all over the desk, you find out this isn't the right office. Then you repeat the whole procedure. It doesn't get any easier.

"I finally got . . . $78 a month for the four of us. That's why there is no soap, no medicine, no needles, no hot water, no aspirin, no hand cream, no shampoo—none of those things ever.

"You say there are schools? Sure there are, but my children have no paper, no pencils, no crayons, no clothes, no anything worthwhile or useful. All they have is worms, pinkeye, infections of all sorts all the time. They aren't hungry, but they are undernourished.

"Poverty is an acid that eats into pride until pride is burned out. It is a chisel that chips at honor until honor is pulverized. You might do something if you were in my situation—for a week or a month. Would you do it year after year, getting nowhere?

"Even I can dream. I dream of a time when there is money—money for the right kind of food, for medicine, for vitamins, for a toothbrush, for hand cream, for a hammer and nails, for screens, for a shovel, for paint, for sheets, for needles and thread, and . . . but I know its a dream, just like you know it's a dream when you see yourself as president.

"Most, though, I dream of such things as not having wounded pride when I'm forced to ask for help. I dream for the peace of sincerely not caring any more. I dream of a time when the offices I visit for help are as nice as other government offices, when there are enough workers to get to you quickly, when those workers don't quit in defeat and despair just as poor folk quit hoping. I dream of the time when I have to tell my story just once each visit, to just one person. I'm tired of proving my poverty over and over and over.

"I leave my despair long enough to tell you this: I did not come from another place, and I did not come from another time. I'm here, now, and there are others like me all around you."

It is to the analysis of the plight of the millions of people like this woman, and the problems of culture and structure in dealing with their situation, that this chapter is dedicated.

Source: Victor Ficher and Herbert S. Graves, *Deprivation in America*, Beverly Hills, Cal.: Glencoe Press, 1971, pp. 1–7.

C H A P T E R

8

THE PROBLEM
OF POVERTY

Inequality in America has created a large poverty sector. Millions of Americans live at or below current standards of subsistence. The plight of these Americans has periodically been a topic of concern by the more affluent, but this concern has yet to be translated into a series of programs or social readjustments that would eliminate widespread poverty in the most affluent land in the world. Poverty is one of America's most enduring social problems.

There are two major levels of poverty: (1) being deprived and (2) being impoverished. Both of these levels is determined by how far below an established level of subsistence a family or individual lives. Establishing a national level of subsistence for individuals and families in different regions is never easy, but presently an income of about $8,500 can be considered the national subsistence level for a family of four. Naturally, this level is lower for smaller families and single individuals. *Deprived* families or individuals fall somewhat below this subsistence level, whereas the *impoverished* are considered to have less than half that needed for subsistence. A deprived family is thus constantly pinched to make ends meet; and should a crisis, such as an unexpected medical bill or a period of unemployment, hit the family, it would be unable to survive without public assistance. An impoverished family, on the other hand, has a perpetual and chronic need for assistance; it is among the impoverished that widespread hunger and starvation occur (Kotz, 1971).

How much deprivation and impoverishment exist in the United

Two types of poverty

223

States? Have the numbers of the poor increased or decreased? Such questions cannot be answered in absolute terms because standards of bare subsistence have escalated over the last 30 years. It is, therefore, difficult to compare the present with the past in terms of a fixed line of poverty. The poor, like anyone else in America, are not going to be satisfied with a fixed standard of living when the level of those around them has, until recently, been going up at a rate of about 2.5 percent per year. If the poverty line were not constantly adjusted upward in accordance with increasing affluence in the society, such "necessities" as electricity, flush toilets, automobiles, and television sets would be luxuries. What was once a luxury quickly assumes the status of basic necessity in a constantly expanding economy.

Using the standards of deprivation and impoverishment in each of the last four decades, two conclusions concerning trends in poverty emerge:[1] (1) The proportion of the population that can be classified as *deprived* has remained about the same over the last 25 years—hovering at about 20 percent of the population; and (2) the proportion of *impoverished* has decreased over the last 25 years from around 15 percent to 10 percent of the population. Thus, while abject poverty has decreased somewhat, a below-subsistence living is still common for many families and individuals.

Depending on whether deprivation or impoverishment is used as the criterion and depending on whose figures are used to establish a subsistence level of living, estimates of the number of poor range from a low of 25 million to a high 50 million. Even using the low figure, it is clear that poverty is not just an isolated problem in the most affluent society in the world.

How many poor in America?

THE PROFILE OF POVERTY

Some widely held beliefs about the poor include:

1. The poor are the lazy and shiftless who do not want to work.
2. The poor are composed primarily of single males out of a job or unwilling to work.
3. The poor are "social leeches" who live off welfare and exploit its benefits.
4. The poor are composed mostly of blacks and other minorities.
5. The poor are isolated in just a few places: the cores of large cities and in the rural South.

Each of these statements is incorrect, and yet, many affluent Americans would probably agree with them. In reality, the poor are located in all regions and in all sizes of cities; nearly 80 percent of the poor are white; they are poor not because of inadequate motivation, but because of few opportunities; most of the poor work and want desperately to work when they are unemployed; most of the poor are heads of families; and, the majority of the poor receive no welfare of any sort. Although data are imprecise, the poor can be categorized in the following way (H. Miller, 1965; Harrington, 1963, 1968, 1971; Seligman, 1965, 1970; Starnes, 1976; Turner and Starnes, 1976):

Inaccurate beliefs about the poor

1. About 8 million families and 5 million unattached individuals can be considered poor in that their incomes are below established subsistence levels. Of these individuals and families, around 78 percent are white, although minority populations are overrepresented (in comparison with their numbers in the general population) among the poor.
2. About one-fourth of the poor families in America are headed by females.
3. Another one-fourth of these poor families are headed by persons who work full time, but whose wages are insufficient to meet subsistence requirements. This figure indicates that low wages are still a major cause of poverty and that the poor are willing to work.
4. Over 1.5 million family heads work full time, but are laid off during the year—indicating that another large group of the poor want to work, but are at the mercy of economic cycles.
5. Nearly one-fourth of the poor families have an aged head whose retirement income is not sufficient to meet subsistence needs.
6. A majority of the single poor are young, uneducated, unskilled, and want to work, but cannot find jobs because of their lack of job training.
7. Of all the poor, only around 40 percent receive public assistance. Many are too proud to receive it; others are bewildered by the complex welfare system; still others do not know that they are eligible; and many do not qualify under the sometimes arbitrary rules of welfare agencies.
8. One-half of the nation's poor live in rural areas, but receive less than one-twentieth of the federal funds made available to the poor. These rural poor are concentrated in Appalachia (extending from southern New York to central Alabama and Georgia), California, the Ozarks, Wisconsin, and Minnesota—revealing a broad geographical profile of rural poverty.

Facts about the poor

While some individuals and families move in and out of the major poverty categories listed above, most Americans born poor are likely to stay deprived or impoverished. Unlike rural migrants and immigrants of previous generations, the current population of poor appear

To be born into poverty is, in most instances, to be condemned to a life of poverty. What chance will this child have to "make it" in America? How many "opportunities" will present themselves? Will this child have an equal opportunity?

to have less chance for movement to a better standard of living. In Michael Harrington's words (1968:vii), these poor are the "internal aliens in this affluent country," because unlike previous generations of migrants, they have little hope for upward mobility. They are the farmland refugees, the unskilled worker who has been replaced by a machine, the old and infirmed, mothers of dependent children, high school dropouts, farm and menial workers whose wages cannot keep up with the costs of living. Because these poor and their offspring are likely to remain in poverty categories, a search for the reasons *why* this should be so has been undertaken by both social scientists and political decision makers.

One of the most prominent explanations invokes the concept of a *poverty cycle*—a circular chain of events that perpetuates poverty from generation to generation. Daniel P. Moynihan (1969:9), who is both a social scientist and political figure, has schematically summarized this notion as presented in Figure 3. Limited income results

The poverty cycle

Figure 3 **The Poverty Cycle**

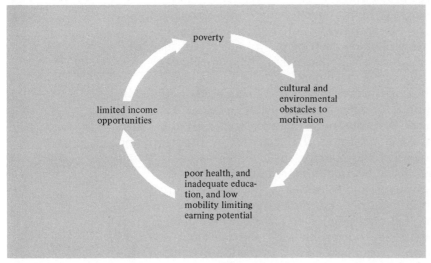

From *On Understanding Poverty*, edited by Daniel P. Moynihan, chart "The Poverty Cycle" (New York: Basic Books, Inc., Publishers). © 1969 by the American Academy of Arts and Sciences. Reprinted by permission.

in poverty; poverty somehow creates a physical and cultural environment that suppresses the poor's aspirations, motivation, and capacity to achieve; without these, the poor do not acquire sufficient education, resulting in limited earning potential; with little earning potential, there is limited earning opportunity; thus, the poverty cycle is completed.

This vision of poverty certainly captures some features of the poverty problem but it is also incomplete. As many scholars have noted, it tends to underemphasize the broader cultural and institutional forces within which this cycle operates–a fact to which our cultural and structural approach should alert us. For example, it would be difficult to address the issue of limited income opportunities without focusing on the political and economic processes in the broader society that limit opportunities. Limited income is not solely the result of a poor education, or inadequate motivation to work, but also because of governmental reluctance to redistribute income, to attack the tax structure that favors the affluent, to finance better schools in poverty areas, and to provide jobs for those who cannot find them in the private sector. Obviously most investigators, including Moynihan, recognize the importance of these societywide forces; but for those who have relied on cycle-of-poverty explanations, critics have pointed out that they have inadvertently diverted attention away from the forces in the broader stratification system that perpetuate poverty.

One result of this diversion is the use of piecemeal solutions to

Criticisms of the poverty cycle concept

address the poverty problem (Fernbach, 1965). For example, if poor children are seen to have inappropriate values and low aspirations, then a separate school program is initiated; if the poor require skills, then a hastily implemented job training program is established; or if racial discrimination is involved, then a new civil rights law or "affirmative action" program is developed. All such programs are no doubt necessary, but rarely have they been coordinated or guided by a true understanding of the deep-seated cultural and structural forces perpetuating poverty. Poverty is not a phenomenon easily eliminated by superficial laws and programs that change the life-styles and presumed pathologies of the poor or by laws and programs that suddenly give the illusion of equal opportunities.

Thus, the real causes of, and solutions to, poverty can only be discovered by exploring in more detail the cultural and social forces of the broader society that maintain poverty. Rather than being a cycle of poverty, it is more appropriate to refer to a national "cycle of inequality," of which poverty is the result at the lower ranks. In this way, attention is drawn not just to the life-styles of the poor, but also to the political, economic, and cultural forces that allow a cycle of poverty to persist.

GOVERNMENT PROGRAMS AND POVERTY

All levels of government in the United States have attempted to cope directly with poverty. Urban renewal, public housing, the war on poverty, the once giant Office of Economic Opportunity bureaucracy, divisions in the Department of Health, Education, and Welfare, and the sprawling welfare system all document the involvement of the federal government as well as state and local agencies in eliminating poverty. While the data on the poor reveal that various programs have probably helped cut the percentage of people in abject poverty or impoverishment from around 15 percent to 10 percent, the percentage of deprived individuals and families who must live below subsistence has remained about the same over the last 25 years. Overall, it must be reluctantly admitted that the government has failed to dramatically reduce the number of poor in the United States.

There are several reasons for this failure: (1) Federal programs have often been based upon questionable cultural premises; (2) the programs have been typically underfinanced; (3) federal programs have been piecemeal, overlapping, and fragmented; and (4) none of the current programs confront the real source of poverty—the persisting pattern of societywide stratification and inequality.

Why government programs fail

CULTURAL PREMISES OF GOVERNMENT PROGRAMS

Government programs proceed on several cultural beliefs that can at times undermine their effectiveness. One cultural belief revolves around the sanctity of private enterprise and competition and is justified by what we termed the trickle-down beliefs. For example, even the New Deal of Franklin D. Roosevelt in the 1930s and the New Frontier of John F. Kennedy in the early 1960s held a vision that economic prosperity would somehc v filter down to the poor. However, in light of the institutional forces that maintain inequality, this is only partly true. Instead of directly subsidizing the poverty sector, a typical governmental approach, as in the New Deal and New Frontier, has been to pour billions of tax dollars into the economy in order to stimulate private enterprise and competition and then wait for the ensuing prosperity that will presumably provide jobs and thus be of benefit to both the affluent and poor. Most typically, however, it is the more affluent who have benefited, with poor receiving comparatively little aid.

Another way in which this cultural belief in private enterprise constrains federal programs for the poor is by assuming that private incentive and open competition must be left intact (Dentler, 1967: 101–124). This belief is consistent with such core values as individualism, freedom, and activism, but it has tended to discourage the government from creating jobs for the poor that might compete with those in the private economy. Moreover, it has operated to restrain the federal government from regulating more closely those industries that employ large numbers of the poor. Since open competition is now greatly mitigated among big companies, and since government regulation and subsidy have become commonplace for large economic interests, it is curiously contradictory to suggest that anything but incentives and open competition for the poor will violate basic American values (Harrington, 1968; Fernbach, 1965).

Another cultural belief inhibiting government programs is the charity ethic which maintains that government assistance, whether through welfare or public works, should be only temporary and custodial. Such beliefs are derived from the values of activism, achievement, materialism, and humanitarianism. And because this belief is so embedded in America's consciousness, most Americans resist permanent public assistance to the poor because it is believed that to do so might undermine the poor's desire for achievement. However, in a society with somewhere around 35 million poor, rapid automation, and an economy incapable of sustaining full employment (due to periodic recessions) and unable to provide subsistence wages for much of its work force, this cultural premise emphasizing the tempo-

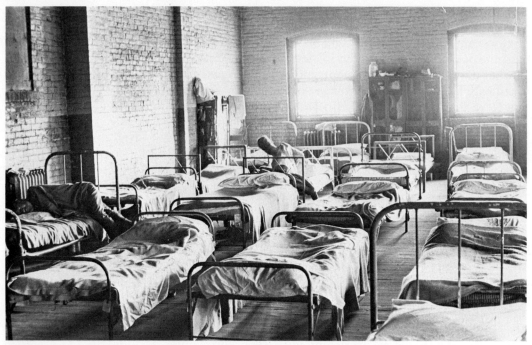

*Most poor cannot work; and yet, current beliefs stigmatize those who
cannot assume work roles and condemn many—like the men
above—to the stigma and degradation of dependency on "charity."*

rary and custodial nature of federal assistance insures that a vast
pocket of poverty will remain. It is more in tune with the realities of
the problem to recognize that certain categories of the poor, such as
the aged, unwed mothers, and the handicapped, will have to be permanently supported by government subsidies. Currently, almost all
government programs spend millions of tax dollars and create
bureaucratic entanglements to ensure that government subsidies for
the poor are not permanent and that "individual achievement" is not
undermined—an unsubstantiated assumption about human motivation that can damage even the most promising federal programs.

A related cultural belief is that a person's income can come only
from work and that esteem and moral worth are degraded if income
comes from other sources.[2] This work ethic has been translated into
provisions, in almost all federal assistance legislation, that require
people to work after a certain time period or when they meet certain
conditions. For example, in the recent legislative proposals for a
guaranteed annual income for the poor, there is an argument over a
requirement that unwed mothers work once their children reach

school age. Thus, in Michael Harrington's (1971) estimate, by some current beliefs it is considered more dignified for an unwed poor mother to perform menial labor for a below-subsistence wage than to be at home, raising her children. Menial labor is considered work and, therefore, highly worthy, whereas raising one's children is not work and, hence, is not *as worthy*. As many commentators have noted, such provisions do little to eradicate the cycle of poverty, because they force people to work at subsistence wages and neglect their families—conditions that are probably not conducive to breaking the cycle outlined in Figure 3.

A final cultural belief which can serve as an obstacle to eradicating poverty is the pervasive belief in local community autonomy and control, as opposed to direct intervention by the federal government. Derived from such values as freedom and individualism, this belief has sometimes allowed local political and economic interests to subvert the good intentions of many federal programs. Moreover, beliefs in local community autonomy have also made it difficult to have a national program or plan for eliminating poverty (Harrington, 1968, 1971). While most Americans firmly believe that federal programs are inefficient and wasteful (Gans, 1964), they fail to grasp that one of the reasons for this inefficiency is that these programs are usually channeled through local community agencies, where the potential for corruption and political patronage is higher.

In sum, government programs are often undermined before they are even initiated. Until the cultural beliefs guiding thought and action become more consonant with structural realities, they will continue to be less effective than would be desired. In a way, a counterproductive cycle has been initiated: federal programs start off on the wrong foot; they are therefore ineffective; ineffectiveness supports people's conceptions that the government cannot really do the job and/or the poor are simply motivationally deficient and do not deserve assistance; and thus, it is easy to justify terminations and cutbacks in programs designed to help the poor.

THE FAILURE OF THE WAR ON POVERTY

There has perhaps never been a more ambitious program to eradicate poverty than the "war on poverty" begun in 1964. Conceived in great haste and rapidly pushed through Congress, this program, with its many diverse projects, was to eliminate poverty in the midst of affluence. In many ways the failure of this massive "war" epitomizes the mistakes consistently made in ameliorative federal legislation for the poor; and for this reason, its structure is worthy of more detailed discussion.

The war on poverty and its administrative agency, the Office of Economic Opportunity (OEO) were, with the wisdom of hindsight, poorly conceived. In 1963 President Kennedy began to conceive of an antipoverty program, spearheaded by a kind of domestic Peace Corps later known as VISTA. When Lyndon Johnson became president, the public and Congress had rediscovered poverty and were receptive to antipoverty legislation initially visualized by Kennedy before his death. In the desire to take advantage of such public receptiveness, the program was rapidly drawn up and passed by Congress. Ideally, the war on poverty was to be a broad frontal attack on poverty encompassing income tax cuts, civil rights, regional development, youth programs, vocational training, and hospital insurance (Seligman, 1970:162–63). In some ways, the broad scope of the program greatly contributed to its demise because it encompassed, duplicated, and overlapped with specific programs in the departments of Labor, Agriculture, and Health, Education, and Welfare (HEW). Supposedly, OEO was to consolidate and coordinate the diverse programs ranging from juvenile delinquency prevention to job training. But in reality, OEO was automatically placed in a situation that inevitably generated squabbles with other executive departments over priorities and program funding.

Emergence of the war on poverty

Furthermore, OEO chose to bypass state governments and the local welfare establishments, with the result that the program immediately came under attack from senators, congressmen, and social workers. Additionally, the program was to encourage "maximum feasible participation" of the poor, but the laws enacted by Congress and the guidelines of the OEO did not specify clearly what this meant and it soon became, in Daniel Moynihan's words, a "maximum feasible misunderstanding." One consequence was for local governments to seek control of each program for purposes of consolidating political power while excluding the poor from decision making. Under these conditions, the OEO soon was in the middle of struggles over control of poverty funds among leaders of the poor, community political officials, and local welfare agencies. Also, despite its lofty claims as a comprehensive program, the war on poverty became oriented primarily to urban blacks even though half the poor live in rural areas and four-fifths of the poor are white. And when the urban riots of the 1960s emerged, Congress and the public suddenly became unwilling to support programs geared primarily to "ungrateful" blacks. Finally, unlike other types of war efforts in American history, the war on poverty was grossly underfinanced considering the magnitude of the problem.

In addition to administrative problems, the war on poverty failed to confront the real issue of income distribution in the United States.[4]

Although a guaranteed annual income was entertained, serious action along the lines of direct cash subsidies to the poor were considered too radical. The result of this major constraint was a piecemeal attack on poverty, with poverty workers isolating single "causes" of poverty and then constructing separate programs to eliminate each cause. In Ben Seligman's words (1970:164–165), "If the poor are untutored, they should be trained; if they withdraw from society, their attitudes must be altered." Unfortunately, despite the good intentions of the program's framers and backers, the result was a fragmented and piecemeal program with a Job Corps (to train the unskilled); Community Action Programs (to generate new attitudes and political awareness); a massive Head Start program (to start children off "right" in school); a Neighborhood Youth Corps (to provide jobs in the summer); an Upward Bound program (to get blacks into college); and a VISTA program (to encourage general involvement in the war on poverty). Since each of these programs was underfinanced, chaos resulted as proponents of the various programs in the OEO, the local community governments, the target communities, the local welfare establishments, and the state governments fought over limited funds. Because programs in the OEO and other executive departments overlapped and duplicated one another, additional chaos stemming from fragmentation resulted. For example, high school dropouts could find themselves in the position of not knowing to whom they could turn: the Office of Juvenile Delinquency (sponsored by the Department of Labor), the Office of Education of HEW, the Neighborhood Youth Corps or Job Corps of the OEO, or the local welfare bureaucracy (Seligman, 1970:109).

The failure to confront directly the pattern of income distribution can be understood in light of American cultural values and economic institutions, but it is remarkable that the program did not seriously approach the issue of job creation. Values such as activism and achievement translated into a "work ethic" would have made a comprehensive job program popular with the general public; for indeed, blacks in ghettos wanted jobs rather than training in a Job Corps Center for nonexistent work. The poverty program's indirect approach of training the young, as in the Head Start or Job Corps programs, tended to ignore the needs of adults with large families; they needed immediate income, if not in the form of direct income subsidies, at least jobs with above-subsistence wages. It was only late in the war on poverty that this failure to provide jobs became evident. But by this time, public and congressional support of the program had turned to either disillusionment or apathy.

Considering the handicaps—financial, administrative, and conceptual—of the war on poverty, it was inevitable that it could not

Many poor faced the confusion of War on Poverty programs with bewilderment. The Job Corps, for example, isolated people in "camps" away from their homes and "trained" them for nonexistent jobs.

meet the high hopes and expectations placed on it in 1964. Almost from the beginning months its demise was inevitable, for even by liberal estimates it reached only 15–20 percent of the poor. Furthermore, the OEO was unable to offer proof, even after several years of the program's existence, that it had changed the lives of the poor whom it did reach. Congress wanted this proof, and even today no such proof exists.

As the Vietnam War began to expand in the late 1960s, coupled with increasing disillusionment with the war on poverty's results, federal funding declined; programs were cut back or absorbed by other executive departments such as Labor, Agriculture, and HEW, and obscurity began to cover the once prominent Office of Economic Opportunity. It would be incorrect to assume, as many have done, that the Vietnam War, with its demands on the budget, destroyed the war on poverty. Like so many federal programs, the war on poverty had many inherent weaknesses that made fulfillment of its goal impossible. We should briefly summarize these weaknesses:

Weaknesses in the war on poverty

1. The goal of the program was vague and far too broad.
2. Insufficient attention was paid to how monies would be administered and how local and state governments, the target communities, the local welfare establishments, and the OEO were to coordinate their activities and resolve their power struggles. For in a federalist political system, resolving these administrative problems is critical for any program's success.
3. It duplicated programs in other executive departments, creating waste and inefficiency as well as power struggles.
4. The program was underfinanced at all stages.
5. It failed to address the fundamental cause of poverty—income distribution. In so doing, it became fragmented into a series of loosely integrated programs revolving around socialization and training for the young. It thereby bypassed all the really significant institutional and cultural causes of inequality.

WELFARE

In addition to the special programs designed to "break the poverty cycle," the federal government, in conjunction with state and county bodies, has bestowed welfare on the poor. Such welfare consists of cash and "in-kind" subsidies (usually medical care, surplus food, and food stamps) to certain categories of the poor. These subsidies are designed to enable "deserving poor" to survive at a marginal level of existence, while inducing them to "better themselves" through work or participation in various governmental programs, such as those of the war on poverty. Much of the current structure of welfare can only be understood by examining the history of charity in America, for indeed, the present welfare system, or as politicians and citizens alike exclaim, "the welfare mess," is the result of a series of historical events. These events require elaboration in order to visualize how the "welfare mess" is a problem of American culture and social structure (Turner and Starnes, 1976; Piven and Cloward, 1971).

As we briefly mentioned in Chapter 7, the history of welfare in America has been shaped by several dominant beliefs that traditionally have reduced perceptions of viable alternatives in relief giving. One constraining belief is the work ethic which proclaims that income should come from work and that nonwork income is undesirable. Another belief reducing alternatives to relief giving is the charity ethic which views welfare as appropriate only for the "deserving" poor who, if they could, would seek their income through work. A third belief dictates that charity is a local community affair and that welfare should be, in large part, controlled by local officials who know and understand the particular problems of "their poor."

Unlike the affluent, the poor must receive their subsidy under crowded and degrading conditions. Few middle class Americans would tolerate the above conditions for receiving their income tax rebates and other forms of subsidy.

Early relief giving in America represented a literal application of these beliefs, with local communities and private agencies solely responsible for welfare, and with the "indolent" poor subjected to the vicissitudes of the community workhouse (these poor were viewed as violating the values of activism and achievement). Not until the Great Depression in the 1930s did the federal government begin to assist states and communities in relief giving, and even then, the federal government intervened most reluctantly. In 1931, for example, President Hoover proclaimed: "I am opposed to any direct or indirect government dole . . ." and even in 1935, after years of massive federal welfare, President Roosevelt maintained that "the federal government must and shall quit this business of relief." Shortly after 1935, the federal government did begin cutting back on its programs but, at the same time, the passage of the 1935 Social Security Act was to forge the profile of the contemporary welfare system. Under this act the federal government would provide "grants and aids" to states for certain categories of poor, such as the aged, blind, orphaned, and dependent children (absence of parent). The "able-bodied poor" were left out of the federal government's "categories," despite the fact that work was unavailable. Between 1935 and 1939, most states took at least some of the grant and aid money, creating the profile of the present welfare system:

1. States were allowed to set their own grant levels, thereby assuring state and regional differences in welfare assistance.
2. State and county governments were left to structure their own offices in any manner they preferred, with only the most general federal guidelines constraining the organization of local welfare bureaucracies.
3. Since the federal government made no provisions for the able-bodied, the states rarely made their own; and only with revision of the Social Security Act in 1961 were families with an unemployed father included in federal grant and aid categories.
4. In all states, work requirements for the poor who could work once their "temporary" need for charity passed were enacted and enforced.

It is this structure, legitimized by beliefs in the work ethic, the charity ethic, and local control, that was to regulate relief giving in America for 25 years, and even today, only a slightly modified version of this structure is in operation. There have been many problems with the welfare system since its inception in the late 1930s, but two stand out as most important: (1) the system has been highly abusive of the poor, and (2) it has perpetuated poverty.

    1. During the years between 1940 and the early 1960s, the welfare

system worked against as much as for the poor. At the state and local levels there are elaborate and excessively complex conditions for securing welfare because recipients must be more than impoverished, they must also be morally "worthy" and eager to work.

Besides the elaborate conditions imposed upon recipients, they also must *continually* prove their need for welfare. The welfare bureaucracy—unlike the social security and veterans' bureaucracies—does not seek out the poor; on the contrary, the poor must seek out the welfare agencies, fending for themselves in a labyrinth of overlapping offices, rules, and administrations. Then, once recipients are on welfare, the bureaucracy continually surveys and evaluates their qualifications or "worthiness." Some surveillance methods violated the recipients' constitutional rights. For example, social workers at one time periodically raided unwed mother's homes, without a search warrant, to check to see if a man was living with her, thereby disqualifying her for welfare. Fortunately, such violations of the recipients' legal rights, such as equal protection under the laws, due process, and immunity from unreasonable searches, are not as prevalent today as in the past (Ten Broek, 1968). Yet, the constant surveillance continues and consumes much of the manpower and money allocated to the welfare bureaucracy. Were this concern over cheating to be lessened the size and cost of the welfare bureaucracy would be drastically reduced.

In addition to the injustices and abuses inherent in the surveillance activities of the welfare bureaucracy, local administrators are often given too much discretionary power in interpreting welfare laws. More than any other body of laws, welfare laws are vague and fail to specify the conditions under which they apply. This vagueness has at times become a license to bureaucratic administrators to implement policies arbitrarily. Until very recently, with the emergence of the National Welfare Rights Organization and various legal groups devoted to helping the poor, these abuses were excessive and there were no channels of appeal for those persons against whom abuses were leveled.

In the early 1960s the various groups representing the poor were able to have the federal courts strike the most abusive welfare practices. For example, the "no man in the house rule" for mothers with dependent children (AFDC) was struck down by the Supreme Court in 1968. Also in 1968, a three-judge panel struck down laws requiring that AFDC mothers be willing and able to work; midnight raids to welfare recipients' homes were declared unconstitutional; and in 1970, the Supreme Court ruled that welfare recipients have the right to appeal termination of their benefits. While many of the abusive features of the welfare system have been eliminated or mitigated,

The "eligibility worker" is the backbone of the current welfare system. Here a sincere and well-intentioned worker "checks up" on a welfare mother.

poverty persists. And in many ways, the current structure of welfare promotes persistent poverty.

2. As presently constituted, the welfare system maintains poverty by providing subsistence or below-subsistence payments to recipients. In turn, the remaining work requirements and below-subsistence benefits force or induce the poor to enter the job market where, for the vast majority, only the most low paying and menial work is available. The decentralized structure of welfare, which allows states to set their own grant and aid levels, operates to keep welfare benefits below low wages. For example, one study recorded that there was a very high correlation between agricultural wages (usually the lowest in an area) and welfare benefits in all regions of the country, leading to speculation that benefits are deliberately kept low in order to induce the poor to work in any job that pays above-subsistence wages (Piven and Cloward, 1971). Such a system also operates as a subsidy for the affluent employer who requires inexpensive and seasonal labor, since workers can be pulled off of welfare when needed and then returned to the welfare roles when the need for their labor subsides. In this way, the welfare system maintains a large unskilled labor pool which can be forced or induced to enter an

The economic functions of welfare

economic system that perpetuates poverty. These practices are legitimized by beliefs in the importance of work and in the temporary nature of public assistance.

While few would argue that the present welfare system is good, there are several obstacles to its restructuring. First, economic interests and the affluent have a "vested interest" in a system that maintains a cheap labor pool; and while it is difficult to know exactly if, or how, they pressure local political and welfare officials to maintain the system, some influence undoubtedly must occur, for the needs of some economic organizations for seasonal and inexpensive labor correspond too closely to the way the welfare system operates. Second, once structured, the welfare system becomes an "establishment" which lobbies actively to maintain its current operation, despite the recognition that it is inefficient and does not improve the plight of the poor. Third, dominant beliefs in local control, the work ethic, and the charity ethic make the public fearful of abandoning a system that personifies basic values of activism, achievement, and humanitarianism. Thus, the obstacles to welfare reform are many, but the growing recognition that the system is both abusive of the poor and inefficient has led to speculation about possible alternatives. The most likely to be implemented of these alternatives is the guaranteed annual income.

THE GUARANTEED INCOME ALTERNATIVE

The guaranteed annual income would establish an income floor for all individuals and families. The federal government would simply subsidize the income of those who fall below this floor. Many current welfare programs, with their conditions, surveillance, and arbitrary administration could (theoretically at least) be subsumed under one national welfare program. The result of such a program would be to cut back the size of the welfare establishment, eliminate its duplication at the local, state, and federal levels, and simplify administrative procedures. If the income floor were set at the subsistence level and constantly adjusted upwared with inflation, abject poverty would be eliminated. The cost of such a program is difficult to estimate, but a figure of $35 billion annually is probably close to realistic. If income tax expenditures were cut, some observers believe that such a program could be financed without seriously affecting the rest of the federal budget and without increases in the structural rate of taxation.

Cost of the guaranteed annual income (GAI)

In late 1974 President Ford "circulated" a tentative draft for a guaranteed income and, at present, this plan is the most likely direction of welfare alternatives. Basically, the plan would completely abolish the traditional "grants and aids" approach to welfare by

Proposals for a GAI

taking much of the financing and administering of welfare out of the hands of state and local governments. Instead of food stamps, surplus food, and conditional cash stipends, the tentative program would bestow a cash subsidy of $3600 on a family of four with no other source of income. While details of the program are not available at present,[5] some income supplement would be available to families that earned outside income, but at a total income level of $7200, income supplements would cease.

Many questions about this program remain to be answered if it is to pass Congress. First, will there be a work requirement? Will some people be forced to work for low wages in menial jobs when they become available? Second, will the $3600 supplement rise with increases in the cost of living? Or, will the poor be forced to live on a fixed income supplement in times of rapid inflation? Third, and perhaps most important, why is the income guarantee so low, when *official* government figures in 1974 placed subsistence for a family of four at around $7000? Would not such a low income supplement force the poor to enter an exploitive job market in much the same way as the current welfare system?

The fate of President Nixon's previous income guarantee program in 1972 can probably offer the best clues as to how these questions would be answered when an income guarantee plan is subjected to congressional discussion and debate. First, if the president did not do so, Congress would probably add a work requirement—despite the fact that such work requirements are unnecessary in a guaranteed annual income proposal. For example, in a major study of the effects of a guaranteed income in a program without a work requirement, there was no perceptible withdrawal of those on income guarantees from the work force.[6] Rather, without the threat of economic disaster over their heads, workers tended to hold out for better paying and more permanent jobs—behavior that is highly conducive to breaking the poverty cycle. Second, the current welfare bureaucracy would be likely to maintain its monitoring or "watchdog" function and, thus, subject the poor to many of the abuses of the present system. Coupled with work requirements, local welfare bureaucracies could continue to revoke benefits if they perceived work to be available to a recipient. Moreover, the fact that the income guarantee is set at about one-half the subsistence needs of the poor would force them to seek work, virtually any work, to supplement meager welfare benefits. The result of these two features would be for the new welfare system to maintain a cheap labor pool that the more affluent could draw upon when they need low-wage or seasonal labor.

Thus, to avoid the problems of Nixon's previous proposal and for the income guarantee concept to represent a real alternative to the present system,[7] an income guarantee plan must, first of all, create an adequate guarantee of at least $7500 per year (in current dollars) for a family of four. Second, work requirements should be abolished. Third, to prevent the proliferation of yet another welfare bureaucracy, watchdog functions should be assumed by the Internal Revenue Service, which would spot-check recipients of this "negative income tax" in the same manner as it does those who pay income taxes. In this way, welfare payments would approximate subsidies to the more affluent through the tax system and subject both groups to similar forms of subsidy. It would be preferable, of course, to eliminate welfare and subsidies through the tax system and simply make all subsidies direct expenditures. In this way, the $35 billion or so spent on income guarantees would not seem so large when compared to the $60–$70 billion spent on subsidies to the more affluent. But realistically, subsidy through tax loopholes is not likely to be eliminated, and thus, equity would dictate that the poor's income guarantee should be no more carefully monitored than the affluent's and wealthy's tax subsidy payments.

Avoiding problems in a GAI program

SOCIOLOGICAL INSIGHTS

Below is a press release by the Associated Press in December of 1974. The areas in color mark improvements in the current system; the boldface type indicates danger areas that will undermine some of the proposed improvements.

FEDERALLY OPERATED WELFARE PLAN PROPOSED BY CONGRESSIONAL PANEL

WASHINGTON (AP)—A new congressional study describes existing welfare programs **as antiwork and antifamily and recommends replacing most of them with a federally administered system.**

The report Wednesday by a panel of the Joint Economic Committee urges that the aid to families with dependent children, *food stamp* and other programs be scrapped. The Ford administration is studying similar changes in the welfare system.

The program of supplemental security income for the aged, blind and disabled should be retained, the report says. Welfare eligibility rules that withold benefits from families headed by males should be scrapped, it said.

The proposal recommends replacing the terminated programs with a system of tax credits and subsistence payments that would be reduced by 50 cents for every dollar earned by recipients.

In addition, states would be required for at least two years to supplement the proposed new program with payments to families that received benefits under the aid-to-dependent-children program as of December 1976, if the families were worse off under the new system.

The congressional study's recommendations are very similar to proposals put forth by Caspar W. Weinberger, secretary of health, education and welfare, earlier this year. The Ford administration currently is studying the Weinberger proposals.

Subcommittee chairman Representative Martha D. Griffiths (D-Mich.), who released the three-year study and its recommendations Wednesday, said the report's proposals would provide more money for most of the nation's 35 million welfare recipients, while providing incentives to work and keep families together.

The report recommended starting the new program in 1977.

The report says current welfare programs are uncoordinated "with gaps, overlaps, cross-purposes, inequities, administrative inefficiencies . . . and wasted taxpayers' money."

The proposed program, to be administered by the Internal Revenue Service, "Will assure a higher level of benefit accuracy at lower cost than relying on separate state agencies," the report states.

Griffiths said the proposal would cost the federal government only $15.4 billion more than the estimated $142 billion that will be spent this fiscal year for what was called income security programs.

These include federal payments for such items as welfare, housing, social services and food stamps. The Agriculture department announced Wednesday that food stamp recipients will pay 30 percent of their monthly income for stamps, beginning March 1. They now pay an average of 23 percent.

The subcommittee said the total value of grants and tax credits would amount to $3,600 for a "penniless two-adult family of four, $3,000 for a penniless one-adult family of four."

The report said the current welfare programs tended to dampen work incentives for beneficiaries by reducing net gain from work to as low as 25 or 15 cents on the dollar in some cases.

"Our program is not going to give them that much money. You're going to be encouraged to work," Representative Griffiths said.

She said the program would encourage families to stay together by doing away with regulations that keep families headed by males from receiving benefits.

"We are destroying family life in America with these welfare programs," she said. "If you are only going to help women with children, then the obvious way to get help is to get rid of your husband."

The study was conducted over three years. Among its findings were that the largest gap in welfare coverage was for low- and modest-income workers, especially men and their families and that benefits varied greatly from state to state.

ECONOMIC PROCESSES AND POVERTY

In Chapter 7 the job market and wage plight of the poor were discussed. We noted then that the poor are in the most competitive of the job markets and that they must compete with each other for very low-paying jobs. As we emphasized, the federal government has not attempted in a comprehensive way to intervene in this situation by providing government jobs or by raising the minimum wage.

Aside from these economic processes, another economic hardship on the poor has become evident: The poor pay more than the affluent in the market for what they get (Caplovitz, 1963). Because their income is low, the poor automatically pay a higher proportion of their incomes than the more affluent for basic necessities such as food, clothing, and housing. What is more significant, however, is that the poor are more likely to get inferior quality merchandise, dollar for dollar, than the nonpoor. For example, the rent paid by the poor—especially racial and ethnic minorities—tends to be exorbitantly high, even for a slum dwelling. It has also been clearly documented that the poor pay much more for food of inferior quality than do those in the suburbs (P. Jacobs, 1970). Since the poor, trapped in cities or in rural backwashes, are not mobile, they cannot shop around as can middle-class buyers, with the result that they are subjected to monopolistic practices of local food and clothing stores. Furthermore, since the poor have little surplus, they cannot take advantage of food and clothing sales by buying in quantity. Another economic bite on the poor comes from sales taxes, which hurt the poor far more than those at higher income levels. A 5 percent sales tax cuts deeply into a $3000 income, whereas it is just an annoyance to those with incomes from $12,000 to $15,000. (Also, the more affluent can use the sales tax as a tax deduction and thus not really pay 5 percent.)

Probably the most prevalent economic problem faced by poor are the various "credit traps" (P. Jacobs, 1970). Because the poor have low incomes, they are considered greater credit risks and hence they

The poor pay more

Credit traps for the poor

The poor—often trapped in a slum—often must pay more to meet their needs. For those who must live under these conditions, the margin of existence is too slim for them to pay more without sacrificing their health and safety.

must pay higher interest rates on money that they borrow. Such a situation might be understandable except for the fact that loan companies *actively solicit* the poor's business since the high risks are not as great as the high profits to be derived from charging high interest rates. Credit managers in poor neighborhoods make little effort to check on the credit of the poor. All that is required is that the applicant have a place of residence and a fixed income. If the borrower cannot meet the payments, the company forecloses, resells the product, and then attaches the borrower's paycheck for the difference. Even in the face of recent "truth-in-lending" laws, merchants in ghetto neighborhoods are at some times ruthless about extending credit. They entice the poor to buy goods—radios, television sets, furniture, and so forth—by offering "easy payment" credit deals. By merely paying "so much per week" (not by the month, as with middle-class buyers), the poor are seduced into buying items with little understanding of monthly costs or high interest rates. One of the principal goals of these merchants is to keep the poor permanently on the credit hook. This goal is realized in a number of ways, the most prevalent of which is to have borrowers come into the store each week to make a payment and then entice them to buy something else on "easy credit."

Paul Jacobs (1970) estimates that the poverty market includes 35 million people having a total income of $28 billion. Poverty, in the aggregate, is "big business," and the poor are simply overwhelmed by merchants and loan companies who, for the most part, take out of the community a large part of the poor's income. Unlike middle-class Americans, who are now "consumer conscious" and very likely to complain about the quality of merchandise, the poor rarely complain and are usually unaware of their consumer rights.

Poverty is big business

A CULTURE OF POVERTY?

Thus far, we have reviewed some of the cultural, governmental, and economic forces in the *broader* society that have perpetuated inequality and poverty in America. Now attention is drawn to a cultural force that has been presumed to exist among only the poor. Many authors have noted that distinct cultures exist among various social strata (W. Miller, 1958, 1965, 1969; Davis, 1952) and that, among the poor, a distinct "culture of poverty" prevails (Lewis, 1968). This culture of poverty is composed of values and beliefs presumed to suppress aspirations and success motivations among the poor. Oscar Lewis (1968), the most persistent advocate of this position, argues that the culture of poverty is not only an adaptation but also a reaction of the poor to their marginal position. Their culture of "nonactivism" and "nonachievement" allows them to cope with feelings of hopelessness and despair that emerge from their realization of the "improbability of achieving success in terms of the values and goals of the larger society." What is crucial to this notion is that, once created, the values of the culture of poverty are *transmitted from generation to generation*. Such transmission puts each new generation in a state of cultural and motivational "unreadiness" to achieve and aspire—even should opportunities for success become available. For those arguing for the existence of a culture-of-poverty, additional behavior patterns among the poor are viewed as further inhibiting the adjustment of the poor to a middle-class, success oriented society. For these thinkers, patterns of "promiscuousness" (unwed mothers, common law marriages), physical aggressiveness, unstable family life, and so on are viewed as detrimental to achievement. These pat-

The culture of poverty hypothesis

Are these people culturally impoverished? Or are they simply in need of money and a job? Do they need "rehabilitation" or income? There are millions of Americans like them and they represent an enduring problem of culture and structure.

terns, they believe, are also passed down from generation to generation and inhibit social and economic mobility.

Reaction against the "culture of poverty" hypothesis has been extensive. Authors falling into this camp can be labeled "situationalists" (Gans, 1969) because they argue that, while the poor evidence distinctive life-styles, these styles are not transmitted in a kind of inexorable and mechanical way from generation to generation. Rather, these distinctive patterns of thought and action among the poor are recreated by each generation as it adjusts to being poor, isolated, discriminated against, and trapped in rural and urban ghettos (Rossi and Blum, 1969; Rainwater, 1969; Valentine, 1968). Furthermore, desires for success and achievement are not absent among the poor; instead they are modified or repressed as the poor attempt to cope with economic and social realities (Rodman, 1963).

The situationalist view of poverty

The distinction between the culture of poverty hypothesis and this situationalist viewpoint is far from trivial. Depending upon the position taken, solutions to the problem of poverty will vary (Rainwater, 1969). If the culture of poverty is the guiding perspective for a government program, then the solution to poverty is personality change and resocialization of the young into dominant American values, because it is necessary to interrupt the transmission of lower-class culture from one generation to another. If the situational view guides ameliorative efforts, government programs should be directed toward income guarantees and other subsidies that will remove people from the situation of being poor and thus allow them to realize repressed desires to be active and achieve. For if the poor are deemed to hold the same success values as the affluent (only somewhat modified or latent), then programs will be directed toward providing opportunities for the poor to realize these values.

Pro and con views on a culture of poverty

Most federal programs have used either the culture of poverty perspective or a position that incorporates at least some of its tenets. For example, war on poverty programs such as Head Start and Upward Bound have been geared to resocializing the poor into dominant American values. Other programs recognizing at least some of the situationalist's arguments have been geared to providing opportunities in the economic, political, and educational spheres (e.g., Job Corps, voting rights legislation, and other civil rights programs). However, one major criticism of such programs is that they do not focus on the broader system of stratification and the structural and cultural forces maintaining the societywide pattern of inequality. A somewhat simplified, but essentially correct, way to make this critique is to note that federal programs implicitly blame the poor for their cultural inadequacies (such as low achievement motivation) rather than addressing the broader causes of the poverty problem—the present nationwide system of income distribution as we described it in Chapter 6 (Valentine, 1968).

Since it is only recently that all the tenets of the situational view have gained prominence, programs derived from its premise appear somewhat revolutionary. Most notable of these programs is the guaranteed annual income, which would subsidize people's income to the point of removing them from the "situation" of being poor. Unfortunately, as we noted earlier, the currently proposed income guarantees are not sufficient to pull people out of poverty and it is unlikely that they will have a great impact on the lifestyles of the poor in either a cultural or situational sense.

Who is right in this debate over the culture of poverty? At this point answers are not available. In all likelihood, each position is accurate for different groups of impoverished at different times and in different places. The poor do not represent a homogeneous population. As Herbert Gans notes, "Despite a middle class inclination on the part of researchers to view the poor as homogeneous, all available studies indicate that there is as much variety among them as the affluent (1969:206)." Some of the poor may be culturally impoverished, others may be realists about their chances in life, and still others may have high aspirations that must lay dormant. Many may need "cultural rehabilitation," others special opportunities, and some just an income that allows a subsistence living.

There is an often quoted conversation that supposedly took place between F. Scott Fitzgerald and Ernest Hemingway. Fitzgerald is reported to have argued that the affluent are, in terms of ability, temperament, and other psychological states, basically different from the poor. To wit, Hemingway replied: "Yes, they have more money." This discussion has been duplicated again and again by social scientists who have debated whether or not the poor are basically different by virtue of a culture of poverty or are simply adjusting to poverty in ways that could easily be changed with more money. If Hemingway and social scientists of the situationalist persuasion are correct, then an adequate guaranteed annual income, coupled with real opportunities for success, would reveal the superficiality of differences between poor and affluent, as the poor quickly assumed the cultural patters of the affluent. If Fitzgerald and social scientists who argue that a true culture of poverty exists are correct, then programs directed at resocialization of the poor should be pursued. Currently, it is impossible to know which position is the most accurate since an *adequate* guaranteed annual income has never been tried and since programs based on Fitzgerald's premise have rarely been sufficiently well financed to determine if indeed resocialization works. Both opinions are probably valid to some extent for *different groups and segments* of the poor. But until adequate action employing both sets of assumptions is taken, poverty will remain one of America's most enduring problems of structure.

SUMMARY

We have explored the problem of poverty in Chapter 8. After distinguishing between the two levels of poverty, we outlined the characteristics of poor people. Our attention then shifted to analyzing the structural and cultural approaches to dealing with the poor. In particular, we focused on the cultural restraints imposed upon the structure of governmental solutions. The war on poverty was viewed as one example of these constraints; similarly, the welfare system and proposed alternatives for a guaranteed income were viewed within the context of present cultural and structural constraints. We also examined some of the economic forces—from high prices to credit traps—which perpetuate people's poverty.

Finally, the "culture of poverty" hypothesis was addressed, and the positions of those criticizing this presumption—situationalists—were presented.

NOTES

1. There are numerous sources that document trends in poverty. For example, see Ornati, 1964; Harrington, 1971; H. Miller, 1965; Orshansky, 1965, 1968; MacDonald, 1968. These figures must be viewed as approximations of the actual numbers of deprived and impoverished because, depending on whose figures are used, the percent of deprived and impoverished varies. This discrepancy in estimates stems from the fact that there is no agreed-upon subsistence and poverty level among analysts.

2. In 1971, echoing this cultural premise, President Nixon was moved to proclaim that "scrubbing floors or emptying bed pans" is as dignified as any other job including the presidency. Apparently impressed by his own words, Nixon went on to say that: "If a job puts bread on the table and gives you the satisfaction of providing for your children and lets you look everyone else in the eye, I do not think it is menial."

3. For a more extensive discussion of the war on Poverty, see Moynihan, 1969:3–35; Seligman, 1970:161–218, 1965; Levitan, 1967.

4. Experimental guaranteed annual income programs have been initiated by the OEO; and since President Nixon proposed a guaranteed annual income, the OEO has become bolder on the issue of income redistribution. But during the initial phases of the war on poverty, OEO was conspicuously silent on this issue.

5. Unfortunately, this book is being written at a time when this plan is only under consideration. Currently, there appears little chance for such a program. Be aware that in several years the guaranteed annual income program that eventually might emerge may deviate somewhat from the one discussed here.

6. See, for example, Office of Economic Opportunity, *Further Preliminary Results of the New Jersey Graduated Work Incentive Experiment*, Washington, D.C.: U.S. Government Printing Office, 1971.

7. For discussions of the guaranteed annual income, see Harrington, 1971; National Welfare Rights Organization, 1969; Rainwater, 1969; Vadakin, 1968; Gans, 1964; Miller and Roby, 1969; and, Rossi and Blum, 1969.

REVIEW QUESTIONS

1. Defend to a friend the argument that most poor cannot or should not work, even if there was a federal job program.
2. Argue against the position that "there are too many people on welfare."
3. What are the strengths and weaknesses of the concept of the poverty cycle?
4. In what ways do cultural beliefs limit the options of government in dealing with poverty?
5. How does the welfare system abuse the poor? Has the situation changed?
6. What alternatives to the present system are being proposed? What are their problems of culture and structure?
7. Is there a culture of poverty?

GLOSSARY

culture of poverty a hypothesis that people who are poor pass on, generation after generation, feelings, values, beliefs, and motivations that keep them from becoming motivated to leave poverty

deprivation the state of living only somewhat below established levels of subsistence

guaranteed annual income the proposal that would replace the current grants and aids welfare system by subsidizing an income floor for all individuals and families in America

impoverishment the state of living at a level considerably below established levels of subsistence

poverty the state of having to live below the established levels of subsistence in a society

poverty cycle the concept that poverty creates cultural and environmental obstacles to acquiring adequate motivation to get oneself out of poverty by working to take advantage of opportunities

welfare the governmental programs that give financial and other forms of relief to those who must live below the level of subsistence

PROLOGUE 9: THE IMPERSONALITY OF RACISM

Following are the comments of a black writer and television newscaster about racial discrimination:

"If you look at the racial problem from a black man's point of view, you can see the jokes as well as the injustices. . . .

"A favorite comic theme among the 'concerned and enlightened' elements of white society is 'Let's Stamp Out Racial Hatred.' Hoo boy! Hatred has very little to do with the central problem, Charlie. What is done to and withheld from black folk day by day in this country is based on neither hate nor horror. On the contrary. It is coldly impersonal. Like the brains of precocious computers.

"Simply put, it seems to me that white folk are convinced, deep in their bones, that the way they run this melting pot—with black folk unmelted at the bottom—is nothing more than the natural order of things.

"What happens quite naturally for example, is that a black *bon vivant* who shows up in a clean shirt at a posh restaurant is approached by white customers who beg him to get them a good table, please. There is nothing malicious about it. They simply think of black men in clean shirts as waiters.

"Similarly, a black man caught on foot near a public building lot is likely to be buttonholed by a pale proud patrician who wants his limousine fetched in a hurry.

"And even the most militant white egalitarians are prone to compliment one another by saying, 'That's real white of you, Edgar.' Obviously, the notion that anything white is inherently superior to its black counterpart is built into the white American idiom, and thus into the white American mind. . . .

"I am exposed to the same basic joke almost every time I walk into an all-white apartment building to keep an appointment with a friend. I see panic in the eyes of the pale residents coming out as I go in—trying to recall whether they locked their doors. And the doorman himself seems to be trying to remember the standard procedure for 'What to Do Until the Cops Come.' (Source: New York *Times* Magazine, September 15, 1968.)

This passage could have been written by a Mexican-American in the West, a Puerto Rican in New York, a Cuban in Miami, or an Indian in Arizona. Each has experienced the more subtle forms of discrimination—that is, the taken-for-granted expectation that they are at the bottom of the stratification system. The impersonality and taken-for-granted nature of discrimination underscores that racism is built into American social structure and culture. It is this structure and culture of racism that will occupy our attention in Chapter 9.

9

PROBLEMS OF RACIAL AND ETHNIC DISCRIMINATION

ETHNICITY IN AMERICA

American society is unique in the diversity of its population. Few nations in history have even sought to embrace a population so varied in its cultural heritage. Blacks, browns, Native Americans, Orientals, and large numbers of "white ethnics," including Germans, Poles, Czechs, Italians, Irish, British, French, Slavics, Jews, and Scandinavians, now seek to enjoy some of the fruits of American affluence. Race and ethnicity are powerful forces in America, for there are large blocks of the population who live in two worlds—that of the broader society and that of their own cultural grouping.[1]

Race and ethnicity are intimately related to the distributive system. The first European migrants who settled America not only came to escape persecution but also to find a better life and a larger share of affluence. The waves of European white ethnic migrants of the last century came for similar reasons. The internal migrations of blacks from the rural South, who came first to the urban North and then to the urban South and West, were in response to a desire to share in affluence. Similar reasons spurred the migrations of browns—Cubans, Puerto Ricans, and Mexicans—and Orientals to America's cities and farmlands. All immigrants have suffered persecution and discrimination in this "land of opportunity." Language, country of origin, skin color, and religion have, for different groups, been the basis for discrimination by the white Anglo majority. Some

America's ethnicity emerges

255

racial and ethnic groupings, however, have fared better in their efforts to overcome persecution and discrimination, and they now are able to claim higher than average incomes and standards of living.

What accounts for their differences in the "success" of ethnic and racial groupings? Length of tenure alone cannot answer such a question, for the most tenured—blacks and Native Americans—now suffer the most. Language certainly gave some ethnics, such as the Irish, an advantage in coping with the new world, but what explains differences among all the varied non–English speaking ethnics? Other factors, such as the origins of migrants, whether from rural or urban backgrounds, can account for some of the differences. So can religious background. Also, the compatability of general values and beliefs with those encountered in America can partly explain the differences. Moreover, family structure and the nature of the areas where migrants settled can help us find answers, and the state of the economy at people's first landing can further assist in understanding the differential access of migrants' and their descendants to income, education, and occupational prestige in America. Problems in assimilation

For each ethnic or racial grouping in America, then, a unique combination of forces have operated to shape their destinies. Many members of ethnic groups are now content with the "American way," but others are frustrated at not achieving what they want. In only a few communities in America are the inequalities associated with ethnicity and race not a force to be considered. The riots of the 1960s and 1970s, the demonstrations against and for the war in Vietnam, the violence accompanying the union movement among farm workers, the pro- and antibusing demonstrations and riots of 1975, and the politics of most big cities were and still are all influenced by the tensions existing among American ethnic and racial groupings.

Understanding the problems of these groups over "making it" is the focus of this chapter. It will be impossible, of course, to analyze the situation of all groups in America. We will, therefore, analyze briefly the overall economic situation of prominent ethnic and racial groups, then we will focus attention on the largest racial group— black Americans—and one of the largest ethnic groups—Mexican Americans. We will draw attention to these two groupings because they have yet to enjoy the levels of education, income, and occupational prestige of most other groups. And an understanding of why this is so will help us appreciate more thoroughly the operation of racial and ethnic discrimination in America.

The patterns of inequality and poverty described in Chapters 8 and 9 have been compounded by a third force in American society: racial and ethnic discrimination. Such discrimination has created and perpetuated a class system with various minority groups such as blacks, Racial and ethnic discrimination

Most ethnics came to America and were "processed" as these immigrants on Ellis Island, New York. Yet, others such as blacks were "sold" as slaves—a fate that put them behind white and brown ethnics in their efforts to be economically mobile in America.

Mexican Americans, Cubans, Puerto Ricans, and Indians at its bottom rungs. Although Anglo and ethnic whites constitute a majority of those in poverty, members of certain racial and ethnic minorities are *over*represented in poverty groupings and are more likely than whites to stay in poverty over several generations. The perpetuation of minority poverty is one of the enduring problems of structure and culture in American society.

THE STATUS OF RACIAL AND ETHNIC GROUPS

In order to understand the situation among members of racial and ethnic groupings, we should examine the available data on their income, occupation, and levels of education. These indicators can offer a relatively clear picture of how some of the prominent racial and ethnic groupings fare in receiving shares of income and wealth. Moreover, by looking at the status of other ethnics, the reasons for our more detailed analysis of blacks and Mexican Americans will be evident.

In seeking to understand the status of various groups, one of the most interesting discoveries is the lack of data on America's ethnics. In a society that prided itself on being the "melting pot" of the world, it is rather remarkable that the data collected by the government census is sparse and inadequate. Data on national origin exist, but these tend to ignore the influence of religion on definitions of ethnicity. For example, Protestant Irish and Catholic Irish are much different in terms of their beliefs, values, and sense of identification. Or, among the census category of "Spanish-speaking" can be found people from such diverse countries as Mexico, Cuba, and Puerto Rico. Thus, in our presentation of the data, we will rely upon survey research results conducted by private organizations. These surveys are done with smaller samples than census reports, and they must be interpreted with caution. They are better, however, than the census reports because they ask more detailed questions and make more accurate distinctions among ethnic groups.[2]

Income figures for selected ethnic groups are reported in Table 9.1. To interpret the table requires some explanation. The figures reported are deviations from the national income average for all Americans in the late 1960s. The data are somewhat old, but they are the most recent data of this sort available. Those figures with plus signs (+) indicate the average amount above the national average earned by the heads of families in various ethnic groups. Minus figures (−) represent the average amount below the national mean earned by the head of an ethnic family. As can be seen, three ethnic (racial) groups

Income and ethnicity

Table 9.1 **Income Among Selected Ethnic Groups: Their Deviation from the National Average ($7,588)**

Ethnic Group	Deviation
Blacks	−$2,163
Spanish-speaking	−$1,443
Jews	+$3,324
Protestant Irish	−$ 566
Catholic Irish	+$1,637
Italian	+$ 391
Polish	+$ 352

SOURCE: Adapted from A. M. Greeley, *Ethnicity in the United States: A Preliminary Reconnaisance*, New York: Wiley, 1974, p. 67.

Table 9.2 **Percentage of White-Collar Occupations Held by Members of Selected Ethnic Groups**

Ethnic Group	Percent Holding White-Collar Jobs
Blacks	18%
Spanish-speaking	24
Protestant Irish	38
Catholic Irish	49
Italian	39
Polish	34
National Average	39%

SOURCE: A. M. Greeley, *Ethnicity in the United States*, p. 42–43.

have average incomes below the national mean: blacks, Spanish-speaking, and Protestant Irish. Unfortunately, even the survey data does not break Spanish-speaking peoples into their constituent ethnic groups. Black and Spanish-speaking income is considerably below that of white ethnics. Such a situation will require further explanation.

In Table 9.2 these income differentials among ethnic groups can be seen as a result of the inability of the black and Spanish-speaking populations to penetrate white-collar jobs. Only 18 percent of the black population and 24 percent of the Spanish-speaking groups hold white-collar jobs.

Table 9.3 presents data on the pattern of change in income during a decade period for selected groups. If a group were making dramatic progress toward income parity, their progress would be reflected in a table such as this. All groups earn more from one decade to the next

Table 9.3 **Changes in the Income of Selected Ethnic Groups During the 1950s and 1960s**

Ethnic Group	Average Income in 1950s	Average Income in 1960s	Amount of Change
Blacks	$2,863	$ 4,860	$1,997
Spanish-speaking	3,870	6,360	2,490
Jews	6,960	10,940	3,980
Protestant Irish	5,110	7,854	2,434
Catholic Irish	5,882	8,907	2,025
Italian	5,263	8,945	3,622
Polish	5,252	8,317	2,061
National Average	$5,050	$ 7,812	$2,762

SOURCE: A. M. Greeley, *Ethnicity in the United States*, p. 60.

Table 9.4 **Education Among Selected Ethnic Groups: Their Deviation from the National Average (10.9 years of school)**

Ethnic Group	Deviation
Blacks	−1.2 years
Spanish-speaking	−1.6 years
Jews	+2.4 years
Protestant Irish	−0.3 years
Catholic Irish	+1.3 years
Italian	−0.2 years
Polish	−0.9 years

Source: Adapted from A. M. Greeley, *Ethnicity in the United States*, p. 65.

because generally rising incomes for the entire work force and inflation would assure increases in the dollar amounts earned by different groups. As can be seen, however, a number of group's average income increased less than the population average, with blacks, Poles, and Catholic Irish making the least progress. More recent data on blacks from the Census Bureau confirms this trend for the present decade (data on Catholic Irish is not reported by the census).

In Table 9.4 the number of years that different ethnic groups lag behind or move ahead of the national average is reported. If a group is to be mobile in American society, education is critical to securing prestigious and better paying jobs. As the data indicate, only Jews and Catholic Irish receive an average education above the national mean. The black and Spanish-speaking population lag considerably behind other ethnic groups and the national average, thus, assuring that it will be more difficult for them to get a better paying job.

Education and ethnicity

Table 9.5 represents the change in college attendance over a decade. Dramatic change would reveal increased access to better jobs and higher incomes. Blacks and Protestant Irish reveal the least change in college attendance, lagging considerably behind the national average for this period. Other ethnic groups reveal much progress in increasing their college attendance.

The data in these five tables reveal progress for many ethnic groups in the educational, income, and occupational spheres. The one consistent pattern is the problems encountered by blacks in all spheres and by Spanish-speaking populations with respect to some facets of education and income (although improvement is clearly evident for income). Many of the problems encountered by these two groups are similar to those faced previously by white ethnics. But there are profound differences. Blacks and browns are often biolog-

Blacks and browns are easy targets of discrimination

Table 9.5 **Changes in College Attendance Between 1950 and 1960 for Selected Ethnic Groups**

Ethnic Group	Percent Attending College in 1950s	Percent Attending College in 1960s	Percent of Change in College Attendance
Blacks	10%	11%	1%
Spanish-speaking	7	18	11
Jews	26	50	24
Protestant Irish	25	24	− 1
Catholic Irish	22	29	7
Italian	9	18	9
Polish	18	29	9
National Average	19%	24%	5%

SOURCE: Adapted from A. M. Greeley, *Ethnicity in the United States,* p. 60.

ically distinguishable from white ethnics and Anglos and, therefore, are easier targets of discrimination. It is this discrimination against such large and identifiable groups that marks many of the current problems of race and ethnicity in America. Not only are blacks and browns subject to intense discrimination from all segments of the society, their efforts to reverse this pattern are often resisted by white ethnic populations who are just beginning to rise above national income and education averages. This difficult situation is presently one of America's most explosive problems of structure and culture.

THE CULTURE OF ETHNICITY IN AMERICA

Some of the most strongly held beliefs in America concern racial and ethnic populations. It would be impossible, of course, for millions to "migrate" to a nation and for a massive black population to have existed in slavery without a corresponding system of beliefs about these processes. Some of these beliefs are derived from basic values, but others stand in contradiction to these values; and it appears that beliefs are changing, creating a situation of intense cultural conflict. In reviewing the culture of race and ethnicity in America, we can observe several general classes or types of belief systems: (1) "melting pot" beliefs, (2) beliefs in cultural pluralism and diversity, and (3) beliefs in the "inferiority" of designated racial or ethnic populations.

"MELTING POT" BELIEFS

The waves of European and Oriental immigrants to America's shores were initially accompanied by the belief that they would become acculturated and assimilated into the American way of life.

Moreover, it was felt that by "melting" together into the "American way," a new vitality for American society would result. Melting pot beliefs reflected the value of conformity, but they implied much more: immigrants must be "active" and "achieve" their "material" rewards, and in so doing, they would not only individually "progress" but they would contribute to the betterment (or "progress") of the society. Thus, intimately connected to melting pot beliefs were beliefs in the work ethic and in taking advantage of the opportunities available in America.

These beliefs are widespread today among both the ethnic (Greeley, 1974; Novak, 1972) and the white populations. And while many ethnics have proved "unmeltable"—to use Michael Novak's phrase—most Americans believe that ethnics have melted into the mainstream of American life. But recent research indicates that ethnics hold two sets of orientations, those constant with the broader American culture and those reflective of a unique ethnic culture. Melting pot beliefs, as a result, capture only part of the reality of ethnic assimilation.

Consequences of melting pot beliefs

One of the consequences of melting pot beliefs, however, has been to condemn those who obviously have not "made it" or become assimilated into America. Most particularly blacks and browns are often condemned for not working hard enough or not taking advantage of opportunities, hence, it is "their own fault" if they do not enjoy the levels of achievement and material success of other minorities who "worked hard and made it." Such beliefs often operate to blind white ethnic and Anglo populations to the current lack of opportunity and to obvious patterns of discrimination. Moreover, they serve as a mobilizing theme for many who resist programs, or "special treatment," that are designed to break down some of the barriers facing black and brown minorities. The recent demonstrations against busing, against minority quotas in unions, and against "affirmative action" all document people's beliefs that those who have not melted into the mainstream have not worked hard enough. Such beliefs inevitably aggravate tensions among white ethnics on the one hand and blacks and browns on the other.

BELIEFS IN PLURALISM AND DIVERSITY

Such core values as individualism and freedom dictate a set of beliefs giving people the right to be different and to reveal cultural patterns that deviate from the mainstream. These beliefs contradict the value of conformity and many tenets of melting pot beliefs, yet, the recent resurgence of ethnic pride—"Polish power," "black dignity," "la raza," and other symbols drawing attention to diversity—docu-

Some beliefs hold that diversity is "good" and that not all ethnics should be "melted" into the mainstream of American life. Such beliefs are used to legitimize and encourage the "Chinatowns" of America.

ments the attempt to use beliefs in pluralism to legitimize the differences and deviations of certain ethnics from the modal American pattern. Such beliefs reflect the realities of ethnicity in which residential segregation among groups is high and where clear differences in life-styles are still evident.

At the same time, however, the failure to make it in America and maintain a separate culture can serve to stigmatize certain ethnic and racial groups. The resurgence in white ethnic cultural identification has come just as ethnics have begun to cross national educational and income averages (see Tables 9.1 and 9.2, for example). For groups who are well below these averages, blacks and browns, for example, cultural differences have often been reinterpreted as a culture of poverty or as a culture inhibiting the realization of such values as activism and achievement.

Thus, beliefs in pluralism are conditional in America. As long as there is evidence that dominant values have been realized (values such as activism, achievement, and materialism), cultural uniqueness is tolerated, and at times, even glorified. For those who have yet to evidence that they have adhered to dominant values in terms of income and education, cultural differences are viewed more suspiciously and, at times, they become the basis for stigmatizing a group. For example, black cultural patterns (values, beliefs, and the lifestyles these encouraged) were for many years codified into the "sambo" stereotype of the "shufflin' nigger" and were used to condemn the black population. On the other hand, the dress and life-style of affluent, "hustling" blacks—primarily those engaged in illicit activities—are now, on occasion, glorified. The mannerisms, exaggerated plumage, large car, and smooth-talking black male—whether a private eye, drug dealer, or pimp—have become in some "white circles" a social pattern to be emulated.

To take another example, the "peasant" image of the "siesta seeking" Mexican was used to condemn the Chicano population as lazy and unwilling to work, and thus, as undeserving of participation in American society. Similar stigmatizing of the culture of minorities has occurred for "wops," "polacks," "chinks," and other ethnic-racial

Cultural differences are the basis for ethnic stereotypes

Ethnic pride becomes more prominent as a group "makes it" in America.

groupings during their years of severe deprivation. Cultural differences, then, are more likely to be tolerated by Americans *after* a group has realized some success in American society.

BELIEFS IN INFERIORITY

Epithets like "nigger," "polack," "wop," "chink," "bean," "spick," and the like are used to condemn not just differences among ethnics, but they have also been used to label a group as inferior. During early contact such beliefs tended to be based on presumptions of "biological inferiority," but with further contact, and perhaps under the influence of social and biological science research, a more "cultural" basis for inferiority is now postulated. The label *culturally impoverished* is often popularly employed to describe a social group's "inferiority." But for biologically distinguishable groups, such as blacks and browns, biological explanation for failing to "make it" in America can still be found. For example, the efforts of such academicians as Arthur Jensen and William Schockley have again rekindled beliefs in black's innate intellectual inferiority; and while their work is widely condemned among scholars, liberals, and intellectuals, it has hit a responsive chord among many Americans.

Thus, both the definition and substance of minority problems are influenced by these three types of cultural beliefs. And depending upon one's beliefs, the identification of the problems of minorities can be based on such things as a "failure to integrate," a "failure to tolerate diversity," a situation of "cultural deprivation," or a failure to "take advantage of opportunities." But beliefs such as these are also intimately connected to the substance of minority problems. Indeed, they are often used to legitimize patterns of discrimination. Such discrimination has been well institutionalized in American society and represents a clear problem of structure.

Beliefs and social problems

THE IMPACT OF DISCRIMINATION ON BLACKS AND BROWNS

Cultural beliefs both reflect and dictate social structural arrangements. For example, beliefs about the inferiority of blacks were initially used to justify the establishment of slavery. But once established, slavery and the patterns of discrimination in the ensuing decades after its demise required rejustification and legitimization through cultural beliefs. Thus, there is a complex and reciprocal relationship between cultural ideas and social structure—a relationship that is not completely understood by social scientists. For our purposes, however, we need only be attuned to the fact that patterns of discrimination in America are related to cultural beliefs. At times, these discriminatory patterns may have caused these beliefs to be developed, while at other times, the existence of the beliefs encouraged discrimination. But once this reciprocity between ideas and social structure exists, it operates as a powerful force in perpetuating the disadvantaged position of certain minority groups. Nowhere is this more evident than in the discrimination experienced by black Americans and Mexican Americans. It is to the analysis of their situation that we now address our attention.[3]

Our discussion of blacks and Chicanos (Mexican Americans) should begin with a brief overview of their common plight (see also Tables 9.1–9.5):[4]

The plight of blacks and Chicanos

1. The average yearly income for blacks and Chicanos is, at best, only around 70 percent of that for whites; Chicanos earn somewhat more than blacks. This income gap has been closing at a very slow rate and has changed little since 1960; and in fact, it has dropped slightly for blacks over the last five years.
2. These income differences are reflected in the fact that members of these minorities are from three to five times more likely to be in a poverty situation than whites.
3. Members of these minorities are all underrepresented in skilled blue-collar and white-collar occupations.
4. In terms of total years of education, blacks lag less than Chicanos behind whites, but as Table 9.4 revealed, both receive considerably less education, on the average, than whites.
5. The life expectancy for members of these minorities averages around five years less than that for whites. Infant mortality rates, while declining, still lag considerably behind those for whites.
6. Members of these minorities are three times more likely than whites to live in housing classified as dilapidated.
7. Among these minorities, death due to disease—especially influenza, pneumonia, and tuberculosis—and accidents occurs at a much higher rate than among white.

While there are differences in income, housing conditions, education levels, and health among blacks and Mexican Americans the similar plight of these groups is more striking than the differences. The exact cultural and institutional forces that have promoted this situation are different, and the interaction between each minority population and the broader institutions of American society has also varied. But the end result has been the same: Relegation to the lowest positions in the distributive system.[5]

DISCRIMINATION AGAINST MEXICAN AMERICANS[6]

THE ECONOMIC CONQUEST OF MEXICAN AMERICANS

Mexican Americans had settled in the Southwest long before the Anglos began to move westward in the nineteenth century. In the early 1800s there were approximately 5,000 Mexicans in Texas, 7,500 in California, less than 1,000 in Arizona, and close to 60,000 in New Mexico (McWilliams, 1949:52). Most of these settlers owned land and engaged in ranching and farming. However, with the initial westward migrations of Anglos in the 1800s and then with the extension of the railroad into the Southwest in the 1850s, and the resulting flood of migrants, Mexican Americans were "hopelessly inundated by the tide of Anglo immigration, reduced to landless labor, and made politically and economically impotent" (Moore and Cuéllar, 1970:20). Thus, initial relegation of Mexican Americans to the bottom of the stratification system in the United States was a reflection of economic and demographic changes of the last century.

The change from independent rancher to landless laborer occurred first in Texas, where the fencing off of large cattle and sheep ranches destroyed the open range upon which smaller Mexican (and Anglo) ranchers depended. One by one Mexicans were forced off their land, and as the cotton industry moved into Texas and later into the rest of the Southwest, displaced ranchers and their descendents became the tenant farmers, or the cheap-wage labor, of the emerging plantation system. In New Mexico a similar process of displacement of small ranchers by large ranch enterprises occurred, although Mexicans were able to retain considerable political power because of their large numbers. In Arizona, where few Mexicans resided, the Anglo economic takeover was quick and resulted in a new pattern of economic exploitation of Mexicans by Anglos. Because the indigenous Mexicans constituted only a small labor pool, it was "necessary" to import cheap labor from across the border to maintain the large ranching and farming enterprises. This process initiated the first of many subsequent waves of immigration that were to place both the indigenous Mexican settler and the new migrant into a subordinate economic position.

Displacing the Chicano

In California Anglo economic domination of Mexicans occurred first in the northern part of the state, where large Mexican landholdings were broken up, initially, by the waves of prospectors during the gold rush and, later, by the steady flow of settlers and squatters. In southern California, Mexicans maintained their landholdings and political power for some time; but with the drought of 1862, followed by a devastating flood, many Mexican landowners were placed in economic jeopardy. Then, as taxes began to rise and cattle prices dropped, the large Mexican estates were broken up. And when Anglos began to flood into the southern part of the state, the now landless Mexicans were used as menial labor for the large, Anglo-owned agricultural enterprises that began to dominate the state.

In all these states, the railroad was of particular importance in subordinating the Mexican resident and immigrant. First, the railroad brought in thousands of Anglos who began to push Mexicans off the land. Second, the railroads required large work gangs of inexpensive, mobile labor, which were gotten by encouraging immigration of impoverished workers from Mexico. As these migrants poured into the Southwest in search of new opportunities, the social image of Mexican Americans who had lived in the Southwest for generations was altered from that of independent landholders and entrepreneurs to one of unskilled, migrant laborers. And it was probably during this time that beliefs about the "sleepy, lazy, siesta-seeking Mexican peasant" began to be developed as a means for justifying their use in menial economic positions. If a group can be stigmatized as inferior and unwilling to work unless subordinated to Anglo domination, it is easier to justify their exploitation.

The early part of the twentieth century saw an extension of the economic forces that were relegating Mexicans to the bottom of the stratification system. The emergence of mass, capital-heavy, labor-intensive, irrigated farming in the Southwest assured that no small farmer could afford either the capital investment or the labor pool necessary to farm melons, grapes, citrus fruit, sugar beets, cotton, and vegetables; the result was that the last of the remaining Mexican ranchers and farmers were forced off the land (Moore and Cuéllar, 1970:20–21). Furthermore, the need for a large, migratory labor force to harvest the crops of these new farms stimulated even more migration of unskilled labor from across the border. And the expansion and extension of the cotton industry west of Texas served as a similar stimulus for Mexican migrations (Waters, 1941). The proliferation of railroads in the Southwest continued well into this century and was also a major force behind the escalated migration of Mexican laborers, who were shipped around in boxcars much like cattle.

Importation of bracero labor

By the 1920s Mexican Americans constituted a migrant proletariat who could harvest crops and work on the railroads. During the same decade small groups of Mexican Americans began to appear in the factories of Michigan, Ohio, Indiana, and Pennsylvania. Many acquired nonfarm skills and settled in large urban areas, initiating the urbanization of Chicanos.

The depression undermined the gains made by these urban, working class Mexicans and further impoverished the migrant agricultural workers. Yet, during the 1930s many Chicanos fled from depressed rural conditions in search of employment in cities, but only with the onset of World War II did large numbers of Mexican workers eventually find employment. Many others enlisted in the army and acquired work skills there. While the offspring of indigenous Mexican ranchers and early migrant workers were urbanizing during the war, the importation of temporary and alien Mexican *bracero* labor for work in the wartime agricultural boom was again accelerated. When demand for bracero labor receded in the postwar period, illegal immigration continued, culminating in the mass deportation of millions of Mexicans during the 1950s. Of those who avoided deportation, many became the current migratory work force that harvests the crops of the massive agrobusinesses in Texas, Arizona, and California. Even under pressures from unionization by Cesar Chavez and the United Farm Workers, and more recently, the Teamsters Union, this labor force works at low wages (yielding only a poverty level of living) and frequently under unsanitary and unsafe conditions. For those who escape to the cities to join the already large urban concentrations of Chicanos in California and Texas, few economic opportunities are available (Kramer, 1970:171; Heller, 1966; Madsen, 1964).

Today urban Chicanos, who constitute a majority of the Mexican-American population, suffer from severe economic discrimination (Moore and Cuéllar, 1970:60–65; Bullock, 1964; Ramirez, 1967). Chicanos get lower pay than Anglos for the same kind of work. They are grossly underrepresented in highly unionized occupations because of union discrimination. Their lack of formal education is apparently used to keep them from even those jobs that do not require extensive education. Even with education, Chicanos receive less pay and lower job status than Anglos with equivalent education.

In sum, the economic forces operating against Mexican Americans display a unique pattern. Initial agricultural development displaced the early Mexican settler; further economic development and the extension of railroads into the Southwest created a demand for cheap and mobile labor which, in turn, stimulated massive migration from Mexico. During the twentieth century Mexican Americans have become highly urbanized and now constitute a large underemployed urban proletariat that is predominantly poor. Like the Indians, Mexican Americans have suffered the economic abuses directed against a colonized, indigenous population; and like the black slaves, Mexican Americans have suffered abuses directed against an immigrant people brought in to perform cheap agricultural labor. The economic exploitation of Chicanos has not been as great as it has been for either blacks or Indians, and yet, the fact that Chicanos have had to endure *both* forms of exploitation has pushed them into the bottom rungs of the American stratification system.

POLITICAL DISCRIMINATION

Except in New Mexico, and for a period in southern California, Mexican Americans have suffered from political discrimination. The original Mexican American settlers became politically disfranchised when they lost their land to the large agricultural, ranching, mining, and railroad interests that controlled state legislators and sought to keep Mexicans in an economically and politically subordinate position. These efforts were promoted by the fact that many migrant Mexicans were aliens and had no voting rights. Over time, as both indigenous and migrant Mexicans became defined *as one social category* (especially with further codification of beliefs about the inferiority of "these peasants from across the border"), the Anglo majority established a variety of procedures—from a poll tax to open primaries—to keep impoverished Mexicans out of the political arena. While these political tactics are no longer legal, Chicanos are now only beginning to enter the political arena which for so long was openly discriminatory.

Early Mexican settlers and migrants also suffered from the lack of a well-developed political structure in the Southwest (Moore and Cuéllar, 1970:33). Unlike the early white ethnic migrants in the Northeast, Mexican migrants confronted a loosely organized political system because there were few large cities to support political machines and because party organization within the southwestern states or territories was only in its incipiency. There were simply no political opportunities, thus, Mexican Americans were not able to acquire training in either big-city or state politics—a condition that greatly facilitated the social mobility of early European ethnic groups, especially the Irish. In Texas and California, where the political structure was most developed, large economic interests controlled the state legislatures and kept Mexicans confined to migrant shantytowns where they remained politically isolated.

The prolonged border dispute between Mexico and the United States further isolated Mexican settlers and migrants from Anglo political institutions. The open war between the United States and Mexico in 1846 placed Mexican Americans in the unfavorable position of being identified with a political enemy. Even after the Treaty of Guadalupe Hidalgo ended the war, border raids and skirmishes between Anglos and Mexicans persisted for nearly 60 years. In many regions Mexican Americans remained politically isolated for fear of

The lack of political opportunities

arousing Anglo resentment stemming from these prolonged border skirmishes.

This legacy of political disfranchisement has followed Chicanos as they have migrated into the growing urban areas of the Southwest over recent decades. Many urbanites have not even had citizenship status. And the rate of naturalization of migrants has been very low because migrants have tended to retain political loyalties to Mexico, while harboring a distrust of the American political system (Grebler, 1966). This distrust was justified in the 1950s during "Operation Wetback," when over 3 million alien Mexicans were apprehended,

Operation Wetback

The United Farm Workers, led by Cesar Chavez, have become a powerful political force in the southwest. Here in Delano, California, a UFW meeting is religious, educational, and political.

without benefit of a court-issued warrant of arrest, and expelled from the country. Aside from illegal apprehension, expulsion was often done illegally—without any attention to due processes of law (a court hearing, the right to a lawyer and to plead a case, etc.). Furthermore, hundreds of thousands of American citizens who "looked Mexican" were stopped, searched, and forced to prove their citizenship—a practice that would not be tolerated by the Anglo population (Moore and Cuéllar, 1970:43).

The distrust of American governmental agencies arising out of Operation Wetback persists to the present day. Although there has been a growing participation of Mexican Americans in state legislatures and Congress, they are still underrepresented in most local, state, and national bodies. This situation is reflected in the lack of federal programs directed at Mexican *barrios* (slums) in the large cities of the Southwest; especially notable was the absence of Mexican American programs during the peak period of the War on Poverty. While various economic and political organizations of Chicanos have emerged over the last 20 years, these groups do not exert the political pressure proportionate to the size of the Mexican American population—the nation's second largest disadvantaged minority. The burgeoning Chicano movement and the rise of national leaders, such as Cesar Chavez, to a position of political prominence have so far done little to balance the historical legacy of political discrimination against, and isolation of, Mexican Americans.

EDUCATIONAL DISCRIMINATION

While their average educational attainment varies from state to state, from a low in Texas to a high in California, Mexican Americans, as an aggregate, lag behind most other minorities in number of years of schooling completed (L. Miller, 1964; Grebler, 1967; Stoddard, 1973). Despite a large increase over the last 20 years in the number of school years completed, Mexican Americans are still far behind blacks, Anglos, and Orientals, even in the 14–24 age group where dramatic changes in educational achievement would be most evident (Grebler, 1967).

One reason for such low educational attainment has been the resentment of Mexican Americans to their confinement as outsiders in a community and to segregated and inferior schools. Originally, and even today in rural communities, Mexican Americans have been forced into labor camps; as the children of farm laborers became resentful of their segregation into inferior schools, they tended to drop out and subsequently find themselves in the same jobs as their immigrant fathers. In urban areas considerable residential and educational segregation persists; Chicano youths must endure inferior teachers, dilapidated school facilities, and a white Anglo curriculum. While these urban students go further in school than their rural counterparts, many still drop out of high school and less than 10 percent go to college (this figure deviates from that of "Spanish-speaking" in Table 9.2 because this category includes many more people than Mexican Americans).

In addition to de facto school segregation stemming from patterns of residential segregation, Chicano youths are often deliberately segregated from Anglos. Such segregation, especially in Texas, is justified by a series of outdated beliefs. Teachers and administrators tend to assume that the bilingual student will automatically have learning problems and that the Mexican American student, as a member of "a traditional, peasant culture," will not be highly motivated to achieve. By using this variant of beliefs about Chicano inferiority, it is then assumed that Chicano youths cannot compete with Anglo children, and until they are assimilated in the melting pot, they must remain segregated "for their own good." The fact that segregation persists through secondary school, where language problems and cultural obstacles would have lessened, reveals the real intent behind school segregation. More importantly, the stereotypes used by teachers and administrators are self-fulfilling in that they are used to justify placing Chicano youths into inferior programs which, in turn, probably lessen aspirations and educational achievement. Such a situation, of course, decreases the ability of Mexican Americans to realize beliefs in the melting pot.

School segregation

Within these segregated schools, cultural assimilation into a white Anglo world is supposed to occur. In accordance with melting pot beliefs, students are often punished for speaking Spanish in the playground; the Anglo curriculum is rigidly imposed; and Anglo dress and behavior codes are tightly enforced in some schools. While in a few places, such as urban California, the schools are more flexible and accommodating to the cultural uniqueness of Mexican American youths (in accordance with beliefs in cultural pluralism), the suppression of Mexican culture remains widespread throughout the Southwest. Faced with such suppression, Mexican American youths simply leave school at the earliest possible age, thus decreasing their job opportunities.

Classroom discrimination

THE LAW AND MEXICAN AMERICANS

Mexican Americans have long been subject to extensive surveillance by local, state, and federal enforcement agencies. Because Mexican Americans constitute an impoverished, physically distinguishable minority living in high-crime rural and urban barrios, local police are more likely to be "suspicious," which increases the probability that they will "watch" and perhaps "question" residents—a practice that may, at times, be necessary in a high crime area but which is deeply resented by Chicanos. We must remember that it was not long ago that Mexican Americans were subject to vigilante law enforcement initiated by ranching, fruit-growing, and mining enterprises in efforts to "resolve" labor disputes. This legacy of vigilante law, coupled with current police practices, has created a "culture of suspicion" of Anglo institutions that has contributed to Mexican American withdrawal into ghetto areas in both rural and urban areas (Lohman, 1966:55). In some states, particularly Texas, Chicanos have had to confront special state units, such as the Texas Rangers, which were originally established to deal with the "Mexican problem" (Moore and Cuéllar, 1970:89). It was only recently, after the abuses of the Rangers were exposed, that the Rangers were reduced to a token force.

The most unique feature of Chicano relations with the police revolves around the issue of citizenship. Since many Mexican Americans were imported as alien labor and then deported *en masse* by the federal government during the 1950s, Mexican Americans have always been subject to regulation by the federal Border Patrol. The officers of the Border Patrol have wide authority under federal law, an authority often used to check up on the citizenship status of Mexican American families. For example, officers can stop families on highways, go to their homes, enter their places of work, and engage in extensive questioning. Realizing the power of the Border Patrol to disrupt the lives of Mexican Americans, some local and state police officers "threatened to call the Border Patrol" to achieve compliance (sometimes illegally) with their demands, such as search, seizure, and detention. Thus, Mexican Americans are subject to a kind of triple jeopardy from federal, state, and local police forces, all of which have the power to intrude into their lives and demand proof of not only innocence to a crime, but also of their citizenship.

The "culture of suspicion"

DISCRIMINATION AGAINST BLACK AMERICANS[7]

ECONOMIC DISCRIMINATION

While it is not clear just when slavery became institutionalized, by 1670 most blacks in America, and their offspring, were condemned to perpetual servitude. Whether the expansion of slavery was encouraged by the emerging plantation system in the South or the exis-

Slavery as economic oppression

tence of slaves allowed for the development of the plantation system can never be known (Genovese, 1965; Fogel and Engerman, 1974). The relationship was probably reciprocal, but the increasing reliance of the Southern economy on labor-intensive agricultural crops, such as cotton, tobacco, hemp, rice, wheat and sugar, caused the rapid expansion of slavery. Once a large slave population existed, fear of revolts from oppressed slaves probably perpetuated slavery, even if it became a less efficient form of economic organization.[8]

The importation of blacks and the creation of slavery was justified and legitimized by well-developed beliefs about their "inferiority" (Turner and Singleton, 1976). The institution of slavery stood clearly at odds with basic values of freedom and equality, and thus, only by viewing blacks as inferior beings who were "less intelligent" and prone to "animal instincts" could their subjugation be justified in the South. Such beliefs were, of course, challenged by more progressive beliefs that slaves could be capable of understanding white ways and they could thus be free. Even progressive beliefs, however, did not seriously question the assumption of black inferiority.

While the importation of slaves was outlawed in the early years of the nineteenth century, the large size of the black population was sufficient to provide labor for not only agriculture, but also for the growing industrial sectors of the southern economy (Starobin, 1970). Slavery is, of course, the most oppressive form of economic discrimination since a slave is "property" that can be used, mistreated, bought, or sold at the owner's discretion. Moreover, as property slaves possessed few familial, legal, political, and personal rights (Stamp, 1956). And while various northern groups opposed slavery as an institution, little was done to change this economic situation, except for a very brief period in the post–Civil War period.

Although the period of Reconstruction after the Civil War saw many blacks participating in political and educational spheres, white conservatives soon regained control of state legislatures and were able to destroy Reconstruction programs. By 1900 blacks had been forced off their land (given to them during Reconstruction) onto tenant farms owned by whites, or they had become part of the cheap labor pool that provided the muscle and the menial services for white enterprises. Such tactics were justified by beliefs that, without supervision and subordination to white control, blacks would degenerate into "their natural state:" they would be "inactive" and "unwilling to work," they would be "prone to crime," and they would tend to "lust after white women."

Postslavery economic discrimination

With the onset of World War I and the increased opportunities in northern industrial cities, blacks began to leave the South in search of new economic opportunities; they encountered the same white violence and economic discrimination that they had left in the South. Except during the height of wartime production, blacks were excluded from skilled jobs in industry and relegated, once again, to a cheap and menial labor force.

During the depression black migrations to urban areas stopped, while those in both rural and urban areas suffered enormously from unemployment and hunger. In the mid-1930s great masses of blacks received some form of public assistance; but even so, welfare allocations were differentially bestowed on blacks and whites (Pinkney, 1969:33–34). The New Deal marked a change in beliefs and policies toward blacks; politicians and legislators were now becoming "concerned" about their plight. The Joint Committee on National Recovery—a combination of various black rights groups—revealed the differential wages paid to black and white workers in both the private economy and the federally run public works projects. Yet discrimination continued, for it was only under the threat of a massive march on Washington did President Franklin D. Roosevelt issue an executive order banning discrimination against blacks in the growing number of government-financed wartime industries. The large labor unions, particularly the Congress of Industrial Organizations, allowed some blacks into their ranks, although separate locals for blacks and whites were often maintained.

"Cultural inferiority" replaces "biological inferiority"

Such changes were justified by beliefs that blacks were not innately inferior, but because of their long period of servitude, they were "culturally inferior" and in need of both job opportunities and "cultural rehabilitation" to assure that they would take advantage of opportunities.

In the post–World War II period, with the persistence of racial discrimination in employment and white supremacy practices, even in the face of changing beliefs about innate inferiority, blacks became increasingly militant and began to press for equality. In response, President Harry S Truman integrated the heretofore segregated armed forces and established the National Committee on Civil Rights. Several states enacted antidiscrimination laws—most notably the New York Fair Employment Practices Law of 1945. Furthermore, the U.S. Supreme Court began to evidence an antidiscriminatory profile, culminating in the 1954 decision prohibiting racial segregation in public education.

Although the economic plight of blacks improved in the postwar period and in the early 1950s, the last decade has seen only slight change in their economic situation. Blacks are still overrepresented in menial, farm, and service occupations; they are underrepresented in professional and managerial positions; black unemployment has remained at twice that of white unemployment; blacks tend to be unemployed longer than whites in equivalent job categories; they earn less in the same job as whites; college-educated blacks earn about the same amount of money as high-school-educated whites; and black income as a percentage of white income has actually dropped from 61 percent in 1969 to 58 percent in 1973.[9]

    The relatively deprived economic position of black Americans cannot be explained solely in terms of inadequate education, cultural impoverishment, unstable family life, and similar forces. Rather, economic discrimination remains—over 100 years after slavery—a major cause of black unemployment and underemployment.[10] State and private employment agencies still discriminate against blacks eligible (in terms of education) for white-collar work. Blacks are often assigned occupational classifications not commensurate with their skills; they tend to receive fewer referrals than whites to employers; they are rarely referred to openings in banks, loan firms, and other commerical establishments; and they are less likely than whites to be referred to retail stores and other businesses (Schaffer et al., 1970:44). Blacks have at times been excluded from blue-collar occupations because of the discriminatory policies of trade unions, including those of the plumbers, carpenters, electricians, printers, metal workers, and machinists (Schaffer et al., 1970:44). Typical craft union strategies for discriminating against blacks include: (1) excluding blacks from apprenticeship programs and (2) insisting, in collective bargaining agreements and contracts, that the union—not the contractor or builder—maintain control of the hiring and firing of workers (Seligman, 1970:50–51). Industrial unions that incorporate diverse workers on an industrywide basis sometimes still engage in discrimination by forcing blacks into the lower-paying jobs and by segregating blacks into separate locals. The instances of this latter tactic have declined under pressure from the federal government. Yet, the legacy of both these tactics now haunts blacks who are unskilled and hence unable to join unions and, in many cases, unable to "qualify" for apprenticeship programs. The lack of skill among black workers is a result of a historical legacy of discrimination by many unions; this lack of skill has then been used by some unions to justify exclusion of blacks. For example, the U.S. Commission on Civil Rights reported that in the late 1960s, of the 1667 apprenticeships available in St. Louis craft unions, only 7 were held by blacks; or of the 750 building trade apprenticeships in Baltimore, 20 were black; and in both Atlanta and Baltimore, there are no black apprentices in the plumbers, iron workers, electrical workers, sheet and metal workers, and painters unions (Turner and Singleton, 1976). Even among industrial unions organized on an industrywide basis and in which blacks are proportionately represented, discrimination still

Present forms of economic discrimination

occurs in the recruiting of apprentices for the better-paying jobs. For example, in one Detroit auto plant, 23 percent of the workers were black, but only one black was involved in the 289 apprenticeships (Knowles and Prewitt, 1969:23).

Employers are also engaged in discrimination against blacks. For example, in the South separate white and black pay scales have only recently been outlawed. In many industries in both the North and South, even those with government contracts, blacks are simply excluded from certain occupations. These practices clearly violate the 1964 Civil Rights Act, but enforcing the law has proved difficult. The Civil Rights Division of the Department of Justice is simply too small to prosecute all the violations reported by the Employment Opportunity Commission (created by the 1964 Civil Rights Act). More importantly, the government has been hesitant to prosecute companies on whom it depends for "vital" defense contract items, especially those companies located in the districts of powerful congressional committee chairmen (Schaffer et al., 1970:53). Even within the federal government, there are signs of employment discrimination against blacks. While blacks are overrepresented in government jobs, they are underrepresented in the higher-paying government jobs (Pinkney, 1969:80).

POLITICAL DISCRIMINATION

The Civil War was ostensibly fought over the slavery issue,[11] and the fact that it was one of the bloodiest wars in American history might, to an outsider, give an indication of a strong governmental commitment to emancipation. However, the commitment was short-lived and ultimately resulted in the federal government's abandonment of the "black cause" by 1880 in the name of political stability and unification. After this betrayal there followed decades of neglect, resulting in the creation of a black "caste" that only recently shows signs of breaking down.

After the Civil War, President Abraham Lincoln conceived of the Rconstruction in the South and the emancipation of blacks as a presidential function.[12] With his assassination and the ascendance of Andrew Johnson to the presidency, Reconstruction efforts began to ignore the situation of blacks in the South. White violence against blacks again became widespread, and a series of oppressive *Black Codes* were enacted at the state and local level. To counteract this presidential neglect, Congress took over the responsibility for Reconstruction and proceeded to engage in a comprehensive program for assisting the newly emancipated slaves. During this period of Radical Reconstruction, the South was divided into military districts and ex-

Radical
Reconstruction

slaves became temporary wards of the government. The Black Codes were suspended by the Freedman's Bureau in 1865, and in 1866, to supplement the Thirteenth Amendment (abolishing slavery), Congress enacted a Civil Rights Act (later to be the Fourteenth Amendment), which gave blacks full citizenship rights. Other federal legislation encouraged blacks to register and vote, with the result that widespread participation of blacks in state and national politics became typical. Although black legislators never controlled any southern state and no black ever became a governor, blacks could be found in high-ranking positions throughout state governments. Coupled with these new political freedoms, blacks began to enter schools and skilled occupations and hence initiate movement up the stratification system.

However, this new freedom and social mobility began to decline as federal troops were withdrawn in the 1870s, stimulating a wave of white violence against blacks. By the middle of the decade, blacks had been pushed out of schools, skilled jobs, and many governmental positions. Then in 1877 the presidential election of 1876 became deadlocked and was thrown into Congress; the Republicans, in order to secure the election of Rutherford B. Hayes, agreed to abandon all Reconstruction efforts and leave the matters of race to the South to decide. Very quickly, blacks were forced once again into almost totally subservient social and economic positions that differed little from those of pre–Civil War days.

The Great Betrayal

After this second betrayal the situation of black Americans was ignored by the federal government. During the depression, some federal assistance was provided for blacks, and President Roosevelt appointed a black committee—known as the Black Cabinet—to advise him on the plight of blacks. But little was really done to assist those who remained in the South or who were trapped in the slums of northern cities. Even during the post–World War II period extending into the 1950s, comparatively little federal assistance to blacks occurred, despite the 1954 landmark school desegregation decision of the Supreme Court and the integration of the armed forces. Although public housing and urban renewal improved somewhat the housing conditions of blacks in urban areas, they also confined blacks to the urban cores of large cities, where educational and job opportunities were not as great as in the suburbs. While the federally backed welfare establishment grew during this period and provided many black families with desperately needed assistance, the multitude of abuses and injustices leveled on blacks negated many of its more benevolent features.

Probably the most comprehensive effort to assist blacks since Radical Reconstruction has been the war on poverty initiated at the mid-

point of the 1960s. Coupled with a more vigorous federal commitment to the Supreme Court school desegregation ruling of 1954, some
assistance to blacks occurred, but in less than a decade the federal
commitment to both these goals, especially the war on poverty, has
waned. The conspicuous projects of the mid-1960s—Operation Head
Start, the Neighborhood Youth Corps, the Job Corps, Upward Bound,
VISTA, and even the Office of Economic Opportunity itself—have become increasingly obscure (see Chapter 8 for details on the war on
poverty).

EDUCATIONAL DISCRIMINATION

Prior to the Civil War, most black Americans received no formal
education, although a few were given training in an effort to extract
more skilled labor from them. In the brief period of Radical Reconstruction following the Civil War, however, blacks began to enter the
emerging system of public schools, but with the demise of congressional Reconstruction in the 1870s, virtually all blacks were expelled
from southern schools, although a few did manage to secure education in segregated public facilities and church schools.

Since the 1870s the black population has made significant gains in
years of education completed. The percent of illiterates has dropped
from 80 percent in 1870 to less than 7 percent in 1970, although this
figure is still nearly four times higher than that for whites. The total
number of years in school for blacks is higher than that for Mexican
Americans (see Table 9.4), although it lags considerably behind that
for whites. Most of the educational gains of blacks have occurred at
the primary level, where today 99 percent of black youths are
enrolled, and at the secondary level, where nearly 90 percent of black
youths are still in school. Even though a larger proportion of blacks
attend college than ever before, the proportion of whites attending
college has also increased, maintaining the educational gap (see
Table 9.5).[13] Despite the educational gains of blacks, their economic
positions relative to whites has remained about the same: In 1974 a
black high school graduate still earned roughly the same as a white
dropout, and a college-educated black earned not much more than a
white high school graduate.[14] These data clearly reveal the operation
of discriminatory forces in the broader society that cut off opportunities for educated blacks.

Even in this decade of awareness over inequality in the schools,
blacks still must endure discriminatory practices. While school facilities at the lower education level, even in segregated schools, appear
to be becoming more equal, the middle-class environment of the
school tends to alienate many black students. The emphasis by white

Black educational gains

Economic stagnation

teachers and administrators on verbal skills and competitive examinations, as well as the use of IQ and achievement tests normed to white populations, apparently suppress the achievement of children who come from somewhat different cultural backgrounds.

Blacks also suffer from educational abuses at the college and university level. In 1968 over 50 percent of the black college students attended all black colleges, accounting for 80 percent of the degrees earned by blacks. These colleges are grossly underfinanced (only 3.5 percent of the $4 billion in federal aid given to higher education in 1969 went to predominately black colleges), and their need is much greater than that of white schools. Furthermore, black land-grant colleges do not receive their share of federal and state funds. For example, federal and state aid to white colleges averaged out to $2300 per student, whereas the corresponding figure was $1365 for blacks in 1969. Coupled with the fact that students in black colleges come from poor families with average incomes of $4000 per year, tuition costs must be low and hence cannot finance, to any great degree, black college facilities. The result of these financial squeezes on black colleges is an inferior education. Teachers' salaries are low; physical facilities are barely adequate; and the curricula are narrow and do not allow for training in professional occupations, except teaching (Seligman, 1970:47).

Thus, in terms of quantity and quality of education, blacks still lag behind whites despite some educational gains—reflected by the fact that blacks are better off than Chicanos in terms of educational attainment.

LEGAL DISCRIMINATION

By 1650, several American colonies had enacted laws distinguishing white and black endentured servants, for blacks were increasingly consigned to servitude for life. Beliefs about black inferiority and "bestiality" had become sufficiently codified that by the early eighteenth century they were enacted into similar groups of laws in all southern states:

1. Blacks were to be slaves for life.
2. Slaves were property *and* persons; owners held property rights, while incurring some responsibilities to blacks as persons.

The legal tenets of slavery

3. Black children were to inherit their mother's position.
4. Marriages between blacks and whites were prohibited.
5. Blacks were not allowed to acquire property.
6. Blacks were not allowed to enter civil contracts, engage in litigation, testify against whites in court, or sit on juries.

In the North, laws were not nearly so severe and varied enormously from state to state. In the early 1800s, the existence of free blacks in the North and total slavery in the South was increasingly debated, and with the entrance of Missouri to the Union in 1821, a vague congressional proclamation allowed northern and southern states to enact entirely contradictory laws, with the North increasingly enacting "liberalized" laws and the South ever more severe laws. Even with liberal formal laws in the North, however, informal "Jim Crow" practices—restricting black access to jobs, education, recreational facilities, transportation, and housing—often guided actions more than the formal law. Thus, at the dawn of the Civil War, formal law and informal practices in the South were highly correlated, whereas in the North, liberal formal laws were frequently contradicted by informal Jim Crow practices.

"Jim Crow" practices

With the demise of Radical Reconstruction, Jim Crow practices were extended to all regions of the North and South, especially with respect to black access to public accommodations, public conveyances, and amusement facilities used by whites. Indicative of their

Until very recently, a visible evidence of Jim Crow could still be found. Discrimination is now more subtle.

broad use and support is the fact that they were sanctioned in a series of landmark decisions by the Supreme Court. For example, the Supreme Court declared unconstitutional the Civil Rights Act of 1875 which had made it a crime to deny people equal access to public places; and in 1896 the Court ruled that segregated facilities for blacks and whites were not a violation of the Thirteenth and Fourteenth Amendments. As it declared: "If one race be inferior to the other socially, the Constitution cannot put them on the same plane" (Pinkney, 1969:28). As a result, white supremacy beliefs on black inferiority became institutionalized by the Supreme Court and discrimination in virtially all spheres of social life became the tacit law of the land. It was not until the post–World War II period that Jim Crow began to recede; and only with the 1954 school desegregation decision and with the civil rights acts of the last decade did the American legal system *explicitly forbid* Jim Crow laws and practices. Yet much damage had been done—nearly a century of legal discrimination had forced blacks into the bottom ranks of the stratification system. And even today, with civil rights laws on the books, the Justice Department has at times failed to enforce the legal rights of black Americans.

In criminal cases, police discrimination and abuse, as well as disproportionately strong indictments and long jail sentences for crimes against whites, are typically imposed upon blacks by a legal system staffed predominately by whites. As a number of studies reveal, blacks in urban ghettos list "police practices" as their most intense grievance, revealing the still uneasy accommodation between black Americans and the legal system. And while police and community groups have made significant efforts to reduce tensions, considerable estrangement between the enforcers of the law and black Americans remains.

Thus, the history of black Americans' treatment under the law is one of inequity. Unlike most minorities, blacks have experienced formally sanctioned discrimination. As a result, blacks have been segregated and excluded from all major social, recreational, and institutional spheres—a situation that forced them to the bottom rungs of the stratification.

SUMMARY

This chapter should be read within the context of the forces maintaining inequality and poverty in American society. Running through the general pattern of inequality and poverty are the additional forces of racial and ethnic discrimination. Discrimination at an interpersonal level often reveals people's racism and bigotry, but *it also re-*

flects broader institutional and cultural patterns. While basic social institutions are, in part, a reflection of people's beliefs, the relationship is reciprocal: Beliefs are also shaped by basic institutional arrangements. What is more, institutions have a kind of autonomy and capacity to perpetuate themselves, even when values and beliefs change.

These facts should indicate that discrimination transcends "just plain folk" interacting with one another. People are only actors in a script written by the structure of basic American institutions: the economy, government, education, and the law. To understand why certain racial and ethnic groups are disproportionately represented at the lower end of the American stratification system required an examination of the historical forces that have shaped current institutional arrangements. These forces have operated somewhat differently on the two minority populations discussed in detail (Chicanos and blacks), but there are many similarities in the general pattern of institutional discrimination.

In the economic sphere blacks and Chicanos have suffered from somewhat similar abuses. Whether as *bracero* labor or slaves, these groups have been used as a low-wage, unskilled labor pool. Until very recently, Attempts to remedy this stiuation were (and are still) resisted by those economic interests dependent on such labor and by the beliefs of many white ethnics that blacks and browns have not worked hard enough or taken advantage of opportunities. These minority peoples have thus been kept from joining unions in proportionate numbers; and even when they were able to crack the union barrier, they were often forced into the lower job classifications. Coupled with employer discrimination, they have been kept economically deprived and dependent on the welfare programs of government.

Politically, blacks and Chicanos have traditionally been disfranchised. Members of each group have been treated at various times as somewhat less than full citizens—a practice that has delayed their involvement in the political process where they can better press for their interests. As less than full citizens and as economically impoverished groups, they have had to rely on federal programs that are notable for their inadequacy and insensitivity to the needs of these populations. Furthermore, these programs have typically addressed the more superficial conditions of the minority poor and have avoided the hard issues such as housing integration and income redistribution.

Educationally, minority populations still endure discrimination despite clear recognition of the importance of education for realizing values of achievement and materialism. Several common patterns of discrimination are encountered by blacks and Chicanos. First, these minority groups tend to be residentially segregated as outcast populations from the rest of society. One result of segregation is that minority young are likely to attend segregated schools in urban enclaves and rural backwaters that are inferior to schools serving suburban white students. Overcrowded classrooms, lack of teacher credentialing, poor texts, and rigid curricula are still typical of schools serving minority students, even though the gap between facilities serving *poor* whites and minority populations has now closed. Second, when minority students attend integrated schools, they are most likely to suffer teacher and counselor discrimination and to be tracked into separate and inferior lanes on the presumption that they are "culturally inferior" and, therefore, cannot compete with whites. Third, schools rarely accommodate themselves to the diverse cultural backgrounds of minority students; rather, in accordance with melting pot beliefs, they attempt to assimilate students and force them to abandon their cultural uniqueness and conform to a white, middle-class images of the "good student." As a direct outgrowth of these discriminatory practices, minority students are more likely to drop out of school and less likely to go on to college than are their white counterparts, thereby decreasing their job opportunities and ability to ascend the stratification ladder.

Even in the aftermath of a series of civil rights acts and sympathetic Supreme Court decisions, the institution of law remains a discriminatory force in America. The highly publicized civil rights legislation of the federal government is often not enforced at the local community level, where police and courts often discriminate against minority groups. More importantly, decades of legal abuse have preceded current attempts to legislate equality. For example, restrictive legislation, discrimination in hiring, separate wage scales for minorities, union discrimination, segregated schooling, poll taxes, and other discriminatory practices were allowed to continue even though they violated basic constitutional rights. Even today legal action against such policies is sometimes slow and ineffective.

Today in American communities, minority-group individuals can still expect to find that (1) they are more likely to be viewed as "suspicious" by police than lower-class whites; (2) they are more likely to be arrested than whites; (3) they should be prepared to be charged with a more severe crime than a white for the same alleged behavior, especially if the crime is against a white; (4) because of their poverty and inability to afford legal defense, they are more likely to be forced to "cop a plea" (even when innocent) and plead guilty to a lesser charge than are whites; and (5) they can expect longer jail sentences than whites when they commit a crime against a white.

The impact of tacit legal sanctioning of economic, political, and educational discrimination is obvious: it blocks access to those institutional spheres necessary for mobility out of poverty, and it prevents the minority poor from realizing dominant American values. The consequences of more direct discrimination of police and courts against individual members of minority groups are more difficult to assess. At the very least they deprive an individual of basic constitutional rights, and at the most they generate fear, distrust, and hatred among large segments of minority populations—not only toward the legal system, but also toward the broader institutions it sanctions. While changes in the position of minorities is occurring, racial and ethnic relations will remain, for many decades, one of America's most enduring and intense problems of structure.

NOTES

1. The topic of ethnicity has recently become recognized as important to understanding American society. For recent efforts to deal with the topic, see: Glazer and Moynihan, 1975; Novak, 1972; Greeley, 1975, 1974.

2. For the most pertinent census report, see the U.S. Department of Commerce's *Subject Report: National Origin and Language*, 1973. For more detailed survey data, see Andrew M. Greeley's (1974) excellent summary analysis.

3. In focusing only on blacks and Chicanos, we should not underemphasize the discrimination experienced by other large minority groups: Cubans, Indians, Puerto Ricans, and Asians, as well as "white ethnics." However, the growing political protests among young blacks and Chicanos make these groups currently more visible than the others and, hence, more likely to be considered a social problem. Also, since black Americans represent the largest racially identified minority, and Chicanos comprise the largest ethnic group in the United States, it is appropriate that our detailed analysis focus on these two groups.

4. For information on income and education levels for these minorities, see *Census of the Population, Characteristics of Population*, 1960, and 1970, vol. 1. For secondary analysis of statistics on characteristics of these minority populations, see Moore, 1970; Pinkney, 1969; L. Miller, 1964; Brophy and Aberle, 1966; Spicer,

1962; Special Subcommittee on Indian Education, 1968; and Knowles and Prewitt, 1969.

5. For more theoretical analyses of such relegation, see Turner and Singleton, 1976; Blauner, 1972; W. Newman, 1973; and Daniels and Kitano, 1970. The analysis offered in this chapter is more of a description of what happened, only partial answers as to why it happened are given.

6. For basic reference works on Mexican Americans, see Stoddard, 1973; Grebler et al., 1970; Steiner, 1970; and Moore and Cuéllar, 1970.

7. For basic references on the history of white racism against blacks, see Turner and Singleton, 1976; Glasurd and Smith, 1972; and Feldstein, 1972.

8. For more detailed descriptions and analyses of slaves and the slave community, see Blassingame, 1972 and Feldstein, 1971.

9. For data on black income during the 1960s, see U.S. Department of Labor, Bureau of Labor Statistics, *Recent Trends in Social and Economic Conditions of Negroes in the United States 1968;* and Current Population Reports, *Consumer Income*, U.S. Department of Commerce, 1970. For somewhat dated, but still accurate portrayals of black economic plight, see Pinkney, 1969:77–90; Moynihan, 1965; Siegal, 1965; Batchelder, 1964; and Seligman, 1970.

10. For a more detailed discussion, see the 1968 U.S. Department of Labor report on *Equality of Opportunity in Manpower Programs.*

11. However, as many commentators have noted, the war may actually have been fought over political and economic issues as much as over slavery. Emancipation may have been a convenient justification to suppress the South politically and economically.

12. For basic references on the Civil War and the period of Reconstruction, see Franklin, 1961; Trowbridge, 1956; Simkins, 1959; Woodward, 1951.

13. More recent data than that in Table 9.5 indicates that during the early 1970s black college enrollment increased dramatically. Black college enrollments now appear to be approaching a rate close to that recorded for whites; however, these new data are very tentative. It will take close to a decade to determine if a clear trend is evident.

14. This situation may change, however, since black graduates from white colleges are now in great demand because of pressure from the federal government and from the genuine concern of many corporations. But it will be at least a decade before these improvements are reflected in income data for blacks. In fact, black income as a proportion of white income has declined. However, a recent government survey reveals that among younger, *employed* blacks (we must remember that blacks have high rates of unemployment), *salary* differences appear to be declining. Thus, changes may be forthcoming over the next decade.

REVIEW QUESTIONS

1. How do cultural beliefs operate to stigmatize blacks and browns in America?
2. Explain the differences and similarities in the structured discrimination against blacks and browns in regard to the following institutions:

    economic   legal
    political   educational

3. Discuss the history of a white ethnic group, and compare cultural and structural discrimination against that group, on the one hand, and blacks or Chicanos on the other.
4. How does racial and ethnic discrimination aggravate the overall pattern of inequality in previous chapters?

GLOSSARY

barrio the urban slums inhabited by Mexican Americans

caste a system of social stratification in which social standing is almost completely determined at birth

Chicano a term used to describe Mexican Americans, especially younger urban groupings

culture of suspicion the beliefs of Mexican Americans that they must be distrustful of certain institutions in America, particularly the legal structure.

discrimination the process of behaving in ways, and of creating social structural arrangements, that deny certain groups the same options available to others

ethnicity the term used to describe cultural differences among groups in America

Jim Crow the term used to describe formal and informal laws, rules, and practices that prevented black Americans from participating in the mainstream of American society

racial group a group that can be biologically, as well as culturally, distinguished from the rest of the population

white ethnics those groups of Americans who migrated from Europe to America during the eighteenth century

PROLOGUE 10:
HER STORY

Certain semantic conventions reveal the extent to which it is a "man's world." They are indicators of cultural and social arrangements.

Take the word *history* for example. The recording of events in the past is "his story," not "her story." If one doubts this, ask: How many women are prominent in "his story?" A few queens, here and there. A few current political leaders. One scientist, Madam Curie. A handful of writers. But "the great" scientists, artists, literary figures, leaders, composers, conductors, athletes, and almost any category of "greatness" in a field are stories of men, not women. What were women doing throughout history? Apparently, from the point of view of "history," not much.

Is this true? To some extent it is because social and cultural conditions prevented women from having the opportunities to achieve. This is true not just of the past. It is also true today. And for this reason, Chapter 10 is "her story." This is not a happy story, because it is a story of discrimination against women. Much of this discrimination is blatant, but as we will come to see, much is subtle and invidious. It is so built into our cultural and structural arrangements that we often cannot see the discrimination, for it appears "in the natural order of things."

Language again can reveal the subtlety of our expectations and orientations. If you read the sentences below honestly and supply the first pronoun that comes to your mind, I think that you will realize some interesting things as you reread the list of sentences:

The surgeon knew _____ could save the patient.

The detective's gun was in _____ left hand.

The scientist smiled graciously as they awarded _____ the Nobel
Prize.

No matter what the spy did, _____ could not get away from
_____ pursuers.

_____ was always strong and confident.

_____ was the most intelligent student in law school.

_____ pleaded with _____ to help _____ fix the car.

After _____ cleaned the house, _____ did the shopping.

Everyone knew _____ was afraid to be alone.

_____ always prepared the income tax returns because _____ was
too easily confused by all those figures.

_____ was silly and scatterbrained, but attractive.

It is to achieving a better understanding of why most of you placed
the pronouns where you did that Chapter 10 is dedicated.

10

SEXUAL DISCRIMINATION

THE OPPRESSION OF THE MAJORITY

The analysis of discrimination and inequality usually concentrates on the plight of racial and ethnic "minorities"—the black, brown, white ethnic, and impoverished. Over the last decade, however, we have seen a dramatic change of perspective: the recognition that a numerical majority in America—women—are more likely to suffer discrimination than American males. For years Americans accepted the exclusion of women from certain jobs and governmental positions as normal and correct. Their place was, after all, in the home taking care of children, household, and husband. To even phrase the issue this way now seems "chauvinistic," and yet just a few years ago, there was widespread consensus among men and women over the man's and woman's "place" in the scheme of things. As we observed in the chapter on the family, female roles, and associated cultural beliefs, are undergoing rapid change and now pose a conflict for many. This ambiguity in family roles and beliefs is but one indicator of the growing awareness among women, and to some extent, men, of the past oppression of females and of the need to have greater equality between the sexes.

As with other social problems, sexual discrimination has its roots in the American institutional structure—in economic, political, legal, familial, and educational arrangements. These arrangements have seemed correct and proper because of legitimizing cultural ideas. But

The nature of sexual discrimination

today, these ideas are being called into question, and as a result, the basic institutions they legitimize are under pressures to change. As we see, however, institutions are not easily changed, especially when many women accept and believe in the ideas that traditionally have legitimized them. And yet, for those women who seek equal participation in economic, legal, governmental, and educational institutions, they often find themselves in the same situation as minorities: they desire to participate, but are subject to negative stereotypes and outright discrimination. The result is for women to be denied access to the same sources and amounts of income, prestige, and power as men. And it is in this sense that sexual discrimination is a problem of the distributive system.[1]

ECONOMIC DISCRIMINATION

In 1940, approximately 28 percent of American women participated in the labor force. Today close to 45 percent of women work. In 1940, only 36 percent of women in the labor force were married; now close to 65 percent are married. In 1950, 12 percent of married, working women had children under six years of age; today, over 30 percent do.[2] The trend is thus very clear: a greater number of married women with young children are entering the labor force. And increasingly, the composition of the female labor force is beginning to resemble the general composition of the female population (Blau, 1975:218).

The smaller proportion of women as compared to working men is perhaps one indicator of discrimination. For we may ask: Why don't as many women work as men in a society which bestows prestige and honor on those who work? (Recall the power of the work ethic discussed in Chapter 7). Many women select themselves out of the labor market, and thus, it is sometimes difficult to document overt and blatant economic discrimination, although we shall discuss in later sections the subtle forms of discrimination which make women choose family over work roles. Probably the most direct way to document overt economic discrimination is to ask: What happens to the women who do work? What kinds of jobs do they hold? How well are they paid?

In looking at the kinds of jobs women can hold, it becomes immediately clear that women are excluded from many occupations. Apparently, much as in the home, there is "woman's work" and "man's work." In 1971, over one-third of all employed women worked in clerical jobs of low prestige and pay, and an additional 22 percent held even lower-paying service jobs (Whitehurst, 1977). In contrast only 7 percent and 8 percent, respectively, of the male labor force were em-

Economic exclusion of women

Women have only recently begun to question and protest wage inequalities. And employers have begun to yield only under pressure from the federal government.

ployed in these occupations. One way to document the pay differences between men and women is to note that a full-time working woman will earn, on the average, about 60 percent as much as a full time working man (Whitehurst, 1977). To phrase the matter differently, 40 percent of working women, compared to 14 percent of working men, earned less than $5,000 in 1970; whereas, 1 percent of the working women and over 13 percent of the working men earned over $15,000 in 1970.

These differences in pay reflect the exclusion of women from prestigious and well-paying professional occupations. While women's participation in the general census category of "professional and technical workers" has increased with growing numbers of women in the labor force, such increases occur primarily in the lower-paying and lower-prestige "women's professions," such as nursing, social work, and elementary school teaching. In Table 10.1, this confinement to, and exclusion from, professions are documented between 1910 and 1960 (Epstein, 1971:8).

Table 10.1 **Proportion of Women Among All Workers in Selected Professions**

	1910	1920	1940	1960
Lawyers	1.0%	1.4%	2.4%	3.5%
College Pres., Prof., Instructors	19.0	30.0	27.0	19.0
Doctors	6.0	5.0	4.6	6.8
Engineers	—	—	0.3	0.8
Dentists	3.1	3.2	1.5	2.1
Nurses	93.0	96.0	98.0	97.0
Social Workers	52.0%	62.0%	67.0%	57.0%

It is evident from Table 10.1 that up until 1960, many high prestige male professions remained impenetrable to females. Even when women do enter traditionally male professions, several studies indicate that they are likely to be at the lower end of the salary and prestige scale. In college professions, for example, women are more likely to be at lower academic levels, locate at smaller, less prestigious schools, and hold less prestigious research (as opposed to professorial) positions (Eckert and Stecklein, 1971). In medicine, to take another example, women are found to specialize in pediatrics, psychiatry, and public health, while avoiding surgery (Kosa and Coker, 1965; Epstein, 1971). Or, women in law, for instance, tend to be excluded from judgeships and are overrepresented in less prestigious forms of practice, such as Legal Aid and family law. In contrast, women are highly underrepresented in high paying and prestigious tax, corporate, and real estate law (Epstein, 1971:161). Perhaps even more indicative of the discrimination evident in the professions is the fact that, even in professions dominated by women, they are underrepresented in the top level positions within these professions. For example, in 1969 only 11 percent of the deans and directors of social work schools—a profession where close to 60 percent are women—were females. In elementary teaching, where over 88 percent of teachers are women, men dominate the administrative positions of school principal. Or, even among college libraries—staffed 85 percent by women, they hold only 50 percent of head librarian positions, and even less among larger libraries (Blankenship, 1971:93–102).

Male dominance of "female professions"

Thus, in looking at the data on woman's participation in the economy, it is clear that women are segregated from the better-paying and more prestigious occupations, even in those professions where they are overrepresented. Such economic discrimination is the result of several interrelated structural and cultural forces in our society.

SOCIOLOGICAL
INSIGHTS

THE CONTRADICTIONS OF "WOMAN'S WORK"

There is a clear sex-typing of occupations in the American economy. Most of these occupations are extentions of the female role in the family: servicing someone else, secretary to a male boss, nursing, counseling, public health, and social work. Women are said to have "special qualities" that make them more qualified for these kinds of jobs.

What is interesting is that sex-typing occurs for low-paying jobs, but these "special qualities" do not apply for high-paying, prestigious jobs. For example, women are said to be well equipped for the detailed, fine, and tedious work of assembly at electronic plants. After all, their fingers are smaller, they have greater dexterity than men, and they can withstand the pressure of monotony. These same women, however, do not have the dexterity or powers of concentration to perform surgery—the statistics on the number of women surgeons reveals there are even less than the number of women doctors. Men, who are too clumsy to thread a needle or do detailed electronics work, are not considered the more skillful at surgery—a high paying and highly prestigious occupation (Whitehurst, 1977).

WOMEN AS A MARGINAL AND RESERVE LABOR POOL

Since well over one-half of all working women are employed in clerical and service jobs, this fact should reveal something about their place in economic arrangements. One explanation of the "woman's place" in the work force is that she is primarily a marginal employee who, during times of recession and cutbacks, can be laid-off. The fact that over one-half of all unemployed are women, even though they constitute about 40 percent of the work force, would lend some support to the contention that they are likely to be a marginal work force. Moreover, this figure is probably somewhat conservative since they do not include many who have simply given up looking for work. Women are restricted to a relatively few occupations, and since they have such a high unemployment rate, it is argued by some that they represent a reserve labor pool that is called upon to work when needed, but that can be discharged when no longer needed; and because women have fewer job opportunities, they must often accept this situation (Blau, 1975).

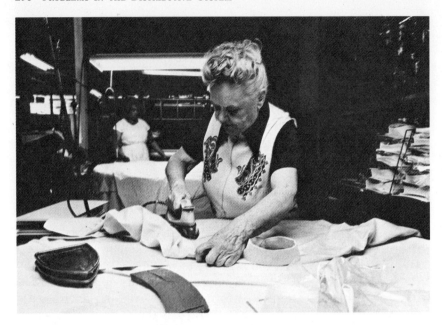

Women still perform in work roles which are defined as "woman's work." These roles are typically menial and ungratifying.

The economy in general is perhaps dependent upon a low-paid service and clerical sector of female employees. Should service and clerical salaries increase, then costs and prices would rise. Or, should women begin to enter, in massive numbers, "male occupations," then more competition for jobs would ensue, thus decreasing pressures for higher wages as the supply of workers exceeded the demand. Thus, to raise the salaries of women or to open new opportunities would require considerable economic adjustments in costs and prices as well as in labor-management relations. For most sectors of the economy, it is in their interests to avoid such alterations.

The consequences of economic parity

THE FAMILY CYCLE AND EMPLOYMENT

One problem facing women in the labor force revolves around child bearing and child rearing. Dominant beliefs hold that the mother should raise her young children—a belief that places the working mother in personal conflict over her career and her children's well-being. Equally significant is the interruption of a career for child bearing—an event that can take a number of weeks, if not months, from a job.

At present, there are few ways to deal with these issues. Employers are not always willing to give women time off to have a baby, especially if the woman wishes to be with her child during its first year.

Career versus child bearing and rearing

Child care facilities for the working mother are expensive, particularly for very young children, and not always available. Thus, the economic system has yet to accommodate itself to the family cycle of women and this fact represents a barrier to their participation in the economy. Since child bearing and rearing comes at just the time when careers are initiated, women are placed at a severe disadvantage in starting a career. And if they stay out of the labor force while they raise their children, reentrance into the labor market will be when prejudices about "older" employees operate against them.

THE "STAG" ECONOMY

Since men dominate the majority of economic positions, and certainly most of those where decisions are made, women are placed at a disadvantage in their competition with men. Much of this kind of discrimination is subtle, and yet, it has profound consequences for a woman's career. For example, many professions have "white male" norms about how a job is to be conducted, and even though there may be many alternative ways to do the same job effectively, an employee is forced to approximate the white male style of performance—a situation that places women (and many minorities) at a disadvantage. To illustrate further, much information about the availability of jobs, about ways to be effective, or about closing a "deal" is acquired informally outside an office in social activities (bars, golfing, etc.) among men. Since women are likely to be excluded from such activities, they are also excluded from valuable sources of job and career information.

Finally, since some men in the economy are likely to hold traditional views of man's work and woman's work, some are also likely to be hostile toward career-oriented women. Also, because successful women in many occupations must be exceptional if they are to overcome barriers, many male employees, and decision makers, can be insecure and jealous. Employers are likely to avoid such conflicts between male egos and career-oriented women; and since men constitute a majority, they are often likely to keep the peace by excluding women.

Conceptions about "woman's work"

SOCIALIZATION BARRIERS AND EMPLOYMENT

To some extent, women select themselves out of occupations because they feel that they "cannot compete with men" or "handle the pressure" of a well-paying, prestigious job. As we will discuss in more detail in later sections, these feelings are the result of the socialization experiences of women in America. For example, in most families,

The psychological consequences of sexual socialization

girls are not encouraged to think of an occupational career: they play "house;" they observe their mother in a household role; they are discouraged from being aggressive and "masculine." Socialization in schools further reinforces that in the home: Girls are discouraged from taking the sciences and shop; and counselors are likely to steer girls away from "masculine" careers. Media socialization can exert a similar discouraging effect since in most television shows, movies, and children's books, women are cast in domestic roles and are rarely portrayed as assuming traditionally male occupations. Thus, most girls are subtly discouraged from having high occupational aspirations, and equally important, most do not receive the socialization experiences that could give them the interpersonal and cognitive skills to enter a "man's occupation."

CULTURAL BELIEFS AND EMPLOYMENT

Two dominant beliefs are currently used to justify confining women to particular occupations and to paying them comparatively low wages (Whitehurst, 1977): (1) Women should get less pay because they require additional facilities and incur extra costs due to their

Women are often socialized to assume ornamental roles (left) *and to believe that they must be passive with men* (center). *Such orientations will handicap them as adults—often forcing them to assume ornamental jobs* (right).

higher rates of absenteeism, turnover, and the likelihood that they will quit the labor force, marry, and raise a family, and (2) women should get less pay because they are not the principal breadwinners and are just working for extra luxuries. Both of these beliefs do not correspond to the actual facts of the working woman, yet they are consistently used to justify employment discrimination against women.

1. There is no evidence that, except for the most demanding physical chores, women are less productive than men, and there is some evidence that they perform better at monotonous production work and assembly (Whitehurst, 1977). But despite productivity records equal to men, it is assumed that they cost more—a belief that is not substantiated. For example, a U.S. Public Health Department survey revealed roughly comparable days of absenteeism per year for men and women—5.6 days for women, 5.3 days for men. And these small differences disappear when men and women in comparable jobs are compared; the highest rates of sick leave recorded were for *all*

Inaccuracies in beliefs about working women

workers in the lowest salary levels (where, of course, women are most likely to be). With respect to employee turnover, rates per 100 employees reveal a figure of 5.2 for women, 4.4 for men. Of these, 2.6 per 100 were work quits for women, 2.2 for men, with the remainder the result of lay offs. As for changing their jobs, 10 percent of the men held different jobs from one year to the next, 7 percent of the women.

Thus, there is little evidence to support the belief that women employees "cost more." And were women not employed in the lower paying jobs, where all employees evidence dissatisfaction, the small differences between men and women would disappear.

2. Do women need to work? The data reveal that a large proportion of working women need to work. Twenty-three percent of working women are single and need to support themselves (Blau, 1975). Another 19 percent are divorced, widowed, or separated, and thus, in need of work to support themselves. Among the remaining married 58 percent, 23 percent of these married women have husbands with incomes only just above the poverty level. It is obvious, then, that the clear majority of women work because they must either support themselves or provide necessities for their families.

In sum, then, people's position in the economy determines, in large part, their access to money and prestige. Women are denied access to these scarce resources, and in a society which values activism and achievement, especially in the work sphere, women are forced to endure not just fewer financial rewards but the stigma of being less "active" and less "achieving" than males. Women are thus often forced to live at variance with dominant values, or at very best, they can realize these values only within a highly limited set of options, family life and menial work. Such are the consequences of economic discrimination.

LEGAL DISCRIMINATION: THE PAST AND CHANGING PRESENT

Much as with minority groups, women have suffered legal discrimination in that the law has explicitly denied them certain rights and privileges enjoyed by others in the society. The most obvious form of legal discrimination was the denial of women the right to vote until 1920. In being denied the vote, women were considered less than full-fledged citizens, but more importantly, it assured their exclusion from the political process—the very processes which could have reversed other patterns of discrimination. Since men have dominated the political arena for so long, it is difficult even today for women to make significant inroads into politics, especially at the federal level.

The Nineteenth Amendment

After the Nineteenth Amendment granting women the vote, the legal status of women did not change dramatically until the 1960s and the early 1970s. In 1964 Title VII of the Civil Rights Act prohibited discrimination on the basis of sex. In 1965 an Executive Order from the President extended the provisions of the 1963 Equal Pay Act to include sex, in addition to race, religion, color, or national origin. These changes in the law make it illegal to discriminate on the basis of sex in job hiring and in pay scales. Moreover, some provisions require "affirmative action" by employers to recruit women for a full range of job classifications. These laws, for the first time in American history, provide women and women's organizations with a legal basis for challenging employment practices of employers. However, the law places much of the burden on individual women and organizations representing them "to prove" discrimination—an expensive and arduous task; and because proof is often difficult to establish, many informal and subtle practices of the past are allowed to continue.

Recent legal actions

While these changes in federal law have improved the legal status of women, many subtle forms of legal discrimination persist. Some of this discrimination involves not assuring women certain rights, such as securing credit independently, receiving full pensions, insurance, and survivor benefits, and being allowed maternity leaves from work.

SOCIOLOGICAL INSIGHTS

WOMEN'S RIGHTS, CIVIL RIGHTS, AND THE SOUTHERN STRATEGY

When Title VII of the 1964 Civil Rights Act was proposed (barring sexual discrimination), many liberals felt that this would make the bill difficult to pass. Since the bill was primarily directed at minority discrimination, there was concern that the sex discrimination amendment to the Act would hurt the civil rights of minorities.

In an ironic twist of politics, southern congressmen supported the amendment because many felt that it would hamstring the agency charged with administering the act, thereby, depleting the resources for dealing with racial discrimination. Thus, with strong southern support, Howard W. Smith of Virginia submitted the amendment to the House Rules Committee despite objections by the U.S. Department of Labor and the House Judiciary Chair, Emanuel Celler, who proclaimed the amendment "illogical, ill-timed, ill-placed, and improper" (Whitehurst, 1977).

Laws designed "to protect" women can also discriminate; for instance, in some states protective laws favor women in giving them rest periods, better working conditions, and lighter duties, but these same laws restrict their overtime work and, hence, the opportunity to make the same premium wages as men. However, these same laws do not protect women from night nursing, cleaning, and entertaining (Whitehurst, 1977).

Many of these subtle forms of legal inattention and discrimination could be immediately eliminated with the ratification of the Equal Rights Amendment (ERA). This amendment, which simply states "equality under the law shall not be denied or abridged by the United States or any state on account of sex," has been introduced into Congress every year since 1923, but it did not pass both houses of Congress until 1972. At this writing, 34 of the necessary 38 states have ratified the Amendment. Should the Amendment be ratified, it would eliminate the special "protections" granted women as well as the discrimination against them. Because the Amendment has generated such controversy, some of the pro and con arguments surrounding it should be addressed.

The Equal Rights Amendment

ARGUMENTS AGAINST ERA

The major thrust of the arguments against ERA come from those who see it as threatening the family and crucial family relations. These arguments include: (1) A wife will have to assume an independent status and lose the right to be supported by her husband. (2) The husband's role as breadwinner and household head will be undermined. (3) Wives could lose alimony. (4) A mother could lose her "right" to almost automatic custody of children in the event of divorce. Another line of argument concerns the issues of women's status outside the family: (1) Women will lose protective legislation in the job market; (2) Women will be subject to the draft and insertion into combat zones during war; (3) Rape laws would be difficult to enforce; (4) Public restrooms and sleeping facilities could no longer be segregated for men and women.

ARGUMENTS IN FAVOR OF ERA

The most persuasive argument in favor of ERA is that it would give women equal rights and that it would require all levels of government to treat people, both males and females, as individuals. With regard to the specific objections raised against ERA, many of them represent misinterpretations. Common Cause—the nonpartisan "people's lobby" in Washington—has done research on some of the consequences of ERA and drawn these conclusions: Women will not be deprived of alimony, custody of children, or child support, but men *will* be eligible for these under the same conditions as women. Women will still have the right to choose being a housewife, and under these conditions, husbands will still be obligated to support their wives and children. Protective laws which discriminate will be invalidated, but where meaningful, they will be extended to men. ERA would have no effect on rape laws, since these laws do not condone discrimination. Men and women would not have to share restrooms and sleeping facilities because of the state's right to regulate cohabitation and all people's constitutional right to privacy. However, women will be eligible for the draft and combat obligations, but they would be eligible for the same exemptions and benefits as men.

ERA would thus eliminate the need for piecemeal legislation on women's rights, while not seriously changing the rights of women who choose to remain in the traditional household role. It would eliminate, however, many forms of discrimination against women who wish to seek equal participation with men outside of the home. Until ERA is ratified, it is likely that a considerable amount of subtle discrimination will occur, thereby maintaining the disadvantaged position of women in American society.

FAMILY OPPRESSION OF WOMEN

Many commentators have noted that what was once a biological necessity has become institutionalized in family roles and now operates to oppress women. The problems of child bearing and rearing were indeed protein for the first human societies, and it was perhaps more natural then for male-female roles to be divided along economic-household lines. In these societies, there was no reason to view female roles as inferior to male hunting activities, but in contemporary America where the values of activism, achievement, and individualism dominate, and where a strong work ethic prevails, child bearing and rearing and household roles can, for some men and women, be defined as demeaning, unachieving, and suppressive of individual creativity.

The structure of the isolated nuclear family (see Chapter 3) aggravates these problems of realizing dominant American values. Women are isolated from kin, from their husbands, and thrust into child rearing and housekeeping chores that can consume enormous amounts of time and energy, while producing few tangible achievements. In many ways, the fact that men resist performing these activities underscores how little fulfillment they offer to individuals

Dominant values surrounding the family

having sources of fulfillment and achievement outside of the home. Life cycle patterns among females further compound the problem of finding meaning in female household roles: Because women live much longer than previously, they will spend a majority of their adult life without children, who will have grown and established their own family. As a result, the wife is left with only her household duties—few of which offer intrinsic rewards or a sense of achievement or accomplishment. Women, thus, run the risk of the "empty-nest syndrome" of depression and neuroticism stemming from the loss of one of the few female roles—childrearing—where it is possible to court some sense of accomplishment.

Not only are female roles in the family lacking in meaning for many women, they also operate to inhibit women from seeking sources of gratification outside of the home. In American society today, beliefs about motherhood and wifehood take precedence. Most women want children and they want to be good mothers and wives. Yet, the current definition of what constitutes a good mother and wife comes into conflict with desires and aspirations for work and career outside of the home. The desire to be a "good mother and wife"—concerned, loving, caring, responsive—place a ceiling on the energy and emotional involvement a woman can invest in a job and career (Janeway, 1971). When these distracting obligations are compounded by housework and daily chores (laundry, cooking, cleaning, dishes, etc.) it takes an exceptional woman to pursue a career with full energy and commitment. While over 40 percent of women work, it is difficult for them to make the same commitment as their husbands to a career or profession, as long as their motherhood and wifehood duties loom as major responsibilities.

A number of studies on dual career families highlight some of the problems of women who seek to realize their home, wife, *and* career aspirations. One study, for example, revealed that wives who sought to have full-fledged careers, while at the same time raising a family, were under enormous physical and emotional strain (Rapaport and Rapaport, 1971). Another study of women engaged in law, medicine, and college teaching reported considerably less emotional strain, apparently because this sample of women sacrificed much of their career to meet home demands. By defining their situation as "work" (as opposed to "career"), with an emphasis on family, these women achieved more emotional tranquility (Poloma, 1972). Another study reported that working women developed a "tolerance for domestication" in which women keep their occupational sights low, while not training for a specific field, or if they do train for a field, not becoming too involved. Most of these women were thus sacrificing their careers to the demands of family life (Poloma and Garland, 1971). In

Problems of career women

another study of twenty dual career professionals, a considerable degree of compromise between husbands and wives was observed. The woman's career influenced the husband's career decisions, but in almost all cases the wife made the career sacrifices when decisions about where to live were made (Holmstrom, 1972). In yet another study of career women, it is evident that women tend to choose careers which will allow them to be mobile and accommodate themselves to their husband's plans. Careers such as nursing, teaching, social work, psychological testing, accounting, or real estate can usually be "picked up" in new areas as the husband moves in pursuit of his career (Bird, 1968).

Thus, from the available data it is evident that the women's child rearing, domestic, and wife obligations, obligations that most women were socialized to accept as natural, require her to (1) lower her career aspirations, (2) channel them into careers that can be "picked up," or (3) sacrifice full commitment to a career. These structural features of the family which inhibit even seeking a career or, as the above studies show, making clear career sacrifices, are often made to seem "right and proper" or as "necessary" by several dominant cultural beliefs.

One such belief emphasizes the "glory and creativity" of childbirth and stresses that it is one of a woman's more creative acts. This belief can subtly communicate that since this is one of the female's most noble and significant tasks, she need not seek further gratification outside the motherhood-household role. A related belief emphasizes that "only the mother" can provide the love and nurturance so necessary in raising healthy children. It is the mother's love, according to this belief, that is most important, thus, women should make job and career sacrifices, especially during children's formative years, in order to provide the emotional support that "only a mother can give."

The data on working mothers and its psychological impact on children are ambiguous and no clear generalizations are possible (Hoffman, 1963). From all the available evidence, however, no study has documented that the mother must be *the* nurturer, and no studies have documented a "natural" mother-child bond. There is also no evidence that women are necessarily better child rearers than men. The data clearly document that children need nurturance and will suffer psychologically without it, but there are no data to support the belief that only a woman can provide this nurturance. Thus, what has always been has to now become translated into what is "natural" and "necessary." The result of these beliefs is to make it partiularly difficult for women to leave the home and pursue with the same vigor, energy, and commitment a career. It is in this sense that the family operates to oppress the options of females in American society.

Working mothers and children

EDUCATIONAL DISCRIMINATION

Many of the discriminatory practices against women in the economy, law, and family are reinforced in the educational system. As students move through the educational hierarchy, sex-typing and channeling of girls and boys into different roles occurs. By the time girls become adolescents and young adults, many career options have been closed off. One way to visualize this process of closing off options is to examine some of the discriminatory patterns faced as females move through the educational hierarchy from primary school to college and graduate studies.

DISCRIMINATION IN PRIMARY SCHOOLS

In examining discrimination in primary schools, the full range of the educational process needs to be examined, especially since so much of the discrimination is subtle and unintended. We should, at the very least, look at teacher-student interaction, the content of textbooks, the curriculum, and classroom activities.

A number of studies on teacher-pupil interaction exist and they all document a consistent pattern: Teachers direct more attention to boys in terms of formal instruction, encouragement, and praise (Whitehurst, 1977). Moreover, they are more likely to encourage independence and autonomy among boys, while encouraging docility and passivity among girls. One study, for example, of New York City school teachers revealed that teachers wanted boys to be dominant, assertive, and independent, while they voiced clear preferences for unassertive and submissive girls who are concerned about their appearance (Levy, 1972). Thus, in terms of those qualities valued by the society—activism, achievement, individualism—teachers subtly place these expectations upon male students, while encouraging more "feminine" patterns of docility and submissiveness among girls. Such interaction better prepares boys for the higher education and professional occupations.

Education reinforces role-playing

Many studies on the content of elementary school textbooks have been undertaken, all revealing similar findings. Women and girls are depicted in major roles less frequently than men and boys; there are few females ever cast into professional roles; and girls are usually depicted as dependent and passive (Whitehurst, 1977). Other data on textbook discrimination comes from the American Library Association list of notable books that lists two books about boys for each one about girls, and more importantly, content analysis of such books portrays boys as independent, competent, and engaged in exciting tasks, while girls are pictured as domestically inclined or as

Textbook sex-typing

"watching" boys (Epstein, 1971). Even animal characters in children's books put males and females in these stereotyped roles (Donlon, 1972). Sometimes the sexism is more subtle as was the case in a study of arithmetic books where boys were pictured in photographs, examples, and problems as making money while girls were portrayed as buying supplies or cooking (Howe, 1971). As children read, a subtle sex-typing of their "appropriate" roles occurs—a process that reinforces existing stereotypes of how men and women are supposed to behave.

Research on the curriculum of elementary schools reveals similar patterns of sexism. Girls are expected to like reading while boys are supposed to excel in math and science. Such expectations constitute subtle pressures which channel male and female intellectual activities. It is perhaps in sports and physical education that sex-typing is most evident: Boys and girls are segregated in these activities, even though elementary school girls are as big and strong as boys. Moreover, boys' exercises revolve around team games involving the use of muscles and energy; girls' activities stress less cooperative and more individualistic activities such as muscle exercises and simple games involving little team activity or competition.

Curricular discrimination

Even in classroom activities, sex-typing often occurs. Boys are to move furniture and desks, while girls set tables and put out refreshments (Whitehurst, 1977). At these ages, girls are as strong as boys and thus could easily lift furniture, but they are encouraged to stay away from such masculine activities. Moreover, many activities involving competition—spelling bees, math games, races, and the like—often segregated into boys' and girls' competitions, thereby communicating to females that they should not or cannot compete against boys. Even in the noise levels tolerated by teachers, boys are assumed to be noisier in their activities than girls. Or, in extra-classroom activities, girls become school nurses, boys traffic monitors; or girls are elected class secretaries, boys class presidents. Thus, the sex typing of boys' and girls' activities works against girls, who are kept less active and quieter, and who are prevented from acquiring as much experience in individual and team competition with and against boys. Such typing communicates to girls that they should not compete, while depriving them of the practice in competition that they will need later in life to participate equally with men.

Classroom discrimination

DISCRIMINATION IN SECONDARY SCHOOLS

The subtle forms of sex-typing evident in student-teacher interaction, in the textbooks and curriculum, and in school activities continue in secondary schools. But because of the close proximity of high

Females who seek to participate in "boys'" activities are often subject to ridicule in secondary schools.

school to decisions about college or work, patterns of discrimination begin to have direct consequences for the placement of males and females in the broader society. Examples of how the discrimination becomes more explicit include: Girls are encouraged to take homemaking or secretarial skills courses, boys shop courses; boys are encouraged to compete in interscholastic or intramural sports, girls in cheerleading and pep clubs; boys join math and science clubs, girls future homemaker clubs.

Sex-typing in high school

Counselors reinforce these sexual stereotypes by guiding girls into feminine occupations by assuming: (1) girls will probably organize their life around marriage and family, (2) girls will have so many obstacles in a "man's world" that they should be spared this hardship (Chafetz, 1974).

HIGHER EDUCATION

Women receive about 51 percent of the high school diplomas, but only 40 percent of bachelor's degrees. Thus, a considerable amount of self-selection from the college race probably occurs after high school and then during the early years of college (Roby, 1972). A number of discriminatory practices have prevailed against women seeking a college education (Roby, 1972): Admissions policies have tended to favor men, since they represent less of a "drop-out risk." Such policies also discriminate against older women who seek to begin their education after their children are in school, or are actually gone from

Women in colleges

the home. Scholarships aid has been more likely to go to men because men are better risks and because many women "have someone to support them."

Coupled with many of the difficulties of taking themselves seriously as career-oriented students—difficulties stemming from prior family, media, and educational socialization—females are more likely to avoid career-oriented curriculums where they must compete with men (science, engineering, and mathematics). Colleges also reaffirm the stereotype of the "husband seeker" and the "drop-out" who gets married and/or follows a husband as he pursues his career.

For these reasons, even fewer women reach graduate school. Women receive 34 percent of the masters' degrees—many of which are in sex-typed vocations such as teaching and social work or in comparatively nonvocational fields such as English literature, music, and the like—and they receive only 12 percent of the doctoral degrees. These figures reveal further self-selection out of the credentials race with men. The same discriminatory processes with respect to admissions and financial aid also operate at the graduate level, and in many ways, serve as a self-fulfilling prophecy. As women see the barriers to their achievement, they are more likely to drop out which reaffirms the belief, among those who establish the barriers, that women are poor risks. And since it is during the years of graduate training that women are likely to begin their family, the same household, wifehood, and child rearing pressures that keep many women out of the job market operate to discourage women pursuing graduate degrees. In the end, without a graduate degree, many professions—doctor, lawyer, dentist, and the like—are closed forever.

Graduate training among women

In sum, at each stage in the movement from elementary to secondary and from secondary to college and post-graduate education, women face severe barriers. Some of these are explicit, but many are psychological and are the result of being subtly told from the first grade on that a career equal to a man's is perhaps undesirable and certainly very difficult to achieve. It is in this sense that the educational hierarchy discriminates against women in America.

POLITICAL DISCRIMINATION AND THE WOMEN'S MOVEMENT

Changes in institutionalized patterns of discrimination will occur through two related processes: (1) the raising of both the male and female consciousness about the overt and subtle forms of discrimination, and (2) the use of political power to change discriminatory structural arrangements. The second of these processes is currently difficult since women self-select themselves out of professions, and are excluded from political decision making in America. And the first of these processes is only just beginning as various women's organizations have emerged to educate the populace and politicians as to the extensiveness of sexual discrimination. We need to describe these two processes in order to complete our overview of institutionalized sexism in America.

WOMEN AND POLITICAL POWER

Potentially women as a group possess considerable political power. In 1972, for example, women cast 53 percent of the votes—a pattern that reflects their greater numbers in the general population (Bureau of Census, 1972). The fact that women have not used their voting power to elect women candidates can be easily documented because the number of women in positions of political power is few: There has never been a female president, vice president, or Supreme Court Justice; there have never been more than two women senators at a time; women represent about 2 percent of the House; there have been only three women cabinet members; there has been only one mayor of a large city; only three women have ever been elected to governorships, and only one who was not the wife of a former governor; about twelve women have been ambassadors to foreign countries; and less than a dozen hold federal judgeships.

Exclusion of women from politics

While the 1974 elections slightly increased the number of women in the House of Representatives and gave women their first nonnepotistic governorship (Ella Grasso in Connecticut), their first major-city mayor (Janet Hayes in San Jose, California), and their first elected state Supreme Court Justice (Susie Sharp, North Carolina), these gains are not great and certainly do not portend a significant increase in political power for women in America.

Women are not suddenly becoming political; women have been active in political campaigns for decades, but their participation has been, in many ways, an extension of their household duties. As volunteer workers, they tend to perform the office work—mailing, licking envelops, running mimeograph machines, typing, phoning and the like (Chafetz, 1974:148). Men, on the other hand, tend to be the candidates and field managers of the candidates. Why do women stop in these routine, menial roles? Why are they not at least field managers? Why are they not candidates? And why do they not vote in great numbers for women candidates when they do run for election? The answers to these questions appear to reside in both discrimination and women's definition of their place in politics.

Several studies have documented that both men and women feel that it is not right and proper for women to enter such a "competitive, dirty, and difficult world as politics" (Whitehurst, 1977). As Patsy Mink of Hawaii, one of the few long-term female members of Congress notes: "Politics may be the last and most difficult area of 'breakthrough' for women, . . . the barriers . . . are mainly based upon custom which no court can eradicate." Women themselves are likely to view the female role—one of being passive and feminine—as counter to the qualities required of being a politician. Moreover, females in America are more often than not accustomed to dominance by males, whether in their jobs, schools, or families, accordingly, females have had few opportunities to hold leadership positions in an educational and occupational system that is so discriminatory. Not only do perceptions of the female role and a lack of leadership experience inhibit political participation, but women's household, wife, and child-rearing roles often preclude political activity in much the same ways as they inhibit career commitments in the job market.

Thus, the same barriers operating to inhibit women's participation in other than marginal labor and household roles also operate to suppress political ambitions. But we can ask: Why don't women at least vote for the few women candidates who do run for national political office? Much of the answer lets in the psychological orientations of women who have been conditioned to exclude themselves from serious, nonfamilial roles. A number of studies have reported, for example, that women vote much like their husbands (Safilios-Rothschild, 1974); and, few women possess a high degree of consciousness about their situation and of the barriers to their achieving fulfillment outside the home.

THE WOMEN'S MOVEMENT AND POLITICAL CONSCIOUSNESS

Since the passage of the Nineteenth Amendment in 1920, little organized political activity by and for women had been evident until the 1960s when, with the creation of the National Organization of Women (NOW), the woman's movement was reborn. Although its membership was small, NOW received considerable publicity and its ranks grew rather quickly. The goal of NOW was to work within the present system to break down many of the discriminatory barriers operating to oppress women. To pursue this goal, NOW revealed a traditional organizational structure: a central national office with local chapters, a national president and officers paralleled by local chapter offices, the collection of dues, and the use of revenues to lobby for women's causes.

National Organization of Women

Partly in reaction to the traditional structure of NOW and partly as an alternative, perhaps complimentary tactic, "radical feminism" emerged in the early 1970s. Rejecting much of the tight, centralized structure of NOW, local *consciousness raising* (CR) *groups* were formed in an effort to awaken women to the nature and extent of their oppression. CR is a combination of group therapy (where efforts are made to raise women's self-esteem) and group instruction on the multiple sources of discrimination. The loose organizations and groups of the radical movement have as their ultimate goal the reorganization of the "sexist society," that is, a basic change in institutions and cultural symbols supporting these institutions. Rather than reforming the system, the goal is to radically change it. To achieve this goal requires awareness and consciousness on the part of women, hence, the emphasis on CR.

Both the reform approach of NOW and the approach of the radical movement, however, reveal common goals:

1. the consolidation of political power,
2. the elimination of negative sexual stereotypes,
3. the reduction of the need for artifice and other unnatural symbols,
4. the creation of alternatives, whether through reform or radical change, for women that are equal to those available to men,

Consciousness raising

Goals of women's movement

Twenty thousand women marched for suffrage in New York in 1918 (left). After the Nineteenth Amendment was passed, the women's movement became dormant. Only recently (right) has a new consciousness emerged.

5. the development of a sense of sisterhood and solidarity,

6. the improvement of women's self-images of themselves, and

7. the humanization of both men and women as well as the structures in which they participate.

The goals are somewhat lofty and vague, but they are more reflective of dominant American values than the present situation. Through political and CR activities, women are seeking the right to be active, to achieve, to be individuals, to be free, to be equals, and to realize a more humane society. One of the curious ironies is that those who pursue goals consonant with basic American values are often resisted and ridiculed. The reasons for such resistance reside not just in the oppressive and discriminatory arrangements that we have thus far reviewed, but in a set of cultural beliefs about women that contradict basic American values. And curiously, Americans have become so accustomed to the contradiction that attempts to change beliefs about women appear "deviant" and strange. They appear deviant, of course, because these beliefs have legitimized, a set of institutional arrangements that favor men and that have convinced many women of the naturalness of their inferior status.

THE CULTURE OF FEMININE OPPRESSION

In most institutional spheres, women are not expected to live up to dominant values of activism, achievement, and individualism. When women do seek to be active and achieving individuals in the economic or higher educational spheres, they are often labeled as "overly oppressive," "men haters," "old maids," and other negative stereotypes. The application of these stereotypes reflect the existence of two general beliefs about what women are and what they should be:

1. Women are "naturally" more expressive, emotional, and affectionate than men.

2. Women are "naturally" less aggressive and more submissive and dependent than men.

There is no evidence that such beliefs accurately describe woman's biology, but they do serve as a means for justifying educational, economic, and political discrimination, while condoning family oppression. If women are defined as more emotional, affectionate, and less aggressive and independent, then they should not compete with men in the educational, economic, and political arenas; rather, they are best in the family and home where their "natural" talents allow them to give warmth, affection, and support to children and husband.

It is often assumed that women are less aggressive then men. Could this not be a result of early socialization of males and females?

To the extent that women can realize dominant values, they are usually forced to do so in the home and in community activities: One achieves by raising a family and supporting a successful husband; one is active only in community service and recreational activities; one expresses individuality in ornamental ways such as in dress and home decorating; and, even if one works, it is not so much an achievement as "something to do" while raising a family and maintaining a household. Thus, women are denied the gratifications that can come with realizing the basic core values that most Americans hold. More significantly, they must endure the negative psychological consequences of living at odds with these dominant values.

These negative psychological consequences—frustration, depression, lowered self esteem, for example—as well as the inevitable strains created by beliefs and structural arrangements that are in conflict with dominant values can serve as a force of social change. Eventually these psychological strains and sociocultural contradictions will force pressures for social change. It is in this sense that sexism is presently a problem of social and cultural structures, and it is a problem that promises to initiate widespread social change in America.

SUMMARY

This chapter has examined the structure of discrimination against females in American society. In our analyses we discovered that while 40 percent of women work, they are more likely to hold inferior jobs. Even in professions dominated by women, men are still more likely to occupy high-ranking positions. Some of the forces accounting for this pattern are the existence of a reserve labor pool, the "stag" economy, socialization experiences, and cultural beliefs.

Women continue to suffer legal discrimination, and are also faced with barriers to equal employment stemming from the traditional definitions of the female role in the family. The discriminatory forces built into the educational system represent additional factors in female discrimination. The subtle ways females are encouraged to be feminine and assume feminine roles sometimes results in women being less prepared psychologically to compete with men in the job market. Finally, our discussion of structured discrimination examined the political processes in which women have little power to press for their interests and are just beginning to initiate a movement geared toward raising women's consciousness of their mutual interests.

Two prominent cultural beliefs legitimize these structural patterns of discrimination: (1) beliefs that women are "naturally" more expressive than men, and (2) beliefs that women are "naturally" less aggressive than men; hence, they should assume expressive and supportive roles in the family. Such beliefs support current institutional arrangements and reveal the extent to which sexual discrimination is a problem of culture and structure in America.

NOTES

1. This chapter is heavily indebted to Carol Whitehurst's (1977) excellent analysis of women in America. For more detailed analyses of the problem, see Deckard, 1975; Bardwick, 1972; Sinclair, 1965; and Oakley, 1972.

2. Department of Labor, *Statistical Abstracts*, tables 348 and 353, Wash. D.C.: Government Printing Office, 1972.

REVIEW QUESTIONS

1. Using the two cultural beliefs about women's "natural" tendencies, indicate how these beliefs are institutionalized into economic, legal, educational, and political arrangements in America.

2. What are the pros and cons of ERA?
3. How does early family and educational socialization pose barriers to the occupational achievement of women as adults?
4. Why is the women's movement often re-

sisted and ridiculed by men? By other women? Does the explanation lie in cultural and structural forces?

5. What do you see as the most important barrier to achieving equality between the sexes?

GLOSSARY

CR consciousness raising in which women are encouraged to understand the broader forces in the society, as well as those in their daily lives, that limit their options and force them to define their own activities as demeaning

empty-nest syndrome the sometimes difficult emotional situation that females, who have devoted their energies to raising children, must endure when their children have left the home

ERA the Equal Rights Amendment that would guarantee women equality under the law

labor force the sum total of labor that is ready and willing to assume work roles

NOW the National Organization of Women—the most prominent political and social group seeking to alert women to their current position and to the options available to them

reserve labor force the labor force of surplus workers who can be placed in temporary and/or low-paying jobs

self-selection the term used to describe many women's "decision" that they cannot and should not attempt to compete with men in a "man's world"

sexual discrimination discrimination against females, that is, practices which limit the options of females in comparison to those available to men

IV
PROBLEMS OF COMMUNITY ORGANIZATION

As we noted in Chapter 2, communities are self-governing geographical areas where people live and meet their needs through interrelated and partially coordinated work activities (Boskoff, 1970:3–37). Communities determine people's geographical location in society while influencing many of their actions, such as when and how they work, where and how their children are educated, and where and how they use their leisure time.

Over the last 150 years, under the pressures of industrialization, the United States has become an urbanized society. Residence, work, and social life, for well over half the population, now occurs within a few hundred large urban and metropolitan areas. This majority of the population is crowded into less than 2 percent of the land expanse of the United States—a population density rivaling India, Egypt, Japan, and Java. During the transformation from a rural to urbanized society four notable trends have been evident:

1. the great rural to urban migrations of indigenous whites into the cities during the middle of the last century
2. the massive immigrations into cities of Europeans and Asians during the latter part of the nineteenth century and the early years of the twentieth century
3. the internal migrations of southern blacks from rural areas to cities in the North

4. the rapid exodus over the last 25 years of white, middle-class
  Americans out of the cities into the suburbs

These trends highlight an incredible series of shifts in the way
people live in American society. Associated with these
transformations is a host of social problems confronting the
giant metropolitan areas. A number of such problems are related
to the physical ascendance and subsequent deterioration of
major American cities, to the burgeoning of white suburbs, and
to the creation of vast patterns of residential segregation. We
will thus discover in Chapters 11 and 12 that *built into the
structure* of American communities is a set of enduring problems.
   We can also use the concept of community in a broader sense.
Humans are only one part of a much larger unit: the national
and international ecological community. Ecological communities
are composed of functional relationships among and between
species and their physical environments.[1] While the complexity
of these relationships can be enormous, one fact is clear: Each
species is dependent on at least some other species and some
elements of the physical environment for survival. No matter
how ascendant humans believe themselves to be, they cannot
extricate themselves from this dependency on other life forms and
minerals in the global ecosystem (Iltis, 1970). It is this dependency
that makes the study of interactions between the ecosystem and
society critical.

Over the last 10,000 years humans have evolved increasingly complex social systems that have allowed their populations to grow at incredible rates. As a result, humans organized into urban, industrial societies like the United States have been able to disrupt, on a scale never before possible, basic relationships within the world ecosystem. The inevitable trend toward complexity and diversity of ecosystems in nature has been reversed with the cultivation of single crops, the use of pesticides, and the stripping of soil and plant life. The basic cycles of materials, involving the circulation of life-sustaining elements such as carbon, nitrogen, and phosphorus, may have been disrupted. Air has been altered chemically in ways harmful to people's lives. Crucial life forms, such as the ocean's phytoplankton (life forms that give mammals most of the air they breathe), have been invaded by chlorinated hydrocarbons like DDT, and the life-sustaining capacity of water has been reduced in many parts of the world.[2]

These events are a familiar story and we need not dwell upon them here. What is crucial for our understanding of the impact of human societies on the environment is the fact that changes introduced in one part of the world "ecological community" have consequences for other areas, always extending and magnifying disruption of the environment. The amount of damage that has already been done and the long-range disruptions that will show up in the future cannot be precisely estimated since the chains and cycles of the ecosystem are too complex. It is evident, however, that considerable ecological damage has already occurred and that, unless existing patterns of human social organization are altered, the point of no return from an ecocatastrophe could soon be passed. It is thus appropriate that we close the discussion of community problems with an analysis of how American social structure and culture pose problems for the world ecological community. Patterns of stratification, institutional adaptation, and community organization in America can perhaps be viewed as posing the ultimate problem of structure: The potential destruction of all species through massive alteration of the ecological community.

[1] For more detailed, yet readable discussions of ecosystems, see Ehrlich and Ehrlich, 1970:157–199; Odum, 1969; Duncan and Schnore, 1964; Murphy, 1967:49–108. For more technical discussions, consult the bibliographies of these works.

[2] For more technical discussions of the impact of pollutants on the ecosystem, see Revelle, 1968, and Ehrlich and Ehrlich, 1970:117–198.

PROLOGUE 11: LIFE IN THE METROPOLIS

On any typical day in America's metropolitan areas, the following events occur.

· It's 6 A.M. and Mr. Commuter must hurry if he is to catch his 6:25 train to the city. He rushes past his kids and wife who will spend their day in a well-groomed house, modern schools, and pleasant shopping centers. As the commuter train approaches the city, the backs of old brick and wood buildings become evident. Most are occupied by blacks, although browns, such as Chicanos, Cubans, and Puerto Ricans, may occupy many of these unpleasant places. The train stops in the downtown station, and a quick bus ushers Mr. Commuter to the tall glass building where he works. At 5:07 that evening, Mr. Commuter takes his earnings to his wife and kids, even though he earns his money in, and uses the services of, the inner city. His money will support his town—its police, fire units, schools, parks, shopping centers, and all the facilities that Mr. Commuter moved to the suburbs to receive.

· Meanwhile, back in the city, black and brown children, as well as their white fellows whose parents could not afford to move out, will face another night fearful of what occurs outside their tenement. The next day they will go to an old school, with fewer books, movies, and recreational facilities than their counterparts in the suburbs. Their teachers will be suspicious, if not fearful, and will fantasize that they too can join others in a suburban school.

· On a corner in the black ghetto, men of all ages can be found standing about. Some are school age, but they have dropped out. Others are much older, but they all share a common plight: no jobs and no hope for the good life that they see on television each evening.

· In a nearby brick building, an old lady sits in front of her TV, mesmerized by its dulling effects. She watches because she has no place else to go and because she is fearful of the dangers outside.

· In city hall, city workers—many of whom live and pay their taxes in the suburbs—worry about the eroding tax base and the problems of meeting the payroll, financing the schools, providing police, fire, and health care, while attempting to maintain roads and parks. They realize that those who live in the city need many services, but they also face the problem of dwindling resources.

As the buses and cars rush by outside among tall glass needles rising amidst old wood and brick buildings, it is perhaps difficult to view the big city, with all its busy commerce and monuments to the sky as deeply troubled. But few American cities do not face profound problems of paying their bills and dealing with the unique problems of those who have stayed behind. These problems are built into the cultural premises and structural conditions under which the cities initially developed, and with growing suburbanization, they have become profoundly disturbing to all Americans. Chapter 11 examines these problems of the city in the midst of the suburban metropolis because the events recorded above are but an indicator of one of America's most enduring problems of culture and structure.

CHAPTER

11

PROBLEMS OF THE CITY

While all individual cities evidence social problems, it is the large cities of America's metropolitan areas that reveal the most critical problems—blight, pollution, corruption, racial tensions, poverty, and potential insolvency. These problems have their sources in the history of urbanization in America, for it was during early urbanization that the basic culture and structure of America's large cities was formed.

As we examine the problems of the city in metropolitan areas, we should recognize that, even if we do not actually live in the city or in one of its suburbs, much social life and activity in America is shaped by the problems of these large metropolitan areas. Indeed, much of the economic, political, media, educational, and recreational activities of Americans occurs within these areas, and increasingly, the population of the society is becoming concentrated in metropolitan regions. Thus, both the present and future life of Americans will be conditioned by the problems of the city in metropolitan areas. It is for this reason that we should understand how these areas first emerged and why they present us with many enduring problems of culture and structure.

THE CULTURE OF COMMUNITY IN AMERICA

Nowhere are basic values of individualism, freedom, and activism more powerfully manifest than in beliefs about what communities in America should be. As we noted in Chapter 4 on education, Ameri-

Local autonomy and control

cans believe that there should be local control and autonomy of their community: Communities, through their active efforts, should be free to determine and shape, in accordance with their individual preferences, basic living patterns—their zoning laws, roads, schools, form of government, public works, and community services. Federal control of such matters is considered inappropriate and undesirable.

Contradicting these beliefs is the fact of federal intervention into the affairs of American communities. In accordance with the necessities of societywide planning and the human needs of many residents, the federal government has increasingly become involved in community life. But the *pattern* of intervention has been influenced by widely held beliefs in local control and autonomy. Federal assistance to cities has tended to be indirect and piecemeal. Much assistance is in the form of grants and aids for specific categories of activities—housing, police, fire, welfare, flood control, and education, for example. By offering monies (which communities must at times match) in specific areas and by giving local communities much control over how the monies are administered, the federal government's intervention has kept a low profile, hence, it has not been viewed as violating local autonomy and control beliefs.

When intervention is direct, obligatory, and manifest, however, resistance is evident. For example, many suburban communities have fought and stopped the building of public housing projects. Or, to take a more recent example, the busing of school children to achieve equal educational opportunity is, in part, a response to people's perception that they have lost autonomy and control of their community (of course, bigotry and racism are also factors influencing people's resistance).

Thus, it would be difficult to understand the profile and problems of America's cities without appreciating the extent to which people in America believe in local autonomy and control. Such a belief is strongly embedded in the core values of freedom, individualism, and activism; and it operates to define for many what is "wrong" with the cities, while being intimately connected to the substance of their social problems. For indeed, the structure of community problems has been, as we will come to see, heavily influenced by this dominant belief.

THE STRUCTURE OF COMMUNITY PROBLEMS

THE EMERGENCE OF THE METROPOLIS IN AMERICA

In 1800 only a few cities in the United States had a population over 25,000; none of these exceeded 100,000 (Strauss, 1961:91). Compared

Rapid growth of America's cities

America's "cities" were little more than small towns at the beginning of the nineteenth century. It is in this rapid growth from settlements, like the one above, to the giant metropolitan areas of today that current problems inhere.

to London with 800,000 or Paris with 500,000 residents, Philadelphia (70,000) and New York (60,000) were little more than small towns. However, by 1860 New York had a population of more than 800,000 inhabitants (not including Brooklyn) and was the third largest city in the Western world, behind London and Paris. Philadelphia, with over 500,000, had surpassed Berlin in size, and six other American cities had swelled to over 100,000 inhabitants (Schlesinger, 1951). By 1880, with the vast immigrations from southeastern Europe only beginning, 20 American cities had surpassed the 100,000 mark in population (Strauss, 1961:91).

This spectacular emergence of large American cities can be attributed to several interrelated forces: (1) industrialization and the creation of urban jobs, (2) the resulting massive internal rural to urban migrations of people in search of these jobs in industry, (3) the immigration of peasants from rural Europe into the cities in search of a prosperous life, and (4) the natural increase of urban residents stemming from the high birthrates of rural migrants and immigrants.

The first large cities in the American colonies, (New York, Boston, Baltimore, Philadelphia, Charleston, and Newport), were commercial seaports that marketed goods from Europe while distributing indigenous agricultural goods from their own hinterlands. Migrations westward from these initial cities resulted in the emergence of cities beyond the Appalachians, as in Ohio and Indiana. Unlike those in the East, these cities were populated not so much by rural migrants as by sons of city residents on the eastern seaboard. The westward expansion of urban communities altered the commercial profile of eastern cities to one centered around the manufacture of goods for these new territories. At the same time, industrialists began to establish factory towns along the banks of rivers from which power could be easily derived. From 1815 to 1850 these industrial towns grew and greatly extended urban industrial communities into the interior of the nation along major waterways—a pattern that persists until the present day. As the factories in the seaboard and river cities grew in number and size, farmers from the surrounding rural areas moved into them in search of opportunities not available in the increasingly unprosperous hinterland. This rural peasantry was rapidly transformed into an urban proletariat and became crowded into the tenements surrounding the factories. In the 1850s the railroad allowed further urban development in the West, most notably in Chicago and Toledo, and stimulated increased industrial manufacturing in the East, thereby initiating new manufacturing in the Midwest.

> The urban-industrial profile of early America

By the 1850s the urban-industrial profile of American communities was becoming clearly evident. With further industrialization, the demand for unskilled factory labor began to exceed the supply available from rural migrations and natural population increases in the city. Fleeing from impoverished conditions in Europe in search of these job opportunities, waves of immigrants began to pour into the cities, resulting in a new and persistent pattern of urban organization: the ethnic ghetto or enclave. The influx of foreign immigrants was so great that the cities became overrun, creating incredibly crowded and unsanitary living conditions. Housing was scarce, so rents soared as buildings became increasingly crowded and deteriorated. Thus, by 1850 the ethnic slum and its absentee slumlord were permanent fixtures of the American city.

> The emergence of slums and ghettos

Concomitant to the development of urban slums was the emergence of middle-class residential areas of white-collar workers who managed the factories and provided the services necessary to keep them running. Also, extensive downtown shopping and commercial areas developed to service both the factory and white-collar worker, as well as to distribute and market many of the products of the industrializing economy. Thus, within a comparatively small geographical region, working-class tenements, impoverished ethnic slums, middle-class neighborhoods, factories, and an extensive downtown commercial center typified most urban-industrial cities by the turn of the century.

While the ethnic and cultural diversity, as well as the concentration of so much human activity around a prospering central business district gives, in retrospect, an image of a vibrant polis, today's cities, with all the problems imputed to them, are much safer and more sanitary places to live in *in absolute terms* than they were at the turn of the century. By 1910, with the development of the automobile, cities became highly congested because the streets and their patterning were not designed for the use of cars and trucks. Furthermore, as industrial production increased, as the sewage facilities of the city were overtaxed by the urban masses, and as the concentration of cars and trucks into the narrow city streets multiplied, pollution of the air and water was initiated—although at that time few considered it a serious social problem.[1]

Partially because cities in America developed so rapidly and spontaneously, they were unplanned and went unregulated by the federal government which, in accordance with beliefs in local autonomy and control, did not think it appropriate to intervene extensively in the internal affairs of cities. Hence the dangers, unsanitary facilities, grievances of the urban peasants from Europe, and deteriorating conditions of the inner city were viewed as outside the province of the federal government. Furthermore, the vast capital needed to plan cities more rationally was unavailable to the federal government in an era when there was no federal income tax. Thus, reflecting dominant values and beliefs, cities, from their outset, were politically decentralized and autonomous from the federal government. This tradition of local autonomy—buttressed by a laissez faire ideology in economic activities (see Chapter 6)—makes federal involvement in city problems difficult and often ineffective, even today.

Lack of planning in early urban America

This lack of national policy for cities created a pattern of urban city politics that dominates many large eastern and midwestern cities to this day. The wave of immigrants from rural areas in Europe and the outskirts of urban areas encountered many problems of adjustment that were partially resolved by the local ward heeler of the big-city political machines—Tammany Hall in New York, Crump in Memphis, Hague in Jersey City, Curley in Boston, and Pendergast in Kansas City (Dynes et al., 1964:55). Ward heelers provided help, comfort, and vital services to the new city residents who were poor and insecure in the new urban-industrial complex. They became intermediaries between the slumlord and resident (usually at a price unknown to the resident), and eliminated the bureaucratic entangle-

City politics in early America

ments—residency requirements, red tape, and delays—in securing assistance for families requiring aid. The big-city machine was thus established on the principle of a personal relationship between its local representative and the new urbanite, but for a great price: The urbanite agreed to vote for the machine's candidate in elections and, hence, perpetuate the machine and its capacity to render great profits for its leaders. While most of the big political machines in large urban areas have diminished, a *pattern* of political control was established and persists today. The persistence of widespread political corruption and patronage, as well as control of a city's resources by a few elites, has persisted and has often inhibited federal involvement in a city's internal affairs; when such involvement has been allowed, as in urban renewal, local corruption has often been the result.[2] What is important for our present purposes is to emphasize that big-city politics had been institutionalized and *built into* the structure of American communities by the early decades of this century.

From 1910 to 1930 a new form of internal immigration from rural America became conspicuous: The rural, southern black began to migrate to northern cities in search of work. For decades rural conditions in the South had deteriorated, and with the boll weevil's devastation of the cotton-farming industry, along with the industrial expansion and changes in immigration policies accompanying World War I, blacks began to pour into northern cities in search of job opportunities. Because of their poverty and because of racial discrimination, black migrants were forced into the most dilapidated and crowded tenements, the result was the birth of the black ghetto. Out of these conditions, fanned by white attacks on black residents, emerged the first urban race riots and interracial conflicts. Between 1915 and 1919, Allen and Adair (1969:31) conclude, 18 major race riots occurred. For example, between May 28 and July 2, 1917, a total of 39 blacks were killed in East St. Louis, Illinois, because they had been used as strikebreakers. Reports indicate that the intense violence, burning, and disruption were subdued only by the use of the National Guard and escalated police activity. By 1920 urban segregation and exploitation of blacks and its resulting racial tensions were clearly *built into* the structure of major cities in the United States.

Shortly after the turn of the century, the following conditions were endemic to the structure of the American city:

1. overcrowded and impoverished slums with substandard housing and unsafe sanitary facilities
2. ethnic and racial segregation of neighborhoods
3. industrial pollution of the air and water
4. community pollution of waters stemming from inadequate sewage facilities

The black ghetto and racial turmoil

The problems of early cities

5. extreme congestion from trucks and automobiles
6. corrupt big-city politics
7. racial tensions and riots

These conditions began to appear as soon as large cities emerged in the early 1800s and were well known by scholars and residents of the time. If current city conditions are compared to those at the turn of the century, it is clear that things have gotten better, on an absolute standard. In fact, congestion, housing, and sanitation are clearly much better than at the turn of the century, but current urban conditions are not judged and evaluated on a fixed standard. They are judged on a constantly escalating standard—a yardstick that compares city life with the affluence of white, middle-class suburbia. The big city was thought pleasant, or at least endurable, as long as most people were of the working class, but as the ranks of the middle classes began to swell, cities became thought of as abhorrent (Banfield, 1970:66). This sense of relative deprivation may help account for the myth about the "golden age" of cities, for in reality they were never very pleasant places to live by any standards. Cities, from the beginning, have been unplanned, heavily industrial (at least in the East and Midwest), overcrowded, congested, unsanitary, and great polluters of the environment.

The large industrial city that was the hallmark of urban America at the turn of the century was an inevitable by-product of the technology of the times. The technology of early industrial societies did not allow for the flexible movement of energy over long distances by electrical cables. Factories had to be located near sources of energy or at least near railroads or major waterways, where coal and oil could be easily supplied. Since work was concentrated in cities so was the work force, which, because of limited transportation facilities, had to remain close to the factories. The markets for industrial goods were in the central cities, therefore, the commercial and trade industries also became tied to cities in the form of central business districts.

Just as the imperatives of early industrial technology stimulated the growth of large cities, changes in that technology and the resulting changes in the economy created a new form of urbanism in the twentieth century: metropolitan areas composed of large decaying cities inhabited by the poor and surrounded by suburbs inhabited by the white and the more affluent.

Creation of the metropolitan area

TECHNOLOGY AND SUBURBANIZATION

Shortly after the turn of the century a technological revolution occurred. In 1915 there were 2.5 million automobiles, but 20 years later assemblyline production had increased the number of cars exponen-

Early American cities were designed to accomodate horse-powered transportation, as depicted in Boston in the 1880s (left). *But today these narrow streets must accomodate automobiles, creating extreme congestion and pollution problems—problems that are evident in the Boston scene of the 1970s* (right).

tially. Cars made it possible to adapt transportation facilities to where people wanted to live, rather than the reverse. Heretofore, residential areas had to be adjusted to the existing and fixed trolley and rail transport systems, but with the increasing development of roads and highways, more flexible living patterns outside the city limits could be enjoyed by those who could afford a car and the costs of commuting to work from the suburbs (Dentler, 1967; Green 1965).

Transportation and suburbanization

There were other technological forces contributing to the outward growth of urban areas (Banfield, 1970). Mechanical refrigerators, wide varieties of canned foods, and high-voltage electrical transmission cables allowed people to have the amenities in the suburbs that previously were available only in the central city. Furthermore, the communications revolution involving first the radio, then television, enabled suburban residents to remain psychologically tied to cities while being geographically separated from them.

Technological changes also allowed, and in some cases forced, industry to follow residents out of the central city. The development of extensive assemblyline techniques of production required more space than was economically feasible to buy in the central city. The rapid proliferation of a road and highway system and the emergence

Industrialization and suburbanization

of a trucking industry allowed producers to disperse their production facilities without losing access to raw materials and markets. These and other kinds of technological changes had a profound impact on the way the American economy in the twentieth century became organized. In turn, these changes in the economy facilitated suburbanization.

ECONOMIC ORGANIZATION AND SUBURBANIZATION

As people began to move into the suburbs, marketing and service organizations also relocated to serve the affluent suburbanites. This movement created jobs for white-collar workers, with the result that even more white-collar residents migrated out of the city to take advantage of new jobs and better services. As ever more white-collar, middle-class residents relocated to suburbia, so did more marketing and servicing enterprises in search of a more lucrative market. In this way, a cycle of suburbanization of economically prosperous residents and skilled, white-collar industries was initiated and perpetuated.

As the buyers for many industrial goods located in the suburbs, manufacturing corporations also began to relocate near these affluent markets. Since land was cheap and taxes were low in the suburbs, many industries could increase their profits by relocating beyond the city limits. One result of the movement of servicing, marketing, and manufacturing enterprises to the suburbs was to drain the central city of its skilled and affluent work force, as well as some of its major enterprises in the central business district.

The flight of business and affluent workers

GOVERNMENT POLICIES AND SUBURBANIZATION

State, local, and federal governments have contributed to the mass exodus of white, affluent, middle-class city residents to the suburbs. During the 1930s the Federal Housing Administration (FHA), and in the 1940s the Veterans Administration (VA), encouraged the construction of single-family dwellings in the suburbs by insuring mortgages. This policy overcame traditionally conservative banking practices and enabled people who had a little economic surplus to purchase their own homes in the suburbs. The FHA thus kept the urban exodus alive, even during the depression years. During World War II housing, building, and rent controls were established, and many industries in the cities were revived, resulting in migrations back into the cities. After the war, however, with the help of the VA home loan guarantee and FHA guarantees, movement out of the city became truly massive and led to the present day dramatic transformation of American cities. (Harr, 1960).

Housing policies and suburbanization

State and local governments also contributed to the emergence of suburbia. Initially the central city annexed the new residential areas along its borders, but eventually shortsighted city leaders began to feel that the suburbs were a liability because the taxes they yielded did not pay for the services the city had to supply (police, fire prevention, sanitation, streets, etc.). By the time large city governments began to realize that their tax base had vanished to the suburbs, suburban communities had begun to incorporate in order to determine their own fate, patterns of land use, allocation of tax monies, and just who their neighbors were to be. In state after state legislators from suburban areas, who craved self-government, joined forces with rural legislators, who saw the growth of large cities as a threat to rural power, to enact legislation that made the annexation of the suburbs by central cities very difficult. By the end of the 1920s the delineation between suburb and central city was well established in American metropolitan regions (Greer, 1966).

THE DEMOGRAPHIC IMPERATIVES
OF SUBURBANIZATION

As people migrated into the first American cities, city boundaries inevitably had to expand. In 1790 only 5 percent of the population lived in urban areas; today 75 percent live in urban areas; and by 1980, 90 percent of the population will live in urban regions. Naturally, a demographic transformation of these proportions made sub-

The result of urban forces has been the creation of suburbia and exurbia, as in the photo at left. This change in urban patterns has created many problems for the large central city.

urbia almost inevitable. Since there are limits as to how far city boundaries can be extended, autonomous and yet contiguous suburban communities were necessary to accompany the natural growth and migration of the urban population. The migrations of city residents to the suburbs remained highly selective, however, and usually involved only the white and the affluent, whose place in the central city was taken by blacks, Puerto Ricans, Chicanos, and other impoverished minorities who had migrated from rural regions. Many of the problems inherent in urban America derive from the concentration of the minorities and other categories of poor in the central cities and the affluent whites in the suburbs.

The city-suburban color line

PROBLEMS OF THE CITY IN METROPOLITAN AREAS

In light of cultural beliefs advocating federal nonintervention into cities, as well as the technological changes, specific housing policies, patterns of economic organization, and demographic imperatives surrounding urbanization in America, the growth of a large metropolitan area with a core city encircled by white suburbs was inevitable. Whether the consequences of these forces were also inevitable is now a moot question, but the problems of the cities are to a very great extent the result of the white exodus that created the metropolitan area and of the still well-entrenched belief that communities should have local control of their affairs and autonomy from federal dictates.

POLITICAL FRAGMENTATION

One of the major consequences of the growth of metropolitan areas and the resulting incorporation of separate and autonomous suburban communities was the political decentralization of decision making in urban America. In the old big cities, political machines represented a highly centralized form of decision making with the result that policies—both good and bad—could be easily implemented across the whole city. In contrast, the multiple communities in a modern metropolitan area now make unified and concerted political action difficult (Greer, 1966), especially with the dominance of local control and autonomy beliefs. Each separate community has its own local officials and city government, which, on the one hand, represents a traditional American ideal of a decentralized and democratic polis, but also, on the other hand, makes planning across an entire metropolitan region difficult. While local governments act autonomously, they are in reality part of a larger urban system that, in order to remain viable, probably needs to engage in metropolitanwide

Local government waste and inefficiency

planning. From this perspective, American metropolitan areas can be visualized as having *built into* their structure and culture the *inca*pacity to respond politically and administratively to problems of housing, crime, traffic, pollution, sanitation, and police and fire protection.

In addition to fractionalizing political power, suburban incorporation and the persistence of local autonomy and control beliefs has resulted in the duplication of many public services. Such duplication often represents an enormous waste of the financial resources of a metropolitan region since vital services, including police and fire protection, public works, sanitation, and pollution control, can be financed less expensively and administered more efficiently at the metropolitanwide level than at the local level. One consequence of this is that resources that could be used for attacking many problems, such as pollution, congestion, poor housing in the cities, and crime in the streets, are spent in duplication of services. Thus, in addition to political fractionalization and the resulting decrease in the capacity to act at the metropolitan level, resources necessary for resolving metropolitan problems are sometimes unavailable for either the large core cities or their suburbs.

Political fragmentation is a continual dilemma facing a federalist political system. Decentralization of political power has many advantages, the most notable of which is to minimize the gap between political leaders and the citizenry. Centralization has many disadvantages, the most prominent of which is to create a wasteful bureaucracy that is out of touch with those it is supposed to serve. The dilemma facing America's metropolitan areas, then, is how to restructure government so that the benefits of decentralization can be realized, while, at the same time, maintaining some degree of adminis-

trative centralization to deal with metropolitanwide problems. Such a formula calls for a delicate balance that is difficult to effect in the first place, and even more difficult to maintain.

THE ECONOMIC PLIGHT OF THE CITIES

The white, middle-class exodus to the suburbs has created an economic crisis in the cities. First, the movement of industries, businesses, and commerce to the suburbs has frequently led to the decline of the central business district in many large cities. In turn, the decline of this area has undermined the tax base which the city needs to survive and prosper. Second, the high-income resident, in moving to

The large city can often no longer afford to clean its streets, assist its indigent, protect its people, or provide services for the young.

the suburbs, no longer spends money in or pays taxes to the city, resulting in an even greater erosion of the revenue necessary to maintain a large city. Third, state and federal tax formulas typically create a situation whereby the city pays more in taxes than it receives in services such as education, police protection, highway benefits, transportation funds, and public service revenues. The overall result of these three forces is to make it increasingly difficult for cities to finance and supply necessary services (Grier and Grier, 1966). They can no longer afford "to educate and train their underprivileged, support their unemployed and elderly poor, police their streets, mend their sick, or operate their courts, jails, utilities, and garbage plants" (Abrams, 1969:38).

Reasons for the economic crisis

The city is an integral part of a metropolitan area, and yet, it has a decreasing base of tax revenue. Coupled with the fact that public services cost more than ever, an economic crisis of severe proportions has emerged. In addition, the residents of contemporary cities—the poor, the minorities, and the aged, not to mention the more affluent city-dwellers who can exercise greater control over their place of residence—are requiring an increasing number of services in the form of housing, welfare, police protection, and health care. Under current conditions, the city is decreasingly able to pay the rising costs of these necessary services. In 1932 municipalities were collecting more taxes than the federal and state governments combined. Of all tax monies received, cities received 52 percent (Abrams, 1969:39); today the intake of cities is less than 10 percent of the total. With rising costs and increasing demands for services in the burdened cities, new fiscal formulas for financing America's large core cities will become increasingly necessary.

SUBURBAN EXPLOITATION OF CITIES

Among America's large cities only New York, predicts Mitchell Gordon (1963), will have a majority of its work force residing within the city limits by 1980. Even if this prediction is inaccurate, it points to a trend of utmost importance for the cities: The large city has increasingly become solely a workplace for the suburbanite. This likelihood means that the commuter will derive a livelihood from the city, use many of its facilities (police, transportation, sanitation), and yet pay no personal taxes to it. The city may well become, as it already has in many instances, a service area for the affluent middle-class suburbanites who return home to their suburban community, where they deposit their money, buy their wares, and pay their taxes. Since this trend is likely to continue, new sources of tax revenue and city financing will have to be found.

The commuter and city services

THE DECAYING URBAN CORE

The movement of much industry and commerce as well as many middle-class residents out of the city has been paralleled by a substantial migration of the poor into the city. While some descendants of many early immigrants have vacated their ethnic enclaves for residence in suburbia, or in more prosperous areas of the large city, the rapid influx of blacks and other impoverished minority groups into the city's tenements has perpetuated the urban slum. To illustrate how rapid these migrations of blacks into the cities have been, it can be noted that in 1910 73 percent of the black population lived in the rural South, whereas by 1960 73 percent resided in urban areas (Taeuber and Taeuber, 1965). Similar migrations of rural Puerto Ricans and Chicanos have occurred.

The massiveness of the influx of the poor into the cities has created extensive demands for low-cost housing which is available only in the decaying tenements that were constructed around the turn of the century. Since the demand for low-cost housing has been great and the supply low (especially for blacks, who have been openly discriminated against), landlords have maintained the tradition, first initiated in the last century, of charging comparatively high rents and providing little property maintenance and few improvements. While in absolute terms the quality of ghetto housing is now superior to that at the turn of the century, the standards of what constitutes decent housing have risen as the level of affluence in the broader society has escalated. Thus, housing is still a major social problem for the urban minorities who are forced to live in dwellings that are substandard and dilapidated by escalated standards.

Entrapment of the poor

While the persistence of substandard housing at the city's core is often the result of personal greed by landlords and of the inability of the poor to afford better living conditions, the urban housing blight has other sources—many of which are *built into* the structure of American institutions and communities. Inhibited by beliefs in local control, the federal government has never really (until very recently) approached the question of housing on a national level. For example, in a society with a federally conceived and financed highway system and with a national farm policy, there currently is no national urban policy, even though American society has been urbanized for half a century. There has traditionally been no national research—until the last few years—on how to deal with the construction and distribution of housing. Research financed by the federal government on housing lags by billions of dollars behind that financed by the government for agriculture, manufacturing, medicine, and other areas of applied technology. Even massive federal programs such as Urban Renewal,

Recent immigrants to the city are forced to adjust to a decaying urban core.

Public Housing, and Model Cities have had little impact on housing blight. In many cases, as with the FHA and VA housing mortgage insurance programs, the federal government has encouraged urban blight by stimulating the building of new houses in the suburbs rather than in the cities. Probably the best demonstration of how unsystematic and uncomprehensive the federal government's approach to urban problems has been is the fact that the Department of Agriculture has existed for 100 years, while the Department of Housing and Urban Development was initiated only in 1965 (Dentler, 1967:291–319). If one compares the funds available to each of these cabinet offices, and their respective power, the neglect of urban conditions by the federal government becomes even more marked.

The structure of the housing industry also helps to account for the current blight in the cities (Dentler, 1967:302–319; Greer, 1966). The building industry is a private enterprise system that, naturally, seeks to make a profit. Contractors are therefore likely to build in middle- and high-income areas in the suburbs, where profits are greatest. The housing industry is also a *local* industry with few national corporations of the magnitude of the Ford Company and General Motors. Yet the housing industry provides one of the most important commodities, a home; does an annual business of close to $25 billion; employs over 5 million workers; and, creates a vast market for other industries. However, because the housing industry is so decentralized, it goes comparatively unregulated by the federal government, with the result that clear national housing policies—should they ever be initiated—would be difficult to implement, as has been the case with the Urban Renewal program, Model Cities, and other federal programs.

Other features of the building industry prevent the introduction of money-saving innovations and technologies that could reduce costs to a point where it would be profitable for contractors to build low-income housing. For example, current technology would allow for mass production and assembly of almost all components for a house—from the roof to the plumbing—in factories. Most trade unions in the building industry, however, require in their contracts on-the-site assembly (and production) of houses. The production of current housing in factories would, of course, displace many workers; and until new jobs could be guaranteed for workers in the building industry, unions are naturally going to resist changes in the present mode of home construction. Also, many *local* building codes prevent the introduction of new building materials that could reduce the cost of home construction. Like the entire building industry, building codes are locally established. Typically, the requirements of these codes pertain to the use of specific materials rather than the performance of materials. Instead of stipulating that building materials be of a certain strength and durability, local codes usually specify the actual *material* that must be used by a contractor and architect. Local contractors, subcontractors, and building suppliers, operating as a powerful vested interest, can often assure a material emphasis in building codes by exerting pressure on local officials who establish these codes. At times the FHA reinforces this roadblock to the introduction of new building materials by requiring certain materials in homes before it will insure a mortgage.

RACIAL AND ETHNIC SEGREGATION

As the affluent whites moved out of the cities, the poor, especially blacks, migrated into the cities. Because they came from rural areas and had few industrial skills and because of racial discrimination, blacks were confined to the worst jobs in the most dilapidated parts of the city. Currently racial and ethnic minorities are locked into the decaying city core and are surrounded by the more-affluent whites in the suburbs. Furthermore, within the core cities segregation of the racial and ethnic minorities into ghettos, like that of their immigrant predecessors, remains extremely high. The explosiveness of such "urban apartheid" is all too apparent—as is explored extensively in Chapter 12. For the present, it can be noted that residential segregation of blacks continues to be high within cities and between the city and suburbs (Taeuber and Taeuber, 1965; Farley and Taeuber, 1968). Such segregation is the result of more than racial bigotry; it has been built into the structure of the federal government's policies and the demographic forces accompanying American urbanization.

Urban apartheid

ATTACKING URBAN PROBLEMS

As the affluence of the broader society has increased, those trapped in the cities inevitably have an escalated sense of deprivation. Although slow to respond and somewhat ineffectual when it did, the federal government began to recognize the deprivations of residents in the core cities, as well as the deteriorating physical conditions of central business districts. Over the last 25 years this recognition has been translated into a series of programs designed to "cure" city problems. Some "cures," however, have been mitigated by beliefs in local autonomy and control, and have made federal intervention highly conditional and somewhat ineffectual.

THE PUBLIC HOUSING PROGRAM

One of the first programs for providing housing to the poor was the federal public housing program (created by the Housing Act of 1937). The initiation of this program must be viewed in the context of the

FHA and VA mortgage insurance programs, which encouraged whites to move into single-family dwellings in the suburbs; while the federal government was building large public housing complexes in the core city, usually in ghetto areas. Such dual programs furthered residential segregation by confining impoverished minorities, especially blacks, to the core city, while subsidizing the migration of whites to single-family dwellings in the suburbs.[3] Furthermore, until the early 1950s the FHA often kept affluent blacks from migrating to suburbs, by warning realtors, FHA authorities, and bankers in its manuals that racially integrated neighborhoods were likely to deteriorate rapidly and were poor financial risks. The FHA backed up this warning by refusing to insure housing developments that were racially integrated—resulting in the emergence of racial covenants in early American suburbs (Abrams, 1967:59–64; Grigsby, 1964:223). Since this policy existed during the great postwar exodus of whites and the in-migrations of racial minorities to urban areas, it established a pattern of suburban-city segregation. It is in this context that the public housing project was initiated—usually a large, monolithic, concrete and brick structure erected in the middle of the decaying city core. At a time when American values, tastes, and preferences were shifting to the single-family dwelling, the federal government was forcing the poor to live in "supertenements." As Catherine Bauer Wurster (1966:247) commented: "Life in the usual public housing project just is not the way most American families want to live. Nor does it reflect our accepted values as to the way people should live." Furthermore, public housing is *government-managed* housing—a situation that violates people's values of freedom and individualism. Compounding this situation is the overall architectural design of housing projects: They have a standardized institutional appearance, much like that of a hospital or prison. For example, the Robert Taylor Project in Chicago, where 28,000 people are confined to several huge high-rise buildings can be typified as a $70-million ghetto that residents refer to as the "Congo Hilton" (Schaffer et al., 1970). Even though public housing projects may be initially clean, the lack of maintenance funds coupled with their high population densities, often make older projects dirty, unsanitary, and trash strewn.

Problems with public housing

In addition to their physical appearance, public housing projects, by imposing income ceilings on their residents, create income homogeneity, which adds to the projects' institutional profile. Furthermore, in a society that values freedom from government constraint, the whole concept of a government-managed home is automatically stigmatizing. The result is that those who can afford to would often rather live in a dilapidated "private enterprise slum" where more diversity is possible and where the possibilities for local autonomy and control are greater.

Recently, recognizing the error of the original public housing program, new legislation has been passed in an attempt to remedy some of its deficiencies. For example, the Turnkey Program allows public housing to be built and managed by private corporations and encourages the building of more dispersed, low-rise buildings. While these new kinds of projects may mitigate the institutional and managed character of traditional public housing, two fundamental problems remain with such programs: (1) The black poor are not encouraged to *own their houses* as are whites in the suburbs,[4] and (2) projects still encourage the segregation of blacks in the cities from whites in the suburbs. New approaches to public housing will not quickly or effectively undo the inequities that have existed between 1935 (when the FHA was created) and the 1950s (when FHA policies changed). The reason is that for close to 20 years whites have had their ownership of single-family dwellings in the suburbs subsidized by the federal government (FHA and VA), while blacks and other minorities have been shunted into public housing complexes where only their rent was subsidized. Even as recently as 1967 the FHA continued to discriminate against the poor by affirming that "blighted areas" in the core of cities could not be insured for mortgages, preventing blacks and other minorities from owning even dilapidated homes and forcing them into slum rentals or public housing. Only after the Detroit riot of 1968 was this policy modified (Harrington, 1968).

THE URBAN RENEWAL PROGRAM

The Housing Act of 1949 created the Urban Renewal Program, which focused on the overall physical and economic needs of the cities. The goals of the program were stated somewhat vaguely: (1) to provide a decent home for every citizen; (2) to assure well-planned, rationally organized neighborhoods; (3) to beautify American cities and communities (Greer, 1966).

Problems with urban renewal

As lofty and laudable as these goals would appear, they were implemented within constraints that made their realization most difficult. First, America's large cities had expanded under pressures of early industrialization when sources of power and transportation were limited, resulting in a centralized-city pattern of land use. It is unlikely that patterns of land use appropriate to the nineteenth century are always viable in light of the massive technological, economic and demographic changes over the last 50 years (Greer, 1966; Banfield, 1970). The Urban Renewal Program was therefore committed to basic goals which, at times, went against fundamental patterns of reorganization of American urban life. Second, urban renewal was constrained by beliefs in local control and was, accordingly, initiated on what are perhaps questionable premises: (1) The existing private enterprise facilities—banks, construction companies, real estate firms, and trade unions—were to provide the vehicle for each project's implementation. Buildings were, therefore, built by private corporations for a *private market*. Since these same private enterprise processes were responsible for many of the current urban problems—from racial segregation to exploitation of the poor—the wisdom of the government's policy to preserve the sanctity of, and in many cases to subsidize, private enterprise in this sphere can be questioned. (2) Each urban renewal project was to be initiated at the local level and run by the local city government. Considering the political tradition of American cities for corruption and patronage, this provision of the Housing Act was also of questionable wisdom. Indeed, it soon became apparent that urban renewal was, at times, the political tool of big and little city governmental machines. Third, urban renewal projects tended to be concerned only with physical restoration of the cities, not with changing the social pattern of community life.

The structure of urban renewal has often subverted the implementation of its goals. Generally, in accordance with beliefs in local autonomy, the city must initiate a program through a local agency, which is to work up an urban renewal plan to be approved by the regional and federal renewal agency. If approved, the federal government will supply most of the money needed to acquire necessary land and subsidize the demolition of buildings. Once the land is acquired, the approved plan is contracted to a private developer who implements the plan, while being supervised by the local, regional, and federal urban renewal agencies. One of the main shortcomings of this structure is that political biases and pressures from local political officials, as well as from local real estate and business enterprises, greatly determine what is to be renewed in a city. The federal government oversees the project, but the local redevelopment agency is under heavy pressure from local political and economic interests. One consequence has been that downtown areas, where business interests are strongest, have been renewed at the expense of the poor. For example, downtown blight has frequently been eliminated by displacing the poor from their slum residences and forcing them into either public housing or into even worse slums. When new housing is finally built in the former slum, it has tended to be in the form of upper- and middle-income complexes since this kind of housing is most profitable on a *private* real estate market.[5] Even when low-income housing has been built, it is typically more expensive than the

Urban renewal has often leveled the poor's housing—forcing them to compete even more for slum residences or to enter sterile public housing projects. In place of housing, the giant edifice designed for the affluent has emerged.

old and often suffers from the same drawbacks as public housing.

Because urban renewal has been, since its incipiency, committed to reviving the old urban polis, many cities have "renewed" their downtown areas into culturaleconomic centers of office and civil buildings as well as cultural attractions such as music centers and museums. These projects have been designed to entice middle-income residents to move back into the city, but unfortunately these residents have tended rather to visit the renewed facilities, leaving their tax money in suburbia. Oftentimes, the net impact of urban renewal has been to provide new recreation areas for the suburbanite, while displacing the poor who lived in the renewed area and forcing them into other, already overcrowded ghettos or, even worse, public housing projects (Anderson, 1964). Since the poor have not been as well organized or as powerful as the political and economic elites of cities, restoration of downtown areas has usually taken precedence over low-income housing, with the result that "at a cost of more than three billion dollars the Urban Renewal Agency has succeeded in materially reducing the supply of low-cost housing in American cities" (Greer, 1966:3).

Where attempts at slum elimination and restoration do take precedence over political and economic interests, blacks and other poor, as in public housing, are still forced to stay in the core city. Furthermore, while there can be little doubt that, in terms of physical facilities, urban renewal has improved the conditions of many ghettos, it has not attempted to touch upon the social problems such as crime and drug use. In their desire to plan neighborhoods rationally, local agencies have often ignored the social and human side of a neighborhood in the name of mere physical restoration. Social isolation in towering, impersonal complexes and victimization in untended elevators and corridors are tragically recurrent themes.

Perhaps many of the problems of urban renewal stem from its failure to focus on the whole metropolitan area, for if one considers the cities to be "sick and decaying," the solution to their problems can probably best come from metropolitanwide programs. In focusing only on the symptoms of decay, urban renewal has often ignored the "disease" that is built into the technological, economic, and demographic underpinnings of the modern metropolis.

THE MODEL CITIES PROGRAM

In 1966 Congress enacted the Demonstrations Cities Act in an effort to overcome some of the deficiencies in the Urban Renewal Program. In general, the Model Cities Program created by the act attempts to revitalize a city's economy by strengthening its tax base while providing for improved low-income housing. Unlike urban renewal, the Model Cities Program requires a more comprehensive plan to improve the housing, employment, business, and social service picture in a city. Furthermore, cities must select for development districts that evidence a large proportion of deteriorating housing (Schaffer et al., 1970). The resulting renewal or development plan must receive the approval of local groups and leaders *in the renewal area;* it must provide adequate relocation procedures for those displaced; it must involve and employ local residents in the program; and it requires attractive building design utilizing the latest technology and the altering of building codes if necessary. City governments that submit a plan that includes these provisions are awarded a cash bonus or subsidy to pay for up to 90 percent of development costs. Additional grants can be obtained from the government to improve various municipal services, such as libraries, schools, and sanitation and recreation facilities in the development area.

While the Model Cities Program eliminates many of the problems of urban renewal, several drawbacks remain (Greer, 1966): (1) The program still is initiated by local officials who are more often interested in development of the business area than the slums. The program also is subject to pressures from local vested interests, such as

The poor, trapped in their slums and at the mercy of federal and city government, seek meaning and purpose.

building and real estate industries. Yet the program, in requiring low-income housing development and local residential involvement, does represent a significant improvement over urban renewal. (2) When the Model Cities Program is initiated in large cities, rarely does it cut down on the degree of residential segregation of racial and ethnic groups. While improvements in the downtown area may help recruit middle-income residents back into the city, it does little to break down walls of discrimination and segregation. (3) The program, like urban renewal, focuses only on the city and not on a whole metropolitan area and, therefore, goes against the tide of suburbanization. In doing so, it subsidizes the downtown business district in its competition with suburban shopping centers. At the same time it perpetuates the segregated position of ethnic and racial groups within the core city, albeit in somewhat improved housing. One of the basic problems of local programs initiated only in the city is that they do little to help the poor migrate out to the suburbs and thereby eliminate urban-suburban segregation.

Problems with model cities

THE HOUSING SUBSIDY PROGRAMS

After 33 years of subsidizing (under FHA and VA programs) middle-income homeowners, the federal government, with the passage of the Housing and Urban Development Act of 1968, initiated a subsidy program for lower-income residents. The act provides for interest-rate subsidies for home purchase among families with incomes between $3000 and $7000. The subsidy comes in the form of a cash gift ranging from $40 to $50 a month to be used for mortgage payments. One problem with the program is that it does not reach the most impoverished, those with incomes below $3000, trapped in the worst urban slums. Another problem is that it does not provide the poor with sufficient funds to meet the high costs of home maintenance.

Problems with housing subsidies

Another subsidy program initiated with the Housing Act of 1961, but significantly bolstered by the 1966 and 1968 acts, provides for rent subsidies. The poor inevitably have had to pay a very high proportion of their monthly income into housing at the sacrifice of clothing, food, and medical care (Schorr, 1963). The rent subsidy program attempts to keep the proportion down by paying the difference between the actual rent and 25 percent of the monthly income of low-to moderate-income families.

While subsidies may carry little stigma in slum or ghetto areas in large cities, it is not clear what would happen to minority families who attempted to use the benefits of the program to buy or rent in the suburbs, where a subsidy would perhaps carry a burdensome stigma

(Glazer, 1967). Coupled with what are often discriminatory practices of developers and real estate agents, the program will have minimal impact in moving ghetto residents into the suburbs.

GRANTS-IN-AID AND REVENUE SHARING

Over the last decades, states and cities have received much grant-in-aid from the federal government. *Grant-in-aid* is the mechanism by which the federal government and local governments—state, county, city—share financing and administering vital programs. There are a wide variety of grant-in-aid programs, but they reveal a number of common features: (1) Federal tax revenues are given to states and local communities for specialized activities, such as education, welfare, health care, city development, and housing. (2) State and local governments are to administer the programs financed by grants-in-aid, but there are usually clear guidelines as to how, for whom, and for what the combined federal and local monies can be used. Moreover, there are usually specified auditing procedures for determining if local governments are conforming to federal conditions and guidelines. (3) Early grant-in-aid programs required the local government receiving federal grant-in-aid money to "match" each federal dollar with locally derived dollars, but during the 1960s the great majority of grant-in-aid programs were enacted with more than 50 percent federal participation, with some totally financed by the federal government.

Grant-in-aid has now become one of the principal ways federal monies are channeled back to state and local governments. Since the mechanisms of subsidy and the administrative control by the federal government under grants-in-aid is somewhat hidden from the general public, it has been accepted despite the persistence of local control and autonomy beliefs. There are now close to 600 grant-in-aid programs, and this form of assistance constitutes over 25 percent of federal outlays for domestic assistance, with much of this assistance going to cities.

The grant-in-aid program has established useful relations among federal, state, and local governments, but despite its many accomplishments—public housing, model cities, welfare, education, health care, community development, and the like—a number of problems are built into the system (Reagan, 1972:86–88).

First, much grant-in-aid money is bestowed as a "project grant" which allows those governments with professional staffs, who are good at "grantmanship," to receive favorable financial treatment. Such cities will tend to be the most affluent, and thus, the least in need of federal monies. Large cities represent an exception because

Problems with grants-in-aid

they have extensive needs for revenue and they do have effective professional staffs, but suburban governments—the least likely to have need—are equally effective in securing grant money, thereby denying cities and poor communities of monies.

A second problem is that grants requiring matching monies can force local governments to channel their limited monies into programs that are less than essential. To some extent, the proliferation of large numbers and varieties of grant-in-aid programs has lessened this problem, but this proliferation has created a third problem with grant-in-aid: The creation of so many overlapping programs has caused severe administrative problems. Local governments are often confused about which of several overlapping programs, each with different requirements and administrative procedures, to select for their particular needs.

Finally, grant-in-aid money can do little for communities whose needs lie outside the aid categories. Many intense needs—especially in the large cities and poor communities—are not covered by a grant-in-aid. Moreover, these cities may have used monies that could address these problems to match less essential programs which do provide grant-in-aid money.

Recognizing these problems, *revenue sharing* has been implemented in the 1970s as a supplement, and in some cases as an alternative, to the grant-in-aid system. In 1972 Congress passed and the President signed the State and Local Assistance Act which provided for the distribution of $30.2 billion from 1972 to 1976 to 40,000 state and local governmental units. The amounts to be distributed are determined by complex formulas which are affected by such variables as the nature of the governmental unit (state, county, township, city), its population, its per capita income, its adjusted taxes, and the number of intergovernmental money transfers it receives. The unique feature of revenue sharing is that the money is given with "no strings" (matching requirements, administrative guidelines, or restrictive categories). Revenue sharing is thus consistent with beliefs in local control, while at the same time it meets the obvious needs of cities for revenues from the federal government. In passing this legislation a number of outcomes were expected: (1) Local government could have the freedom to take diverse approaches to their unique problems. (2) The severe financial crisis in many communities, especially the large cities of metropolitan areas, would be mitigated, thus, many of the present tensions over tax revenues between federal and local government would be lessened. (3) The program would equalize federal expenditures on states and communities by applying the same formula to all local governments. (4) The use of progressive federal income tax revenues to finance local government programs would reduce the reliance of local governments on less-progressive property taxes. (5) In accordance with local control beliefs, decentralization of resources and administrative power would ensue, thereby realizing more completely the original goal of a federalist governmental system.

Despite its promise, and its partial realization in some communities, a number of problems have become evident (Reagan, 1972:123–132): First, the federal government spreads limited monies to all communities, thereby avoiding the difficult decisions about what priorities are to guide federal assistance to the cities. The federal government is, by virtue of its more detached position, better able to see national problems than local political leaders who are much more likely to be influenced by local interests groups—professional administrators (city planners, police, fire, etc.), real estate interests, and the Chamber of Commerce—which are likely to ignore the more chronic needs of many impoverished cities. For example, the most recent evaluation study of revenue sharing reveals that a disproportionate amount of money has been used on capital improvements—city halls, police cars, new fire engines—and not on health, education, and welfare of residents, especially the poor.

Problems with revenue sharing

Second, cuts in grant-in-aid programs have occurred under the presumption that revenue sharing can "make up the difference." Such an assumption ignores the needs of the cities for increased revenues, regardless of their source. Third, revenue sharing may help perpetuate an overall urban pattern that may, in the long run, be fiscally and politically unviable. Revenue sharing might help maintain the problematic political and fiscal structure of metropolitan governments, and thus, it could delay the crisis which could prompt reorganization of America's large urban areas.

The principle vehicles by which the federal government addresses community problems—grant-in-aid and revenue sharing—reveal their own problems of structure. Both grant-in-aid and revenue sharing are probably necessary approaches to urban problems, but unless they are used to induce, and perhaps coerce, fiscal and political reorganization of America's metropolitan regions, their full potential may go unrealized.

HOUSING AND URBAN DEVELOPMENT

In 1965 the Department of Housing and Urban Development (HUD) became a full cabinet-level office. However, it currently does not have the status, tradition, power, or financial resources of other cabinet offices such as the departments of Defense, Agriculture, or Health, Education, and Welfare. Yet, if in the future a national hous-

SOCIOLOGICAL INSIGHTS

THE FUTURE OF CITIES: PROPOSED DIRECTIONS OF CHANGE

The problems of cities are associated with recent decades but they were clearly evident, as noted earlier, by the turn of the century. These problems are, thus, well institutionalized and programs to alter them will probably involve more than accommodation by the federal government to the housing industry and local governments. The reverse will likely have to be the case in the future, for a national program for the cities may well have to be *imposed* on American communities. While such a conclusion may seem regrettable, solutions have been imposed in other areas, such as agriculture, transportation, commerce, national defense, and many other spheres. Moreover, this conclusion goes against the deeply held beliefs of most Americans.

In view of the diversity and extensiveness of its problems, developing concrete proposals for changing and improving the central city in metropolitan areas is difficult. When the conceptual inadequacies of proposals are placed up against the manifold sources of political, economic, and social resistance, such proposals may take on a utopian character. Nevertheless, our structural analysis at least dictates a direction toward which change should move if the cities are to become attractive places to live. While certainly an incomplete proposal and clearly not politically practical at the moment, some desirable directions of change are briefly discussed:

1. A new form of pan-metropolitan governmental authority will probably need to be established over both the central city and the suburban fringe. County governments may have to be eliminated in metropolitan areas and replaced by a metropolitan authority. On the basis of population and other criteria, each city within a metropolitan area could have representation on the decision-making body of the metropolitan authority. The most important function of this authority would be to set the tax rate for the entire metropolitan region, collect and pool the property tax, and redistribute these revenues in accordance with a formula weighted by population size and per capita income of residents. The greater the size and the lower the per capita income of residents, the more revenues a community would receive from the metropolitan authority.

2. In addition to allocating tax revenues, the metropolitan authority could be responsible for financing certain services that can be more efficiently undertaken at a metropolitanwide level. These would include police and fire protection, transportation, health and social services, and pollution control. However, accommodation to local control beliefs could occur by allowing local governments of the metropolitan region to staff and administer these services. Within very broad fiscal and policy guidelines, diversity in the way these services are administered could be encouraged as local governments attempt to meet the unique needs of their population.

3. Aside from administering these metropolitanwide services, local governments would be free to use the liquid tax resources received from the metropolitan authority in any way considered desirable by their elected officials. Additionally, local communities would have administrative control of their schools—schools that would not be financed by regressive property taxes, as is currently the case, but by federal revenues. Also, local communities would have the option of applying for federal urban renewal, model cities, business development, and mortgage subsidy funds, and federal policies would give priority to areas of the core city.

Such guidelines for future action on the cities are devoid of the details that give a proposal other than a utopian character. Yet, it must be recognized that old patterns of city government, outdated fiscal formulas, chaotic and wasteful ways for providing public services, the growing problems of community pollution, and the exploitation of cities by the affluent suburbs may require a radically different form of urban polis. The new forms of government in metropolitan areas should seek to maximize the economies and equities that can come with centralization and at the same time provide for responsiveness of city governments to the unique needs of their residents. Such is the dilemma of structure and culture facing America's cities.

ing policy with adequate financing can be generated within this new department, there is hope that the largely unsuccessful programs of the past will not be duplicated in the future.

The current dilemmas and problems of America's cities will re-

*The city planner, with his impersonal map that will "rehabilitate"
the physical structure of the city, will often ignore the human needs
of the population. America's urban programs are distinquished for
their failure to attack the human problems of the central city.*

quire concerted efforts on three fronts: (1) The development of new
housing technologies; (2) a federal commitment to city development
that regulates more extensively the housing industry; and, (3) the imposition of new political and fiscal organization on metropolitan
areas. A good proportion of HUD's funds are channeled to its Office of
Urban Research and Technology where new ideas and approaches to
home construction and city planning are being developed. For example, mass-produced homes in factories, regional city planning,
and experimental cities are on the drawing boards of this agency.
Unless these technologies can be implemented by the basic reorganization of the housing industry, however, progress in changing housing and city patterns in American communities will probably be
difficult. As long as the building industry remains local and decentralized, with local contractors, local building trade unions, local

Implementing
solutions to
urban problems

building codes, local real estate enterprises, and local government regulation of home construction and city development, there is little possibility for significant progress. While this conclusion may appear somewhat harsh, the federal government will probably have to cease relying on the "talents" and "good will" of local building industries and governments to generate more payoff in its programs.

SUMMARY

In this chapter our attention was drawn to the problems of the large city in metropolitan regions. The shape of the metropolis, and attempts at resolving its problems, is influenced by a powerful belief in local autonomy and control. Cities initially grew under guidance from this belief; and similarly the suburb proliferated as people sought autonomy and local control, but now efforts to help the cities are circumscribed by this belief.

Our analysis of the structure of community problems began with an historical account of the growth of cities and how most of their current problems were built into a particular pattern of growth. These problems were compounded by suburbanization, so our concern shifted to an analysis of the problems of the city in the metropolitan area. Several problems were discussed in detail: (1) Political fragmentation of the metropolitan area, (2) the economic plight of cities, (3) the suburban "exploitation" of cities, (4) the decaying urban core, and (5) racial and ethnic segregation.

Next, we examined the problems inhering in governmental programs dealing with the urban situation. These programs include public housing, urban renewal, model cities, housing subsidies, grants-in-aids, and revenue sharing.

REVIEW QUESTIONS

1. How did the belief in local autonomy and control shape the development of the city and how does it now limit the options available in developing solutions to America's urban problems?
2. List the problems inhering in the cities at the turn of the last century.
3. Analyze how current problems are extensions of the turn-of-the-century problems?
4. What new problems has suburbanization created?
5. List the governmental solutions to urban problems. What are the prospects and limitations of each?

NOTES

1. Obviously people were aware of what was occurring, and most did not like living in the crowded and congested city, but it was firmly believed that some amenities had to be sacri-

ficed in order to make more money and live at a higher material standard.

2. Irving Louis Horowitz (1970) has argued, quite perceptively, that perhaps the old big-city political machines were not so bad after all. They kept people in contact with their leaders—albeit somewhat exploitively—and thereby gave city residents a sense of community. Today big-city political machines have little contact and connection with the people they govern, thus creating the form of city government that is big, heavily bureaucratized, oftentimes corrupt, and detached from its constituency.

3. A 1971 U.S. Supreme Court ruling makes it possible for suburban residents to block the construction of public housing in their communities. This ruling assures that public housing will remain big-city ghetto housing.

4. Some might argue that the poor cannot afford houses and hence should be thankful for the public housing subsidy. What this line of argument ignores is that most whites could not afford houses until the FHA and VA were established. To argue now that the government should not subsidize the poor in home ownership is to contend that the best housing subsidies should go only to the affluent. It is a curious reversal of the concept of subsidy to maintain that it should *not* be applied to those most in need.

5. Building low-cost housing and showing even a small profit is probably impossible for a private developer, especially since building codes and labor unions prevent the use of cheaper assemblyline methods of construction. Clearly such low-cost housing must be subsidized by the federal government so that the poor can afford it and the developer can make a reasonable profit. As of yet no effective fiscal formula has been developed to allow aid for the poor.

6. Unfortunately, data on the uses and impact of revenue sharing are only just becoming available. The most recent published study is *General Revenue Sharing: The First Planned Use Reports,* (1973). For references on current research, see *Proceedings of the Conference on Revenue Sharing Research* (1973).

GLOSSARY

city self-governing, geographical unit where people live and engage in work activities

FHA Federal Housing Authority, which guarantees mortgages to banks for people purchasing homes

ghetto an area where people of a particular cultural orientation are concentrated; such urban areas are frequently slums

golden age the belief that the cities were, at one time, much more pleasant places to live than they currently are

metropolitan area or region an extensive grouping of contiguous cities, usually with one large city at the core surrounded by smaller residential communities

migration the concept describing the movement of people from one place of residence to another

segregation the process whereby distinct groups—usually racial and ethnic groups—live in separate neighborhoods within a city or in separate cities

slum an area where the housing is delapidated and run down

suburbanization the process that creates the metropolitan region, characterized by people leaving the central city for residence in outlying cities.

PROLOGUE 12: THE WHITE BARRIER

On any day in America, the following events could occur:

· It's a gay cocktail party, being tested only by the discussion about the "colored family" which has just moved in down the street. All are concerned about their property values, their children's safety, and of "what will happen to the neighborhood." Some think out loud about moving, but know that they probably will stay. A few recognize that nothing is going to happen to their neighborhood, but the majority are very concerned.

· A young black couple has sought out a realtor in a new town. They will soon look for another, for they are beginning to realize that the housing that they are being shown is all black or "going black." They have the incomes to afford better, but do not seem to be able to communicate this fact to their realtor.

· A black carpenter has earned enough to buy a house in the suburbs. He and his family do not like where they live—it's dangerous and the schools are not good. But they are apprehensive about moving to white suburbia, especially after watching on T.V. the residents of South Roxy in Boston attack school buses of black children. Yet, they know that they must make the move and give their children a better chance. But this realization does not remove their intense anxiety.

· Another black worker, who has been fully employed for years, encounters a hard reality: He cannot afford to move out of the ghetto.

360

Housing in the suburbs has become too expensive, and despite all the years of work and saving, he could not meet payments on a new home. This sad realization may, he fears, keep him in the inner city for the rest of his life.

· A suburban city has just rezoned, for park use, a plot of land on which the federal government contemplated building a lower-income housing project. Residents had packed the city council meeting to protest such a project which would "ruin their property values" and create "too much congestion."

Such is the reality of housing discrimination in America. People believe that their property values will suffer with integration, and they act to protect their greatest investment. From the non-white side, especially for blacks, they experience the frustration of not being able to follow their white counterparts to the better neighborhoods, and even if they are able to do so, they begin their life in the new neighborhood with considerable anxiety about what their neighbors are like. In Chapter 12 we will examine the historical reasons for the creation of segregation in America, with particular concern about the cultural and structural forces which have created urban apartheid in a land that prides itself on being the melting pot of the world's peoples.

12

COMMUNITY SEGREGATION

Where people live in their communities is often influenced by race and ethnicity. For despite beliefs that America is indeed the world's melting pot, much residential segregation still exists. While many members of racial and ethnic groups choose to live in their own neighborhoods, such a choice is often made in order to avoid the possibility of discrimination. Or, as is the case with many minorities, people are often unable to afford housing outside a particular slum area within a community.

Many would argue, however, that racial and ethnic communities are a vital part of America, and rather than constituting a "social problem," they give American society diversity and uniqueness. There can be little doubt that America's ethnic communities do have many positive consequences for both their residence and the broader society. Much residential segregation, however, promotes tensions, conflicts, and hatreds. And much segregation is forced and aggravates problems of inequality in the distributive system. Indeed, many Americans are unhappy with their segregated existence, and as the riots in black ghettos during the 1960s underscored, segregation creates the potential for societal disruption. It is in this sense that community segregation is one of America's enduring problems of culture and structure.

RESIDENTIAL SEGREGATION IN AMERICA

Within any large urban community with residents of diverse cultural backgrounds, some groups are more segregated than others. In Table 12.1, we can observe variations in residential segregation for New York City in the 1960s. More recent data are currently unavailable, but it is unlikely that the pattern outlined in Table 12.1 has changed over the last decade. Interpreting the numbers of Table 12.1 requries some explanation: The numbers represent a residential segregation index which is constructed by examining who lives in various census tracts. For our purposes, all we need to know is that if there were no residential segregation at all in a city, then the index score would be zero. On the other hand, if complete segregation existed—that is, all racial and ethnic groups lived apart—the score would be 100. Therefore, a score above zero reveals some segregation and the closer to 100 the score, the more segregation there is.

Scores for different ethnic groups are computed in order to determine how segregated each is from the other. By looking at the intersection of rows and columns, we can observe the degree of segregation from each other of selected racial and ethnic groups. For example, by finding the "German" row and the "Irish" column, a score of 33.3 is evident, indicating some segregation of the two groups in New York City. More dramatic is the "black" row, for here we can observe a high degree of residential segregation of blacks from all other ethnic groups. Similarly, Spanish-speaking Puerto Ricans are highly segregated from other groups, although somewhat less so from blacks.

This pattern can be observed in other communities: High segregation of blacks from all groups, and somewhat lower, but still high, segregation of Spanish-speaking ethnics. Only black segregation has

Segregation of ethnic groups

The pattern of segregation in America

Table 12.1 **Residential Segregation Among Selected Racial-Ethnic Groups in New York City, 1960**

	Irish	Germans	Poles	Italians	Blacks	Puerto Rican
Irish	—					
Germans	33.3	—				
Poles	51.7	47.1	—			
Italian	48.0	45.6	52.7	—		
Black	80.3	80.6	79.7	80.5	—	
Puerto Rican	76.5	79.7	75.5	77.8	63.8	—

SOURCE: N. Kantrowitz, *Ethnic and Racial Segregation in the New York Metropolis,* New York: Praeger, 1973.

been extensively documented, thus, we will focus our attention on the plight of black Americans. Many of the processes that we will come to understand, however, also operate with respect to other groups, particularly Spanish-speaking ethnics.

In the 1960s, Karl and Alma Taeuber undertook a massive study of the census data on residential tracts. From their studies, they developed the residential segregation index described for Table 12.1. In their studies, they examined 207 large American cities and have now recorded the degree of segregation in those cities from 1940 to 1970. We have reproduced their indexes of residential segregation of nonwhites (virtually all of whom are blacks) in 109 of these American cities in Table 12.2 (Taeuber and Taeuber, 1965; Sorensen, Taeuber, and Hollingsworth, 1975).

Table 12.2 **Indexes of Residential Segregation Between Whites and Nonwhites, 1940 to 1970, for 109 Cities**

City	1970	1960	1950	1940
Akron, OH	81.2	88.1	87.6	82.2
Asheville, NC	88.5	92.3	89.2	88.6
Atlanta, GA	91.5	93.6	91.5	87.4
Atlantic City, NJ	86.9	89.2	94.0	94.6
Augusta, GA	93.3	93.0	88.9	86.9
Austin, TX	84.6	93.1	92.0	84.8
Baltimore, MD	88.3	89.6	91.3	90.1
Beaumont, TX	89.7	92.3	89.6	81.0
Berkeley, CA	62.9	69.4	80.3	81.2
Birmingham, AL	91.5	92.8	88.7	86.4
Boston, MA	79.9	83.9	86.5	86.3
Bridgeport, CT	71.7	69.7	74.4	78.8
Buffalo, NY	84.2	86.5	89.5	87.9
Cambridge, MA	52.6	65.5	75.6	74.3
Camden, NJ	67.4	76.5	89.6	87.6
Canton, OH	82.4	81.5	89.3	89.9
Charleston, SC	86.5	79.5	68.4	60.1
Charleston, WV	74.3	79.0	79.6	80.3
Charlotte, NC	92.7	94.3	92.8	90.1
Chattanooga, TN	89.9	91.5	88.5	86.5
Chester, PA	82.2	87.4	88.1	85.1
Chicago, IL	88.8	92.6	92.1	95.0
Cincinnati, OH	83.1	89.0	91.2	90.6
Cleveland, OH	89.0	91.3	91.5	92.0
Columbia, SC	86.7	94.1	88.1	83.0
Columbus, OH	84.1	85.3	88.9	87.1
Covington, KY	86.9	87.8	85.0	80.6
Dallas, TX	92.7	94.6	88.4	80.2
Dayton, OH	90.1	91.3	93.3	91.5
Denver, CO	77.6	85.5	88.9	87.9

Table 12.2 (continued)

City	1970	1960	1950	1940
Des Moines, IA	79.2	87.9	89.3	87.8
Detroit, MI	80.9	84.5	88.8	89.9
Durham, NC	87.5	92.7	88.8	88.2
East Chicago, IN	79.0	82.8	79.6	74.5
East Orange, NJ	60.8	71.2	83.7	85.3
East St. Louis, IL	76.8	92.0	94.2	93.8
Elizabeth, NJ	75.5	75.2	76.1	75.9
Evanston, IL	78.3	87.2	92.1	91.5
Evansville, IN	88.6	91.2	92.4	86.2
Flint, MI	81.7	94.4	95.3	92.5
Forth Worth, TX	92.6	94.3	90.4	81.3
Galveston, TX	77.4	82.9	78.3	72.2
Gary, IN	82.9	92.8	93.8	88.3
Greensboro, NC	91.4	93.3	93.5	93.1
Harrisburg, PA	76.2	85.7	89.8	87.2
Hartford, CT	77.4	82.1	84.4	84.8
Houston, TX	90.0	93.7	91.5	84.5
Huntington, WV	85.9	88.8	85.8	81.6
Indianapolis, IN	88.3	91.6	91.4	90.4
Jacksonville, FL	92.5	96.9	94.9	94.3
Jersey City, NJ	75.6	77.9	80.5	79.5
Kansas City, KS	84.7	91.5	92.0	90.5
Kansas City, MO	88.0	90.8	91.3	88.0
Knoxville, TN	89.6	90.7	89.6	88.6
Little Rock, AR	89.7	89.4	84.5	78.2
Los Angeles, CA	78.4	81.8	84.6	84.2
Louisville, KY	88.9	89.2	86.0	81.7
Macon, GA	90.2	83.7	77.1	74.9
Memphis, TN	91.8	92.0	86.4	79.9
Miami, FL	89.4	97.9	97.8	97.9
Milwaukee, WI	83.7	88.1	91.6	92.9
Minneapolis, MN	67.9	79.3	86.0	88.0
Mobile, AL	91.0	91.9	89.4	86.6
Montgomery, AL	93.2	94.7	90.5	86.8
Mt. Vernon, NY	78.4	73.2	78.0	78.9
Nashville, TN	89.0	91.7	88.7	86.5
Newark, NJ	74.9	71.6	76.9	77.4
New Bedford, MA	72.7	81.6	86.8	83.4
New Haven, CT	69.1	70.9	79.9	80.0
New Orleans, LA	83.1	86.3	84.9	81.0
New Rochelle, NY	70.7	79.5	78.9	80.6
New York, NY	73.0	79.3	87.3	86.8
Norfolk, VA	90.8	94.6	95.0	96.0
Oakland, CA	63.4	73.1	81.2	78.4
Oklahoma City, OK	81.8	87.1	88.6	84.3

Table 12.2 (continued)

City	1970	1960	1950	1940
Omaha, NB	85.6	92.0	92.4	89.5
Pasadena, CA	75.0	83.4	85.9	84.2
Paterson, NJ	70.3	75.9	80.0	79.8
Philadelphia, PA	83.2	87.1	89.0	88.0
Pittsburgh, PA	83.9	84.6	84.0	82.0
Port Arthur, TX	87.0	90.4	91.3	81.7
Portland, OR	69.0	76.7	84.3	83.8
Providence, RI	72.0	77.0	85.5	85.8
Richmond, VA	90.8	94.8	92.2	92.7
Roanoke, VA	91.8	93.9	96.0	94.8
Rochester, NY	73.8	82.4	86.9	85.5
Sacramento, CA	56.3	63.9	77.6	77.8
St. Louis, MO	89.3	90.5	92.9	92.6
St. Paul, MN	76.8	87.3	90.0	88.6
San Antonio, TX	81.8	90.1	88.3	79.6
San Diego, CA	71.6	81.3	83.6	84.4
San Francisco, CA	55.5	69.3	79.8	82.9
Savannah, GA	91.2	92.3	88.8	84.2
Seattle, WA	69.2	79.7	83.3	82.2
Shreveport, LA	97.4	95.9	93.2	90.3
Springfield, OH	81.1	84.7	81.6	80.9
Tampa, FL	90.7	94.5	92.5	90.2
Terre Haute, IN	82.5	90.1	89.8	86.6
Toledo, OH	86.7	91.8	91.5	91.0
Topeka, KS	74.1	83.5	80.7	80.8
Trenton, NJ	77.2	79.6	83.0	81.9
Tulsa, OK	76.4	86.3	91.2	84.6
Waco, TX	86.8	90.7	87.0	80.1
Washington, DC	77.7	79.7	80.1	81.0
Wichita, KS	85.0	91.9	93.3	92.0
Wilmington, DE	69.8	79.8	86.2	83.0
Winston-Salem, NC	94.0	95.0	93.8	92.9
Yonkers, NY	68.0	78.1	81.7	82.0
Youngstown, OH	74.9	78.5	83.5	80.0

As can be seen by reading the residential segregation score for each city, we can see that nonwhites are highly segregated in all American cities. Moreover, little change has occurred between 1940 and 1970 in these patterns of segregation. Thus, the data on segregation within cities reveal much separation of blacks from others, and moreover,

Black segregation

the data suggest that there is not a dramatic trend toward a decrease in black segregation.

Patterns of residential segregation are even more pronounced when we examine white-black separation across an entire metropolitan area rather than census tracts *with* a particular city. Of the total metropolitan population in the United States, over 80 percent of its black residents live in the core downtown area of the big cities. Since over 40 percent of the black population of the United States lives in the 20 largest of these metropolitan areas in both the North and South, segregation involves the confinement of blacks to the extreme vicissitudes of the decaying cores of America's larger cities. As Charles Abrams (1969:38) once remarked: "An urban society in which there is freedom of movement and which sees thirty-five million people move annually from house to house, city to city, and state to state . . . cannot put up a 'No Entry' sign (for blacks) as many suburbs have done." Thus, in many ways, the wall between the big city and suburbia has become the "new Mason–Dixon line" of American society and represents a form of urban apartheid. Black Americans are confined to large housing tracts in ghetto areas where black-owned homes are three times more likely to be substandard than those of whites, and were black-rented units are twice as likely to be substandard as white-rented units (Taeuber and Taeuber, 1965:140). In order to eliminate such segregation and create racial balance in large cities such as Washington D.C., by the year 2000, George Schermer (1967:120) estimates that every year 1200 black families would have to move out of slums into the suburbs and 4000 white families would have to return to the city. Achieving a balance by the year 2000 in Philadelphia would require that 6000 black families move to the suburbs and 3000 whites move back to the city every year. Similar mass migrations would have to occur in other large cities to significantly break down current urban-suburban apartheid. However, data reveal that large-city residential segregation may have increased during the last decade (Farley and Taeuber, 1968).

The existence of segregation, especially central city-suburban apartheid, lowers minority access to better schools and many job opportunities in the suburbs. Moreover, it exposes the poor to the problems of cities that are increasingly unable to provide many services. The fact that core cities and ghetto areas within any community are often centers for crime, drug abuse, and civil disorders would signal that the confinement of impoverished populations to only certain areas presents problems not only for these areas, but also for a society that values freedom of opportunity for people to achieve and share in America's material affluence. Segregation compounds problems of inequality and poverty, while violating basic values of

Consequences of segregation

freedom and equality. To understand this problem, then, we must examine both the culture and structure of segregation in America.

THE CULTURE OF SEGREGATION IN AMERICA

Segregation of racial and ethnic groups has been a fact of American life since the beginnings of urbanization. Such a long standing social pattern is inevitably justified by beliefs that make discrimination and segregation appear proper. Three beliefs have operated to legitimize discrimination within communities and between the core cities and the suburban fringe: (1) "Live with their own kind" beliefs, (2) "the right to choose your neighbors" beliefs, and (3) "integration lowers property values" beliefs.

"LIVE WITH YOUR OWN KIND" BELIEFS

There are several versions of this belief, but basically it presumes that blacks prefer to live with each other. Whether a biological or cultural basis for differences between blacks and whites is postulated, this belief acknowledges that "differences" between blacks and whites require the separation of the races. In its most benign form, these beliefs assume that blacks would "feel uncomfortable" living in white neighborhoods because their "culture is so different." And thus, it is for "their own good" that blacks remain segregated.

"RIGHT TO CHOOSE YOUR NEIGHBOR" BELIEFS

Related to values of freedom and individualism are local autonomy and control beliefs in people's right to determine who their neighbors are and the ethnic and socioeconomic composition of their community. Unlike "live with your own kind" beliefs, which contradict values of individualism and freedom for blacks, beliefs in the "right to choose your neighbors" are more consistent with basic values, if they were not applied so selectively to ethnics who could be identified by their skin color. Yet, people's belief that "their home is their castle" and that they have the right to actively pursue their free choice in the composition of their neighborhoods and community can make discrimination and segregation for many seem correct and proper.

"INTEGRATION LOWERS PROPERTY VALUES" BELIEFS

Most Americans believe that if blacks move into their neighborhood, property values will decline. Such a belief contradicts the actual facts, but individuals and real estate firms often resist integration for fear of lowering property values in an area. What the data reveal is that when a neighborhood is already deteriorating, property values and rents decline to a point where the poor can afford to live in the neighborhood. Since blacks are overrepresented among the poor, they are likely to move into a deteriorating neighborhood where houses are being abandoned and used as rentals. Thus, there is often a correlation between integration and a decline in property values, but the causal relationship is the reverse of that postulated by beliefs: deteriorating property attracts the poor, many of whom are black. The property must already be deteriorating for the poor to afford it; the poor do not cause the deterioration. In nondeteriorating neighborhoods, integration has no impact on property values since blacks and other minorities who can afford to buy prime property can also pay the costs to maintain it; hence, the property does not deteriorate and property values remain firm.

Beliefs legitimizing discrimination and segregation

These three beliefs represent a culture of segregation, for they were used to justify isolation of minority populations in the core cities of metropolitan areas during suburbanization in America. Even today, they are frequently used to justify exclusionary practices within communities and between suburban communities and the core city. The result of the application of these beliefs has been to create and sustain a structure of residential segregation that is very difficult to alter.

THE STRUCTURE OF SEGREGATION

CREATION OF THE BLACK GHETTO

As late as 1900, three-fourths of all black Americans lived in rural areas of the South (Taeuber and Taeuber, 1958:121–27). Between 1900 and 1970 virtually the entire black population became transformed from a rural to a predominantly urban aggregate, with well over 70 percent living in urban areas. In 1900 over 90 percent of the black population lived in the South, whereas today only about 50 percent do. The extensiveness of the migration into northern urban areas is revealed by the fact that ". . . more Negroes live in the New York metropolitan area than in any single southern state, about as many Negroes live in metropolitan Chicago as in the entire state of Mississippi, and more Negroes live in metropolitan Philadelphia than in the entire states of Arkansas and Kentucky combined" (Pettigrew, 1969:48). Thus, as blacks have moved from rural to urban locations, and as they have migrated from the South to the North, they have been ghettoized and segregated from much of American society.

Urbanization of blacks

Economic and Demographic Factors. Since their beginnings in the United States as slaves, blacks have been economically impoverished. Such impoverishment was perpetuated after slavery by Jim Crow laws that maintained segregated facilities and by decisions of the U.S. Supreme Court that sanctioned such segregation. There was widespread discrimination and violence against blacks in the South, and their subordinate position was woven into the American social fabric (Turner and Singleton, 1976). Most blacks had unskilled farming jobs, whether as tenant farmers or poorly paid labor for large landholders. Around the turn of the century, however, even this marginal economic position of blacks in the rural South worsened (Hamilton, 1964): (1) The high birthrates of rural families began to exceed the obtainable food supply, (2) rapid changes in the form of agriculture were taking place as farms became increasingly mechanized, as new government programs for limiting farm production were enacted, and as the boll weevil devastated the cotton industry, and finally, (3) cotton cultivation began to shift from the South to the Southwest and West.

Combined with these "push" factors forcing people out of the South were a series of "pull" factors from northern cities. The onset of World War I had stopped the massive immigrations from Europe; as wartime production increased—first from European demand and then from internal demand when the United States entered the war—the need for labor in northern factories increased. Recruiters from northern cities began actively to encourage rural blacks to leave the South, with the result that an estimated 400,000 to 1 million blacks left to work in northern industries between 1914 and 1920 (Franklin, 1948:465; Hamilton, 1964). Since industrial jobs were located in the large cities, black migrants began to settle in the cores of densely populated urban areas. In addition to these new economic opportunities, the persistent brutality, lynchings, and intimidation of blacks in the South made almost any new opportunity or hope of a new life seem bright. However, as blacks settled in northern cities, they were again subjected to discrimination, which forced them into the worst of housing slums and which subjected them to white violence (Pinkney, 1969:31). John Hope Franklin (1948:471–76) recounts that the summer of 1919 became known as the "red summer" because of the violence and bloodshed that took place. From June to the end of September, 25 race riots erupted in cities; 14 blacks were killed in one incident, and 23 blacks and 15 whites died in Chicago in another outbreak. Thus, initial migrations of blacks out of the South and into northern cities resulted in the emergence of patterns of residential segregation and a white-black antipathy that persists today.

During the 1930s migration of blacks into the North declined as

Reasons for black migrations

the depression shut off economic opportunities. With the industrial boom stimulated by World War II, migrations again became extensive and marked a massive shift in the distribution of blacks in communities. As with their predecessors, these wartime and postwar migrants were subjected to job and housing discrimination as well as white violence, resulting in their confinement to slums.

Equally important to the plight and entrapment of blacks in the urban slums was the timing of their migrations—the last of the major migrations began around 1820. Since 1910 millions of blacks—6 million since 1950 alone—have come to the ghettos from the South, but they have brought with them few marketable work skills. Because of employment practices in the South, blacks had been kept out of skilled jobs that might have given them the work backgrounds useful in northern cities.[1] Furthermore, blacks came to the cities at precisely that point in time when the need for manual labor was decreasing—new technologies were rendering obsolete, at an escalating rate, unskilled and even some semiskilled jobs. Thus, unlike their white predecessors, black migrants had difficulty even finding unskilled jobs from which they could work their way up and out of poverty. And during the post–World War II period, when wartime production and jobs declined, large numbers of blacks moved into the cities just as new technologies took away jobs that had previously been an economic springboard to other generations of white migrants. Furthermore, as industry began to move to the suburbs, blacks could not move with it because they lacked necessary skills and, more significantly, whites and the federal government blocked black migrations to the suburbs. Even when suburbanization of blacks occurred, they were at times forced into "mini" ghettos where white discrimination and few job skills kept them trapped in poor housing and economic impoverishment.

Today considerable migration of blacks into large northern cities still occurs, but the stereotype of the rural sharecropper encountering the big city is no longer very accurate. The more typical pattern is for young blacks to come to the North from a southern city or from another northern city. Modern migrants are younger, better educated, more cosmopolitan, far more militant, and less religious than their parents (Pettigrew, 1969:49). These migrants have grown up with promises of change and betterment in economic conditions; but as they migrate, it becomes evident that they still must live in a ghetto and that economic opportunities are not that readily available.

Currently, the black population increase in the core of American cities stems as much from high birthrates as from in-migrations. In 1968 15 million blacks lived in metropolitan communities, with 11.8 million of these living in the central core of large cities. Nearly 90

Population increases in the central city

percent of the nation's black population growth, including both migrations and birthrates, occurred in central cities; if this rate of growth continues, around 17 million blacks will soon live in the cores of large cities (Schaffer et al., 1970:31). And if migrations stopped today, the national population increase in central cities would swell the black population to nearly 16 million in the urban cores (*Report of the National Advisory Commission on Civil Disorders*, 1968:227). By the end of this decade, New Orleans, Richmond, Baltimore, Jacksonville, Cleveland, St. Louis, Detroit, and perhaps Philadelphia, Oakland, and Chicago could potentially have a majority of black residents. If industrial migration to the suburbs continues and if patterns of segregation and discrimination in housing continue, American cities could potentially become the most volatile in history. Coupled with the fact that black birthrates did not begin to decline until the beginning of the last decade, the 1970s will see a high proportion of young blacks, and the potential for urban riots will probably remain high (Pettigrew, 1969:50), even though it appears that racial violence has declined in the 1970s.

Racial Discrimination. Discrimination against black Americans is very much a part of the American heritage. Probably the most blatant form of discrimination has been violent acts of intimidation by whites. White violence and lynchings were common practices in the rural South in this century. For example, a crowd of 3000 whites in Tennessee once turned out to watch the burning of a black in response to a notice in a newspaper advertising the event. Similarly, white violence and threats of violence against blacks occurred during the early migrations of blacks into northern cities.

The *pattern* of discrimination in urban America has helped, in fact, to account for the ghettoization of the black population. When blacks ventured into white residential areas, they were often beaten (Pinkney, 1969). For example, in the East St. Louis riot of 1917, the Chicago riot of 1919, and the Detroit riot of 1943 the whites initiated violence against the blacks (Allen and Adair, 1969:31–37). For fear of intimidation by the white majority, blacks moved into racial enclaves where housing was the most deteriorated.

White violence

Housing discrimination has greatly contributed to racial segregation in the United States. Blacks have typically had to pay high rents for deteriorated housing. For example, Taeuber and Taeuber (1965:139–140) have documented that, in northern metropolitan areas, the median monthly rents of whites and blacks are not significantly different; however, the difference in the quality of housing is extremely great, with black rentals twice as likely to be substandard. Similarly, a study of housing costs of blacks and whites in the Chicago area, disclosed that on the whole nonwhites had to pay around $15 per month more than whites for the same quality of housing. Given the large differences in family income for blacks and whites, blacks must devote a much larger proportion of their total income to secure housing—even substandard housing—than whites. The Taeubers (1966:140) conclude that in 1960 about 33 percent of blacks spent over one-third of their income on housing, whereas around only 20 percent of whites had to do so. Black families, then, must sacrifice such things as quality food, health care, and recreation to secure housing that on the whole is of poorer quality than that for whites who earn comparable incomes.

Housing discrimination has been as intense in the suburbs as in the city. In accordance with beliefs about lowered property values, as well as those about the right to choose one's neighbors, housing developments in the suburbs initially had restrictive covenants excluding blacks. When these were declared illegal and proved unenforceable, communities used new discriminatory strategies, such as

Housing discrimination

SOCIOLOGICAL INSIGHTS

SURVEY FINDS THAT LENDERS DISCRIMINATE

The federal agency that regulates institutions making the bulk of the nation's home loans reported yesterday that lenders refuse mortgages to blacks more than twice as often as whites.

The Federal Home Loan Bank Board, which drew no conclusions from a survey of lending practices in five cities, said that black home loan applicants experience the highest rejection rate of any racial or ethnic group.

The Federal Reserve Board reported in May that its six-area survey showed minority applicants were rejected about twice as often for home loans.

The comptroller's study, which broke down rejection and acceptance rates by income level, showed that even among applicants with assets in excess of $20,000, blacks were rejected 21.6 percent of the time and whites 14.1 percent of the time.

The Home Loan Bank Board, which regulates savings and loans but included all types of home loan institutions in its time survey, said blacks were rejected 18 percent of the time and whites 8 percent of the time.

Source: San Francisco Chronicle, August 19, 1975. Reprinted by permission of United Press International.

changing zoning regulations in order to prohibit black housing developments. For example, Charles Abrams (1966:516) reports that when a union tried to build houses for its black members in Milpitas, California, the area was rezoned for other than residential use, and when a private developer submitted plans for integrated housing in Deerfield, Illinois, the proposed land site was condemned for use as a park. Such practices were justified by beliefs in the right to choose one's neighbors and to maintain local control over community composition.

Resistance of white suburban governments to entrance of blacks into better housing is one of the most oppressive forms of racial discrimination in American metropolitan areas. This resistance has been reinforced by presidential policy statements and a 1971 U.S. Supreme Court ruling. In 1971 President Richard Nixon pledged that, while the government would "vigorously enforce laws against racial discrimination in housing," it would not force affluent suburbs to accept housing projects intended for the poor. Since most poor blacks probably cannot get out of the ghetto without such housing projects, this policy statement condemns most blacks to the large ghetto of the central city. A Supreme Court ruling buttressing this policy upheld state laws giving voters in a community the right to block the construction of low-rent housing—thus making it easier for communities to exclude poor blacks. Again, such actions were justified by the belief that communities have the right to determine their own destiny.

Government Policies and Practices. In Chapter 11 we reviewed some of the federal programs designed to rescue the cities. On the whole these programs have been less successful than anticipated and have at times worked at cross-purposes with other programs. Moreover, many of them have contributed to racial segregation within cities and between large cities and their suburbs.

The Federal Housing Administration (FHA) was established under the New Deal in the depressed 1930s. The philosophy behind the FHA is that the building industry relies on a constant flow of mortgage money which the federal government must guarantee. The outgrowth of this philosophy was for the federal government to insure mortgages lent out by private banks and loan associations. If a borrower forfeited on a mortgage the federal government agreed to buy the mortgage up. Under this program, lenders and builders have been able to make profits with little risk or real investment, for the FHA, and later the Veterans Administration (VA), was to serve as a stimulus to the building industry, while becoming "a sales tool for realtors" (Abrams, 1969:37). While there is little doubt that the FHA and the VA mortgage insurance programs stimulated the building in-

Racism in FHA policies

dustry and subsidized lending institutions with close to $4 billion in bought-up mortgages, they did little to improve the housing conditions of the poor. In fact, they actively discriminated against blacks in several conspicuous ways:

1. FHA refused to underwrite racially integrated neighborhoods because, as its manual (until 1950) proclaimed: "If a neighborhood is to retain stability it is necessary that properties shall continue to be occupied by the same social and racial classes" (Abrams, 1966:523). Such a policy reflected the inaccurate belief that racial integration of neighborhoods would lower property values. From 1950 to 1962 the FHA was officially neutral on racial integration, but in practice it was segregationist (Pettigrew, 1969:58). Not until President John Kennedy's executive antidiscrimination order in early 1962 did even the tone of federal housing policy change. But even then it remained, as Pettigrew summarizes, "ineffectively integrationist."

The government subsidized whites by insuring their mortgages in single-family dwellings in suburbia. In contrast, blacks had their rent subsidized in sterile and dangerous public housing projects in the slums of the central city.

2. The FHA subsidized the white middle-class exodus to the sub-urbs while preventing blacks from joining in the suburbanization of communities. Without FHA, and later VA, insurance, lending institutions would not have allowed moderate-income whites to assume home mortgages. By subsidizing the lending institutions in home mortgages, the FHA thus encouraged whites to move to the suburbs, where single-family dwellings could readily be built.

Public housing, also initiated during the New Deal, was designed to alleviate substandard housing for whites in large cities. Only with the extensive migrations of blacks into American cities during the post–World War II period did it come to effect profoundly the pattern of segregation in America. Originally, public housing was run exclu-sively by the federal government in an effort to keep it out of the hands of the big political machines of the cities. Furthermore, public housing was initially set up, much like the FHA, to stimulate the sag-ging building industry; not until 1937 did it acquire the social pur-pose of eliminating substandard housing for the poor. About this same time, public housing was taken out of the exclusive control of the federal government and was turned over to local city govern-ments, which, it was thought, could do the job "quicker, cheaper, and better than [the] federal bureaucracy" (Abrams, 1969:35). The change in policy had two consequences for racial segregation: (1) It probably forestalled indefinitely the possibility of federally initiated and con-trolled public housing projects in the suburbs. Once turned over to the cities, public housing was built almost exclusively in their cores. (2) Because public housing tended to be built in existing black slums, it perpetuated patterns of racial segregation within the city by pro-viding the only low-cost housing available for blacks; in doing so, it kept blacks from migrating to the suburbs. Such confinement was done, at least partly, under the belief that blacks would prefer to "live with their own kind."

Inequities in public housing

So far, urban renewal has largely been a subsidy for the downtown business district and private developers of middle- and upper-class housing in cities. Urban renewal has cleared vast tracts of city land and has managed to displace blacks from their slum homes into the equally degrading and dehumanizing public housing projects. While slum housing is not pleasant, many residents have preferred to live in it rather than in standardized, high-rise, and government-run housing complexes.

Abuses of urban renewal

Over the last decade Congress and the Supreme Court have moved to break down housing discrimination. The Civil Rights Act of 1968 prohibits discrimination in either the sale or rental of apartment complexes or housing developments. Real estate brokers are also pro-hibited from discriminating in the sale of individual, single-family

More recent "housing projects" are tasteful and benign, but they still promote segregation.

homes. While the law did not prohibit discrimination on the part of owners selling their own property, the Supreme Court, in *Jones* v. *Mayer*, did. Such policies can perhaps lead to the breakdown of discrimination in the suburbs. Coupled with rent and home ownership subsidy programs (Chapter 11), mobility out of the cities may become increasingly possible, for the first time, among the minority poor.

However, three constraints operate against any immediate changes in residential patterns: (1) Enforcement of open housing laws is difficult since the Civil Rights Division of the Department of Justice is grossly understaffed and underfinanced; (2) these laws operate at cross-purposes with the urban renewal and model cities programs of the government, which tend to confine the poor to the core city; and (3) these policies go against strongly held cultural beliefs about the impact of integration on property values and the right of people to control their neighborhoods. And to the extent that the government fails to back up the open housing laws, some have argued that it *actively* discriminates against blacks and other minorities trapped in the core cities.

SOCIOLOGICAL
INSIGHTS

SUBURB'S DOORS SHUT TO POOR

Washington—After almost a decade of effort, federal, state, and local housing programs have made virtually no progress in increasing access by low-income city dwellers to American suburbia.

And powerful economic and social forces appear to be making significant success even less likely in the future, according to experts who gathered recently at the Center for the Study of Democratic Institutions.

From New York to California, with only a handful of exceptions, suburban housing integration programs for the poor have been the victims of intense resistance by middle- and upper-income communities, of federal court decisions that for the most part have upheld the rights of local communities to establish restrictive zoning and land-use controls, and of policies of the Nixon and Ford administrations that have drastically curbed low-income housing subsidies.

According to government and private housing experts, two other obstacles of potentially equal importance are now dimming even more the hopes of poor persons' finding housing in the suburbs.

They are soaring construction and land costs for new housing that are making a home, or even an attractive apartment, in the suburbs less and less attainable not only by poor people but also by those with moderate incomes of $10,000 to $18,000 a year or more; and a spreading philosophy of "no growth" or "slow growth" around the country that is increasingly limiting residential construction and raising the cost of existing homes.

"This is called 'power to the people who got there first,'" said Herbert Franklin, a housing specialist for the Potomac Institute, Inc., a Washington research organization.

THE BLACK GHETTO

In everyday language, the terms *slum* and *ghetto* are used interchangeably. However, in a more specific sense, the two terms denote different features of communities. *Slum* refers to the physical and economic conditions of a residential area, such as its population density, quality of housing, the poverty level of its residents, sanitation facilities, and other public services. *Ghetto* pertains to the degree

Slums and ghettos

The black and brown ghettos meet in New York City. Most blacks and browns must live in slums, but the degree of cultural unity and social organization varies enormously from slum to slum.

of residential isolation of a minority population and the degree of organization and cultural unity among that population, such as Jews in Europe before World War II or blacks in the United States today.[2] A ghetto is an isolated and segregated neighborhood in a larger community structure where distinct patterns of leadership, neighborhood organization, and cultural identity among residents are evident.

In the United States, black residential areas in both urban and rural communities are almost always slums of substandard and overcrowded housing, poor sanitation facilities, and low-income residents. The degree of social organization and cultural unity within these slums appears to vary greatly in different areas within a city and from city to city. In the past the label *black ghetto* has not always been completely accurate because in many cases patterns of social organization and cultural unity in black neighborhoods were weak.[3] But recently, with the blacks' growing political awareness of cultural bonds and conditions of economic exploitation, black slums can increasingly be labeled ghettos.

Ghettoization of Rural Blacks. Perhaps the most cohesive black ghettos are those in small, rural southern towns. In these towns, with their segregated residential slums, housing for blacks is generally unpainted and poorly constructed, in need of repairs, and often without indoor sanitary facilities. A civil rights volunteer described a typical black ghetto in a rural town in Mississippi: "The Negro neighborhood hasn't got a single paved street in it. It's all dirt and gravel roads. The houses vary from beat-up shacks to fairly good-looking cottages. The beat-up places predominate. There are lots of smelly outhouses, and many of the houses have no inside water" (Pinkney, 1969:56).

The conditions of black neighborhoods reflect the incomes of their residents. The majority, often nearly 80 percent, earn less than $4000 per year. To earn even this small sum, rural blacks are usually dependent on the white community, for the best jobs available are usually those of sharecropping for white farmers and menial ones in homes and businesses owned by whites.

Rural southern ghettos pivot around the church. Although this situation is changing rapidly with politicization of rural blacks, the church has traditionally provided an approved and tolerated (by whites) place "for social activities, a forum for expression on many issues, an outlet for emotional repressions, and a plan for social living" (Johnson, 1941:135). It is because of such organization around the church that the Reverend Martin Luther King, Jr., in the 1960s, could mobilize rural blacks for many movements, such as voter registration and boycotts (Pinkney, 1969:57). (Conversely, because of the lack of a single communitywide organization—such as the church—in urban communities, Dr. King was less successful in organizing city blacks.)

Lack of communitywide organization

It is from the rural slums that the original black urban migrant came in hope of finding new opportunities. However, they were soon to find that dilapidated, unsanitary, and crowded housing conditions, white discriminatory practices, and white control of black economic fates did not change with their movement to urban slums. At times, they had to endure these conditions without the benefit of a well-organized church. This situation can help explain why much of the political activity in black urban ghettos over the last decade has revolved around finding an alternative to the church in generating ghettowide social organization and cultural unity.

Urban Slums and Ghettos. Just how much social organization and cultural unity exists in black urban areas is not clear. Kenneth Clark has described the high degree of social and cultural *dis*organization in Harlem, as well as that area's economic and political dependence on the surrounding white community. He emphasized that, because black males in Harlem cannot secure well-paying jobs, high rates of family instability are evident: "One out of every five men is separated from his wife, and about two out of every seven women are separated

Pathologies of the slum

In some slums the most organized group is the violent youth gang. One can only speculate about the life chances of this young child in such a milieu.

from their husbands" (Clark, 1965:47). Family structure in Harlem is thus highly unstable, with only about one-half of all children under 18 living with both parents. Clark also documented the high degrees of mistrust and suspicion among Harlem residents: For "the residents of the ghettos," he reports, "who have learned from bitter experience, any form of altruism appears to be a ruse, a transparent disguise for the 'hustle'" (Clark, 1965:70). In an environment dominated by such mistrust, leadership and community organizations have proved somewhat ineffectual. Clark completed his picture of disorganized Harlem by emphasizing the high rates of delinquency, venereal disease, narcotics addiction, illegitimacy, homicide, and suicide.

Economically, Clark continued, Harlem is a consumption rather than a production based community. There are few wholesaling or manufacturing enterprises, virtually no office buildings, and only a few corporations, which are, characteristically, owned by whites. Even the "numbers racket" and other enterprises of crime are run by whites and provide few job opportunities for economic advancement among blacks. On the other hand, black-owned businesses tend to be small and to provide few employment opportunities, for they are primarily consumption, as opposed to production, enterprises (bars, liquor stores, pawn ships, beauty parlors, fortune-telling establishments, and storefront churches). Thus, Harlem does not manufacture anything of significance, concluded Clark, for the New York urban area or for the nation. Economically the ghetto remains tied to, and dominated by, white enterprises, while the surrounding white community controls its vital public services, such as schools, police "protection," garbage collection, and welfare. Slum buildings are owned by absentee white landlords.

Clark used the metaphor of a *colony* to describe Harlem's relations to the white community. "The dark ghettos are social, political educational, and—above all—economic colonies," he said. "Their inhabitants are subject peoples, victims of greed, cruelty, insensitivity, guilt, and fear of their masters" (Clark, 1965:11).

How accurate is Clark's portrayal? Is it a true description of all black slums? Even if it is assumed that domination of economic opportunities and public services by the white community appears to be a common condition of black slums, are they all also disorganized, filled with mutual distrust, and leaderless? A study by Hill and Larson (1969) of a Chicago slum, called "Old Annex" by the investigators, revealed a pattern of slum organization in marked contrast to Clark's portrayal. Like Harlem, Old Annex is economically depressed and displays high rates of family instability; but unlike Harlem, there is clear-cut community leadership, extended kinship and friendship patterns, an absence of fear and distrust, and many formal organizations and membership groupings engaged in community action. Hill and Larson (1969:160) concluded that, "Just as we have learned that stereotypes are not valid with respect to individuals, so we must constantly guard against the use of stereotypes in referring to . . . ghettos."

If the nature of community organization in ghettos varies so drastically, it seems logical that different strategies for slum and ghetto aid should also vary for different types of ghetto organization. To "renew" a highly organized ghetto such as Old Annex by leveling buildings and relocating residents would probably be self-defeating, for it would not take advantage of community leadership and organization. In fact, it could actually undermine these viable community patterns. It would perhaps be more appropriate to allocate a lump sum of money through revenue sharing to the community and let it organize its own self-assistance programs in welfare, housing, and education.[4] On the other hand, to the extent that Clark's portrayal is

Vibrant ghettos

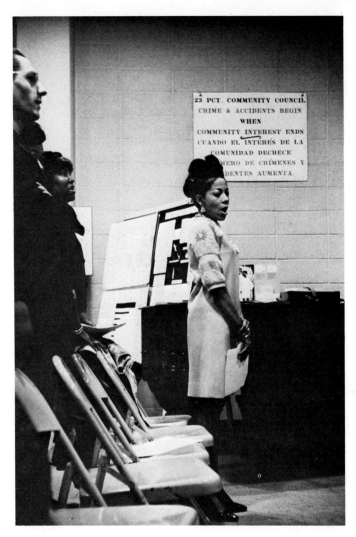

23 PCT. COMMUNITY COUNCIL
CRIME & ACCIDENTS BEGIN
WHEN
COMMUNITY INTEREST ENDS
CUANDO EL INTERÉS DE LA
COMUNIDAD DECRECE
[MERO DE CRIMENES Y]
[DENTES AUMENTA]

Residents of many slums have sought to create unity and organization. A typical community council meeting, where people seek control of their own destiny, is depicted here.

accurate, this strategy would be inappropriate in Harlem, for it appears to have fewer organizational and leadership patterns. In Hill and Larson's words (1969:160):

> Clark's Harlem may need to be rescued. Old Annex does not. Old Annex needs to be allowed to test itself, to use its strengths, and to grow stronger through such use. Old Annex deserves the right to exercise responsibility to debate and select its own programs, to choose its own consultants, and to act like any other viable segment of a city.

One of the main difficulties of federal assistance programs, especially urban renewal, is that they have used the white community's leadership and organizational resources *to impose* solutions on viable black communities. Moreover, programs have probably been too uniform and have thus ignored wide variations in the communities being affected, with the result that black residents have at times become further alienated from federal and local governments. Such alienation has at times led to violence in many of America's ghetto communities.

RIOTS IN URBAN AMERICA: PAST EVENTS AND FUTURE PROSPECTS

In the 1960s, the militant black leader H. Rap Brown is reported to have said that "violence is as American as cherry pie." In a more tempered tone, historian Richard Hofstadter (1968:112) drew the same conclusion: "The historical catalogue of American violence is a formidable one." The destruction of the American Indians and their culture, the white supremacy practices against slaves and freedmen, the bloody confrontation between early trade unions and police, and the student-police confrontations of the 1960s and early 1970s are sufficient to illustrate the violent clashes among segments of American society.

After the bloody 1917 and 1919 riots, blacks, who had heretofore been relatively nonviolent, began to retaliate against whites during periods of racial tension; and in fact, one critic has argued that they were acculturated into the American tradition of violence. As late as 1943, in the Detroit riot, self-defense and retaliation against whites were the most characteristic features of black civil disturbances. The decades after World War II were comparatively peaceful, but in the 1960s black civil disorders in ghetto areas erupted more frequently. Contrary to previous race riots, however, these contemporary disorders were not direct retaliations to massive white violence, but rather, spontaneous outbursts against whites stemming from seemingly "minor" incidents between small numbers of white police and blacks. The Kerner Commission's report on civil disorders (1968) emphasized the many unique elements in each of the recent racial disorders, but the race riots of the 1960s nevertheless displayed a similar profile.

White-black violence in America

Scenario of Recent Race Riots.[5] It is a summer evening in the ghetto, and many people are out on the streets to escape their hot and overcrowded living quarters. The police arrest a black for a relatively minor crime. Prior to this incident tensions between police and

Police and ghetto riots

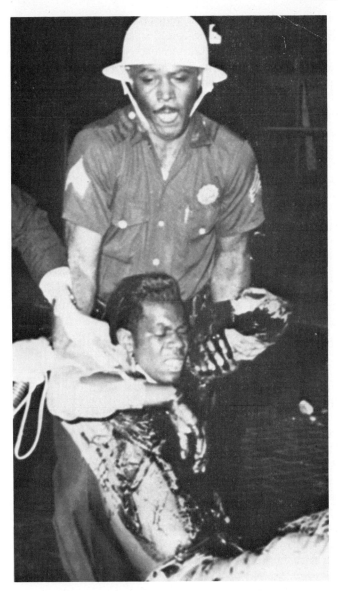

The riots of the 1960s produced many dead. Here, a wounded youth in New Jersey is carried off the battleground.

ghetto residents had escalated because of verbal abuse and efforts at social control by the police. A crowd begins to gather around the policemen in reaction to what they perceive as another act of harrassment. They shout abuses and then begin to throw rocks and bottles at the patrol officers, perhaps even attempting to rescue the police "victims." As the crowd swells, the disturbance grows noisier, and attention shifts to surrounding stores. Windows are broken and looting starts. Police reinforcements are called in in an effort to control the disturbance, resulting in escalated crowd activity, which goes from window breaking to burning. The riot gathers momentum, with widespread burning, looting, and, in some cases, sniping at police and firemen. If local police agencies cannot control the riot, the National Guard is called in to suppress it. When troops are brought in, promises to ameliorate ghetto conditions are made by local political officials. Eventually, the riot is suppressed, leaving behind burned buildings, a score of dead and injured, and ruined businesses.

The key question in presenting this brief scenario of a 1960s riot is: Could it happen again? And would it take the same form? In many ways, riots are spontaneous outbursts stemming from accumulated frustrations. They are most likely when there are few organizations and channels for social mobility and expression of grievances (Turner, 1976b). The slum of the 1970s is perhaps better organized than that of the 1960s, and there are more channels for expressing grievances. However, the sources of frustrations that erupt into civil disorder remain; and thus, it is clear that the potential for protest—even violent protest—remains high. In an economy with high unemployment, especially among teenage young adults, there is always potential for protest activity and perhaps violence. Such activity may be more organized, less spontaneous, and perhaps less destructive than previously, but it is difficult to determine, at this time, if ghetto organizations and new political sophistication among residents are sufficient to prevent violence, or to channel it in different and less violent directions.

Who were the rioters? Was rioting the work of criminal gangs? Of political activists? Or was it the collective outburst of a wide spectrum of ghetto residents? Almost all evidence points to the fact that rioters received wide support from the whole black community and that a large proportion of ghetto residents, from 15 percent to 35 percent, actually engaged in looting. Rioters were not a "lunatic fringe," outside agitators, or a revolutionary cadre, but a mass of relatively young and long-term residents of the ghetto. As the Kerner Commission summarized:

> The typical rioter was a teenager or young adult, a lifelong resident of the city in which he rioted, a high school dropout; he was, nevertheless, somewhat better educated than his nonrioting neighbor, and was usually underemployed or employed in a menial job. He was proud of his race, extremely hostile to both whites and middle-class Negroes and, although informed about politics, highly distrustful of the political system.

Police "practices" are the most intensely resented aspect of slum life. Many communities and the police have initiated programs to defuse the tensions between police and slum residents.

Why did these blacks riot and why in the pattern portrayed? The Kerner Commission (1968:81–84) found that many grievances are held by blacks, but at different levels of intensity:

Grievances of ghetto residents

First level of intensity

1. police practices
2. unemployment and underemployment
3. inadequate housing

Second level of intensity

4. inadequate education
5. poor recreation facilities and programs
6. ineffectiveness of the political structure and grievance mechanisms

Third level of intensity

7. disrespectful white attitudes
8. discriminatory administration of justice
9. inadequacy of federal programs
10. inadequacy of municipal services
11. discriminatory consumer and civil practices
12. inadequate welfare programs

The most intense of these grievances probably still exist, although the police in many communities have altered some of their abusive practices. But the employment, income, and housing picture of black Americans has not improved, thus, many of the intense grievances that moved people to civil disorder remain—indicating once again the potential for future disorder.

Two overlapping, and yet clearly distinguishable, arguments about the general social *structural conditions* causing riots can be discerned: (1) The first concerns the *caste* position of blacks in American society. Riots seen from the caste perspective are interpreted as a demand for a redistribution of wealth and opportunities for mobility into the middle classes. (2) The second views riots as attempts by blacks to escape "colonial" rule by whites. This argument sees blacks reacting to their dependence on the white community for jobs, education, welfare, housing, and subsistence. The colonialism point of view sees riots as a liberation movement against the occupying army—the police and whites. The caste and colonialism arguments overlap, but the solutions to ghetto and riot problems that each one implies are vastly different, if not contradictory. And depending upon which view is taken, predictions about future ghetto disturbances vary.

Structural conditions causing riots

Riots as a Caste Revolt. There is a large body of literature describing the conditions under which conflicts, revolts, and revolutions by an oppressed population are likely to occur (e.g., Davies, 1962; Erickson, 1966; Brinton, 1965; Williams, 1947; Marx and Engels, 1848). Common to all these perspectives are three important conclusions: (1) Revolts do not come from the totally oppressed and downtrodden, (2) revolts come, rather, from those whose lot has been getting better in absolute terms but worse relative to the standards of the broader society, and (3) revolts are directed toward the goal of redistribution of wealth in a society.

What causes violent revolt?

From this perspective, it is argued that even under the impact of judicial decisions and legislation to promote racial equality—such as the 1954 Supreme Court decision and the Civil Rights acts of 1964 and 1968—little progress has been made to close the gap between the position of blacks and whites in American society. Blacks in cities receive fewer years of education than whites; they are twice as likely to be unemployed, and when they are unemployed it is for a longer duration than for whites; blacks in cities are three times as likely to be in unskilled and service jobs as whites; they earn only about 60 percent of the income of whites; they are twice as likely to live in poverty as whites; blacks pay more than whites for poorer housing; they are three times as likely to live in substandard and overcrowded housing than whites; and so on (Kerner Commission, 1968). Although the current condition of blacks, in absolute terms, is better than it was before the Civil War or at the turn of the century, many blacks justifiably feel *relatively* deprived because of the growing white affluence they see all around them. The selective looting in riots of television sets, furniture, and appliances—all symbols of middle-class affluence—is perhaps the most visible sign of a caste demanding access to that affluence (Dynes and Quarantelli, 1968). Judicial decisions, legislation, and various government programs have raised expectations that things would improve, but the lack of dramatic improvement in ghetto conditions creates an intolerable gap between expectations and reality.

Proponents of the caste perspective argue that if riots are exclusively actions directed toward admittance to the broader society, programs designed to break down discrimination and provide educational opportunity are the key to stopping riots. Suppression by police and the military represents only a short-run solution. To guarantee equal opportunity, well-financed federal programs providing educational, housing, and economic opportunities will have to be implemented more efficiently and with more foresight than in the past, and current civil rights legislation will have to be more seriously enforced than is currently the case. In regard to the future, the recent drop in black income as a proportion of white income, as well as the failure to improve housing, educational, and job opportunities would argue that revolt is still a likely occurrence in many ghetto areas.

Implications of the caste revolt position

Riots as a Colonial Revolt. Contradicting these solutions—and predicting their failure should they ever come into being—is the "colonization" perspective in which riots are seen as more of a liberation movement against "white imperialists." From this perspective, much of the traditional philosophy and strategy for helping the poor in ghettos is called into question.

Richard Rubenstein (1970) has developed an extensive colonial perspective for examining violence in America. In general, his thesis is simple: "Groups become conscious of their independence when they lose it, and resort to violence when violence seems the only alternative to total dependence on more powerful groups or individuals." Revolt and violence occur only after a subpopulation, such as blacks in America, first becomes an internal colony of the dominant population. This process of internal colonization and revolt occurs in a series of stages: (1) Groups become isolated from the economic and political spheres. These groups usually have a collective identity, but they remain loosely organized, isolated from the mainstream of social, economic, religious, and political life in a society, and economically dependent on that society. (2) This outcast population is drawn into closer contact with government and powerful economic interests. Realizing the abuses of government and economic organizations, the population begins to pursue political activity along nonviolent lines under the leadership of middle-class members who seek to integrate them into the larger society. (3) The outgroup secures a local power base and can enter into coalition politics on a national level and thus derive its share of power and privilege. (4) These initial political gains do not eliminate the outcast's dependence on the broader society, and members feel themselves losing control of their community and slipping into permanent servitude and dependence. It is at this stage that riot and revolt become most likely and community leadership becomes increasingly militant. If the dependence of the groups on the society is not changed, a war of liberation, which can involve paramilitary mobilization and guerrilla activity, is initiated (Rubenstein, 1970:45).

Such processes of internal colonization and revolt can be used to visualize civil disturbances of the 1960s in the urban ghettos of American society. Proponents of the colonial perspective argue that the twentieth century has seen the progressive colonization of blacks into ghettos, resulting in increasing exploitation by and dependence upon white institutions, despite political movements in the nation's ghettos to alleviate this state of affairs. For example, among the high intensity grievances of blacks reported earlier, police practices, underemployment, poor housing, ineffective political structures, and inadequate education were all prominent. These grievances may reflect not so much perceived inequalities as intense dissatisfaction with black dependence on whites for housing, jobs, political favors, police protection, and education.

The grievances of blacks probably reflect not only dissatisfaction with black dependency, but also outrage over what is perceived to be white *exploitation* of black colonies. For example, police policies directed toward restoring law and order in ghetto areas are more like police occupation of a colony than serious and sensitive attempts at law enforcement. Since police forces in most urban areas have only token integration, it is not unlikely that the platoons of patrol cars moving through the ghetto with their white occupants would be perceived as a white occupation force. With respect to housing, real estate agencies and developers are so thoroughly entrenched in federal programs—from public housing and urban renewal to model cities—as to make housing programs often little more than slum takeovers (in the minds of residents) by white interests. In addition, the abuses of white absentee landlords aggravate black outrage, as do such white economic institutions as the white-owned store and the white-controlled finance company, with its high interest rates.

To exacerbate matters, political machines in most large cities have only recently been concerned with the welfare of ghetto residents, and when they are, there is little that financially depressed city governments can do about many of the problems of ghetto residents. Even black mayors of large cities are often inhibited by the high degrees of patronage and corruption in the governmental bureaucracy from doing even what little they can do to ameliorate ghetto conditions. In fact, the whole welfare system—predominately staffed by white civil servants—sometimes forces blacks to suffer indignities and invasion of privacy by an intruding and questioning federal bureaucracy. And finally, with only a few exceptions, the school systems in ghettos have been controlled and run by white-dominated school boards and school administrations. Thus, as Rubenstein (1970:127) summarizes:

> The same invasion which raised group expectations by offering a vision of middle-class life in an integrated America deepened the dependence of blacks upon the white community, for whether the colonizer was a venal slumlord or a do-good welfare worker, the result—increasing dependence—was the same.

Young blacks, who are aware of their colonial status, are the most outraged by their lack of control over their lives, by their inability to secure and keep jobs, by their need to "send their women out to clean floors," by self-destructive dependence on alcohol and drugs, and by their participation in white exploitation of "their brothers" (Rubenstein, 1970:128).

If riots are a revolt of a colony led by the angry young, the implications for governmental policies are far reaching. Government-created jobs, more government welfare, a government takeover of ghetto schools, and more government housing are more likely to feed, not quell, anticolonial forces in ghettos. Whether the colonial revolt has

Implications of the colonial rule position

or will reach the stage of paramilitary forces and guerrilla warfare in urban areas is not yet clear. What is clear is that a leadership struggle is currently underway in black ghettos, and the way this internal conflict is resolved will greatly influence the course of ghetto organization and urban violence in America.

The direction of black leadership in the late 1970s and early 1980s will reflect the sensitivity of the federal government to the anticolonial forces in ghettos. If federal programs increase black dependency while subverting self-determination, leaders advocating more violence could gain a wider following. Government programs, at the very least, must allow black residents in each ghetto to have control of the ghetto business structure, housing program, law enforcement, and schools. Ghettos will have to become economically and socially viable communities under black control and regulation. In response to the caste situation of blacks, the federal government will have to move to eliminate economic, social, housing, and educational barriers to blacks. Federal policies will thus have to strike a delicate balance (something that the monolithic federal bureaucracy has rarely done) between allowing greater self-determination in ghettos and breaking down barriers to economic and social mobility through massive federal intervention *in the white community*. Such is one dilemma of structure in America; and it is a dilemma that must be resolved if riots and other forms of violence in American communities are to become a problem of the past.

SUMMARY

In this chapter we have seen that the segregation of ethnic and racial groups is a fact of social life in America. The isolation of minority populations, particularly the black and brown population, occurred during the suburbanization of whites and the initial urbanization of blacks and browns. Dominant beliefs that whites had the right to control their own neighborhoods, that blacks preferred to live together in slums, and that property values would decline with integration helped justify overt practices of discrimination by individuals, real estate agencies, employers, local municipalities, and the federal government.

The result of this legacy of discrimination is the black ghetto and the brown barrio, which exist in contradiction to basic values of freedom and equality, while posing the spectre of civil disorder. Rather than breaking down, residential segregation appears to have stabilized, and perhaps even increased; and as we have analyzed in detail for the black population, segregation will thus continue to be one of America's persistent problems of culture and structure.

NOTES

1. There were many skilled blacks in the South, but they represented only a small proportion of the total black population. However, these skilled blacks were underrepresented in the migrations to the North.

2. Many authors use the term *ghetto* (in a sense not used in this book) to refer to the existing degree of *community:* primary and diffuse relations, strong in-group feelings of solidarity, social organization along kinship lines, social control by custom and tradition, and norms enforced by the entire community. These denote features of a ghetto, but we will refrain from terming them *community.* See Wirth, 1928, for an illustration.

3. Obviously *some* social organization exists, but the *degree* of social organization and cultural unity varies enormously.

4. Even if ghetto leadership were not of the high quality evident in Old Annex, it is not clear whether welfare bureaucrats and government planners are any more competent than lower quality leaders. It is probably better to let leadership conflicts within the ghetto work themselves out rather than impose absentee leadership from the federal government.

5. For a more detailed analysis of the riot process, see the Report of the National Advisory Commission on Civil Disorders, 1968; Rainwater, 1967; Allen and Adair, 1969, 51–139; and Blauner, 1967.

REVIEW QUESTIONS

1. Why do Americans believe so strongly that "their home is their castle"?
2. How were black ghettos originally created in America?
3. List and summarize the types and varieties of housing discrimination.
4. Define *ghetto* and *slum.* How is it that a slum is not always a ghetto?
5. Are all black slums alike? If not, how do they differ?
6. Compare and contrast urban riots from the caste revolt and colonial revolt theories? What implications for corrective action do these theories suggest?

GLOSSARY

colony the exploitive use by nonresidents of the residents of a particular housing area or tract

FHA Federal Housing Authority, which systematically refused to underwrite loans for integrated neighborhoods until 1962

ghetto the degree of social organization and cultural unity of a population inhabiting a particular residential tract or area

housing discrimination the practice of denying certain groups access to housing that is available to others of comparable income

segregation index a means of using census tract data to estimate the degree of residential separation of people from different racial and ethnic backgrounds

slum a tract of highly deteriorated housing

VA Veterans Administration, which underwrote no down-payment loans to veterans of the armed services with the same restrictions as FHA

PROLOGUE 13: ECOCATASTROPHE: IS IT POSSIBLE?

In 1988, the oceans died. Pesticides and other destructive materials had accumulated in the ocean so as to disrupt the photosynthesis process in marine plant life. The source of the vast majority of the world's air had been destroyed.

For years, people had worried about the runoff of pollutants into the oceans. Now, the world faced the prospect of a gasping end to much life. Not that the air was all that enjoyable to breathe. For other pollutants emitted into the sky from cars and factories had made it unpleasant to take a deep breath in much of the nation. But now humans faced the prospect of *no* air, even bad air.

Even if the oceans had not died, it would have been only a few more years until other disasters occurred. The land in many parts of the world had been overused. The natural diversity of the ecosystem had been taken away by single crop agriculture and the extensive use of pesticides, which, as it turned out, only encouraged more resistant pests. Then, with the natural resistance to disruption that diversity provides, these superpests became a severe problem, causing famine in much of the Third World.

Marine life could not provide a safe substitute for failing crops because pesticides had accumulated in fish to such a degree as to make them dangerous to eat. And now, with photosynthesis disrupted, there will soon be very little marine life, and in a few decades, very little life at all.

Governments reproached each other for failing to take note of the disruptive impact of their pollution. The United States blamed Russia and the Third World for seeking to modernize at any cost, while the rest of the world pointed out to U.S. leaders that the United States had caused most of the pollution in the world for the last 50 years.

Suddenly, people who had been suspicious of the Sierra Club, the Environmental Defense Fund, and even the Audubon Society wanted to know what they could do. Membership tripled in these organizations whose leaders, only a decade earlier, had been proclaimed as alarmists and doomsday prophets. But there was little that increased membership could do to save a dying planet.

Could these events occur? And so soon? Probably not as early as 1988, but they could occur. Just whether they do or not depends upon how well the nations of the world resolve the problem of cleaning up the substances that they discharge into the environment. Since America is the world's largest polluter, our concern is with how pollution has become structured into our culture and social patterns. Chapter 13 will initially take us through an examination of the basic principles of the ecosystem and then to an analysis of how cultural beliefs interact with community, distributive, and institutional systems to cause the discharge of pollutants into the ecosystem. Just what harm these have done is a debatable question, but the scenario outlined above is not totally implausible.

13

PROBLEMS OF THE ECOLOGICAL COMMUNITY

In this chapter we will shift our attention beyond human communities, because humans are a part of a much larger community: the ecological community. This *ecological community* can be defined as the complex system of interdependencies among species and minerals that sustain life. These interdependencies can be visualized as chains, flows, and cycles among species and minerals; and as such, they constitute a highly dynamic community in which various life forms actively seek the niche allowing for their survival. Continuity is necessary for the survival of the life forms comprising the ecosystem, for it is through continuity that species evolve those traits necessary for survival in their niche. As we will come to appreciate, however, highly modern societies like the United States now pose a threat to this continuity. In so doing, they could potentially sow the seeds of destruction. It is this potential that presents America with its ultimate problem of culture and structure.[1]

THE NATURE OF ECOSYSTEMS

If we are to understand the operation of the ecological community and how American culture and social structure pose a problem for its maintenance, we must first explore some of the critical patterns of interdependence in the world ecosystem. One of the most essential flows in ecosystems involves the transference of energy from the sun

The ecological community

Figure 4 **The Energy of the Ecosystem**

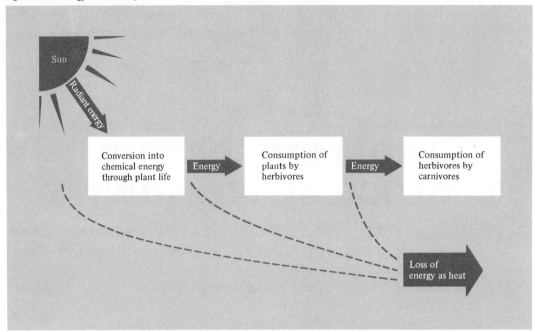

to all life forms. In this process, the sun's radiant energy is converted to chemical energy by the photosynthesis process in plants; this chemical energy is then passed through the ecosystem in extended *food chains* as varieties of herbivores consume plants, and in turn are eaten by carnivores. Within such chains, consuming life forms extract the chemical energy of the plant or animal and utilize it to sustain their life. In this way they store the energy for another organism in the food chain. At each juncture in these incredibly extended and complex feeding chains, some energy is always lost as heat, because energy transfers are always incomplete. This basic process of energy transfer is schematically represented in Figure 4.

Food chains and energy flows

A second crucial process in the ecological community involves the cycling of basic substances. Of the many such cycles, the conversion by plants of carbon dioxide (released by respiring organisms) into oxygen is one of the most fundamental since it enables all animal life to exist. Another important cycle involves the circulation of such critical minerals as nitrogen, phosphorus, sulfur, magnesium, and some fifteen other essential nutrients.These minerals cycle because billions of microorganisms, such as bacteria and fungi, release enzymes produced by their bodies into dead plant and animal material in order to facilitate enzyme absorption into their bodies. In addition to

Mineral cycles in the ecosystem

supplying the energy needs of their own bodies, however, these "de-composers" mineralize organic matter and make it available directly to plants, and indirectly, to herbivores and carnivores. In the process of photosynthesis plants not only require water and the carbon di-oxide released by animals, but they also need varieties of inorganic compounds, including nitrogen, phosphorus, sulfur, and magnesium. In contrast to the energy in these feeding chains, these mineral nutri-ents are not lost, since the activities of decomposers reinsert them back into the energy chain. In Figure 5 the cycling of basic substances is represented.

To the extent that the flows and cycles summarized in Figures 4 and 5 are disrupted, the capacity for life within the ecological community is reduced (Woodwell, 1967). While the complexity of these interde-pendencies of the ecosystem presently defies complete under-standing, we know that life forms are dependent upon each other, since no species can ascend above its dependency on other life forms.

The complexities of these mutual dependencies in the world eco-logical community represent a source of stability, or more accu-rately, orderly change. Because the web of interconnections among life forms is so vast and diverse, local changes in any part of the eco-system will encounter resistance. At the very least, sudden and rapid change will be unlikely, thereby giving plants and organisms time to adjust and adapt to changing environmental conditions. If change is rapid, however, inhabitants of the ecosystem cannot readily adapt to new environmental exigencies, with the result that widespread destruction is likely as the sudden death of some species sets into mo-tion the successive destruction of other dependent species. It is for this reason that "simplified" ecosystems, which have been stripped

Figure 5 **The Fundamental Cycles of the Ecosystem**

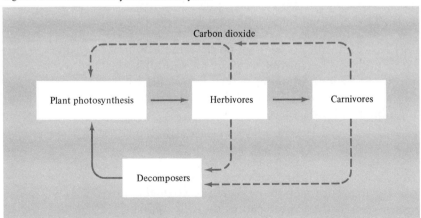

of their natural diversity, are highly vulnerable to rapid and disruptive changes; and since the web of interconnections is so simple, it poses less resistance to change than complex webs. However, the interconnection among life forms of ecosystems assures that changes will eventually reverberate far beyond their source. Such amplification of effects will, of course, encounter resistance, often allowing species sufficient time to adjust to their new environment. The fact remains, however, that a change in one element of an ecosystem will ultimately have implications for the flow of energy and cycling of minerals among many more species than those originally subjected to the change. This inevitability should underscore the *lag effects* of changes introduced into ecosystems—the full implications of a change may take a considerable amount of time to become evident. These change processes may be summarized as the fundamental principles in the ecological community:

Principles of ecological disruption

1. Simplified ecosystems are subject to more rapid change than highly differentiated systems composed of diverse relations among a wide variety of species. The simplification of ecosystems will thus increase their instability.
2. Alterations in relations of ecosystems will be amplified over time and space, with relatively small changes potentially being amplified into large-scale ecological disruption.
3. The ultimate outcome of changes introduced into ecosystems is difficult to determine due to lag effects. This fact can create a situation in which the "point of no return" in the destruction of an ecosystem can be passed before it is recognized that a destructive chain of events is irreversible.

These principles of change make it difficult to assess just how severe current ecological problems are. It is not presently known how simplified the world's ecosystem has become with the extensive use of single-crop agriculture and chemical pesticides. Nor can the amplified effect of currently observable changes in the quality of water, air, and soil be accurately assessed. And, of course, no determination of the lag effects, to say nothing of determining a "point of no return," is presently possible. But sufficient change, alteration, and clear disruption of the ecosystem has occurred to warrant its investigation as one of America's problems of structure.

SOCIETY AND THE ECOLOGICAL COMMUNITY

The culture and structure of modern societies like the United States clearly have the most disruptive impact on the world ecological community. It is in societies such as the United States that the appropriateness of high levels of consumption and the utilization of knowledge to manipulate the environment is emphasized. And it is only in such societies that the capacity to extract massive quantities of resources, to create high levels of energy, and to produce large quantities of commodities is evident. The results of these capacities can potentially be destructive, as is outlined in Figure 6.

In Figure 6 the cultural values and structural arrangements of an industrial society are seen as encouraging high levels of consumption, as is indicated in column 2. Consumption creates demands for industrial and agricultural goods which, reciprocally, stimulate levels of production requiring large quantities of energy. As the arrows in column 2 underscore, these influences are also reciprocal: An extensive productive system encourages consumer demand and sustains the cultural values and structural arrangements in the society that first gave impetus to initial industrialization in modern societies. The consumption, production, and energy use of modern, industrial economies generates vast quantities of waste residues, as is indicated in column 3. In turn, these residues are discharged into the renewable resources of air, soil, and water. These resources are renewable, because each is capable of rejuvenation through the flows and cycles of energy and minerals. While substitutes for stock resources (column 1) can be found—albeit at high cost—there are no substitutes for renewable resources; thus, to use them as a refuse for waste residues (column 4) will disrupt those ecological processes (column 5) that maintain these renewable resources and the vitality of life forms (column 6). Indeed, without air, water, and soil, life is not possible.

The three principles of ecological change enumerated earlier offer a general clue as to the potential dangers of using renewable resources as a refuse. Single-crop, large-scale agriculture using chemical fertilizers and pesticides has reduced the complexity of the ecological community. In so doing, its vulnerability to rapid change and destruction of life forms—including humans—has increased. Moreover, the chemicals of large-scale agriculture run off the soil into the water, mixing with other residues of urban-industrial societies, and can potentially suffocate wide varieties of life including, it appears, even the phytoplankton from which 80 percent of the world's air is produced. These processes of simplification do not, of course, presently reveal their amplified consequences. And in accordance with the principle of lag effects, some biologists now assert, perhaps prematurely, that the point of no return on the road to ecocatastrophe may be reached within the next decade (Ehrlich, 1970).

Precise and exact knowledge on the disruption of the world ecological community is not available, but it is clear that a considerable

Figure 6 **Society and Ecological Disruption**

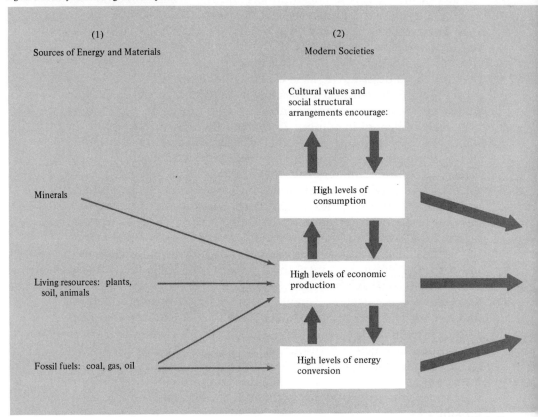

Source: Adapted from J. H. Turner, "The Ecosystem: The Relationship Between Society and Nature," in D. Zimmermand and L. Weider, eds., *Understanding Social Problems*, New York: Praeger, 1976.

amount of disruption has already occurred and that, in light of the culture and structure of modern societies, the potential for further damage is manifestly evident. As the world's greatest polluter, the analysis of the culture and structure of American society becomes critical if the causes of ecological disruption are to be understood. With less than 6 percent of the world's population, America extracts 35 percent of the world's minerals and energy and is responsible for one-half of the pollutants emitted into the world ecosystem.

America is the world's greatest polluter

THE CULTURE OF POLLUTION IN AMERICA

Many of the dominant values that facilitated the development of America into the world's most affluent society have become translated into a series of beliefs which legitimize those structures that

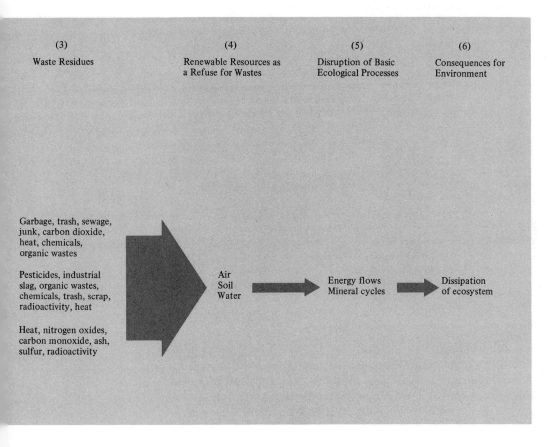

(3)	(4)	(5)	(6)
Waste Residues	Renewable Resources as a Refuse for Wastes	Disruption of Basic Ecological Processes	Consequences for Environment

Garbage, trash, sewage, junk, carbon dioxide, heat, chemicals, organic wastes

Pesticides, industrial slag, organic wastes, chemicals, trash, scrap, radioactivity, heat

Heat, nitrogen oxides, carbon monoxide, ash, sulfur, radioactivity

Air
Soil
Water

Energy flows
Mineral cycles

Dissipation
of ecosystem

cause the discharge of harmful wastes into the ecosystem. These beliefs can be grouped into four general complexes which, for simplicity of exposition, can be labeled the (1) growth ethic, (2) consumption ethic, (3) technology ethic, and (4) plentiful nature ethic.

THE GROWTH ETHIC

During initial industrialization in America, a growth ethic was perhaps necessary to encourage heavy investment of capital in the productive apparatus. Indeed, such basic values as activism, materialism, and progress provided the impetus and justification for economic growth and expansion. During this process, the economy became structured around a belief in growth: the more the better (Rienow, 1969:25–34). This belief was consonant with an underpopulated, early industrial society where renewable resources such as air,

Values and the growth ethic

Americans believe in growth. New houses are constructed, despite the ecological problems involved, while old houses are allowed to decay. Note the disruption to the ecosystem that "development" causes.

water, and soil were in plentiful supply. Discharging wastes into them saved money, time, and effort and thereby escalated growth in production and consumption. It is now questionable whether these vital resources can continue to renew themselves in the face of the ever-escalating demands being placed on them. To avoid severe ecological problems, many ecologists argue, the growth ethic will need to be replaced by new cultural beliefs emphasizing stability, recycling, and maintenance of the natural forces of rejuvenation in water, air, and soil (Boulding, 1966, 1970; Ehrlich and Ehrlich, 1970). However, the supports for continued growth emanating from the economy, polity, and consumption habits of the family make any shift in beliefs in American society difficult.

THE CONSUMPTION ETHIC

Americans value materialism; that is, the consumption of ever-increasing quantities and varieties of economic commodities. Such consumption is considered to generate both progress and prosperity, while being an indicator of people's realization of such values as activism and achievement. The coalescence of these values into a consumption ethic—the belief that increasing consumption is good and proper—was an important force behind America's economic growth and expansion. And once a large productive apparatus exists, it has a

Values and the comsumption ethic

America's thirst for material goods is personified by the Christmas rush at department stores (left). *The young, at the sleepy end of a typical rock concert, continue the "throw away" tradition of their parents* (right).

vested interest in manipulating the value of materialism by stimulating needs for consumption. In turn, such stimulation generates greater economic demand leading to increased production, and so on in a consumption-production cycle. But production and consumption in American society now occur on such a scale that a serious waste residue problem has been created. For as Figure 6 underscored, economic production results in the discharge of slag, pesticides, trash, heat, nitrogen oxides, and scores of other harmful residues into the ecosystem. When high levels of consumption are encouraged by such extensive production of goods and commodities, a disposal crisis is created; as for example, when the phosphates flowing into sewers no longer can be absorbed or when the American landscape becomes scarred with vast quantities of solid wastes.

THE TECHNOLOGY ETHIC

Traditionally, the American experience with a wide number of problems has had an easy solution: more technology. There pervades a strong belief that the application of more scientific knowledge can meet any challenge. Such beliefs reflect basic values of activism in

Values and the
technology ethic

which people are to rationally and efficiently use knowledge to master the environment. Such faith in science and technology is now more problematic than in the past, for it delays immediate action on ecological problems while potentially allowing them to intensify to a point where scientific and technological endeavor will be less effective than would be the case if one presumed that no technological solution could be found.

Even today, in the midst of widespread concern over pollution, science is at times seen as the ultimate cure. For example, the problem of generating enough food to feed the world's population has been turned over to the agricultural experts who, through the selective breeding of grains and intensive use of fertilizers and pesticides, have succeeded in feeding the world *in the short run*. But many have argued that this is being done at a long-range cost of simplifying ecosystems, hence, creating new problems while forestalling the imperative of an international program of population control.

Ecological problems are much more than a technological problem; they may require changes in basic values, beliefs, and institutions. Generating the technology is perhaps the least of the obstacles in meeting current ecological problems. In fact, to continue to wait on a technological breakthrough is probably unnecessary because, as the President's Council on Environmental Quality noted in 1971, the knowledge to solve many ecological problems is currently available. The technology ethic thus poses a curious dilemma: It will assist in the solution of ecological problems, but at the same time, blind faith in its powers diverts attention away from the real source of the problem: the basic structure and culture of American society.

THE PLENTIFUL NATURE ETHIC

All over the world, and particularly in the United States, nature has been considered a "free good" (Murphy, 1967). As such, using renewable resources such as air and water as a refuse has been allowed to occur, free of charge. The use of nature as a free good represents a pioneer conception of unbounded and inexhaustible resources that can be used to realize such values as progress (Revelle, 1968). In reality, it may be more prudent to visualize renewable resources as a "common good," increasingly in very short supply.

Values and plentiful nature ethic

Even with widespread ecological consciousness, changing this belief may not be as easy as it appears in the abstract. It will cost the public money to visualize nature as a common good: Industries will have to pay for their pollution, which in turn will mean that they will raise prices; the federal government will have to engage in expensive monitoring and control of pollution emitted by industries, with the

Nature is no longer so plentiful, as even the ocean can no longer absorb America's sewage.

result that federal taxes will be raised; and local communities will have to increase taxes to pay for their pollution and to expand their sewage and garbage treatment facilities. Thus, the belief that nature is a free good may persist for some time as an ideology for keeping prices and taxes down.

These beliefs, from growth ethic to the plentiful nature ethic, currently dominate American culture. They shape social action and at the same time are being supported by current structural arrangements in the society. It is this reciprocity between culture and structure that makes both highly resistant to change. For as long as beliefs legitimize arrangements that allow Americans to enjoy the good life, change in either the beliefs or the established modes of conduct that they legitimize will be resisted. It is in this sense that disruption of the ecological community is a problem of structure and culture in America.

THE STRUCTURE OF POLLUTION IN AMERICA

In analyzing the structure of pollution in America, our attention should be drawn to the basic social structures which organize human activities and which have served as a frame of reference in previous chapters: (1) communities, (2) institutions, and (3) stratification. The way these structures shape human affairs are the reasons that problems of pollution ultimately arise.

COMMUNITY STRUCTURE AND POLLUTION

Urbanization involves the increasing concentration of a population into a relatively small geographical area. In the United States the current population of slightly over 210 million is settled on a little over 1 percent of the land area. Such a high degree of urbanism necessarily causes pollution, for the wastes and residues of millions of people and a large industrial complex are being discharged into a very small ecological space. It is therefore likely that the air, water, and land within any large urban area will be polluted and that ecosystem disruption will be high, perhaps setting off chains of events extending considerably beyond the urban area. Were the American population more geographically dispersed, the degree of *noticeable* air and water pollution would be considerably less. As necessary as geographical dispersion may be for avoiding further ecological damage, however, the current *pattern* of urban organization in America, regardless of population dispersion, will continue to cause ecological problems. It now appears that ways of treating sewage, disposing of wastes, transporting people, supplying energy, raising revenue, and governing urban areas have evolved in such a way that they pose serious ecological problems.

The pattern of industrialization within urban areas is one source of these ecological problems. During the last century, the first industries tended to settle along major lakes, rivers, and bays. This pattern provided needed power, sources of transportation for materials and goods, and most importantly, a free dump for wastes, since water was believed to be a plentiful free good. A pattern of urban, industrial organization which, with the expansion of industry, was most likely to cause ecological problems was thus established 120 years ago. Just as water was considered a free good, so was the air into which wastes could be ejected in an effort to realize basic values of progress.

Because of this long tradition stressing the unbounded right of industry to use the environment as a refuse, solving ecological problems will be correspondingly more difficult. However, a number of alternatives are currently available (Revelle, 1968): (1) closed cycle opera-

Urbanization and pollution

tions, in which water is treated and recycled through industrial plants; (2) exportation of wastes to an environment more capable of absorbing them; (3) effluent treatment; and (4) plant abatement, by which manufacturing processes are changed so that no dangerous effluents are emitted into the water and air. The technology for all of these solutions exists and could be used, but it is expensive to implement. It seems clear, however, that the heavy urban concentrations of industry and their disrupting impact on the national ecosystem will eventually necessitate the implementation of these solutions by manufacturers in urban areas. The consequences of this fact will require considerable economic adjustment: Profit margins may be less and consumers will probably have to adjust to higher prices. Such are the costs of the existing pattern of urban, industrial organization.

The *rate* of urbanization in America is now creating ecological problems. As we noted in Chapter 10, the United States moved from a rural to urban profile between 1800 and 1860. New York, Philadelphia, Boston, Chicago, St. Louis, and other large cities went from literally small towns to massive urban complexes in only half a century. Such a rapid rate of urbanization severely burdened the sewage facilities of these urban areas, and they simply dumped untreated organic wastes into adjacent waterways. Even with the adoption of sophisticated treatment methods, many large cities continue to be major sources of water pollution because their drainage systems have been jury-rigged for 100 years. For example, in New York, Chicago, Cleveland, and many older cities, treatment of wastes is accomplished by interceptor sewers that have been built to catch wastes from the original sewer system and carry it to treatment plants (Revelle, 1968). But during rainy seasons or excessively heavy use, these interceptor sewers are overwhelmed by the water coming from the older system, with the result that untreated sewage overflows into adjacent waterways. Technologically, these problems can be overcome, but the costs to the taxpayer make any change in sewage treatment fiscally and politically difficult. America's waters will thus continue to be burdened as a result of a sewage-treatment legacy inherited from the rapid urbanization of the last century.

Initial urbanization in America was accomplished without the automobile, but suburbanization and the creation of the large metropolitan area was, to a great extent, the product of the car (see Chapter 11). Although the automobile gave people more flexibility as to where they could live, its emissions now seriously pollute the urban air. For example, it has been estimated that 75 percent of all carbon monoxide and 50 percent of the sulfur oxides, hydrocarbons, and nitrogen oxides—the ingredients of smog—are emitted by automobiles (Steif, 1970). As urban areas have become restructured around the car, the

The rate of urbanization and pollution

implementation of alternative, nonpolluting modes of urban transportation has been made economically infeasible. For example, in Los Angeles the entire metropolitan area is almost completely dependent on automobile transportation, creating a severe smog problem and making alternative forms of transportation economically difficult. Other large cities are not so dependent on cars, but most urban transportation still revolves around their extensive use.

To attack the pollution generated by the urban structure will require some very comprehensive political decisions extending across entire metropolitan areas and into rural areas. Unfortunately, as was noted in Chapter 11, a pattern of community political decision making has been established that presently precludes this possibility (Greer, 1966). American metropolitan areas grew during a period when laissez faire, states' rights, decentralization of government, and local control were valued, with the result that it is most difficult to have unified political decision making over a large urban region. As long as political power in metropolitan areas remains fragmented among suburban communities surrounding the central city, there will be a lessened political capacity to deal with urban pollution. It will be difficult to have planning, waste standards, industrial waste monitoring and enforcement procedures, land use controls, effluent- and sewage-treatment facilities, and alternatives to automobile transportation systems *on a regional level.*

Should the federal government, through additional revenue sharing or grants-in-aid, assist this political system in an effort to abate pollution, much of it could be lost on duplication of effort and financial squabbles among competing municipalities. To avoid this eventuality, it may prove necessary to abandon traditional concepts of urban government, for pollution problems do not end at a community's border, rather, they extend throughout an urban region and well into its rural fringe. Governmental boundaries may thus have to be established with respect to ecological regions, rather than political boundaries. The fact that such governmental reorganization would violate strong beliefs in local control, as well as established political and economic arrangements indicates the extent to which pollution problems are built into the culture and structure of community government in America.

In addition to these political decision-making dilemmas, American urban communities have what may now be an antiquated revenue-raising system—a system that makes financing pollution control at the metropolitan level impossible. Property taxes are probably not a viable way to generate the massive amount of capital needed to address pollution problems. Moreover, financial solutions will probably require more than just new sources of revenue; an entirely new

Problems in attacking pollution

system of deriving revenue to finance cities may be required. To use forms of revenue sharing from the federal government to supplement this system will probably be ineffective within the context of the fragmented political structure of urban areas. But to rely on taxes from assessed property evaluations is likely to prove inadequate for already burdened cities. As the present financial problems of cities reveal, the entire tax structure in cities will probably have to be revised: Property taxes may have to be supplemented by commuter taxes on those coming into the central city from the suburbs; pollution taxes may have to be assessed on older cars and on industries that produce wastes; tax incentives and rebates may have to be created to encourage industries to move out of urban areas and cut down their pollutants; sewage treatment costs to the public will probably have to be raised to support research and investment in new sewage systems and treatment facilities; a better formula for sharing state and federal income tax revenues will have to be devised; and most importantly, all these tax reforms will probably have to be metropolitanwide instead of confined to local municipalities. Again, the possibilities of all these reforms, at present, seem remote.

In sum, we can see that ecological problems in the United States are intimately connected to current patterns of urban organization. Urbanism per se creates pollution problems since it concentrates the wastes of large numbers of people and industrial complexes into a small ecological space. Equally significant, however, are the existing forms of urban industrialism, the modes of sewage treatment, the basis of transportation, political organization, the system for raising revenues, and the cultural beliefs legitimizing these patterns of organization. Until these features are changed, it is most likely that pollution and ecological disruption will continue to be built into the American community structure.

POLLUTION AND THE STRATIFICATION SYSTEM

In absolute terms, the lowest income and poverty groupings have a better standard of living than ever. This increase in the standard of living, however, has not been accomplished through a redistribution of the wealth; on the contrary, the poor of today receive no greater a share of the total wealth than they did previously (Chapter 7). The poor's demands for more affluence has, therefore, been met by the trickling down the stratification ladder of increased economic output that, in turn, has resulted in increased industrial pollution. Were the wealth to be redistributed, such increased output and the resulting pollution would not be necessary to meet the demands of the poor to share in American affluence. The United States has thus made the

The poor, who must endure many forms of pollution, are likely to see programs for them cut back with increases in antipollution efforts by government.

poor more affluent not by making the rich poorer (Boulding, 1970).

The respective amounts of pollution also vary by social class in American society. The greatest polluters are the affluent, who generate the greatest economic demand (and, hence, stimulate industrial pollution), consume the most polluting goods, and dispose of the majority of nondegradable or nonrecyclable wastes (Wald, 1970). Yet, it is the poor who are most likely to live where land, water, and air have been polluted by the needs of the affluent. Another inequity stems from the fact that programs to eliminate pollution will wear most heavily on the poor, not the affluent. The affluent are in the vanguard of the ecology movement not only because they are sincerely concerned but also because they can afford to be. It is the poor who are likely to have to pay a greater *proportion* of their limited income in the higher prices and taxes that will inevitably result from an attack on America's ecological problems. Furthermore, since it is likely that much of the money to fight pollution will be taken out of the domestic rather than the military budget, the poor will see many of the programs that directly benefit them cut back under future efforts to clean up the environment. As one ghetto resident cynically observed, "friends of the earth are not the friends of the poor." It is therefore not surprising that the poor have been slow to join the ecology bandwagon; they have much to lose (Ehrlich et al., 1970; Sprout,

The affluent are the greatest polluters

1970). The poor also have much to gain from a serious attack on pollution problems, since it is they who tend to live in the most ecologically disrupted areas. But unless the poor are exempted from the costs of such an attack, the fight against pollution could aggravate the present levels of inequality that exists in the United States.

Present ecological problems, and their solution, are thus connected to the stratification system. The affluent are the big polluters, and it is they who are able to make the sacrifice in income and standard of living that a cleaner environment may require. Until the poor and disfranchised minorities can be assured that monies directed toward the environment are not coming out of domestic programs, they could resist federal and state environmental legislation—and thus pose another structural roadblock in the way of pollution control in America.

POLLUTION AND THE INSTITUTIONAL STRUCTURE

The Economy. Economic processes in any industrial society have three principle consequences for the environment: (1) They deplete *stock* resources, such as oil, coal, gas, and various metals and minerals; (2) they consume renewable resources, such as air, water, soil, and plant life; and (3) often, as a result of depletion of renewable resources, they disrupt necessary cycles, flows, and energy chains within the ecosystem (Figure 6). While the depletion of stock resources presents short-run economic problems, it is not as serious as is the exhaustion of renewable resources and disruption of the ecosystem. In the long run, substitutes can probably be found for various stock resources, but there is no substitute for life-sustaining resources like air and water, as well as those ecological processes upon which human health and food supplies depend.

The exhaustion of renewable resources and ecosystem disruption can be intentional, such as when massive doses of pesticides are dumped onto crops or when the by-products of industries and consumers are emitted as pollutants into the soil, air, and water. Some of this "economic fallout" directly disrupts the environment and then dissipates; but much of it accumulates in the environment as is the case with DDT and other chlorinated hydrocarbons, thus increasing its disrupting impact over time. In either instance, it now appears that considerable damage is being done to vital resources and ecological processes.

In accordance with basic values and beliefs in expansion, growth, and progress, the American economy is structured around growth and continual expansion, as is revealed by the fact that economic health and prosperity are now defined by the annual increase in the gross

Values, economic growth, and pollution

national product (Boulding, 1970; Murphy, 1967; Hill, 1970; Miles, 1970). More substantively, full employment, monetary stability, and political processes are intimately connected to continued growth of the economy. Therefore, to assure this "necessary" growth, economic enterprises frequently engage in extensive advertising to stimulate needs and desires in the public for more and more goods. Moreover, many industries continually bring out new models of products to instill a sense of psychological obsolescence in the consumer; products are constantly being packaged in "new, more convenient," and often nondegradable ways in order to stimulate additional consumer demand; manufacturers sometimes build in obsolescence so that goods will self-destruct at a rate compatible to continued economic growth; consumers have been cajoled into thinking that for each task they must perform, from opening a can to making an ice cube, they need a special gadget; an enormous credit industry has emerged to stimulate purchases beyond the immediate capability of consumers; and if such artificially stimulated demand is insufficient to assure growth, appeals are sometimes made to the government to provide a subsidy, impose a protective tariff, or buy surplus goods. All such techniques for assuring growth have generated economic prosperity for most Americans, but they have also caused economic fallout. Economic growth means increased energy conversion and hence greater quantities of carbon dioxide, ash, sulfur dioxide, nitrogen oxides, heat, and carbon monoxide. More production creates greater residues of pesticides, fertilizers, slag, chemicals, scrap, and junk. And more consumption will generate increased levels of trash, sewage, garbage, and carbon monoxide. At the same time, however, economic growth assures close to full employment; and as recent recessions have disclosed, a drop in the rate of growth, or even an actual decrease in growth, produces severe unemployment and other economic dislocations. Thus, the stability of the present structure of the American economy, and the fate of many workers, now depends upon growth, setting into bold relief one of America's most difficult dilemmas: environmental stability versus economic stability. At present, it appears that, in the absence of visible ecological catastrophies, economic stability is preferred by both the public and political decision makers to ecological stability. Many times, of course, the two issues may not come into conflict, but more often than not, there is a clear conflict between these two desirable goals.

It is between the "horns" of this dilemma that government efforts to control pollution must be viewed. While stricter governmental controls could probably cut down dramatically the amount of harmful economic fallout, more extreme measures may be necessary to stop agricultural and industrial pollution. Economic growth will

Political problems in stopping pollution

The factory—symbol of economic growth. Note its location on the water into which it can discharge its pollutants.

probably have to be drastically slowed down, since it is likely that with continued economic expansion the benefits of increased governmental regulation would be negated by increased energy conversion, production, and consumption. To slow the rate of growth will require some far-reaching adjustments within the economy. For example, in the face of population growth, full employment within the structure of the existing economy may be impossible; therefore new ways, from outright welfare to governmental subsidies and "make work" projects, might have to be devised to get income to people so that they could buy products and hence maintain the economy. A new system of corporate taxation would probably be necessary to derive the revenue required by the nonworking populace. America's habits of consumption would also have to change: People would have to get used to recyclable and degradable packaging, planned resistance to obsolescence, and fewer gadgets. To effect this change in consumption habits would, in turn, require more government control of the market to regulate demand and supply of only those goods that would improve the quality of life and the environment. Yet, the very fact that these solutions to economic pollution would probably cause severe short-term, perhaps even long-term, economic and perhaps political disruption underscores the built-in roadblocks to easy ecological solutions. Further, such changes would go against deep-seated beliefs of many Americans in growth and consumption, once again indicating resistance to solutions for ecological problems.

The existence of such roadblocks would thus require more "practical" but probably less effective solutions to ecological problems. While only a stopgap measure, one short-term approach would be for the government to subsidize, as it has done for many industries such as the railroads and airlines, a waste recovery industry that could recycle many of the current residues back through the economy (Ehrlich and Ehrlich, 1970). However, recycling should not be viewed as a cure-all for problems of industrial pollution. If only by examining Figure 6, it should be clear that the wastes generated in energy conversion and in many productive processes are not recyclable. While federal standards limiting the emission of these nonrecyclable wastes would certainly improve the pollution picture, it is improbable that all of these wastes can be eliminated; and with rapid economic growth, the impact of federal regulation could prove minimal. Such a possibility reveals that government subsidy of pollution-fighting industries and the strict regulation of emissions by polluting industries may not be the panacea that many experts believe it to be.[2]

Government intervention may have to be much more extreme, involving policies that limit economic growth; at the same time, the government would have to cope with the economic and social problems stemming from such a radical alteration of the economy.

To change the economy, however, will require that the public find ways to overcome the power of economic interests and/or to build its own base of power. The largest and most powerful corporations in America emit the most wastes and produce the most polluting products, such as cars and gasoline. Given the current structure of the American government (Chapter 3), these corporations are able to press their interests more effectively than the public or environmental groups. Despite the impressive pro-ecology advertising campaigns mounted by industrial corporations (another indicator of their power to shape public opinion), they will quite naturally continue to lobby against any pollution legislation that would threaten their profits. Thus, the narrow interests, but enormous political power, of America's corporate structure represent yet another major obstacle to pollution control.

The Legal System. Ultimately, the control of pollutants will be done by administrative agencies operating under regulatory laws. The only partially effective laws presently on the books, and the problems with formulating future pollution control laws can repre-

sent another institutional force that can either forestall or foster ecological problems in America. We should, therefore, analyze the difficulties and dilemmas of creating coherent and effective pollution
control laws.

One of the difficulties in developing effective laws against pollution resides in the lack of a legal tradition supporting environmental
law. In light of the plentiful nature ethic and the growth ethic, such a
situation was perhaps inevitable, for it was well into the twentieth
century before serious conservation laws were enacted in America.
The Bureau of Reclamation was established at about the turn of the
century, and the National Park Service was expanded, stimulating
the passage of limited numbers of conservation laws by state and federal governments. It was not until the Dust Bowl of the 1930s, however, that legislators began to realize the potential dangers of unregulated use of renewable resources; and, with this realization came the
enactment of the Soil Conservation Act (Boulding, 1970). But, after
this promising beginning, the thousands of conservation laws that
have been enacted over the last 40 years have proved, by and large,
ineffective in dramatically abating ecological disruption. Even a cursory purview of the federal codes and statutes reveals that most "conservation" laws represent an "administrative handbook" telling corporations and individuals how to apply for resource extraction. With
some noticeable exceptions, these laws do not prevent harmful extraction.

With this short-lived and largely ineffective legal tradition in "conservation laws," it is perhaps inevitable that recent law enactment
has suffered from a number of defects:

1. Traditional conservation laws and more recent antipollution
laws are often phrased in ambiguous language. Coupled with the
court system's traditional favoritism of economic interests, state and
federal agencies charged with enforcing these vague laws are naturally reluctant to press charges and take violators to court for fear of
having even these weak laws, and perhaps the agency's very function,
invalidated (Murphy, 1967).

2. Existing antipollution laws typically mandate weak civil penalties and hardly ever carry criminal sanctions. The frequent result of
this situation is for companies faced with relatively minor fines to
view pollution penalties as just another cost to be absorbed and
passed onto the consumer in the form of higher prices. It may be that,
until companies are confronted with criminal penalties and heavy
civil damages, antipollution laws will not be as effective as they
might be in preventing ecological disruption. For example, the most
comprehensive and unambiguous federal antipollution law ever enacted, the Clean Air Act of 1970, carries no criminal penalties, hence,

Antipollution
laws

it can be wondered how effective a law without criminal penalties will be. As recent events have underscored, corporations may be able to weaken even this clearly written law as they exert pressure upon legislators. If the penalties for violation of the Clean Air Act can be circumvented, then weaker pieces of federal legislation will probably prove even less effective, especially when the federal government is subject to pressure by corporations seeking to avoid higher costs and a public reluctant to pay higher prices and taxes.

3. The vast majority of laws do not typically address the sources of pollutants; they more frequently require treatment of pollutants *after* they have been created. For example, because there are few state laws prohibiting the use of phosphates and other chemicals in consumer products, the burden of cleaning the water into which these chemicals are dumped must fall upon sewage treatment facilities. To take a further example, the Clean Air Act did not specify that the internal combustion engine must be replaced but only that the ultimate emissions of this engine must be reduced.

4. Finally, many state antipollution laws are enacted with "grandfather clauses" which allow established industries to continue their harmful activities. One result of such clauses is to encourage outmoded and highly polluting industries to stay in an area, while discouraging the new industries which must utilize expensive antipollution equipment from becoming established. Thus, in the end, these laws often perpetuate the very industrial processes that the law was designed to discourage.

This ineffectiveness of state and federal antipollution laws is compounded by the inducements to polluting found in other types of legal statutes. Present tax codes, for example, sometimes encourage unnecessary pollution; traditional depletion allowances, which allow corporations extracting resources to deduct from their taxes the "depletions" of these resources, encourage rapid and sometimes wasteful resource extraction to obtain the highest depletion allowance. Or, to take another example, property tax laws support depletion allowance laws by allowing lower assessed evaluations for land as resources are extracted, once again providing a potential inducement to careless and rapid extraction (Murphy, 1967). Even when corporations are found liable for their pollutants, they are, under some circumstances, allowed to deduct as a business expense the costs of cleaning up their effluents; and under some state statutes, even legally imposed fines for pollution can be deducted as a business expense. These kinds of laws encourage pollution by offering incentives for wasteful resource extraction and by mitigating the costs incurred by companies that disrupt the environment.

In sum, then, it must be reluctantly concluded that the present legal structure in America cannot control and regulate the pollution of the environment. The many state and federal conservation codes often facilitate as much as inhibit harmful resource extraction; tax laws sometimes provide incentives for pollution, rather than the reverse; and explicit antipollution codes are sometimes circumvented by political pressures from the polluters and an economically squeezed public. To overcome these problems, a comprehensive national body of laws carrying severe criminal and civil penalties will probably be necessary. This new federal body of law will have to involve more piecemeal legislative acts, for a coordinated writing and rewriting of pollution, conservation, and tax laws will probably prove necessary. If present trends continue there may come a time when the environment can no longer be maintained by the current maze of state and federal codes whose ambiguities, conflicts, and overlaps have made legal solutions to ecological problems problematic.

The need for comprehensive laws

What may be needed from federal legislators is a set of clear *national* quality standards for the air, soil, and water, with no region in America able to tolerate pollution levels exceeding these standards. Aside from the reluctance of federal legislators to enact such bold legislation, however, there are equally fundamental problems: What are the standards to be? What level of pollution is tolerable? At what point does pollution begin to harm the ecosystem? What are the short-run versus the long-run consequences of various pollutants? These are difficult questions to answer, for despite the heightened scientific concern with ecological problems, a great deal of ignorance exists with respect to the impact of pollutants on the environment. This lack of knowledge places legislators in the position of setting renewable resource quality standards without clear scientific guidelines.

Problems in creating effective laws

In such a state of ignorance, legislators will tend to avoid enacting expensive laws, or if they do enact laws, they will write ambiguities into them, especially when pressured by well-organized lobbying interests (Graham, 1966). For example, the Water Quality Act of 1965 established rather vague water quality standards that could be voided upon a "due consideration to the practicability and to the physical and economic feasibility of complying with such standards . . . as the public interest and equities of the case may require." Coupled with many courts' sympathetic attitude toward communities and industries, the Water Quality Act has proven difficult to enforce because arguments as to how pollutants serve the public interest by keeping taxes low or by providing jobs for workers in polluting industries are rather easily made.

The only significant piece of legislation which explicitly sought to

New cars headed for the freeway and destined to cause more air pollution. Will the Clean Air Act stop their harmful pollutants?

redress these deficiencies was the Clean Air Act of 1970. In this act, tolerable emissions were stated with deadlines for compliance to these standards being explicit. The auto makers have now been granted several extensions in meeting required standards (excluding California); and currently, with energy problems and the specter of more economic dislocations resulting from enforcement of the standards, there is considerable pressure to suspend or weaken the law. If unambiguous standards for clean air cannot be maintained, it is less probable that similar standards can be set for emissions into the soil and water which, in both the short and long run, pose a more serious threat to the ecosystem than air pollution. Arguments about the "public interest," the threat of an economic recession, or higher taxes can be used to weaken, and even suspend, the enforcement of any future standards for the water and soil. This prospect is particularly likely because pollution of the soil and water is not as directly observable as air pollution, and thus, not as disturbing to the public. Equally significant, the interaction of pollutants with the water and soil is more complex than with the air, with the result that legislators will not know just what standards to establish.

Assuming that minimal quality standards for the air, water, and soil could be enacted, the next legislative problem revolves around the question of how to induce communities and industries to pay for *all* remaining pollutants that they discharged into the environment. These laws will probably reveal the following basic formula: The more pollutants emitted within minimum standards, the more offenders must pay in penalties, and when offenders are corporations, the more they must pay in fines which cannot be passed on to consumers. Such laws might serve as incentives for industries to clean up the last of their harmful effluents. Enacting this kind of law, however, poses a major dilemma: How are the formulas for assigning these costs to be created? As already noted, there is considerable ignorance as to how pollutants interact with each other in different environments over varying lengths of time to cause varying degrees of harm to different ecosystems. In light of this situation, then, just how are costs for emissions into the air, water, and soil to be assessed? Such is one of the problems of enactment in environmental law; and yet, unless tentative legislative efforts to construct these formulas for assigning costs are made, industries and communities will have few economic incentives to restrict their effluents.

To further remove current inducements for pollution, extensive and broad programs of law enactment may be necessary. It would seem necessary, for effective pollution control, that depletion allowances and lowered tax assessments for harmful resource extraction be stricken from federal and state laws. Accompanying the elimination of these incentives to pollute should come laws encouraging research on pollution control and installation of emission control devices. One approach would involve high tax write-offs for these antipollution activities, although any such law would have to be monitored carefully by the Internal Revenue Service to prevent industries from simply renaming previous research activities in unrelated areas, "antipollution research, development, and implementation." Another strategy might create laws requiring polluting companies to reinvest a certain percentage of their profits into effluent control, while at the same time, preventing these corporations from passing their increased costs on to consumers.

To add legal weight to these kinds of new laws, and to facilitate their enactment where legislative bodies hesitate, some have proposed a constitutional amendment containing an Environmental Bill of Rights (Nader, 1970; Ehrlich, 1971). In the absence of clear legal precedents for controlling emissions, such an amendment would enable the courts to rule against polluters in environmental lawsuits. Bringing industrywide and class action suits against polluters is presently most difficult because there are few unambiguous legal doctrines that can provide the necessary legal precedent. In this relative legal vacuum, the doctrine of "balance of equities" has evolved and now guides many pollution suits.

An Environmental
Bill of Rights

This doctrine charges the courts to consider the "good" consequences (a clean environment) against the "bad" effects (higher taxes and unemployment, for example) of rules favoring environmentalists. The result has often been for the courts to rule that the economic benefits of pollution outweigh the alleged costs to personal health and ecological disruption. A constitutional amendment containing a forceful Environmental Bill of Rights could potentially rebalance legal precedents in favor of the environment.

Without such a constitutional amendment, there are few legal traditions with which to press environmental lawsuits. Probably the most applicable of existing legal traditions are the doctrines of "nuisance" and "trespass" (Ehrlich and Ehrlich, 1970:267–274; Landau and Rheingold, 1971). It is not completely wrong to consider pollutants as a "nuisance" to public health and as a "trespass" on individuals' air, land, and water. Yet this argument does appear to stretch traditional conceptions of trespass and nuisance; thus, these doctrines are not likely to prove effective. Equally as significant as this lack of legal tradition is the fact that one of the key legal weapons of environmentalists—the class action lawsuit—was redefined in 1973 by the Supreme Court. In a landmark water pollution case, the Court ruled that in pollution suits involving several states, the citizens of each state bringing the suit in a federal court must demonstrate $10,000 in damages to their property or health. This ruling will severely limit the capacity of environmental groups to bring class action suits in federal courts since each plaintiff must now document $10,000 in damages.

The law, therefore, can be both a tool to deal with pollution problems and a roadblock to the resolution of these problems. We have emphasized the obstacles to effective laws in order to highlight the extent to which pollution is built into the present legal system in America. Such need not necessarily be the case, of course, but the problems of calculating ecological damage and of writing pollution control formulas present formidable obstacles to those who seek to write effective laws. And coupled with the economic, social, and political dislocations that the enactment and enforcement of such laws would have, the problems of using law as a tool for pollution control become even more acute. These problems may indeed be surmountable, but they will need to be attacked with political resolve to prevent ecological disruption. Such resolve will reflect the priorities, decision-making processes, and administrative capacities of the federal government.

The Government. To seriously address environmental problems will probably require reordering of national priorities, for the costs of a comprehensive environmental program will be enormously high, perhaps as much as $50 billion per year for a decade, to restore present environment disruptions and close to that amount thereafter

The cost of antipollution programs

just to maintain these restored ecological balances in the face of an expanding economy. The sources of such high costs are many: For example, tax incentives for polluters will be expensive and inevitably raise federal, state, and local taxes; revenue sharing and grants-in-aid to cities attempting to revamp their sewage systems will cost a great deal; and the large federal bureaucracy needed to implement, monitor, and enforce antipollution codes will also be expensive.

Conflicting with these costs are the ever-increasing revenue demands in the domestic sphere (Sprout and Sprout, 1971a). For example, welfare costs will continue to rise; proposed national health care systems will be expensive; education costs are likely to continue to increase; law enforcement costs will not remain stable; perpetuation of agricultural and industrial subsidies will continue to tax federal revenues; foreign aid will remain high; and the total revenue needs of the executive departments like Interior, Labor, Commerce, and Housing and Urban Development will expand. While considerable revenue can be raised from closing tax loopholes, raising corporate and individual taxes, and expanding the economy and, hence, tax revenues, it appears that it will still be necessary to reorder national priorities to generate the large sums of money needed to preserve the ecological community.

If the nation is to maintain current standards of living *and* address pollution problems, the only available source of revenue is the Pentagon's budget. Presently, the military and related agencies receive at least 35 percent (probably closer to 50%) of all federal tax revenues, thereby making it the largest single source of nondomestic monies. To maintain the present military budget *and* address pollution problems would require drastic increases in taxes; or, to maintain the military budget, keep taxes down, *and still* attack pollution problems would probably involve, for example, poorer schools, expensive private health care, less police protection, widespread poverty, continued urban decay, and inadequate transport systems. As Chapter 3 documents, the political influence of the Pentagon, and the corporations and labor organizations receiving its contract dollars, is great. This situation underscores the dilemma of addressing ecological problems, for unless the military budget can be tapped, Americans will have higher taxes and lessened social services. The public is not likely to accept these, while the military is not likely to have its budget cut drastically, thus revealing the extent to which pollution problems are built into the political problems involved in reordering priorities. When these political problems are compounded by the economic consequences of reordered priorities—short-term unemployment for workers and falling stock prices for the owners of corporations doing business with the Pentagon—then the difficulties of

Protest has often been the only way to initiate political action by government.

changing priorities to maintain the ecological community become even more pronounced.

Even if Congress could render priorities and enact comprehensive quality standards for the air, water, and soil, a new set of political obstacles would probably emerge. These revolve around the present pattern of governmental administration in America (Revelle, 1968). As was emphasized in Chapter 5, the United States is a federalist political system with considerable power residing in city, county, and state governments. While there are many advantages to such a system, one of the current problems facing all types of national legislation is the coordination of city, county, and state governments with the federal agencies that administer national legislation. It is perhaps inevitable, in a federalist system, and perhaps desirable from one viewpoint, that state and local governments will often have conflicting interests, but one less positive result is to make difficult implementation of national legislation. In order to avoid these conflicts among and between various levels of government, it may be necessary for antipollution agencies to have considerable power over local governments. However, existing governmental agencies, state and local government, well-organized interests, and even the public in the post-Watergate-domestic spying era are likely to resist the allocation of such power. There are many sound reasons for resisting the concentration of power in administrative agencies, but one of the di-

Problems in governmental antipollution programs

lemmas of a federalist system is that without this power, it is more difficult to cut through the rivalries and antagonisms among diverse governmental bodies and effectively implement a national pollution control program.

Another problem with the current pattern of administration in America is that, even when they have considerable power, agencies frequently fail to implement and enforce regulatory laws. One type of misregulation involves a failure to maintain various quality standards. For example, the U.S. Department of Agriculture has, on numerous occasions, not held the line on the use of certain dangerous pesticides. A second source of misregulation is the cooptation of federal agencies by those very industries they are established to regulate. For instance, the Department of Agriculture is frequently an advocate of the chemical pesticide industry that it is supposed to regulate. The public record reveals quite clearly that it has consistently pushed the use of pesticides, while underemphasizing research on and use of alternative forms of pest control (Ehrlich, 1971). A third source of administrative incompetence can be seen in the reluctance of agencies to argue for tougher standards where the standards are weak or ambiguous (Nader, 1970). Sometimes the reason for this reticence stems from the fact that if agencies push for tougher standards, they could potentially expose their previous laxity in enforcement. A final administrative obstacle to effective administration of regulatory law can be seen in the reluctance of existing agencies to use even the limited sanctions at their disposal. Should an agency finally take action against an offending industry or community, it usually secures a cease-and-desist order which requires the violator to stop its illegal activities. Most typically, only after such an order has been ignored will minimal (rarely maximum) civil penalties be sought by regulatory agencies.

This pattern of administration now appears to be well institutionalized, with the likely result that its failings will be repeated even if antipollution laws are enacted. To avoid these administrative problems, it is likely that the current Environmental Protection Agency will be less successful than anticipated. A "supra-agency" with power over all other agencies in the federal government might well be necessary for effective enforcement of antipollution laws. Establishing an agency with such far-reaching authority, however, will create many problems. One of these will revolve around opening and maintaining lines of authority to other executive departments in the federal government, as well as to state and local governments (Goldman, 1970). For at a minimum, a supra-agency will probably require authority over the other executive departments, such as Health, Education and Welfare, Commerce, Interior, Agriculture, Transportation, and Housing and Urban Development. In light of the history of rivalry, duplication of effort, and jealousy among these agencies, it will be difficult to create a new agency with authority over all of them. Various departments would probably oppose the creation of this supra-agency in the first place, and undermine its effectiveness should it even be created. In July 1970, President Nixon formed the Environmental Protection Agency to consolidate pollution control policy and activity, but the record of the last seven years with respect to enforcement of the unambiguous Clean Air Act reveals that it has had a difficult time asserting authority over other executive departments. If this situation is to prove typical, then the difficulties in the administration of environmental law will be compounded.

The prognosis, then, for an effective administration of antipollution laws reveals many problems, most of which inhere in the current structure of government in America. These problems are exacerbated by the complexities of the task with which an environmental agency would be charged. Laws and their enforcement cannot simply prohibit the emissions of all pollutants, for such a prohibition is not economically, politically, or socially possible. A more reasonable approach is that, within quality standards set by the law, a way must be devised to induce polluters to cut back their other harmful activities. This inducement can come only by requiring polluters to pay for all their emissions within the tolerable limits of national quality standards. As was emphasized earlier, there are problems with writing legal formulas for determining what the costs should be since an understanding of the short- and long-run consequences of pollutants to the ecosystem is far from complete. The administrative problems involved in just creating the accounting system represents a roadblock to monitoring and controlling pollution in America; moreover, the governmental agency charged with enforcing what initially—in light of current ignorance—would be somewhat arbitrary cost formulas, will quite naturally be resisted by industry and communities. One result of this situation could be endless legal battles as polluters seek to document that their pollutants should not cost as much as dictated by existing formulas (Sprout and Sprout, 1971b).

In evaluating the political capacity of the United States to regulate its emissions into the ecosystem, then, it is clear that there are a number of structural obstacles. The reordering of national priorities in the direction of environmental protection will be difficult due to the Pentagon's power. And even should these obstacles be surmounted, the pattern of governmental administration in America reveals an additional set of problems that could potentially reduce effective environmental protection. While these same conditions may have positive outcomes for other sectors of the society, they represent severe problems of structure in resolving the problems of the ecological community.

POPULATION AND THE ECOSYSTEM

Humans are multiplying at an accelerating rate. For example, from 1850 to 1930, the world population doubled from one to two billion (Appleman, 1965). Currently the world's population is set at 3.5 billion and will soon double again (Ehrlich, 1970; Hardin, 1969; Miles, 1970; and Wald, 1970). A rapidly expanding population poses a problem for ecological balances since it creates ever-increasing demands for industrial and agricultural goods. In the agricultural sector of the economy, the demands for food cause the use of the pesticides and chemical fertilizer that kill many organisms necessary for life-sustaining energy flows and mineral cycles. Moreover, in order to keep abreast of growing demand, single-crop or a limited-rotation agriculture becomes necessary. Such agricultural techniques strip the ecosystem of the natural stability stemming from diversity, while at the same time making crops extremely vulnerable to pests and disease. In turn, this susceptibility intensifies reliance upon pesticides and various chemical killers. Thus, the short-run demands for agricultural products created by an expanding population can force a pattern of agricultural production that potentially could decrease the soil's capacity to feed the human species in the long run.

Population and pollution

In the industrial sector of the economy, population growth escalates demands for consumer goods which increases the discharge of pollutants into renewable resources. This demand is likely to be particularly severe as the "revolution of rising expectations" among populations of Third World nations stimulate the production of increased numbers and varieties of industrial goods.

The rate of population growth in modern industrial societies is much slower than that in Third World nations, and perhaps, once these latter societies become industrialized, their population growth will begin to level off. Yet, the population base of perhaps as many as 15 billion to be served by mass industrial and intensive agricultural production could create economic demands that can only be met by further ecological disruption. Presently, these large populations of the undeveloped world do not pose an ecological problem, but with rapid growth and industrial expansion they could represent a severe ecological problem in the future. In the immediate present, the comparatively small populations and low rates of growth of industrialized nations represent the most evident threat to ecosystem balances. As was outlined in Figure 6, the demands of these small

Population and pollution in the Third World

populations are met with the techniques of mass agriculture and industrial production which deposits large quantities of waste residues into the ecological community (Miles, 1970; Stockwell, 1968).

The patterns of population growth now evident in the United States and elsewhere in the industrial world will perhaps become more prevalent in the rest of the world, but the changes which now appear to be associated with a drop in the birth rate—industrialization, urbanization, and mass production—can be potentially harmful, especially as they serve as expanded population base. For example, some statistics can perhaps underscore the dangers of the Third World developing the same consumption habits as Americans: Consumption of goods by polluting industrial and agricultural processes, as well as the disposal of wastes by each American, is 50 times that of a person in the nonindustrial world (Wald, 1970). Or, to phrase the matter differently, the United States causes more pollution with its current population of 210 million than the 2.5 billion inhabitants of the underdeveloped world combined. The prospect, then, of an "Americanized" Third World is disquieting. But for the present, the population patterns of American society are of most direct relevance to current ecological problems. The critical question becomes: What are these population patterns?

Considerable publicity has been given to the sudden decrease in the birth rate to a "no growth" level. From an ecological standpoint, it can be hoped that this recent trend will endure. And yet, even if it does, it will not become translated into a stable population, since the current childbearing population will live for another fifty to sixty years, with the result that their children, grandchildren, and great grandchildren will be added to the population. Hence, even should the birth *rate* stay at the zero level, it is inevitable that the United States will grow to perhaps as much as 300 million before it finally stabilizes.

One difficulty with extrapolating from birth rates is that in the past they have fluctuated considerably. During the 1930s, for example, concern with the low birth rate was pervasive; and then suddenly with the onset of World War II, all projections of a declining population were rendered inaccurate with the baby boom; and now with new values and birth control technologies, a marked drop in the birth rate has occurred. Is this a long-run trend or simply a low point in a cycle? While no definitive statement in this area is possible, it would appear that the long-range trend is toward a decline in the birth rate with periodical reversals. It is these periodic reversals that are of concern because they increase the population base and hence the demand for industrial and mass agricultural goods.

America's
no-growth
birth rate

**SOCIOLOGICAL
INSIGHTS**

POPULATION DOWN

Young American women expect to have fewer children. As a result, population projections for the United States for the year 2000 have been revised downward.

At the end of this century the population of this country will range from a low of 245 million to a high of 287 million. Current population is 213 million.

Young American females questioned by the Census Bureau indicate that they plan to bear from 1.7 to 2.7 children.

In the United States, then, population policy must be directed to preventing any reversal, even one of short duration, of the current rate of zero population growth. With an equally concerted effort at pollution abatement, perhaps the world's ecosystem can support an American population of 300 million, but if the rate jumps suddenly, even if only briefly, world ecological problems would be correspondingly intensified, especially when coupled with the industrialization of the Third World.

How safe to drink is this water? Or any water in America? This girl is wise to hesitate.

SUMMARY

As we have seen, only by understanding the basic elements and processes in social and ecological systems is it possible to comprehend the ways in which society has interacted with the ecosystem to create what could potentially become the ultimate problem of structure. The ecological community is composed of highly complex flows of energy and cycles of minerals through the millions of life forms inhabiting the planet. Social systems are composed of humans organized into complex webs of interrelationships mediated by cultural symbols. As Figure 6 outlined, this organization of the human species into sociocultural entities could threaten the flow of energy and cycling of minerals in the ecosystem, creating not just a crisis of human survival, but one for many other life forms as well.

While completely definitive data on the matter do not exist, it appears that the structure of many ecosystems is now vulnerable to change from the pollutants of human societies, whereas the structure of social systems appear less likely to change in ways that might restore more harmonious relations between society and nature. While the details of ecological disruption are ultimately biological questions, even a cursory appreciation of the nature of the ecological community reveals that human society has (1) lessened, to some unknown extent, the diversity and stability of the world ecosystem; (2) altered, in ways not fully understood, the flow of energy and cycling of minerals, perhaps to the degree that the amplified impact of these alterations will be intense; and (3) perhaps already generated unknown amounts of irreversible destruction to plant and animal species.

Because of its enormous productive power and habits of consumption, American society is largely responsible for this disruption which, by itself, is problematic, but equally problematic is the worldwide process involving restructuring many human societies along the American pattern. While there are notable differences over ideology and forms of political organization among the societies of the developing world, they all reveal a similar pattern of community and institutional organization. For indeed, all are guided by cultural beliefs emphasizing economic growth, higher levels of consumption, the extensive application of technology, and the utilization of nature as a refuse dump. All, therefore, reveal the beginning of community structures and institutional arrangements that will generate large quantities of waste residues.

In closing, it can properly be asked: What are the future prospects for resolving this ultimate problem of structure? And, what will corrective action require of Americans? It does appear that there is some awareness of ecological problems in America; and this awareness may well become translated into actions which reduce the discharge of pollutants into the world's renewable resources. But it could take several ecological disasters, or clearly visible crises, for consciousness to shift into concerted social action. At the very least, there is hope in the fact that Americans realize that some action is necessary. Corrective action, however, may well require difficult adjustments for most Americans: Pollution control will cost money in the form of higher taxes and prices; it probably will require distortions in the job market; it could make "luxuries" of many taken for granted goods and services; and it will no doubt require a willingness to save, conserve, and recycle. These actions represent major changes in the American way of life, and it is an open question as to whether or not Americans are willing, at this time, to begin making the necessary sacrifices. The next two decades will probably reveal America's capacity to deal with this problem of culture and structure.

NOTES

1. For a more detailed analysis of world ecological problems, see Turner, 1976a.

2. Another interesting consequence of subsidizing companies involved in waste recovery, plant abatement technologies, and effluent treatment procedures is that the government would also be subsidizing companies that do the polluting, since some of the big polluters are also manufacturing and selling antipollution equipment to other polluters.

REVIEW QUESTIONS

1. Summarize the fundamental principles of the ecological community.
2. How do each of the cultural beliefs facilitating pollution reflect dominant values in America?
3. How do each of the structures listed below cause pollution *and* inhibit implementation of pollution control measures:

   communities
   social classes
   economy
   law
   government
4. Why is population size still a potential pollution problem in America, even as birth rates approach the zero growth level?

GLOSSARY

amplification the process in which disruption at one point in the ecosystem can, over time, become more extensive and extend to other points in the ecosystem

ecosystem the patterns of interrelationship among animal species and the physical materials of the environment

food chains the process whereby energy is passed through the ecosystem: The sun's energy is stored in plants which are consumed by herbivores that, in turn, are consumed by carnivores

lag effects the process whereby the full extent of ecological disruption is unknown or unrecognized until a point of massive disruption is reached.

mineral cycles the processes by which crucial minerals, which are never destroyed, are cycled through plant and animal forms in such a way as to provide support for life

pollution waste residues that can disrupt mineral cycles and food chains

renewable resources the air, water, and soil, which are capable of maintaining their own vitality through the cycles and processes of the ecosystem, the basic resources on which all life depends

simplification the process in which human use of the ecosystem strips the system of its natural diversity, making it more vulnerable to disruption

waste residues the discharges from society into the ecosystem

V

DEVIANCE: PROBLEMS IN THE SOCIETAL REACTION

While most human action is organized by the institutional, distributive, and community systems, people often deviate from the norms of these basic social forms of human organization. Such deviations frequently go unnoticed, but at times, the reaction can be severe. In fact, this reaction is codified into cultural beliefs and structured responses to some deviants.

It is this cultural and structural reaction to deviance that will occupy our attention in the three chapters of this closing section. In a society valuing freedom and individualism, while putting great pressures upon individuals to be active and to achieve, it is inevitable that some people will be different, that some will seek success illegally, that some will withdraw, and that some will become personally disorganized. Such is inevitable in a large, urban and industrial society holding a profile of values that place great burdens and expectations upon individuals.

In the chapters of this section, we will select three forms of deviance for study: crime, drug use, and mental illness. Other forms of deviance could be selected and perhaps are equally deserving of coverage; however, we will focus on these three problems, but not for reasons of parsimony. These problems, in particular, have generated an extensive societal reaction embracing many people and involving the expenditure of vast sums of money. Moreover, intensely held cultural beliefs have

developed around these "problems." A book on social problems in America is obligated to cover topics subject to such intense debate and commentary.

In Chapter 14, we will examine the crime problem. Americans worry about rising crime and often fear for their lives and property. As we will discover, however, this fear has set into motion a societal reaction among legislators of law, the police, the courts, and correction programs that is, at times, counterproductive. It is in this sense that crime is viewed as a problem of societal reaction.

In Chapter 15, we will shift our attention to the drug problem. As we will see, drug abuse is often a matter of social definition and the reaction to drug use can range from a tolerant response to one defining the problem as in the province of medical professionals or criminal enforcement agencies. The drug problem is, thus, one of definition—a definition that, as we will come to appreciate, has little to do with a drug's addictive power, its extent of use, its harm to society, or its effect upon individuals. These facts will enable us to visualize "drug abuse" as a problem of the cultural and structual reaction.

We will examine mental illness in America in Chapter 16. The very notion that some deviations are an *illness of the mind* is a matter of social definition. And as we will see, the reaction to deviance of the mind is based upon a medical definition of the problem. Such a definition has many consequences, some of which are counterproductive in eliminating this form of deviance.

As we approach the study of deviance we must remain attuned to our personal biases. For indeed, these biases define for us the problems and their solutions. As sociologists, however, our task will be to examine the reasons for the particular definition of deviance as a problem. We will then have to discern how extensive the problem is, using the dominant *cultural definition.* Next, we will need to explore how the society has become structured to react to the "problem." And finally, we will have to ask, especially in a book on social problems, whether the problemness of the deviance resides in the deviants themselves or the way they are treated in society.

PROLOGUE 14: THE REALITY OF CRIME AND JUSTICE

A television news announcer reports to an alarmed public that crime has increased 10 percent according to FBI statistics. Neither the reporter nor the public know how these statistics were gathered or whether they are accurate. They accept them as just another confirmation of "rising crime" and the need for "law and order."

The police have just arrested a lower-class youth. Reluctantly, they read him his rights; then, they book him and put him in jail. There he will wait for two days, despite his constitutional right to a speedy arraignment where formal charges must be read against him. But he does not know about this right, and even if he did, he could not do anything about it. He has no money. His friends have suddenly disappeared. And his family is as ignorant and intimidated by the law as he.

When it comes time to make a plea of guilty, or not guilty, our suspect will plead guilty. He knows that he is not guilty, but the court-appointed attorney has advised him to plead guilty to a lesser charge and be placed on probation. The attorney has too many cases to go to court, and he is interested in collecting his small fee with a minimum of hassle. The district attorney does not want to go to court; he too is busy, but he wants a conviction even if the offender does not go to jail.

In the court, before the supposedly aloof judge, a plea of guilty is entered. The judge passes sentence: three years probation. The judge also is busy and wants to process this case quickly, so he agrees to go

440

along with the district attorney's suggestion that three years of probation is preferable to three years in jail for this "first offender."

For the next three years, our "convicted criminal's" life will be monitored by a busy probation officer. Our "convicted criminal" will now have this stigma around his neck for the rest of his life. His activities for the next years will be guided by restrictive rules which, in his youthful exuberance, he will likely break. If he gets caught, and if his probation officer is strict, he could go to jail. If he goes to jail or prison, his chances of being a criminal the rest of his life, and of ending up in prison again, will be very high.

This is the reality of crime and justice in America. Middle-class people with money can avoid much of the harshness of this reality, but the majority of criminals who get caught are from the lower and working class. And for them, this is the justice system. As the middle classes watch the reports of rising crime on TV, they remain oblivious to this reality. Moreover, they are convinced that criminals are being let off too easily, a belief that contradicts the facts. They do recognize, however, that the court and jails are not working.

Chapter 14 will examine the problems of crime and the societal reaction to crime. As we will come to appreciate, the definition of the problem is influenced by cultural beliefs which have created a system that does very little to reduce crime and is highly abusive of defendants.

CHAPTER

14

THE CRIME PROBLEM

Crime is an act that violates criminal laws.[1] Since most people violate the law, everyone has probably been a criminal at one time or another. For example, a survey of 1700 persons in the New York area revealed that, in response to a list of 49 criminal offenses, over 90 percent of the anonymous respondents admitted they had committed one or more offenses for which they could have received a jail or prison sentence.[2] The majority of these "criminals" were never detected in their crime, nor were many of their crimes reflected in official statistics. These findings reveal that criminal behavior and its consequences for society cannot be understood without focusing attention on the nature of laws that would formally define 90 percent of the population criminal, and on the structure of enforcement and administration of those laws which, as we will come to see, make only a few people actual criminals. Crime in America is thus not just a problem of capturing criminals; much of the problemness about crime stems from uncertainty, ambiguity, and inconsistency in how those charged with "controlling crime" react. And it is in this sense that we will come to view crime in America as a problem of culture and structure.

CRIME IN AMERICA: AN OVERVIEW

PROBLEMS WITH CRIME STATISTICS

The 1967 President's Commission on Law Enforcement (hereafter referred to as President's Commission) noted that "there has always been too much crime. Virtually every generation since the founding of the nation has felt itself threatened by the spectre of rising crime and violence." Indeed, current official statistics document a rapidly rising crime rate. The most comprehensive statistical summary of crime in America comes from the yearly publication of the *Uniform Crime Reports* (UCR) by the FBI. Using three types of property crimes (burglary, larceny over $50, and motor vehicle theft) and four types of crimes against persons (willful homicide, forcible rape, aggravated assault, and robbery), an index is constructed to reveal the amount of, and trends in, serious crimes. The data for this index represent "crimes known to the police" and are gathered from local and state police officials throughout the country. Although usually cautious about claiming that this index reveals *all* crime, the yearly report, as interpreted by the media and the public, is at times accepted uncritically and without necessary qualifications as a rough revelation of crime in America. The report portrays the following picture of crime over the last 20 years:

FBI "Uniform Crime Reports" (UCR)

1. Each year the number of crimes against persons, especially aggravated assault, robbery, and forcible rape, show a sharp increase. Willful homicide appears to remain fairly constant, showing only small increases in recent years.

The UCR trend since the mid-1950s

2. The number of crimes against property show an even more dramatic increase each year.
3. While the volume of crime is greatest in large cities, property and personal crimes are up everywhere, in the biggest and smallest cities, in the suburbs, and in rural areas.
4. Even when increases in the size of the population are taken into account (i.e., there are more people than ever), the *rate* of crime per 100,000 people shows a large increase.

What do these figures actually reveal about crime in America? Unfortunately it is difficult to know exactly what they tell because a number of problems are involved in their collection.

Problems in UCR statistics

First, the study cited earlier reveals quite clearly that most crimes are not reported, indicating that crime is considerably more widespread than revealed by official crime statistics. A number of data sources also underscore this fact. For example, the National Opinion Research Center (NORC) of the University of Chicago surveyed 10,000 households and asked if the person questioned had been a victim of a crime and, if so, if the crime had been reported to the police. Upon comparison, it became apparent that the survey crime rates, except for willful homicide and motor vehicle theft, were higher than the UCR crime rate. Overall, the amount of personal-injury crime was nearly twice as high by the NORC survey as by the UCR index, while property crimes were well over twice as high by NORC as by UCR tabulations (Biderman, 1967; President's Commission, 1967:21–22). More detailed surveys by the Bureau of Social Science Research in high- and medium-crime-rate areas in Washington, D.C., Chicago, and Boston portray a similar pattern (President's Commission, 1967:20–23). A more recent study by the Law Enforcement Assistance Administration in 1973 reveals that from a survey of 125,000 citizens and 15,000 businesses, several conclusions can be reached about crime in the general population: Of the 16.6 million major crimes in the first six months of 1973, only about 5.3 million persons reported them to the police. Moreover, only 3.9 million of these were relayed to the FBI from local police departments. Thus, it is clear that official crime statistics *under*report the amount of crime in America.

A second problem with the official FBI statistics is that they do not incorporate crimes committed by organized syndicates (gambling, narcotics, prostitution), police crime, or professional and "white-collar" crime (income tax evasion, antitrust violations, restraint of trade, and misrepresentation in advertising). Just how extensive such forms of crime are cannot be know precisely, but they are certainly more widespread than the "conventional" crimes reported in the UCR index. These forms of crime are committed by the wealthy and by the highly organized and would raise the UCR index by several-fold if incorporated into official statistics.

This underreporting of crime in official statistics poses a number of interpretive problems. With such a vast pool of unreported crime, any change in police reporting practices or any improvement in policing techniques will cause a sharp increase in the amount of crime reported or known to the police. Although it is impossible to determine for sure, it is likely that at least some of the dramatic increase in crime over the last decades reflects not so much actual increases, but rather changes in police practices that have led the police to dip into the heretofore unreported pool of crime. For example, the President's Commission undertook an extensive examination of police reporting practices and found that from 1959 to 1965 a change in the criminal reporting procedures by police was followed by jumps in the crime rate. These represent "paper increases" that are impossible to distinguish from real increases in crime. Another factor causing a seeming acceleration in crime rates is police professionalism, which, as we will discuss shortly, has resulted in greater police efficiency through the use of new technologies and patroling practices. Furthermore, the increasing use of computers, clerical personnel, and statisticians has resulted in more accurate and complete police records which, when reported to the FBI, raise the national crime rate.

SOCIOLOGICAL INSIGHTS

CRIME STATISTICS AND PUBLIC REACTION

Is real crime increasing in America? Or are rising rates a statistical artifact? The statistics are such that it is impossible to know, but it is likely that, while crime has probably increased, some of the increase as reflected in the UCR index is a paper increase. This likelihood indicates that some anticrime legislation and public concern is in response to a crime wave that may not exist except in official statistics and in people's minds. Ironically, legislative and public concern over crime can have the consequence of statistically raising crime rates because political and public pressure usually results in greater police efficiency in the name of "law and order" which, in turn, forces police to dip deeper into previously unreported crimes and thereby raise the crime rate. Such an increase in the crime rate (not necessarily crime) generates more public and political concern, hence, even more pressure for law and order. To some unknown extent, then, public reaction and concern about rising crime may be a self-fulfilling prophecy: the more pressure for law and order, the more diligent the police, and the more they dig into previously unreported crimes—thereby increasing the statistical rate that generated the public reaction in the first place.

RISING CRIME: ITS INEVITABILITY IN AMERICA

What causes increased crime? This question is impossible to answer because many of the answers lay buried in the psychological processes of individuals and in sociocultural conditions. And while there are many "theories" of crime causation, none have received the empirical support that would allow social scientists to proclaim that they know the causes of crime. Moreover, as the above discussion illustrates, it is very difficult to compute accurate statistics, thereby making imputed increases in crime rates, and inferences about a rise in criminally disposed individuals and criminally inducing social conditions, ambiguous. Furthermore, Americans should expect increased crime for several reasons: (1) There are more laws to break than previously, (2) the demographic trend toward a younger and urban population assures increased crime, and (3) Americans own more material goods than ever, thus, there is more to steal.

The causes of crime are unknown

Law Making and Crime. If crime is defined as a violation of criminal laws, then it can be expected that the greater the number of laws, the more crime. Over the last 50 years the United States has undergone profound changes associated with industrialization and urbanization. Accompanying these changes, new laws have proliferated at an incredibly rapid rate so that today there are more ways to violate the law than there were 70 years ago (Allen, 1964). Crimes such as disturbing the peace, traffic violations, automobile theft, cheating on tax assessments, income tax evasion, violation of interstate commerce regulations, and the carrying of a gun without a permit result from law enactment in this century. Thus, an increase in crime is an inevitable by-product of a modernizing society and its ever-expanding body of law. Ironically, as the public and legislators become concerned over "rising crime," they may hastily enact new laws to deal with crime and, by this very process, force crime rates to rise—perhaps setting off a new cycle of public concern, legislative law enactment, and increased crime rates. Just to what extent current increases in crime *rates* are the product of such a process is impossible to assess. Probably only a small impact on crime rates *in the short run* is registered by an expanded body of criminal law, but over several decades the influence on crime rates would be more profound.

Demographic Factors and Crime. Without delving into the "criminal personality" and without assuming a shift toward a more crime-oriented cultural ethos, increases in crime can be seen as inevitable in light of basic demographic trends in the United States (President's Commision, 1967). One of these trends is the urbanization of the population. Crime has always been more predominant in urban than rural areas presumably because community social control is lessened, while opportunities for committing crimes have increased (again, the increase is not fully understood). Thus, as the American population has become urbanized, crime could be expected to increase. Furthermore, the racial and ethnic pattern of urbanization has forced minority groups into the decaying and impoverished city cores; it would seem inevitable that the crime rate of these slum dwellers, who must remain deprived in the midst of affluence, would be higher than that of their rural ancestors, who did not have to endure such relative deprivation.

Another major demographic trend has revolved around changes in the age composition of the population. Because of the post-World War II baby boom, the younger age groups have increased dramatically as a proportion of the population. Since it is in this age group that crime rates have always been highest (again, the reasons for this

Reasons for
increased crime

are not well understood), it can be expected that as this group increases in size, the national crime rate will rise. For example, using UCR index crimes, over 40 percent of those arrested for forcible rape and robbery and nearly 30 percent of those arrested for willful homicides and aggravated assault are in the 18–29-year-old group. For property crimes such as burglary, larceny, and auto theft, over 50 percent of all arrests are among those under 18 years old. While high arrest statistics for the young may be the result of their criminal inexperience and inability to avoid the police, it is more likely that they just commit more crimes than other age groups, especially those crimes on the UCR index. It is impossible to judge whether crime within younger age groups is rising, but as the young increase as a proportion of the population the national crime rate will no doubt increase. Even without a rise in criminality among youths, the fact that a million additional youths are added to the 18–29 age group each year makes increases of crime inevitable.

American Affluence and Crime. Crimes against property have shown the most dramatic increase (by official statistics). More property is being stolen today than ever before. However, this does not necessarily mean that a larger proportion of the population is prone to theft, robbery, or larceny; rather, these data could reveal that there is *more to steal* in an affluent society and that property is less well protected than formerly (President's Commission, 1967). For example, car theft has become widespread because there are more cars to steal; and since they are insured, owners tend to be more careless. To take another example, the rise in thefts of over $50 may reflect the impact of inflation as much as an increase in serious crime. Thirty years ago $50 represented much more than it does today, with the result that stealing $50 today is really petty larceny, except for the fact that it is recorded as a serious crime and included in the UCR index. If $100 were used as the dividing line between petty and grand larceny, the serious larceny rate would drop and would represent about what a dividing line of $50 did in 1940.

Aside from generating more to steal and inflating the value of what is stolen, affluence creates frustrations among those who, in accordance with values of materialism, desire to participate in that affluence but who are blocked from achieving material well-being. As long as the whole society was relatively poor, the poor could be content knowing that most people were not much better off. But with the growth of affluence and a large middle class, those without much property have an escalated sense of deprivation. Looting during ethnic and racial riots of the 1960s is perhaps the most dramatic example of how such deprivation causes crime, but the less visible day-to-day thefts and robberies among the poor also reflect the desire to be "active" and "achieve" some degree of "material" well-being.

After all these qualifications are tacked onto official crime statistics, the question still remains: Is crime increasing dramatically? Some of the increase in crime rates is probably a statistical artifact, while another portion of the increase appears inevitable as more criminal laws are enacted, as the population becomes urbanized and younger, and as affluence increases the deprivations of the poor while providing more property to steal. Above and beyond these forces, it is impossible to know if individual Americans are more criminally inclined than 10, 20, or 50 years ago. There is simply no way to know.

Is crime increasing? By how much?

THE COSTS OF CRIME

Curiously, the public appears most concerned about one of the *least* costly forms of crime, in terms of dollars lost to individuals and society: crime in the streets—assault and robbery. However, if crime is a social problem because it costs a lot of money and disrupts society, crime in the streets is of less significance when compared to drunken drivers, organized syndicates, fraud, embezzlement, unreported commercial thefts by employees, and willful homicides (70 percent of whose victims are known to their killers).

Crime is expensive in two senses: (1) It involves the loss of property and money, as well as income through death of or injury to the victim. (2) It costs the government tax revenues, since lost money and income cannot be taxed. Most significantly, organized crime dealing in illicit cash flows, narcotics, loan sharking, gambling, and prostitution deprives the government of enormous tax revenues that could be used to help resolve other social problems. From only a cost perspective, then, the crimes that occupy the public's attention—assault and robbery—are less problematic. In fact, UCR index crimes are not nearly as significant as many crimes not included in this index. To quote from the President's Commission on Law Enforcement (1967:32):

UCR Index and the costs of crime

1. Organized crime takes about twice as much from gambling and other illegal goods and services as criminals derive *from all other sources of criminal activity combined.*
2. Unreported commercial theft losses, including shoplifting and employee theft, are more than double those of all reported and commercial thefts.
3. Of reported crimes, willful homicide, though comparatively low in volume, yields the most costly estimates (income loss from death) among those listed on the UCR crime index.

4. A list of the seven crimes with the greatest economic impact includes only two, willful homicide and larceny of $50 and over (reported and unreported), of the offenses included in the crime index.

In Table 14.1, estimates of the respective costs of crime are made by the President's Commission, and although they are almost a decade old, and although the costs are now much higher, the relationship of costs among crimes has probably remained the same.

From Table 14.1 we can see that illegal services, as provided by organized syndicates, and various occupation-related crimes are the most costly.

As we will see in the next chapter, in our analysis of the drug problem, organized crime syndicates derive enormous profits in providing illicit services and drugs. Operating much like business corporations, criminal syndicates have been able to avoid prosecution.[3] One of the principal reasons for the success of organized syndicates is that they provide services demanded by the public—gambling, drugs, quick cash loans, and prostitution (Cressey, 1969).

Organized crime

Table 14.1 **The Cost of Crime**

	Cost (millions of dollars)
Crimes against persons:	
Homocide	$ 750
Assault	$ 65
Subtotal	$ 815
Crimes against property:	
Unreported commercial theft*	$1,400
UCR Index crimes (robbery, burglary, larceny)	600
Embezzlement*	200
Fraud*	1,350
Forgery and other	82
Arson and vandalism	$ 300
Subtotal	$3,932
Other crimes:	
Drunk driving	$1,816
Tax fraud*	$ 100
Subtotal	$1,936
Illegal goods and services:	
Narcotics**	$ 350
Loan sharking**	350
Prostitution**	225
Gambling**	7,000
Alcohol**	$ 150
Subtotal	$8,075

Source: President's Commission on Law Enforcement and Administration, *Crime and Its Impact —An Assessment*, Washington, D.C.: Government Printing Office, 1967, p. 44.
* Occupation-related crime.
** Provided by organized crime syndicates.

Probably the second most costly form of crime is what has been labeled "occupational crime" (Quinney, 1964; Clinard and Quinney, 1967:130–132). A partial list of occupational crimes would include tax evasion, embezzlement, restraint of trade, employee theft, misrepresentation in advertising, black marketeering, misappropriation of public funds, fee splitting, price fixing, infringements on patents and copyrights, unfair labor practices, falsification of records, padding of expense accounts, and corruption in the handling of trusts, receiverships, and bankruptcies. Originally such crimes were labeled "white-collar crimes," because of the high proportion of middle-class professionals and corporate executives involved (Sutherland, 1940, 1967). However, somewhat later it was recognized that "farmers, repairmen, and others in essentially non-white-collar occupations could, through such illegalities as watering milk for public consumption, making unnecessary 'repairs' on television sets, and so forth, be classified as white-collar violators" (Newman, 1958:737).

The public concern for crime is, thus, selective because it concentrates on visible crimes committed more frequently by lower-class individuals. These differences in concern stem from the comparative invisibility of occupational and organized crime (hence, public ignorance about it) and from the power of these criminals to influence law enactment, enforcement, and judicial processes. While data are scarce on the subject, the greatest increase in crime in America is probably among organized and occupational crimes rather than conventional crimes.[4] Currently the public has yet to define these hidden crimes as a serious social problem. Although concern over organized crime is growing, it has yet to reach the magnitude of concern by the general public over crime in the streets.

Not only does crime cost individuals and the society money in terms of lost property, tax revenues, and income, it also costs the society money to control crime. Table 14.2, reports the President's Commission's estimates of these costs.

From a cost standpoint, crime is a costly and, thus severe social problem. Crime is also inevitable; many of these costs are unavoidable. From one perspective, what is problematic about crime is not so

Occupational crime

Visibility and public concern over crime

Table 14.2 **Costs of Crime Control**

	Cost (millions of dollars)
Police	$2,792
Courts	261
Prosecution and defense	125
Corrections	$1,034
Total cost:	$4,212

much its existence, but how the society allocates its resources to control crime. It is in the area of "what to do" and "how much to spend" on crime that controversy, debate, and conflict in America can be found. These controversies stem from different cultural beliefs about how to deal with "the crime problem," as well as established patterns of response that have become institutionalized into American police forces, courts, and correctional institutions. And it is in this sense that we should view crime as a problem of culture and structure. Crime, per se, is inevitable, but it is the reaction to crime that now generates the most controversy, and it is these conflicts and injustices in the reaction to crime that will occupy our attention in this chapter.

THE CULTURAL BASIS OF THE REACTION TO CRIME

Aside from alarm over rising crime, many Americans evidence strongly held beliefs about what the law "should do" and what "should be done" to criminal deviants. These beliefs often come into conflict with those of other segments of the society, especially people of a "liberal" social and political philosophy, and some segments of the law enforcement and corrections professions.

With respect to what the law should do, considerable conflict in beliefs is clearly evident. Some segments of the population maintain that the criminal law should uphold "morality," "the American way," and other conceptions of "what is right." Such beliefs, which may vary among different segments of the population, represent the application of the values of conformity and morality to deviants. Thus, deviants who violate certain moral codes, regardless of whether or not they have harmed some person or property, should be subject to the sanctions of the criminal law. Thus, from this perspective, prostitution, gambling, drug use, and aberrant sex practices should be crimes, even though these acts usually do not harm others or their property. We might label such beliefs about criminal law *beliefs in a moral code.* In contradiction to these beliefs are those of a minority who believe that only deviant acts that tangibly harm others or property should be defined as criminal. Such beliefs represent the application of the values as individualism and freedom to deviant acts, for they emphasize the right of individual citizens to be different. For convenience, we might label these *libertarian beliefs.*

As we will see, the structure of criminal law, enforcement, and corrections in America reflects the contradiction between moral code and libertarian beliefs—a contradiction that mirrors the conflict between the value of conformity on the one hand and the values of freedom

Conflicting beliefs about what the law "should do"

and individualism on the other. For many of the sudden shifts in policies and actions of criminal agencies involves an effort to deal with contradictions in the culture of American society.

In regard to beliefs about what should be done to criminal deviants, we can observe a similar cultural conflict. On the one side are beliefs that criminals should be punished, and the more punishment, the more it will serve as a deterrent to those who might break the law. By recent public opinion polls, the vast majority of Americans hold punishment-centered beliefs about criminals, and a clear majority believes that current levels of punishment are inadequate and that the courts are "coddling the criminal element." Punishment orientations probably reflect the impact of the value of morality as it is applied to the value of conformity. For those who have deviated, especially those who have harmed others or their material property, "society must make of them an object lesson" so that others will not be tempted to commit crimes. Contradicting punishment beliefs are those emphasizing rehabilitation. Such beliefs are held by only a minority of the general public, but a much larger proportion of corrections officials are likely to be concerned with the rehabilitation of criminals. Rehabilitation beliefs dictate that efforts to change criminals—in order to effect their release, as law-abiding citizens, back into the community—is of paramount importance. From this perspective, punishments do not deter criminals, nor do they help those convicted of crimes become noncriminals. Such beliefs in deterrence and rehabilitation represent the application of the value humanitarianism to criminal deviants.

As with the conflict in beliefs over what "the law should do," dissensus over beliefs about what "should be done" to criminals is manifested in contradictory practices and structural arrangements in the courts and corrections agencies. At times, actions against criminal deviants are harsh and punitive, while at other times, rehabilitation of criminals is the prime concern. But in most circumstances, cultural contradictions reflect conflicts in actual structural arrangements that are both rehabilitative *and* punitive.

Conflicting beliefs influence more than the substance of the crime problem; it is this situation of cultural conflict which makes defining the crime problem so difficult: For some the problem is permissive laws and soft punishment; for others, the problem is restrictive laws and too much punishment. In turn, such dissensus over what the problem is aggravates the dilemmas facing enforcement and corrections administrators who, in not being sure of the problem, have difficulty in implementing a coherent and consistent solution. Thus, these cultural forces both reflect, and create, contradictory societal reaction to crime in America.

Conflicting beliefs about "what should be done"

THE STRUCTURE OF THE SOCIETAL REACTION

The societal reaction to crime occurs within four sets of structural arrangements: (1) the law and its enactment by political bodies; (2) the enforcement of the law by police agencies; (3) the adjudication of criminal deviants in the courts; and (4) the incarceration of convicted criminals in jails and prisons. Our goal is to understand the problems of structure inhering in these four phases of the societal reaction to crime.

THE CRIMINAL LAW: THE PROBLEM OF CRIMINALIZATION

What is and what is not crime is ultimately a matter of legal definition. It is, therefore, impossible to separate crime from the legal statutes defining behavior as criminal. At first glance we may think that this conclusion is banal, but in reality, the nature of criminal laws profoundly affect the amount of crime in American society and the way in which it is dealt with by the police and courts.

Crimes Without Victims. Criminal law is supposed to prohibit harms against private property, other persons, and the state. However, in the American legal system a large body of criminal laws has accumulated prohibiting acts that do not directly harm other people, the state, or property. For example, many laws prohibit certain kinds of sexual acts, ranging from "abnormal" sexual intercourse to public solicitation by prostitutes and homosexuals. Another large body of criminal law deals with the use of narcotics and with gambling. These crimes do not have victims in the conventional sense, and their existence is the result of pressure by various segments of the population.[5] As we noted, the existence of these laws reflect the power of moral code beliefs to influence legislators.

In a free society, with its enormous diversity in tastes and lifestyles, there is always a conflict among the values of different segments of the society. Even in the face of legal codes reflecting the "morality" of only some, people still gamble, use drugs, and enjoy all forms of sex. Most persons run little risk of police sanctions because many no-victim laws—especially with respect to sexual acts—are not enforced. As Thurman Arnold caustically observed, they "are unenforced because we want to continue our conduct, and unrepealed because we want to preserve our morals" (Kadish, 1967:161–162). However, many others of these laws *are enforced*, even though no harm to property, other persons, or the state has occurred. The persistence of such laws has presented a number of problems.[6]

    1. Laws denoting crimes without victims, such as those con-

No-victim criminal laws

Are these people criminals? Many states say yes. The existence of "no-victim" criminal laws requires the police—rather than the legislature—to define what will be considered "criminal."

cerning certain forms of sex, drug use, public drunkenness, gambling, and vagrancy are so encompassing and broad that they make potential criminals of everyone. In effect, they hold criminal sanctions over people's heads for behaviors that do no harm except to the precepts of some segments of the population, often the majority. In doing so, such laws potentially limit people's right to self-determination and self-expression, while violating deeply held values of freedom and individualism.

2. Since many people in modern societies appear to enjoy getting drunk, using drugs, having sex, seeking out prostitutes, and gambling, these laws go against widespread behavior patterns. It is always problematic to have vast bodies of laws on the books that people insist on violating. It is possible that, as people violate the law, they lose respect for not only its codes and statutes, but also for those who enforce it.

3. Prohibitions against prostitution, drugs, and gambling have created a vast illegal marketplace for organized crime. Since people demand these services, they tend to be provided by illegal syndicates that derive enormous untaxed profits. In turn, these profits are used to subsidize harmful crimes, such as loan sharking, extortion, and bribery. Additionally, these profits are used to invest and infiltrate legitimate businesses and enterprises—thus making the distinction between law and lawlessness difficult to maintain. From one perspective, no-victim crimes *creates* organized crime. As we will analyze in detail in Chapter 15, it is no coincidence that organized crime in America emerged during Prohibition, when such a large market for liquor existed that criminals needed to become organized in order to deliver the goods demanded by the public and to avoid prosecution by the police. A similar situation currently exists with respect to drugs and gambling; as long as legal prohibitions against these widespread acts remain, organized crime will persist.

4. Perhaps one of the most serious problems created by no-victim laws is the use of manpower and other resources involved in enforcing and adjudicating them. In any large urban area, public drunkenness and disorderly conduct constitute close to one-half of all arrests and thereby clog up the courts (President's Commission, 1967:20). Detective man-hours spent on drug use come close to one-third of the total in large urban areas; court costs for just marijuana offenses run into the millions of dollars each year (Skolnick and Currie, 1970). This diversion of police man-hours and resources, as well as court time, deters the police from catching, and the courts from adjudicating, criminals who commit crimes with victims. It has been estimated that well over 50 percent of total police work and court time is spent on catching and prosecuting people who have not hurt anyone else, taken property, or damaged the state.

5. The persistence of a large body of laws pertaining to crimes without victims creates a situation in which not all of the laws can be enforced; there are simply too many of them and they already consume most police resources. When not all laws can be enforced, *police discretion* in law enforcement is inevitable. The existence of unenforceable laws can, at times, grant the police license to *selectively* enforce the law—a situation that goes against all basic American tenets concerning due process of law. The greatest danger of granting discretion to the police in one area, such as crimes without victims, is that discretion and selective enforcement will be extended into other areas of criminal law. Furthermore, to encourage discretion in police enforcement sets a precedent in that it gives the police the power to remain autonomous from, and at times even in violation of, their legislative mandate. When the police increase their autonomy from the law and

those bodies that enact the law, a society can become subject to the will of agencies and their administrators rather than the rule of law. Finally, unenforced laws can, on occasion, allow the police to use such laws to prosecute persons on grounds unrelated to the evil against which the laws were purportedly addressed. For example, vagrancy laws have traditionally been used to arrest "suspects" from lower economic groups who cannot be arrested or detained on other criminal charges. Thus, no-victim laws not only give the police the power to selectively enforce the law, but they also enable the police to change the intent of law and use it for purposes other than those dictated by the law.

While the police often seek to avoid arbitrariness in their actions, the dangers of their work and the structure of their organizations create pressures for practices that violate the constitutional tenets of American law. It is these pressures, especially as they are compounded by the public's concern over "rising crime," which present the police with a number of dilemmas.

THE POLICE: DILEMMAS OF LAW ENFORCEMENT[7]

In principle, laws define crimes. The police are to enforce *all* laws and thereby deter crime. During enforcement, the police are supposedly guided by the rule of law (procedural law) which, in accordance with the values of freedom and equality, guarantees the civil liberties of suspects and makes the police accountable for their actions. Ideally, just as substantive codes and statutes define criminal behavior for the public, procedural laws define what is criminal for the police. While this principle is simply stated in the abstract, it can at times be violated in practice. The potential dangers of this situation in a free society—police abuse of citizens' rights, police discrimination, police brutality with impunity, police as makers of law through selective enforcement, and police as a political force with sufficient power to overrule the law—need not be dwelled upon.

Dangers of police discretion

The discrepancy between the operation of police in theory and in practice is perhaps inevitable in light of current conditions. First, the broad scope of the criminal law makes the enforcement of *all* the laws impossible, but does not reveal to the police *which ones* to enforce (Lafave, 1964). Lacking a clear mandate from legislatures, the police must use their own discretion in deciding what is and what is not, the law. Second, even though Americans value law and order, resources made available to the police are typically inadequate. Without resources, and burdened with a vast body of no-victim and unenforceable laws, the police must inevitably begin to establish their own policies and priorities of law enforcement; as they do so, they can begin to divorce themselves from their legislative mandate, public scrutiny, and the constraints of procedural law.

While these two conditions help account for police deviations from procedural law, several additional forces also contribute to this situation: (1) police and community relations, (2) the internal structure of the police; (3) police ideology; (4) police professionalism, and (5) police political power.

Reasons for police deviations from procedural law

Police and Community Relations. According to most opinion polls, the American public holds the police in low esteem (Savitz, 1967). Yet, great expectations and demands are placed upon the police within any community. One of these expectations forces the police to engage in a wide range of peacekeeping activities, some of which have little to do with law enforcement. For example, one study found that nearly one-half the requests for assistance received in a police station were for help in health care (such as providing an ambulance service), in handling problems with children and incapacitated persons (a welfare service), and in supervising recreational activities. While such tasks obviously need to be performed, they can divert police attention away from the enforcement of serious crimes and make the policeman, as the authors of this study proclaimed, "philosopher, guide, and friend" (Cumming et al., 1965). One danger in forcing the police to become involved in peacekeeping instead of law enforcement is that their duties are extended beyond the bounds of substantive and procedural criminal law (Wilson, 1968:16–56). As policemen assume the ambiguous role of peacekeepers, they are granted enormous discretion in defining what is necessary to preserve the peace (not to uphold the law). Some suspects, usually from the lower classes, can be arrested to preserve the peace; others, usually middle class, can be let free; and still others can be illegally detained (Esselystn, 1953; Bittner, 1967). Thus, besides diverting resources away from law enforcement, the peacekeeping role can easily be used to justify discriminatory and selective law enforcement—which violates the basic tenets of the rule of law.[8]

Problems in "keeping the peace"

The police in any community are also subject to pressures from the public and local political leaders, who demand that the "streets be kept clear of crime." In any community, the police are highly responsive to this form of pressure, with the result that they can at times violate procedural law and arrest, under various "cover charges," deviant and outcast groups such as homosexuals, prostitutes, drug users, and skid-row drunks, in order to show their efficiency and capacity to keep the streets clear—even though to do so diverts resources away from action on crimes involving injury to persons and loss of property. This need for the police within any community to

**SOCIOLOGICAL
INSIGHTS**

YOUTH AND THE POLICE

A number of studies have sought to determine what characteristics of suspects and circumstances of situations affect the way police will act in the field. The following is a partial catalogue of relevant findings for police and youth encounters (Schrag and Kuehn, 1976):

1. Deference to police by juveniles is just as likely to lead to arrest as an antagonistic attitude, with a civil attitude least likely to result in arrest.
2. Race and ethnicity influenced arrest of juveniles with, for example, black arrests rates nearly twice as high as for whites.
3. Children from broken homes are more likely to be arrested than children from intact homes committing the same offense.
4. The more severe a community defines a crime—and this varies enormously from community to community—the greater the chance of arrest for a juvenile.
5. Females are less likely to be arrested for some crimes than males.
6. Court referrals of juveniles vary by community, with upper, lower, and middle communities having much different referral patterns.

constantly demonstrate efficiency is one of the most persistent conditions promoting procedural shortcuts in the name of maintaining an arrest record that will satisfy the public and various pressure groups in a community.

Internal Structure of the Police. Partly in response to pressures to demonstrate efficiency and partly as a result of the volume of activity, the bureaucratization of police forces is inevitable. Police bureaucracies are basically command hierarchies arranged into major units such as traffic patrols, street patrols, investigative units, undercover units, and quasimilitary units for riot control (Quinney, 1970:101–136). Extensive bureaucratization of the police has at least two consequences for the rule of law. First, bureaucracies tend to develop their own internal rules and procedures in order to generate greater efficiency. However, since these rules are established to increase efficiency, they can sometimes cause violations of the princi-

Problems of police bureaucratization

ples of due process of law. In fact, as Skolnick (1969) has noted, the efficient administration of criminal law *will always* be hampered by the adoption of procedures designed to protect individual liberties. The second consequence is that bureaucratization also allows the police to "hide" their illegal acts. Bureaucracies are always difficult for outsiders, such as civilian review boards, to penetrate or investigate. In addition to the many formal rules of any bureaucracy, a large number of informal rules among law enforcement officials have emerged, emphasizing police secrecy and keeping matters "within the department." This bureaucratic autonomy from public scrutiny can allow the police to remain aloof, if they choose, from both the substance and procedure of criminal law.

Police Ideology. It has been known for some time that, in any large police department, there exists an ideology which, stated in somewhat extreme form, commands the police to (1) maintain secrecy about practices from the hostile public; (2) get respect from the public, even if it must be coerced; (3) by any means, legitimate or illegitimate, complete an important arrest (Westley, 1953; Quinney, 1969). Putting the tenets of police ideology this bluntly is certainly an overstatement; and yet, behind much police activity—especially

In a society where guns are readily available to all, the police have reason to fear the public. Here, a truck stop in Tennessee sells guns along with cigarettes, lighters, aspirin, and other "necessities."

for the poor—these beliefs are prominent. Some might view this ideology as an outgrowth of the authoritarian personality of each policeman. However, several studies reveal that "raw recruits" to the police force are about the same in terms of beliefs and attitudes as their counterparts in the general population (McNamara, 1967; Niederhoffer, 1968). Furthermore, in their training at the police academy, a civil libertarian viewpoint stressing procedural law and the right of the accused is a prominent part of the curriculum. These facts indicate that there is something about the bureaucratic structure of the police force and the nature of police work that soon sours young recruits into veterans who can, at times, harbor a somewhat antidemocratic ideology.

Three facets of police work appear to be responsible for the existence of such an ideology. First, the dangers of police work make the police suspicious of the public, especially in lower-class neighborhoods. Such suspicion isolates policemen from those they serve, while driving them together as a body of close-knit comrades engaged in mutual protection. Second, policemen will at times have to assert their authority to perform law enforcement duties against a hostile public that holds them in low esteem (Savitz, 1967). Maintaining this authority frequently becomes the policeman's on-the-

Police ideology

Police have often had to force compliance from the public.

beat credo, for, as recruits are told again and again by department veterans, "you gotta be tough." The combination of suspicion of the public and the desire to be tough can become volatile when applied to many segments of the population, such as low-income racial and ethnic minorities. Police are already suspicious of these residents; and when they attempt to assert their authority they are resisted, often violently, by minority group members who see such a "get tough" practice as one more abuse not to be endured. The third facet of police work sustaining the police ideology is the internal bureaucratic structure of the force. The bureaucracy must continually demonstrate its efficiency in the eyes of the public and politicians. One indicator of efficiency is the number of criminal cases "cleared" by an arrest. Since the department as a whole, and individual patrolmen, are gauged by their arrest efficiency, policemen are often anxious to make arrests, even if it may mean violating some aspect of procedural law. Another police practice stemming from the need to have high arrest statistics is the "arrest quota" system, whereby police units are required to show a certain number of arrests. One way to fill quotas is to arrest suspects without much evidence, or to clear the streets by arresting vagrants, drunks, and prostitutes. Police vehemently deny the existence of such quotas, but there is too much evidence suggesting their use in some police departments to accept these denials without skepticism. Such concern for arrest is perhaps inevitable in light of the bureaucratic imperative to demonstrate efficiency. It is difficult to document statistically the "efficiency" of the police in preserving civil liberties, and thus by default, the yardstick of efficiency becomes the arrest record.[9]

Police Professionalism. The drive toward police professionalism represents an attempt to overcome the widespread corruption and inefficiency that existed at one time in many police departments in America. Civil service examinations became a basis for promotion; education of the police in academies became required; and the use of new technologies, from computerized auditing to newer and better police cars, became emphasized (Skolnick, 1966:238–240). While these changes have certainly cut down on the amount of corruption among the police, they have caused police professionalism to be based on technological efficiency more than the preservation of procedural law and basic civil liberties. In some police departments professionalism has become defined as using technical gadgetry—telephone wiretaps, police helicopters, computerized files, unlawful buggings, and so on—in fighting crime (Quinney, 1970; Skolnick, 1966). Politicians at all levels of government have supported the direction of such police professionalism by allocating, with little hesi-

Police professionalism has increasingly become defined in terms of acquiring new technologies rather than in developing and creating new capacities for upholding procedural law.

tation, funds to buy technical equipment to be used for riot control and surveillance of citizen activities.

While new technologies can make the police more efficient and competent in fighting crime, a potential danger resides in this definition of police professionalism: Police use of technological devices in the name of law and order can create a climate in which technology, rather than procedural law, dictates the way law enforcement will occur. To maintain core values of freedom and individualism, the use of newer, more technical equipment will have to be supplemented by a new professionalism based on the ideals of a democratic order (Skolnick, 1966:238–239).[10] Yet, under grants from the Law Enforcement Assistance Administration, most federal funds made available to police departments are for technical equipment rather than for research on how to train the police to adhere strictly to the rule of law, even in the face of the many dangers associated with their work.

Dangers of police technocracy

Police Political Power. The police are, to a very great extent, caught in the middle of public demands for law and order, political pressures, the perception of rising crime, and the Supreme Court decisions stressing civil liberties. Under these kinds of cross-pressures, the police have at times retreated behind the walls of their bureaucratic technocracy and are likely to perceive of themselves, in the words of Robert Kliesmet of the Milwaukee Professional Policeman's Protective Association, as "the new niggers of the world." Undeniably the police are subject to a wide variety of pressures; but it is often the police themselves who have exerted pressures on politicians and created the sense of crisis over rising crime. Even though the police can be a defensive organization, they are not passive and have become a powerful political lobby. While such lobbying activities are perhaps necessary for any organization charged with performing a difficult task on limited resources, the current direction of police pressure appears to be lobbying for even more discretionary power. Such lobbying is against the tenets of procedural law which emphasize the "rights of the accused" over and against the needs of the state for order.

THE COURTS: THE DILEMMA OF ADMINISTERING JUSTICE

The Ideal of Justice. The American court system operates under three basic ideals:

1. *Equality Under the Law.* In accordance with such values as freedom and equality, citizens are to be subjected to an impartial application of substantive and procedural law by unbiased judges.
2. *The Presumption of Innocence.* In American courts, suspects are presumed innocent until proven guilty. On the basis of this assumption, suspects are entitled to a speedy arraignment where charges are to be read, a reasonable bail set, and where protection from police harassment and punishment is to be assured.
3. *The Right to a Jury Trial.* It is basic to the concept of American justice that the accused have a right to a trial overseen by their peers. Embodied in this concept is the adversary principle, whereby the accused have a right to counsel, who must be allowed to confront the state and cross-examine those who support the state's accusations. From this confrontation between the defendants and their accusers, the truth is presumed to emerge.

The Reality of "Justice." Few will maintain that American courts do a good job in maintaining the ideals of justice. For indeed, as will be documented, the courts often violate these ideals: Judges are, at times, biased; laws are unequally applied; procedural rules can give way to bureaucratic expediency; suspects are sometimes presumed guilty; arraignment can become slow; bail can be excessive; and few ever have a trial by their peers, much less a full day in court.

Public opinion and the ideals of justice

Just about everybody recognizes that courts need to be overhauled. However, in accordance with punishment-oriented beliefs, most Americans would seemingly reform the courts in a direction that would move them away from the ideals of justice. For example, when asked in a Gallup poll "What ails American justice?" 78 percent of the sample asserted that "convicted criminals get off too easily" (*Newsweek*, 1971). While 68 percent recognized that "it takes too long before accused people are brought to trial," the public appears more concerned with *convicting criminals quickly* than with maintaining the ideal of justice. To the extent that the ideals of American justice are worth maintaining, the problem with the courts is not their conviction rate—which is really quite high—but in *how* they convict suspects. When the problem is phrased in this way, the question of how and where in the criminal court process the ideals of American justice can be suspended becomes prominent.

Arrest and Detention. Within a "short time" after being arrested a suspect *must* be brought before a lower court, such as that presided over by a magistrate or justice of the peace, for a preliminary examination. If the offense is minor, the magistrate often has the power to determine the guilt or innocence of the suspect. However, if the case involves a felony, the function of the magistrate is quite different: to determine if sufficient evidence exists to hold the suspect over for trial, and if there is, to set the bail.

The preliminary examination

Even at this early stage, violations of the ideals of American justice occur. First of all, suspects are frequently detained for much longer than a "short time." One study in Chicago revealed that 50 percent of a sample of prisoners brought before a felony court were held without being booked (formerly charged with a crime) for 17 hours. By the time the magistrate's hearing rolled around, some suspects had been detained in jail for more than several days without bail—a practice that amounts to illegal detention and goes against the ideal of "innocent until proven guilty" (Savitz, 1967:81).

The whole process of setting bail in the magistrate's court can be highly unjust (Goldfarb, 1965; Quinney, 1970; Skolnick, 1966). The Eighth Amendment of the Constitution provides that bail shall not be "excessive;" but what constitutes a "reasonable" bail is left to the discretion of poorly trained magistrates who sometimes set bail in accordance with their own personal, political, and moral biases. Furthermore, the practice of bail discriminates against the poor, who do not have either the collateral to put up their own bail or the money to pay the fee of a bail bondsman. If persons cannot meet the bail set by the magistrate, they must remain in jail until their trial. Bail thus discriminates against the poor and forces them to remain in jail with

Setting bail

The bail bonds "business" is a highly questionable feature of the American judicial system.

others who have been convicted of crimes. It becomes difficult to "presume people innocent" when they must go to jail with those who have been proven guilty. In most cases, rather than endure months in crowded jails awaiting trial, suspects plead guilty to a lesser charge and thereby get their case immediately adjudicated by a judge without benefit of a trial. Thus, bail can be used as a means of detaining suspects in violation of the Eighth Amendment and as a way to coerce defendants to plead guilty. The use of bail against the poor in this way violates almost all the basic tenets of American ideals of justice: equality before the law, the presumption of innocence, and a trial by one's peers. Another injustice occurring in a magistrate's court stems from the fact that magistrates sometimes do not have any formal legal training. They are usually elected and have fixed political ties and social attitudes. As a result, the lower courts in many cities are less than partial, with little decorum and attention to procedural law. Under such conditions, the pretext of impartial justice is difficult to maintain.

Arraignment and Plea. At a pretrial arraignment, the defendant and prosecutor face each other in a court of record. The formal charges are read by the prosecutor, and the defendant is asked to enter a plea of guilty or not guilty. However, it is behind the scenes, outside the courtroom that the real drama of arraignment and plea usually takes place. The pretrial appearance in court is typically just a formality that finalizes a bargain between prosecutor and defendant concerning

Plea negotiations

what the charges and plea will be. By all estimates, from 80 to 90 percent of criminal cases are resolved before arraignment, with the prosecutor negotiating with the defendant's lawyer in an effort to secure a guilty plea in exchange for a reduced charge and/or sentence.

There are three parties in plea negotiations: the prosecutor, the defendant's lawyer, and the judge.[11] The most important of these parties is the district attorney, who is empowered by law to negotiate a plea, drop a case, or push for a maximum sentence. The district attorney, therefore, has considerable discretion in dealing with a case. Prosecutors operate under two heavy constraints that limit their powers, however. They are, first of all, *elected* officials who are sometimes using the prosecutor's office as a stepping-stone to higher political office. Prosecutors are thereby under public, political, and media pressure to appear efficient and effective. They must "win the big ones" to appear effective and dispose of the multitude of minor cases to appear efficient. These factors indicate that the charges in the indictment brought against the accused and the willingness of the district attorney to negotiate pleas are often a reflection of political

Many who are presumed "innocent until proven guilty" must await trial in jail since they do not have the assets or money to secure bail. This fact helps the district attorney in negotiations for a guilty plea.

considerations—a fact that would seem to run against the tenet of equal and impartial justice.

A second constraint on prosecutors comes from the large administrative bureaucracy in which they work. Bureaucracies need to appear efficient; but the court bureaucracy is faced with an overwhelming overload of cases that would impede efficiency if each case were adjudicated by an actual trial. Under these conditions, the only way to maintain the appearance of efficiency is to process rapidly, without trial, as many cases as possible. For this reason the prosecutor must seek to negotiate a plea of guilty in exchange for a lesser charge and sentence—thereby keeping the case from going to trial and jamming the already crowded courts.

To negotiate pleas successfully, prosecutors use a number of strategies, most of which violate the ideal tenets of American justice. In serious felonies, prosecutors usually "recommend" bail pending trial; by recommending high bail, and hence forcing incarceration of the defendant until trial, prosecutors can put pressure on the defendants to plead guilty to a lesser charge. Prosecutors also have influence in selecting the judge; by threatening to select one who is "tough" on the alleged crime of the defendant, they can coerce negotiation. Prosecutors also decide how the indictment, or list of specific charges, at the pretrial hearing will read. Frequently, they use the practice of "multiple indictments," or several different charges for one criminal act, to their advantage in forcing a plea of guilty. For example, a typical indictment for possession of an eighth of an ounce of heroin could read as follows (Blumberg, 1970:56–57): Count 1. felonious possession of a narcotic; Count 2. felonious possession with intent to sell; and Count 3. unlawfully possessing a narcotic. A charge for armed robbery might read: Count 1. robbery, first degree; Count 2. assault, second degree; Count 3. assault, third degree; Count 4. grand larceny, first degree; Count 5. carrying a dangerous weapon; and Count 6. petty larceny. By threatening to "throw the book" at defendants through multiple indictments, prosecutors pressure the accused to seek a compromise—usually to only one of the charges, preferably the least damaging. Finally, prosecutors can threaten to delay bringing the case to court; when coupled with high bail that forces the accused to remain in jail, they can coerce defendants to plead guilty. As is clear, all of these practices are not in response to the imperatives of justice but are a reflection of the political and bureaucratic pressures on prosecutors. The result is that equality before the law, the presumption of innocence, and right to trial can be suspended in the name of expediency.

Supposedly, in terms of the ideology of justice, defense lawyers are to have an adversary relationship with prosecutors. However, in

Negotiated pleas versus the ideal of justice

practice, the defense lawyer readily enters into negotiations with the prosecutor. If the defense attorneys bargained only for their clients, it might be possible to maintain some resemblance of the adversary principle of justice. But as A. S. Blumberg (1970:95–115) describes, defense lawyers are often "double agents" who represent not just their clients, but also themselves and, surprisingly, the need of the court system to adjudicate without trial. The ties of defense lawyers with prosecutors and with the court bureaucracy are often much stronger and binding than are those with clients. A defense lawyer who has been an assistant district attorney at one time may thereby personally know the district attorney; but even when this is not the case, defense lawyers and district attorneys establish personal relationships that must endure beyond the transitory needs of one client or case. Perhaps most importantly, prosecutors must rely on defense lawyers to negotiate in order to keep cases from going to trial, while conversely, most defense lawyers must rely on the court to secure their fee. Collecting fees in criminal cases is always problematic, with the result that lawyers collect in advance for each stage of a trial. The amount of the fee determines the vigor with which they defend their clients.

Much of this vigor is evidenced outside the courtroom, where the defense lawyer pushes extra hard for a negotiated plea and reduced sentence. The defense lawyer is likely to draw upon the obligations for past favors owed by the prosecutor to secure a favorable charge and sentence. Since these negotiations are hidden, the defense lawyer must justify high fees with some form of performance within the courtroom. In this performance, defense lawyers are sometimes aided by the judge and the district attorney, who tolerate excesses and rhetoric. The defense lawyer acquires a vested interest, much like the prosecutor, in a system of negotiated rather than adversary justice; to have a real adversary trial would cost the defense lawyer enormously in time, energy, and fees. Thus, much like the overcrowded courts, the busy defense lawyer comes to rely on "bargain-counter justice" outside the courtroom. To the extent that lawyers rely on this system, loyalties to clients must be balanced with those to the organization and persons with whom they must maintain an adversary relationship.

This system works well for the affluent, who can afford good lawyers who will bargain effectively. But for the poor, who must rely on a court-appointed lawyer, or the public defender, "plea copping" works more to the benefit of the prosecutor and court than to the defendant. Court-appointed lawyers are often the failures of the legal profession. They have little skill or "pull" with the prosecutor, and they are most interested in quickly securing their small fee. The re-

Biases against the poor

sult is a negotiated or "copped" plea that does little for the accused, but much for the court in terms of saving time and money.

More competent is the public defender, who is supported by the county or charitable organizations. But much like the courts, the public defender is burdened by an excess of cases, making it necessary to negotiate pleas with the prosecutor in order to keep up with an awesome caseload. Hence, when public defenders cannot defend clients except through negotiation, they lose the very weapon that could make them effective in those negotiations: the threat of taking the case to trial and tying up court time and personnel. Therefore, the public defender has less leverage against the district attorney than lawyers for the affluent, resulting in a situation in which the poor are more likely to be found "guilty." Because the poor defendants are denied a real trial and presumed guilty (for they must eventually plead guilty in a negotiated system), it is clear that they do not have equality before the law.

The final parties to negotiated pleas are the judges. It is in their courtroom that the pretrial hearing and arraignment occurs. And it is the judge who will ask defendants how they will plead. If defendants plead "not guilty," judges will add the case to an already heavy load and set a trial date. But if the accused pleads guilty, the case can be disposed of quickly. Judges clearly have a vested interest in adjudicating a case without trial for, like the prosecutor, they are part of a bureaucratic system demanding the efficient processing of an enormous caseload. The popular image of the aloof, brooding, reflective, and dispassionate judge is not entirely accurate at the lower-court level, where most criminal cases are tried. In reality a working judge "must be politician, administrator, bureaucrat, and lawyer in order to cope with a crushing calendar of cases" (Blumberg, 1970:122–23). As such, the judge actively, although discretely, is forced to enter into plea negotiations by agreeing to abide by the decisions of the prosecutor concerning the charge and sentence. In fact, under some circumstances, actual meetings may be held behind closed doors in the judge's chambers as the final deal is hammered out. Judges must participate in the negotiated plea, for they must not accumulate too great a backlog of cases. Once the agreement has been struck between the prosecutor and defense lawyer, the judge allows the defendant to plead guilty at the pretrial hearing (Blumberg, 1970:65).

The majority of the cases brought before a judge are resolved in this manner (Newman, 1966:304). This pattern reveals that the judges will have difficulty in remaining impartial, for they inevitably have a vested interest in plea negotiations. The fact that judges enter into the negotiations makes it hard to visualize them as the neutral arbitrator of justice. And the fact that they are likely to encourage plea negotiations reveals a presumption of guilt and an unwillingness to grant every person a trial by their peers. It is likely, of course, that many clearly guilty persons are able to use the court system to avoid the full impact of the law. But it is difficult to separate those guilty who fair well in the system from those innocent who must plead guilty. It is in this sense that the actual operation of the courts can, in many instances, suspend the ideal of justice.

In addition to violating the precepts of justice, the dangers of the current pretrial arraignment and plea process are perhaps obvious: The problem of processing volumes of cases now influences disproportionately how justice in America is administered. Additionally, the whole process of adjudication occurs at times in secrecy, outside the court; thus it does not have to be guided by procedural rules and law. Coupled with the fact that the police are able to hide their enforcement practices (as discussed previously), similar practices of adjudication in the courts reveal a somewhat closed and hidden legal process in America.

Dangers of negotiated justice

Sentencing. After a trial in which the defendant is found guilty, or after a pretrial plea of guilty, the judge is to pronounce sentence.[12] Judges must do so within the limits of the law; but even so, they have wide discretionary powers in imposing the sentence. Many legal innovations, such as the indeterminate sentence and probation, have greatly increased judges' discretion in sentencing, as has the general movement toward individualizing the treatment of criminals (Quinney, 1970:166). Discretion allows for bias on the part of judges. Contrary to their images as impartial figures coldly and rationally

SOCIOLOGICAL INSIGHTS

ALTERNATIVES AVAILABLE TO JUDGES MAKE SENTENCING CHAOTIC

James A. Kidney

Washington (UPI)—In the same courthouse, two men convicted of identical crimes stand before separate judges for sentencing. Both defendants are young, lower-income family men without previous criminal records.

Both black-robed judges are middle-aged men who left prosperous law practices for the bench, thanks to good political connections and impeccable backgrounds.

As judges, both believe they are fair-minded.

Under state law, the crimes for which the two defendants were convicted carry any sentence up to 20 years in prison. There is no other standard.

The first defendent is sentenced to 12 years in prison.

The second is admonished by his judge and gets three years, suspended.

This scene is commonplace in courtrooms across the land, and it troubles the consciences of many jurists and lawyers. Thousands of men and women languish in prison frustrated and angry, knowing that others who committed the same crimes were inexplicably set free.

During trial, defendants enjoy what the Supreme Court calls a "panoply of rights," but once a conviction is handed up, the sentencing process is chaotic.

With almost no standards for a judge's guidance, the severity of a jail term frequently depends on the mood, prejudices, and political pressures of the time. The judge's alternatives are many (including probation, a minimum sentence, or a special rehabilitation program), and are often arbitrary.

Sentencing laws also differ drastically from state to state. A crime might carry a maximum four-year prison term in one state, and a 10-year sentence in a neighboring state.

"The almost wholly unchecked and sweeping powers we give to judges in the fashioning of sentences are terrifying and intolerable for a society that professes devotion to the rule of law," says U.S. District Court Judge Marvin E. Frankel.

The staff of the American Bar Association's commission on correctional facilities and services, which has studied the problem, says reform is not enough that the system must be entirely rebuilt.

A recent federal study of judges in the Second Circuit Court of Appeals in New York acknowledged that sentencing varied widely among jurists, but could offer no immediate solutions.

Reformers find themselves in a quandary because no authority has ever decided what sentencing is supposed to accomplish. Should the sentence reflect the desire to punish? Is rehabilitation the goal? Or, are harsh jail terms meant as deterrents to crime?

Another problem is indeterminate sentencing—best

known in California—where open-ended terms are handed down on the theory that a felon should be released only when he is reformed. A universally used variation involves the legislature setting only a maximum term, with judges allowed the discretion to apply any lesser sentence.

Indeterminate sentences sounded like fair play and drew wide praise at first, but now they are sharply criticized because of the questionable underlying assumption that prisons rehabilitate.

"Jails ruin young men," says Dr. Karl Menninger, Kansas psychiatrist and penologist. "Can't the public grasp this indisputable fact?"

"How can a decent prison attempting a rehabilitation program do anything for a boy who comes to it from a jail where he has been raped, battered, vomited and urinated upon, mauled and corrupted by some of the old-timers in the bullpen?"

Among prisoners sentenced with no fixed release date, hopelessness is fed with despair. Overworked parole boards tend to give cursory attention to each applicant. If a parole request is denied, the inmate often doesn't know why—or what standards he must meet to win his freedom.

Anthony Partridge, of the staff of the Federal Judicial Center, says it is impossible to write a sentencing standard that guarantees reform.

"We may not agree on whether a crime deserves three years or 20 years, but we surely can agree that the sentence should not depend on which judge a person gets," he said.

There are many reform proposals. All have demonstrable flaws and few have been put into use. They include:

- Setting a single sentence for each crime, so judges will have no discretion. Critics say this would leave no room to consider mitigating circumstances.
- Establish sentencing councils in which judges confer with their colleagues in the hope of narrowing the extremes of harshness or leniency. The Second Circuit study also found that councils did not work as well as expected, and they increased court workloads.
- Require more thorough presentencing reports to give judges greater background information before sentencing. The ABA staff, however, said concise reports

would get more attention because most judges base their sentencing on only a few factors.

- Allowing appellate review of criminal sentences in ordinary cases, just as courts allow review of civil damages on appeal. Opponents fear overburdening the courts, but reformers say the loss of individual freedom is no less important than loss of money.
- Establishing computerized data banks for every legal jurisdiction so one judge can see quickly how other judges have treated defendants in similar circumstances.

Partridge said one difficulty with computer banks is deciding how far to go in classifying defendants, such as an auto thief who is an 8th grade dropout with a record of drug addiction. Overclassification would make the system unwieldy.

Whatever the cure, the experts agree the problem goes to the heart of the criminal justice system.

An ABA staff study concluded that because legislatures have failed to decide society's purpose in sentencing, the judges' arbitrary discretion reigns and "equity and justice remain unapplied concepts."

Riverside *Press-Enterprise*, December 8, 1974. Reprinted by permission of United Press International.

applying the law, judges are human and have many of the same biases as anyone else. Nowhere is this more evident than in their sentencing practices.

While personal bias ultimately determines within the broad limits of the law the defendant's sentence, judges can usually legitimize pronouncements in cases that have gone through a trial, or that were set in a pretrial agreement, by invoking the presentence report compiled by the probation department. Frequently, the probation report is the sole basis upon which judges make sentencing decisions. A presentence probation report is compiled by a social worker, who collects data on the defendant from social agencies, relatives, friends, schools, police, employers, psychiatric testimony, and any other available source. Often, they are based on uncorroborated, hearsay data that would not be admissible during the trial. And yet, it is just this evidence that a judge can use to justify a decision made on the

Presentence probation reports

basis of personal biases. If judges use the presentence report as the sole basis of their decisions, they are granting enormous power to an overworked probation officer who has only the slightest familiarity with the defendant and the case. Thus hearsay evidence is used in a court of law to determine the fate of a criminal. What makes this practice questionable is that defendants do not have the right to cross-examine or confront their accuser—the probation officer or the judge.

The U.S. Supreme Court has upheld the use of these presentence reports on the assumption that the probation department functions autonomously from the court and can thereby mediate between the court and defendant (Blumberg, 1970:146). But in reality, the probation department is an adjunct to the court. The budget and the recruitment and supervision of personnel, policies, and administrative directives all flow from the court. As a part of the court bureaucracy, the probation department becomes involved in the processing of large numbers of cases. The ideology, and the desires of most officers, of the probation department stresses concern for the problems and needs of the defendant; but their burdensome administrative mandate forces the quick and efficient categorization of defendants into what can be inaccurate and sterotyped psychiatric categories. To incarcerate a defendant on the basis of such categories, or to use them to justify the biases of the judge, violates basic tenets in the American ideal of justice.

CORRECTIONS: PRISONS, PAROLE, AND PROBATION

No where is the conflict over what should be done with criminals more evident than in society's reaction to convicted criminals. Correctional reactions are, at one and the same time, punishment-centered and rehabilitatively oriented. Americans want criminals punished in order to "teach them a lesson" and to serve as a "deterrent to others." This belief has been translated into the American prison with its harsh authoritarian structure and punitive procedures. On the other hand, Americans want criminals reformed and rehabilitated when they enter or reenter society. This belief has become translated into the increasing use of probation for convicted criminals and parole for prisoners in correctional institutions. Those who favor a punishment-centered reaction regard these measures as "coddling the criminal element," while those holding rehabilitative orientations point out that incarceration in prisons does not deter criminals nor reform prisoners. It is these conflicts in beliefs, as they are implemented in structural arrangements, that make corrections in America an enduring social problem.

Conflicts over beliefs about punishment and rehabilitation

Prisons in America. There are close to one-half million people in America's prisons and jails. It costs almost one billion dollars to run all of these "correctional" facilities. Jails tend to be under county jurisdiction; each state has its own system of prisons; and the federal government has a separate system of federal prisons. It is difficult to typify these institutions because there is wide variability in such critical features as: the physical facilities, the staff to prisoner ratio, the training of the staff, the emphasis or rehabilitation versus punishment, and the nature of the criminals. But prisons usually share a number of features (jails are too diverse to typify):

Common features of prisons

1. Prisoners are confined to cells, with virtually every aspect of their personal life and daily routine subject to control by the prison staff.

2. Prisons typically make at least some efforts to "treat" and "rehabilitate" the criminal. Job training, counseling, and educational programs are the most typical.

3. There is always a conflict between the treatment-oriented and custodial staff, with the repressive actions of guards often working at cross purposes with the professional staff.

4. Prisons are authoritarian hierarchies in which those high in the hierarchy are making decisions without the adequate or accurate information from those low in the hierarchy, guards and other staff. Moreover, directives from the top are selectively implemented by staff. Prisons are thus an ambiguous mixture of formal goals, rules, and directives that are often made in ignorance and which are only selectively enforced.

5. In all prisons there is a viable inmate subculture, composed of different groups and with a clear leadership and patronage hierarchy. This structure has its own internal conflicts—as the incidence of violence in prisons would attest—but it has considerable power to influence the actions of guards and staff. Thus, in addition to the ambiguities of directives, rules, and goals of the formal bureaucracy, there is further ambiguity and the potential conflict within the inmate subculture and between this subculture and the formal bureaucracy.

6. Prisons are political organizations. They are subject to legislative fads and budgeting policies at the state level and Congressional/executive actions at the federal level. Thus, prison superintendents and goals can change dramatically with alterations in the political climate and budgeting policies of legislators and government executives. Such changes can cause amplified disruption in the face of already tense relations among guards, staff, and elements of the inmate subculture.

7. Recidivism rates—that is, those who commit crimes again after their release—are quite high—at least 50% and even greater for

maximum security prisons. While prisons clearly punish—life is not pleasant in a prison—they do not rehabilitate. The reasons for the failure to rehabilitate are not hard to discover:

(a) Prison life is regimented and is thus unlike life in the community. It is hard to learn how to live a normal life in such a repressive atmosphere.

(b) Prisons expose criminals to each other, thus reinforcing criminal orientations, while allowing for the tutelage and acquisition of new criminal skills.

(c) Prisons stigmatize their inhabitants, making it difficult for them to get a job or become an accepted member of the community. Without a job or community acceptance, former prisoners are more likely to turn toward crime again.

Most prisons simply "hold" their inmates. Few are as nice as the one depicted here—the Buena Vista "Reformatory" in Colorado.

The recognition of these problems has led increasingly to efforts by courts and correctional institutions to avoid incarceration whenever possible. Close to two-thirds of convicted criminals are now on either probation or parole. And while the evidence on their recidivism is ambiguous, allowing criminals to live in the community is less punitive and considerably less expensive than incarceration in prisons.

Parole. When prisoners have served part of their court assigned sentence, they become eligible for parole in all states. In some 22 states, it is possible to release prisoners during the day to attend school or hold jobs in the community; and although such programs reach only a small number, recidivism appears to be lower than among regular parolees. Recidivism rates among regular parolees are subject to considerable ambiguity of interpretation. On the surface, parolee recidivism appears about the same as that of prisoners released without parole at the end of their sentence. However, the nature of a parolee's supervision appears to affect recidivism, underscoring some of the structural dilemmas of the parole system.

Upon release, a parolee is assigned a parole agent who is in charge of overseeing the conditions and rules of parolees. Just whether a parole will be revoked appears to depend upon: (1) the personal biases of the agent, (2) the case load of the agent, and (3) the number of technical conditions of parole. Thus, a parolee can be returned because one parole agent is more stringent than another, because the agent has a light case load and can monitor more closely the parolee's activities, or because the agent must work under so many technical rules that violations requiring revocation cannot go unnoticed. Often, parolees have no way to effectively appeal the revocation of their parole. Thus, the system of parole in most states has a series of biases which can subject the parolee to arbitrary practices and which, because of the ease of finding technical (non-criminal) violations of rules, can artificially inflate the recidivism rate.

Problems with parole

Recently, in California, for example, different classes of prisoners are subject to minimal, average, and maximal supervision. Moreover, appeal of revocation is possible. The results have shown no increase in recidivism and the system is considerably less costly. Yet, the ambiguity over the success of parole after incarceration (much damage may have already been done by confinement) has led to an increasing reliance on probation as an alternative to imprisonment.

Probation. Probation is the process whereby convicted criminals serve their sentences in the community under the supervision of a probation officer. This approach to corrections has the advantage of not severing contact with the community, while not unduly stigmatizing the probationer. While some of the differences between probationers and parolees stems from selection at the time of sentencing in the courts, probationers have lower incidence of arrests, better employment records, and more noncriminal social ties.

Yet, problems in the probation system remain: (1) The definition of what is supposed to be done with probationers is vague. Are officers to supervise, counsel, or monitor the probationer? As one criminologist remarked, "casework implies no specific technique of corrections, hence its prescription for crime is as unclear as if medical students were told no more than surgery was the appropriate response to appendicitis." (2) Probation is usually pronounced by a judge on the basis of a probation report which is hastily prepared and often inaccurate. Some criminals may be recommended for probation or prison on the basis of evidence which has little to do with their likelihood of committing future crimes. (3) In both the report and later when under supervision, the probationer is subject to the same potential biases, arbitrary actions, and variable policies of individual probation officers. (4) Most probation officers carry heavy caseloads and thus cannot establish a frequent or intimate relationship with their probationers.

Thus, much as with police enforcement and judicial review, probation and parole are structured in ways which can lead to arbitrary and abusive actions. These actions only seem benign in comparison to a highly abusive prison system which reaffirms beliefs in punishment but which does little to rehabilitate. Correctional action for the nation's one and a half million convicted criminals will thus remain one of America's enduring dilemmas of culture and structure.

SUMMARY

As we have seen, crime is inevitable. Just whether or not criminality in the population has increased dramatically is hard to assess, especially since crime statistics are so illusive. While crime, per se, is a problem, its causes are not understood. Moreover, much of the public debate and commentary over crime does not revolve around the causes of crime but around what to do with criminals and what should be defined as criminal actions.

Much of the "problemness" of crime, then, stems from the societal reaction to crime and criminals. This fact has required us to examine dominant cultural beliefs and their relationship to the problems of the law, police, courts, and correctional agencies. As we have seen, these have their own problems of structure which reflect the conflicts in beliefs about the law and crime in America. Since these cultural conflicts are unlikely to recede in the near future, America's reaction to crime will continue to present many problems of structure.

NOTES

1. Admittedly, this definition ignores much of the debate over definitions of crime from the legalistic one offered here to broader conceptualizations. However, present purposes do not require that the text become involved in this debate, and therefore, the simplest of definitions is offered here.

2. This study is summarized in the President's Commission on Law Enforcement and Administration of Justice, *The Challenge of Crime in a Free Society*, 1967. (Hereafter referred to as President's Commission.)

3. For a detailed analysis of organized crime, see: Cressey, 1969; *Report of the Special Committee to Investigate Organized Crime in Interstate Commerce*, and the President's Commission, *Task Force Report: Organized Crime*, 1967. Also, see Chapter 10 for a more detailed discussion of organized crime in America.

4. Naturally, this statement in no way mitigates the problematic nature of conventional crimes. Being raped, mugged, and robbed is still not much fun.

5. Obviously, some criminal acts, such as heavy narcotics use, can indirectly have victims; those users with expensive habits must commit conventional crimes—usually robbery—to secure the funds necessary to support their habit. However, were drug use not illegal, drugs would not be so expensive and hence users would not have to rob to secure necessary funds. It is likely that those who insist that drug use be a crime are also appalled at the result of their moral crusading: increases in other crimes by those with expensive habits. Unfortunately, they rarely see the connection and the solution it suggests: legalize drug use and make drugs cheap, while providing the facilities to help people get off the habit.

6. See Kadish, 1967; President's Commission, *Task Force Report: The Courts*, 1967:97–

107; Quinney, 1970:86–97; La Fave, 1964:63–84.

7. For basic references on the police in America, see Bordua, 1967; Skolnick, 1966; Niederhoffer, 1968; Wilson, 1963; Banton, 1964; Smith, 1960; Chevigny, 1969; President's Commission, *Task Force Report: The Police*, 1967.

8. One solution to this problem might be to have a large social service staff attached to the police force. This *unarmed* force could perform most of the social services, from amnbulance driver to traffic cop, required by a community. In this way peace keeping, public service, and law enforcement roles would not be confused.

9. One solution to this problem is to have differential weights attached to different kinds of arrests for both the individual policeman and the force as a whole. A cleared arrest for a homicide, for example, should be given greater weight—in terms of prestige, efficiency ratings, promotional considerations, and so on—than for a marijuana case. What is necessary is that the police stop being rewarded for enforcing the law with respect to the least harmful crimes. In fact, the budget of the police force might even be linked to an efficiency rating computed by a weighted system in which clearing the streets would have little reward value.

10. Again, this is not to deny that technical gadgets are necessary enforcement tools in a modern society. What is dangerous is the trend toward visualizing these tools as the *single most important facet* of law enforcement.

11. For a detailed inside description of this process in a large metropolitan court, see Blumberg, 1970, and Newman, 1956. For a secondary treatment of this process, see President's Commission, *Task Force Report: The Courts*, 1967; and Quinney, 1970:140–55.

12. The trial phase in the administration of justice has not been discussed because most cases are adjudicated without trial. Had the trial process been discussed, these facts could be established on the basis of current data: (1) Juries are biased (Robinson, 1950; Strodtbeck, 1957; Bevan et al., 1958; Simon, 1967; Bullock, 1961; Carter and Wilkins, 1967). (2) Witnesses are likely to be unreliable in their testimony (Gerver, 1957; Morris, 1957). (3) Psychiatrists are likely to abuse their medical prerogatives in their evaluations of the defendant (Halleck, 1966; Szasz, 1965; Blumberg, 1969). These facts make it less likely that even a jury trial assures the impartial rendering of justice.

REVIEW QUESTIONS

1. Explain why present crime statistics do not tell us how much crime there is.
2. Why is it inevitable that crime will increase in America?
3. Summarize that conflicting beliefs about crime and what should be done about it.
4. What are the problems of having laws which make criminals of those who have not harmed anyone or the state?
5. What are the dangers in the present trends of law enforcement by the police?
6. In what ways does the present administration of justice deviate from the ideals of justice in America?
7. How has the current corrections system failed to stop crime?

GLOSSARY

arraignment the process of presenting formal charges in a court of record against someone presumed to have violated the law

arrest the process of apprehending a person under the assumption that a violation of a criminal law has been committed

crime an action that violates criminal laws

no-victim crimes actions that violate criminal laws, but which do not harm others, the state, or private property

occupational crime crime committed by employees and businesses in the course of their normal, law-abiding activities

organized crime crime committed by organized syndicates that provide illicit services to the public

parole the practice of releasing from incarceration a convicted criminal before the full term of a sentence has been completed

plea bargaining the process in which charges against a defendant are reduced in exchange for a guilty plea to a lesser crime

police discretion the situation when the police are put in the position of having to decide which laws they will enforce and how they are to enforce them

probation the practice of having a convicted criminal serve a sentence in the community under the supervision of a probation office

probation report the report compiled by a probation officer before sentencing. It is often used as the basis for determining the type of sentence

procedural law laws specifying the proper procedures for enforcing and administering substantive laws

sentencing the process whereby a judge in a criminal court decides upon the punishment to be given a convicted criminal

substantive law laws that specify which behaviors are criminal

UCR abbreviation for *Uniform Crime Reports* collected by the FBI

PROLOGUE 15: DRUG BUST!

The police in Los Angeles have just confiscated hundreds of pounds of marijuana. Three weeks later, the price of marijuana for middle class suburbanites in Palo Alto, California increases fivefold to $220 an ounce.

A heroin addict has just robbed a house. He can now buy his fix, and get through another day. The people he robbed are very unhappy, but they will support increased efforts to stop the flow of heroin into this country. The result will be for the price to go up, forcing the addict to rob in order to get money to support his habit. Moreover, the profits in drug traffic are now so great that organized syndicates will feel the same way as those who were just robbed. As long as the drug is illegal, there are high profits to be made. They will increasingly farm out or franchise the street trafficking, because that is dangerous. They will concentrate on smuggling and refining, much safer operations which are hard to stop.

In any high school chemistry laboratory, LSD can be manufactured. Yet, should you decide to make some LSD, you will find yourself in jail in all states. In fact, no one is allowed to make LSD any more in the United States. Researchers use LSD that was produced by a company which stopped making it several years ago. In fact, researchers cannot make it themselves, or they will find themselves in jail. They can't buy it illegally, or again they will find themselves in jail. But you can buy it on any high school campus in an urban area, and increasingly, in rural areas. In fact as one researcher noted, "the kids can get the stuff in one afternoon; it takes us three months of red tape."

Many people have served several years in jail for smoking marijuana. Most of these are lower class. In 1976, the Surgeon General of the United States announced publicly that marijuana is not as harmful as was once thought and that its effects are less than those of alcohol. And yet, in most states, jail is prescribed for those who partake.

Thus, using drugs is dangerous. You can get "busted." You can go to jail for using something that, if it harms anyone, harms only you—not others, not property, and not the state. This is the way America reacts to drug use. This reaction is supported by cultural beliefs and is implemented through key agencies which have a vested interest in a criminal definition of the "drug problem." In this chapter, we will address the issue: Where is the greater problem? In the use and abuse of drugs? Or in the definition of drug use as a crime? There are no easy answers to such questions, but our discussion will put us in a better position to examine these questions carefully.

15

THE DRUG PROBLEM

No social problem is more illusive than "the drug problem." It is seen as both symptom and cause of other social ills in America, and as such, the society's reaction to deviants using drugs has often been severe. As we will come to appreciate, however, this reaction has been selective: Use of some drugs is defined as a criminal problem, while the use of other drugs is seen as a medical issue. The "drug problem," then, cannot be analyzed independently of the societal reaction to users of different drugs. In fact, as we will emphasize, the social problem in drug use may reside more in the societal reaction than in the incidence of drug use. Indeed, the reaction to drug use has often been counterproductive and has, in some instances, actually increased drug use, while aggravating other social problems. And thus, as we approach the study of drugs in America, we must remain attuned to more than merely the rates, scope, and types of drug use; we must also be alerted to the societal reaction and the problems that different reactions create.

DRUG USE IN AMERICA

TYPES OF DRUGS

   Arriving at a definition of "a drug" is not as easy as it might seem. From a scientific viewpoint, a *drug* is "any substance other than food which, by its chemical nature, affects the structure or functioning of a

Definition of drugs

living organism" (National Commission on Marijuana and Drug Abuse, 1973:9). Such a definition, while scientifically correct, is probably too broad, since many substances affecting bodily structure and functioning are not defined as drugs. Moreover, in the context of the drug problem, this definition does not help us isolate *what* drugs are defined as problematic. For example, the National Commission on Marijuana and Drug Abuse asked a national sample what they regarded as a "problem drug." Some substances, such as heroin and cocaine almost everybody regarded as a drug, but other bodily altering substances, such as alcohol, were not viewed as problematic.

Drugs and "harm"

At one time, of course, alcohol was defined as a "great evil," leading to its outlaw during the 1920s. Other drugs have similarly been labeled as problems. Among these, the most prominent are: (1) alcohol, (2) opiates, such as opium, morphine, heroin, and demerol, (3) stimulants, including such brand names as benzedrine, dexedrine, and methadrine, (4) depressants, such as phenobarbital, seconal, nembutol, and amytal, (5) marijuana and hashish, and (6) hallucinogens, including LSD, mescaline/peyote, psilocybin, STP, DMT, and DCP. Some of the categories are not mutually exclusive—alcohol and marijuana, for example, are also depressants—but they correspond to categories which, as we will see, have formed the basis for extreme societal reactions. Before discussing the problemness of these drugs, we should briefly define the properties, effects, and users of each type.

Alcohol. Fermentation creates alcoholic beverages. Certain yeasts act upon sugar and water to form ethyl alcohol and carbon dioxide, the basic ingredients of all alcoholic beverages. Virtually all plant forms that can be fermented are capable of transformation into alcohol. To increase the concentrations of alcohol in beverages, distillation is necessary. Distillation involves the heating of solutions containing alcohol into a vapor, and then collecting the vapor and condensing it into liquid. "Hard liquor" is created through distillation.

The effect of alcohol is to depress the central nervous system, and while alcohol may increase people's activities, it stimulates only by decreasing their inhibitions. The behavior of those using large amounts of alcohol is difficult to determine, since repressed behaviors and other needs vary from individual to individual. In heavy drinkers, a behavioral tolerance—or greater capacity to "hold liquor" does develop—but among the average to moderate drinker, the following effects can be expected with different levels of alcohol in the blood stream (Ray, 1972:86):

0.05%   lowered alertness; usually a "high feeling

0.10%	decreased reactions; decreased caution and inhibition
0.15%	greatly decreased reaction time
0.20%	marked depression in sensory and motor abilities
0.25%	severe decrease in sensory and motor skills
0.30%	close to unconsious
0.35%	unconsciousness
0.40%	death

Table 15.1 reports the effects of alcohol intake on males and females on blood alcohol levels for ounces of alcohol consumed within one hour. As can be seen, rapid intake of five ounces of alcohol can have pronounced depressant effects, and in smaller individuals, it can cause unconsciousness and death (Ray, 1972:90).

Alcohol is addictive. High levels of consumption over prolonged periods of time create both a biological and physiological dependence that can produce severe withdrawal symptoms. There are many estimates as to how many people drink to excess and become addicted to alcohol. The Department of Health, Education and Welfare speculates that 21 percent of the adult male population and 5

Dangers of alcohol

Table 15.1 **Relationships Among Sex, Weight, Oral Alcohol Consumption, and Blood Alcohol Level**

Absolute Alcohol (ounces)	Beverage Intake*	Blood Alcohol Levels (mg/100 ml)					
		Female (100 lb)	Male (100 lb)	Female (150 lb)	Male (150 lb)	Female (200 lb)	Male (200 lb)
1/2	1 oz spirits** 1 glass wine 1 can beer	0.045	0.037	0.03	0.025	0.022	0.019
1	2 oz spirits 2 glasses wine 2 cans beer	0.09	0.075	0.06	0.05	0.045	0.037
2	4 oz spirits 4 glasses wine 4 cans beer	0.18	0.15	0.12	0.10	0.09	0.07
3	6 oz spirits 6 glasses wine 6 cans beer	0.27	0.22	0.18	0.15	0.13	0.11
4	8 oz spirits 8 glasses wine 8 cans beer	0.36	0.30	0.24	0.20	0.18	0.15
5	10 oz spirits 10 glasses wine 10 cans beer	0.45	0.37	0.30	0.25	0.22	0.18

SOURCE: O. S. Ray, *Drugs*, Society, and Human Behavior, St. Louis: C. V. Mosley, 1972.
* In 1 hour.
** 100 proof spirits.

Alcohol is America's most abused drug. While most alcoholics do not descend to this level, their lives are always filled with tragedy.

percent of the adult female population are "heavy to excessive" drinkers, with close to 10 million individuals being classified as alcoholics—physically addicted to the drug (HEW, "First Special Report to U.S. Congress on Alcohol and Health," 1971).

Alcohol is the most pervasively used drug in America, and in terms of rates of addiction, it is the most problematic. With respect to the economic costs of alcoholism, Bell (1970) estimated that $7.5 billion per year is lost to the economy in employee absenteeism. This figure is compounded by the "human costs" of families with alcoholic members—their frustration, suffering, and psychological impairment.

Opiates. These drugs—including opium, morphine, and heroin —are derivatives of opium poppy leaves, most of which are grown in Turkey. Demerol represents the only synthetic opiate and is produced in large quantities by American drug companies. The effects of the opiates include relieving pain, reducing metabolic rates, producing drowsiness, and in some forms, such as heroin, creating a sense of relaxed euphoria. Opiates have a long history of use, dating back at least a thousand years. In America, opium was smoked by early Chinese immigrants in the last century, while morphine was a vital component in many drugs and cure-alls of the last century.

Currently, much of the drug problem is shaped by public attitudes toward heroin use—a highly refined form of morphine—and yet, by all surveys and accounts, heroin use probably involves the least number of people than any other dangerous drug. Heroin is highly addictive, producing considerable discomfort during withdrawal. However, contrary to public stereotypes, heroin withdrawal does not involve severe pain; rather, as one addict exclaimed, withdrawal is "like getting over a bad cold." Estimates of the number of individuals addicted to heroin range from a low of 200,000 to a high of 500,000.

Heroin is thus the least used dangerous drug, involving the fewest number of addicts. And yet, as we will come to see, its use and marketing carry the severest penalties. The costs of heroin use for the society are difficult to determine, but its high price—primarily the result of its illegality—forces many addicts to commit crimes in order to support their habits.

Stimulants. The nicotine of cigarettes and the caffeine of coffee—both highly abused drugs—are stimulants, but the public concern is with the amphetamines, such as benzedrine, dexedrine, and methadrine. Each of these drugs works their stimulant effect through the central nervous system and each produces feelings of

Heroin and public ignorance of its effects

  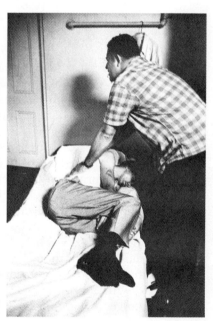

Preparation (left), *injection* (center), *and overdose* (right) *of heroin— a dangerous but not widely used drug.*

well being, increased energy, lessened fatigue, and decreased appetite. Cocaine is another stimulant drug, although of a somewhat different origin than the amphetamines.

The stimulants are not physically addictive, but the loss of stimulation is often accompanied by depression and fatigue, with the result that people frequently continue to take these drugs in order to avoid temporary states of discontent. Cocaine is not widely used, but the amphetamines are; millions of Americans use them in order to diet, keep alert, overcome fatigue, or to have "kicks," and a quick sense of euphoria (injected methadrine is the most typically used to achieve "kicks"). Close to 5 percent of the adult population uses amphetamines for nonmedical purposes (that is, for kicks and euphoria), while untold millions of "average Americans" are highly dependent upon them (National Commission, 1973). One indicator of American's growing reliance on amphetamines is that enough are produced in a given year to "ration" close to 50 tablets to each man, woman, and child. Close to half of this production enters an illegal market and, thus, goes·unregulated by physician prescriptions.

The problem of amphetamine use came into focus during the 1960s as the methadrine "speed freak" became a popular stereotype. More recently, the use of these drugs among high school students—who often get the drugs from their parent's medicine chest—has caused considerable alarm. At the very least, stimulants radically alter the body's functioning in harmful ways, while at the most, overdoses can cause death.

The extensive use of stimulants

Depressants. The most dangerous of the depressants are those classified as barbiturates. They are usually taken as sedatives or tranquilizers, and popular forms include amytal, nembutol, seconal, and phenobarbital. These drugs work by depressing the central nervous system and slowing down bodily functions, thereby producing decreased coordination, drowsiness, a sense of relaxation and symptoms similar to those of drunkenness.

Barbiturates are addictive and withdrawal from them is more severe than that for heroin. Perhaps as many as 1 million Americans are addicted to barbiturates (Weinsaig and Doerr, 1969) and there are enough produced each year to provide 50 tablets for each American. Since the use of barbiturates is often accompanied by excessive alcohol consumption, overdose and death are frequent occurrences among all social classes, particularly members of the middle classes. As with amphetamines, barbiturates are increasingly abused by younger age groups who, because of the vast illegal marketplace, can more readily secure "downers" than alcohol. Barbiturates are now second only to alcohol in the incidence of addiction and they are the most addictive drugs among the younger age groups.

The severe dangers of barbiturates

Hallucinogens. These drugs produce unusual and unconventional visual imagery in their users. Some are synthetic, such as LSD and PCP, while others like peyote and psilocybin are produced from plants. The effects of hallucinogens vary with the drug, its dosage, and the psychological characteristics of the user, but there is some evidence that prolonged use can cause neurological damage to brain cells. Hallucinogens appear to be used primarily by the young, with perhaps 5 percent of the age group under 35 having at least tried them. The pattern of use appears to be experimental, with a user trying the drug, then dropping it or at least cutting down to only occasional use. Hallucinogens are nonaddictive and appear to be taken for "kicks" and in an effort to achieve "new experiences."

Marijuana. This drug is a hallucinogen, but an extremely mild one. Its effect is, thus, much different than other hallucinogens, usually involving increased appetite and a sense of euphoric relaxation. Mari-

Experimentation with hallucinogens

Use of marijuana and hashish is common in America, however, these drugs are not as dangerous as once thought.

Table 15.2 **Incidence of Marijuana Use
by Age, 1971 and 1972**

Age	1971	1972
12–13	6%	4%
14–15	10	10
16–17	27	29
18–21	40	55
22–25	38	40
26–34	19	20
35–49	9	6
50 and over	5%	2%

SOURCE: National Commission on Marijuana
and Drug Abuse, *Drug Use in America:
Problem in Perspective*, GPO, 1973, p. 65.

juana is produced from a form of hemp plant and is typically smoked. Hashish is a derivative drug made from the resin of this plant and its effects are less relaxing and more hallucinogenic.

The use of marijuana is widespread, with as many as 25 million having tried it at least once (National Commission on Marijuana and Drug Abuse, 1973). Marijuana use is not confined to younger populations; there is evidence that over one-fifth of its users are in their thirties. Table 15.2 reports the results of two surveys by the National Commission on Marijuana and Drug Abuse on the use of marijuana by different age groups.

The widespread use of marijuana

Marijuana is nonaddictive and appears to be used by people interested in experimentation and by those seeking a source of periodic relaxation. All socioeconomic groups use marijuana and each group's incidence of use is increasing. The National Commission, however, speculates that the use of marijuana may soon reach its peak level. There are few heavy users, and their use tends to be associated with other features of an alternative or deviant life-style.

THE REACTIONS TO DRUG USE

In Table 15.3 the types of drugs discussed thus far, their effects, their incidence of use, and the societal definition of the problem associated with each are reported. The most interesting feature of Table 15.3 is the nature of the societal reaction: When use is high, there is a tendency for the definition of such use to be defined as a psychological or medical problem (marijuana is the only exception). Where use is not great, the definition of the problem is criminal, involving legal sanctions and imprisonment for users and distributors. The addictiveness of a drug does not help explain the societal reaction since two of the three criminally defined drugs (marijuana and halluci-

Drug dangers do not correspond with societal reaction

Table 15.3 **Types of Drugs, and Their Effects, Use, and Definition**

Type of Drug	Bodily Effects	Addictive	Extent of Use	Societal Definition of Problem
Alcohol	Depressant, loss of co-ordination, sensory control	Yes	Very great	Psychological/medical problem
Opiates	Reduction of pain, lowered metabolic rate, drowsiness, relaxed euphoria	Yes	Low	Criminal problem
Stimulants	Increased energy, alertness, lessened fatigue, and decreased appetite	No	Great	Medical problem
Depressants	Depressant: slowed bodily functions, decreased coordination, drowsiness, relaxation	Yes	Great	Medical problem
Hallucinogens	Unconventional visual imagery; potential neurological damage	No	Low	Criminal problem
Marijuana	Mild hallucinogen; relaxation, euphoria	No	Great	Criminal problem

nogens) are nonaddictive, whereas two of the three most used drugs are highly addictive (alcohol and depressants). Moreover, if the "average person" were asked to name the drugs most responsible for the drug problem, heroin, marijuana, and hallucinogens would head the list. Two of these drugs affect very small populations, and only one of them is addictive.

Thus, the properties and extent of use for various drugs cannot help us understand the drug problem; rather, the nature of the drug problem can only be viewed in terms of the societal reaction, and this reaction is only understandable in terms of certain cultural and structural arrangements in American society.

THE CULTURE OF THE SOCIETAL REACTION

The definition of the drug problem is a reflection of people's beliefs—some of which have become codified into a system of ideas constituting a clear cultural reaction to certain drugs. As we will come to realize, however, these beliefs are often inaccurate and bear little relationship to the actual dangers and incidence of abuse of certain drugs. The inaccuracy of beliefs will, by itself, require explanation, for more than inadvertent ignorance is involved. Certain organizations have sought to maintain this system of beliefs—a situation we will explore after briefly presenting the basic tenets of this cultural reaction.

Much of the negative reaction to drug use in America probably stems from people's perception that drug users violate basic values of activism and achievement. In using drugs excessively, users renounce many of the cultural premises that guide social action for the majority . Moreover, drug users violate the value of conformity, and Americans have always been highly suspicious of deviant behaviors despite their acceptance of the values of freedom and individuals. When deviations from these core values are compounded by perceptions that drug users are "dangerous," "fiendish," "out of control," "freaks," and "criminals," then the basis for the negative beliefs about drug users is clear. The fact that these latter beliefs were deliberately propagated by the Bureau of Narcotics—despite their obvious inaccuracy—will help us understand why the American reaction to drugs is so severe.

Beliefs about drug users

Two general types of beliefs have emerged as a reaction to drug deviation: (1) beliefs that drug users are "fiends" and potentially "dangerous" and (2) beliefs that the use of less-potent drugs leads to the use of stronger drugs that produce "dangerous" behavior. These beliefs now justify the criminal reaction to drug use in America.

THE DOPE FIEND MYTHOLOGY[1]

This belief maintains that drug users must inevitably become addicted to a drug, and that once addicted, they become "crazed" and will do anything and everything to maintain their addiction. Moreover, drug addicts increasingly will become antisocial, losing their inhibitions and heightening their propensity toward crime, rape, and violence.

Such beliefs are inaccurate since most addictive drugs are depressants that lower people's desire to be active. Most addicts seek anonymity, solitude, and quiet in their use. Unfortunately, the criminal sanctions against the sale and use of drugs raises their costs to such a degree that many must resort to crime in order to secure sufficient money to support their addiction. In many ways, then, by defining addicts as "fiendish" and "criminally prone," the society has fulfilled its own prophecy and forced addicts to act criminally in order to support their habits.

Inaccuracy of beliefs about "dope fiends"

THE "SOFT" TO "HARD" DRUGS MYTHOLOGY

The National Commission (1973:152) reported from its 1971 survey that 70 percent of the population believe "marijuana makes people want to try stronger things like heroin." This response typifies a basic and inaccurate belief: use of weaker drugs sets into motion forces—presumably psysiological, and perhaps social—that drive people to desire stronger drugs. One of the tenets of this belief is that all heroin users started with marijuana. In light of this "fact," Americans believe that even less harmful drugs must be outlawed in order to keep people from seeking hard drugs.

This belief is quite inaccurate: Marijuana does not cause people to seek heroin; marijuana is one of those drugs that people who wish to use drugs are likely to try. By the logic of this belief, aspirin, coffee, Coca Cola, and other drugs cause heroin use since all heroin addicts used these first. Moreover, housewives, students, and business executives are not driven to use heroin by their amphetamines or alcohol. This belief, however, propagates a situation where enforcement agencies react severely against all drugs in an effort to keep people from escalating to heroin. The result is for many experimenters and moderate users of nonaddictive drugs—marijuana and hallucinogens, for example—to be subject to severe criminal penalities.

Beliefs about drug use escalation

The spectacular inaccuracy of beliefs about drugs is not a coincidence. Two organizations have a vested interest in a criminal definition of drugs: Those who enforce the criminal laws pertaining to drugs, and those who reap high profits from their sale in the illegal market. The Narcotics Bureau of the Treasury Department has been an active proselytizer of these beliefs, while organized crime has, as contradictory as it may initially seem, been a silent ally. This situation forces us to recognize that beliefs that define the drug problem as a "criminal problem" are the result of active contributions to the perpetuation of not just the harsh policies of the Narcotics Bureau, but also the existence of organized crime syndicates in America. It is in this sense that drug use and the societal reaction are problems of social structure.

THE STRUCTURE OF THE SOCIETAL REACTION

THE NARCOTICS BUREAU AND THE CRIMINALIZATION OF DRUG USE AND ABUSE IN AMERICA

Early negative reaction to drug use—particularly opium and its derivatives—came from religious sources. The smoking of opium by early Chinese immigrants was the initial target of religious leaders who, in a clear case of selectivity, ignored the ingestion of opium by other means by the middle and upper-middle classes; for indeed, during the last century opium and its derivatives were attainable and frequently used by large numbers of individuals. It is

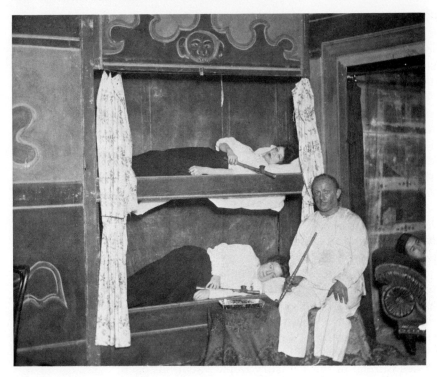

An early opium den at the turn of the century. These dens became the focal point for the first antidrug laws and enforcement agencies in America.

perhaps an indicator of American racism that early efforts to ban its widespread use were directed at a lower-class minority group (Mauss, 1975:257–258).

The first antiopium law appeared in San Francisco and it prohibited the smoking of opium. Far more prevalent was the use, by the white population, of pills, powders, and liquid cure-alls containing opium, but the San Francisco ordinance did not forbid this form of ingestion. Other cities soon followed in banning the smoking of opium.

The first drug laws

In many ways, these ordinances were passed in accordance with beliefs about racial inferiority and the need of whites to protect target racial groups from themselves. By the turn of the century, not only was opium smoking defined as a problem, but the use of cocaine by blacks had emerged as a "problem." Coupled with the fact that drug use was seen to violate basic values of rational and efficient activity in pursuit of achievement, a growing concern over drugs became evident. This concern led to the first international conference on opium in 1908—a conference soon followed by others.

This concern over unregulated opium resulted in the passage of the

Harrison Act of 1914 which placed taxes on the sale of opium, while requiring doctors and pharmacists to keep accurate records on its users and sales. The intent of the law was to assure that opium was used only for "medical" purposes. A narcotics division within the Treasury Department was to be responsible for collecting the tax and maintaining records.

The creation of this agency began the process of criminalization of drug use in America. At the time of the Harrison Act, drug abuse was defined as a medical problem, but during the first two decades of this century the Bureau won a series of court cases prohibiting the distribution of narcotics by physicians—thus taking the problem out of the control of the medical profession. At the same time, the Bureau began to mount media campaigns to propagate the dope fiend mythology, and by 1937, marijuana was added to the list of dangerous drugs that needed to be controlled.

The criminalization of drug use

In this process of gaining the power to regulate drugs, the Bureau sought a criminal definition of the problem. To prevent the spread of the problem, distributors and users of drugs would have to be defined as criminals. Using somewhat self-serving statistics, the Bureau could "demonstrate" that this definition of the problem was successful since, by their records, drug abuse had declined. In the early 1950s, this approach became further institutionalized as a series of laws, such as the Boggs Amendment of 1951 and the Narcotic Control Act of 1956, firmly established a national policy of criminal sanctions for drug use. Such federal guidelines have set the tone for most drug legislation by individual states and local communities.

During the 1960s and 1970s, however, an anticriminal definition of the problem has been posited. Led by reports of several national commissions on drug abuse and crime in America, a more realistic view of the effects of drugs has been presented. However, except in a few states (such as Oregon where marijuana use is now only a minor offense), most states still follow a criminal definition of drug use. This definition has been established by the 1970 Comprehensive Drug Abuse and Control Act which sets forth five categories of "dangerous drugs." The categories were thought to correspond to (1) the potential for abuse and (2) the possible medical utility of different types of drugs. The first category, which outlaws drug use, includes hallucinogens, heroin, cocaine, and marijuana derivatives. Other drugs, such as the stimulants and depressants, are thought to have medical utility and fall within a lower category and are thus dispensed by prescription. Only the nonmedical distribution of these drugs is outlawed.

As we can see, then, the Narcotics Bureau has actively sought to impose a criminal definition of drug abuse. Such a definition allows the Narcotics Bureau to have expanded bureaucratic functions, and this alone is certainly one reason why the Bureau has sought a criminal approach to the problem. Currently, despite evidence to the contrary, the Bureau, and more recently, its allied agencies in the Justice Department, have been able to use the cultural beliefs in the "dope fiend" and "soft to hard drug syndrome" to justify a punitive approach to drug control. The fact that these beliefs were created by the Narcotics Bureau is but one indication of whose interests they best serve.

What are the consequences of the Bureau of Narcotic's criminal approach to the drug problem? One result is for a very large segment of the law-abiding population—especially when the use of marijuana is considered—to be defined as criminal. The use of drugs does not directly harm others or property, and thus, the wisdom of criminal sanctions for drug-related behaviors can be questioned. As we observed in Chapter 14, the existence of such no victim crimes forces otherwise law-abiding citizens into a criminal act, who thereby lose respect for the law, while the government wastes enormous sums of money on enforcement, adjudication, and incarceration of people who often have harmed only themselves.

Consequences of drug use laws

Another result of a criminal approach to drug use and abuse is that it is often counterproductive. By prohibiting the legal distribution of drugs, an illegal market is inevitably created. Because of the risks involved in distributing in an illegal market, prices will be high. For example, heroin prices are so high that people with severe habits must often steal to support their addiction. And the more police "crack down" on heroin distribution, the higher the price and the more drug-related crime. Moreover, the criminal definition of drug use discourages drug addicts from seeking clinical help by forcing them into the criminal fringes of society. Another example of the counterproductivity of criminal policies comes from Operation Intercept in 1969 when a massive federal effort was made to cut down on the importation of marijuana from Mexico. The result was for marijuana prices to rise and for some users to turn to more dangerous drugs.

As the prohibition of alcohol amply demonstrated in the 1920s, people will consume drugs regardless of legal definitions. It is probably not wise to prohibit sale and use of substances in high demand, for in the end, such prohibitions encouraged organized crime. Illegal substances in high demand require efficient organization to deliver in an illegal market. It is no coincidence that organized crime—the Mafia, Costra Nostra, or whatever the name is used to describe these syndicates—greatly expanded their operations during prohibition. With the repeal of prohibition of alcohol, the increasingly criminal definition of drug use provided a substitute market which, along with other no-victim crimes such as prostitution and gambling, has generated a vast network of organized crime. Aside from the problems of organized crime, per se, the existence of syndicates probably encourages increased drug use. The high profits from illegal drugs foster "the pusher" who activeky seeks new drug clients. Without the high profits and organization of the illegal market, much of the incentive behind the pusher's activities would be lost. Thus, once again, the criminal definition of drug use is often counterproductive in terms of decreasing drug use.

The existence of organized crime, however, poses many additional problems. Since it emerged primarily as a result of the societal reaction to alcohol and then to drugs (and other no-victim crimes), we should close our analysis of the drug problem by examining the consequences of organized crime in America.

ORGANIZED CRIME IN AMERICA: ONE CONSEQUENCE OF SOCIETAL REACTION

Organization for the purpose of committing crime has existed since America's beginning. There has always been a vice market, especially in early Protestant America, and there was no lack of will and talent to provide desired services and commodities. Much of early organized crime involved providing immigrant labor to industry, commerical ships, and the military (usually through illegal means). Contrary to current beliefs, the Irish rather than Italians were probably the first to create criminal organization. As the Irish were able to move into positions of real political power, however, their involvement in organized crime began to recede. Accidents of settlement in each community pretty much determined who would assume control of crime syndicates. In some communities, eastern European Jews came to prominence in the early twentieth century, while in other communities Italian immigrants assumed control.

Until the Volstead Amendment to the Constitution in 1919—outlawing alcohol—crime syndicates were not large, nor tightly organized. But with this act, a set of conditions favoring large and well-organized crime syndicates emerged (Keuhn, 1975):

1. legislation outlawing a good or service in high demand was initiated
2. an economic system where a market mechanism allowing for high profits existed
3. there were groups of people willing—in light of their subordinate economic positions—to risk legal penalties to supply these goods and services

Drug use laws benefit organized crime

4. the organizational skills to create large organizations for marketing illegal goods existed

Without the Volstead Amendment, it is unlikely that large-scale crime syndicates, and confederations of syndicates, could have emerged in America. Organizations would have probably been confined to large cities, with little coordination among them. However, once the syndicates existed and were well organized, they sought to maintain and expand their organization and profits. Organized crime syndicates and confederations, thus, have a vested interest in criminal definitions of illegal goods—drugs, for example—and services, such as gambling and prostitution. When goods are illegal, and organized groups can control, through violence, the market for these goods, high prices can be charged, competition can be eliminated, and profits can go untaxed. Moreover, untaxed monies can often be used to infiltrate legitimate enterprises for purposes of creating "fronts" and "laundering" illegally procured money. For example, the Bonnano family used trucking firms, auto repair shops, and a Wisconsin cheese factory as fronts for gambling operations. Or, at times, mob-controlled real estate and finance firms became repositories of illegally received monies, and after a period of laundering, the monies are returned to the syndicates. More recently, organized syndicates have become interested in labor unions, particularly the Teamsters. By controlling unions, organized syndicates can "legally" extort concessions from business and industry by threatening a strike or other "labor" problems.[2]

The dangers of organized crime

Thus, once syndicates exist they tend to expand their activities and often enter both legal and illegal markets. Today, organized crime provides such illicit services as sex, drugs, high-interest loans, untaxed alcohol and cigarettes (in high tax areas such as New York), contraband retail goods (such as meat, TV sets, furniture), and "protection" against all varieties of malady from personal safety to labor disputes.

Such organizations will inevitably persist as long as Americans believe that certain substances and activities must be outlawed. While the massive alcohol market provided the potential for such profits that organization became necessary, drugs have been one of the mainstays of organized crime since the repeal of the Volstead Amendment. With strict enforcement of drug laws, however, organized syndicates have increasingly "franchised" risky drug operations to other ethnic groups—Chicanos, blacks, Puerto Ricans, and Cubans. In this way, the syndicates avoid the risks, while enjoying the high profits that come from the drug trade.

While gambling activities generate the most income for organized crime, distributing illegal drugs remains a highly profitable venture.

*Two reactions
to drug abuse.
Community
members
protest the drug
traffic in their
neighborhoods,
while children
learn the facts
about drugs
and antidrug
attitudes in
school.*

This venture is organized on an international basis, since opium must be smuggled into the United States from the Near East, Mexico, and South America and then wholesaled to local distributors who cut, refine, and distribute heroin. Organized syndicates have recently provided the raw drugs, leaving it to others to engage in the risky refining and distributing process. Other drugs, such as the barbiturates and amphetamines, are marketed in much the same way. Since only one-half of these legally manufactured drugs are ever sold in drugstores, the other half must be secured in a black market, white markets in Latin America, or through the highjacking of trucks and train cars. Organized syndicates coordinate this phase of distributing and then franchise the higher risk distribution to the local wholesalers of the street "pushers." Marijuana and hallucinogens are not extensively marketed by organized syndicates since marijuana can easily be grown and hallucinogens readily manufactured in a high school chemistry laboratory. The manufacture and distribution of these drugs tends to be performed by local entrepreneurs.

In sum, then, some illegal drugs present a favorable profit picture to crime syndicates. These syndicates can control markets and eliminate competition, therefore, keeping prices and profits high. These profits can then be used to finance other activities, including infiltration of businesses and unions, loan sharking, protection rackets, gambling organizations, and prostitution rings. Such is one consequence of the societal reaction to drug use and abuse.

SUMMARY

Chapter 15 has examined drug use in America. After reviewing the nature and effects of different drugs, we drew attention to the fact that the societal reaction bears little relation to the effects of drugs on people. The "problemness" of drug use resides in cultural beliefs, and it is the structural reaction—rather than in the activities of individuals who, for their own reasons, seek comfort and excitement in drug use and abuse—that perpetuates the beliefs that drug use is criminal. This reaction, as was emphasized, does not abate drug use, and in fact, it appears to escalate abuse. Moreover, criminal definitions of the problem have encouraged the expansion of organized syndicates that infiltrate many other legitimate spheres of the American economy. It is in this sense that we have viewed the use of drugs as a problem of culture and structure in America.

NOTES

1. For an excellent treatment of this mythology and how it was created by the Bureau of Narcotics, see Armand Mauss' excellent social problems book (1975:255). For the earliest criticism of this belief, see Linde Smith (1940).

2. For basic references on the structure and operation of organized crime, see Albini, 1971; Cressey, 1969, 1972; Ianni, 1972, 1974; and Keuhn, 1975.

REVIEW QUESTIONS

1. What are the major classes of drugs? Which of these drugs have the most harmful effects on their users?
2. Using the list of drugs that you developed, summarize how the use of these drugs is defined by legal authorities.
3. How do dominant beliefs about drug use influence the reactions of legal authorities?

And, how do the actions of legal authorities encourage these dominant beliefs?
4. Why is organized crime inevitable as long as drug use is defined as illegal?
5. From the analysis in this chapter, can you propose alternative drug policies that might reveal fewer problems of structure?

GLOSSARY

alcohol the substance produced when plants are converted, through fermentation, into ethyl alcohol and carbon dioxide; a depressant which decreases neuromuscular activity

depressants drugs that act to depress the functioning of the central nervous system and slow down the functioning of the body

drug a substance other than food that affects the structure and functioning of the living organism

hallucinogens drugs that produce unusual and unconventional visual imagery in their users

marijuana a mild hallucinogen processed from the leaves of the hemp plant

opiates although synthetic forms are available, most forms are derivatives of the opium poppy leaf; a depressant which relieves pain, reduces metabolic rate, and relaxes its users

stimulants drugs that increase the metabolic rate and activities of the central nervous system

PROLOGUE 16: A MYTH OF MENTAL ILLNESS?

How often have we uttered the phrases: "You're crazy," "you're out of your mind," "he has a few loose nuts up there," or a hundred such phrases which impute "mental problems" to people who do not behave or act in the way that we expect them to. These phrases and an elaborate vocabulary about mental problems and the mentally "sick" and "ill" so pervade our thoughts and perceptions that we never seriously ask: Are people in our mental hospitals really "sick in the mind"? Do they need medical assistance?

Our culture and society treats them as if they were "sick" in the "mind." But are they? Perhaps they just do not get along very well with other people, but does this mean that they are sick? And is the medical profession the best help available to people who have difficulty adjusting to others around them?

Who is to decide if someone is "ill"? As long as we assume that they are ill, we will grant this right to the medical profession. But are they always the best qualified? For example, until recently, the medical profession—that is, the American Psychiatric Association—defined homosexuality as one form of mental illness. Are homosexuals really ill? Are they sick in their heads? Now the APA says no, but for thirty years they said yes. Thus, definitions of illness by experts can vary from time to time. What would we say about the medical profession if it proclaimed, tomorrow, that cancer is not an illness? We'd probably say, "they're crazy," but this is exactly what can happen with definitions of mental illness. For what is true of

504

homosexuals can also be true of others who do not act the same way as "normal people."

How accurate are diagnoses of mental illness? Most people who enter mental hospitals are labeled schizophrenic which, as it turns out, is a global label that includes any behavior which an expert views as loss of touch with reality and convention. Unfortunately, if you ask ten different experts about what specific type of schizophrenia a person has, you will get different answers, that is, you will get different diagnoses of "what's wrong." This means that our schizophrenic has several "illnesses" or that the science of diagnosis is not very precise. Yet, Americans have given enormous power to these medical professionals to decide if any of us are "sick in the head."

These problems with definition and diagnosis have led many to proclaim a myth of mental illness. Maybe many of those labeled sick by medical professionals are not sick. Perhaps, they just don't like people. Maybe, they do not interact very effectively. And just perhaps some relatives do not like them and want to "put them away." The medical profession is structured to find and treat illness; and thus, if people behave in unconventional ways, they are likely to diagnose illness in the mind. And so it will be, as long as they are given the power to decide.

This chapter will explore the problem of mental illness. We will have to be cautious, however, about assuming that people's inability to get along in conventional interactions is a sign that they are ill or sick in the head. This whole conception of behavioral maladjustments is so ingrained in American culture and in its structured reaction that we never question the assumption of mental illness. In Chapter 16 we will examine the culture and structure of mental illness and let you decide to what extent we have relinquished the power to decide if we are "sick in the head."

16

THE PROBLEM OF MENTAL ILLNESS

Throughout history, people have been labeled "mentally disturbed." Whether they have been viewed as "witches," "possessed by the demon," or as "schizophrenics," society has always had a label and an established way of reacting to the mentally disturbed. So it is in contemporary American society: There are official labels for deviance residing "in the mind" and there are prescribed reactions to these forms of deviance.

We must emphasize the societal reaction to mental illness and the structures established to deal with the problem because the definition of *illness* reflects dominant cultural beliefs. In any society there is a range of behaviors defined as normal, eccentric, and as grossly deviant, hence, requiring a societal reaction. There are, however, no absolute standards of normality or deviance; each society has its own cultural values, beliefs, and norms to use as yardsticks for measuring deviations.

We must examine not so much the causes of mental illness—these are not really known and there are a bewildering array of hypotheses—but the societal reaction to certain forms of deviant behavior which presumably are caused by "mental problems." Thus, after examining the established definitions of mental illness and the official rates of this malady, our attention will focus on such questions as: Who establishes these definitions and what are their consequences? What kinds of reactions to deviants do these definitions allow? How

Mental illness is an unknown

are these reactions legitimized by cultural beliefs? And what is the structure of the reaction?

From all we know about societies, "disturbances of the mind" are inevitable. The problemness of mental illness, therefore, resides less in its existence than in how the society treats the deviant. It is in this sense that we will come to view "mental illness" in America as a problem of culture and structure.

WHAT IS MENTAL ILLNESS?

What is mental illness? As glib as this answer appears, mental illness is "whatever those professionals licensed to deal with the problem define as mental illness." Even when legal definitions of insanity exist—for example, did the person know right from wrong—certain professionals are asked to determine whether or not the person is insane under the law. Thus, in answering the question What is mental illness?, we must first look at the "official" definitions. The most commonly used are those of the American Psychiatric Association which, while subject to constant revision, reveal a six-category system for classifying types of mental problems:

Experts decide what "mental illness" is

I. Mental Retardation
II. Organic Brain Syndromes
    A. Psychosis
    B. Nonpsychotic disorders
III. Psychoses Not Related to Organic Causes
    A. Schizophrenia
    B. Major affective disorders
    C. Paranoid states
IV. Neuroses
V. Personality Disorders and Other Nonpsychotic Mental Disorders
    A. Personality disorders
    B. Sexual deviation
    C. Alcoholism
    D. Drug dependence
VI. Psychophysiological Disorders

Categories of mental illness

To appreciate the range and scope of these six classes of labels, we should begin with a brief definition of each:

I. Mental Retardation. This problem involves the diagnoses of subnormal intellectual functioning, correlated with impairments in learning, social adjustment, and maturation. Sources can be brain disease, chromosome abnormality, or environmental deprivation.

II. Organic Brain Syndromes. When damage to brain cells and tissues occurs, many facets of a person's actions and emotions can be affected. Patients are described as "psychotic" when their "mental functioning is sufficiently impaired to interfere grossly with their capacity to meet the ordinary demands of life. . . ." (American Psychiatric Association, 1968:23). Less severe behavioral manifestations of brain damage are simply termed *nonpsychotic disorders.*

III. Psychosis Not Related to Organic Causes. The definition of psychosis remains the same as above, but the causes lie not in brain damage, but in people's social experiences. There are three principal subcategories of psychosis: (1) *Schizophrenia*—which, contrary to

A severely psychotic woman living in her unconventional world and unable to participate in the conventional world around her. Note the shabby conditions in which she must live.

stereotypes of a split personality, usually involves the loss of coherent and conventional thought, the withdrawal from ordinary social interaction, and the maintenance of unconventional conceptions of "reality"; (2) *affective disorders*—which invoke disabling disturbances of people's feelings, temperament, and mood; (3) *paranoia*—which concerns people's beliefs that they are being persecuted or excessively grandiose convictions about who they are.

IV. Neurosis. This problem is defined as high states of "conscious or unconscious" anxiety which do not involve the massive distortions of reality among psychotics, but which do cause behavioral maladjustments. Prominent types include: (1) *Anxiety neurosis*—where people have a pervasive and diffuse sense of anxiety without apparent cause or source; (2) *hysterical neurosis*—where individuals lose the functioning of a part of their body, or where they lose states of consciousness, such as with amnesia; (3) *phobic neurosis*—where people develop an intense fear of an object or situation that is recognized to present no real danger; (4) *obsessive-compulsive neurosis*—where a patient is preoccupied with certain thoughts or compulsion to repeat specific acts; and (5) *depressive neurosis*—where an individual feels a deep and prolonged sense of sadness.

V. Personality Disorders and Other Nonpsychotic Mental Disorders. This category is essentially a residual category in which "mental problems" are presumed to cause such deviant behaviors as drug abuse and sexual deviaitons. Just what is included in this category is subject to changing definition, as was the case recently when the American Psychiatric Association voted to remove homosexuality from the category of mental illness.

VI. Psychophysiological Disorders. Physical disorders, such as asthma, ulcers, impotency, and skin hives that are caused by "emotional factors."

As can be seen, the list of disorders that can be labeled as "mental illness" is broad. Some are biological in origin; others sociocultural in genesis. Most importantly, the scheme is so broad as to include almost any noticeable form of deviation as a sign of mental illness. Such breadth gives those charged with diagnosis and treatment enormous latitude in applying one of the above labels to a person and then classifying the person's "symptoms" as a sign of mental illness. Moreover, the categories are subject to change as certain forms of deviance, such as homosexuality, become more acceptable to the general public and mental health practitioners. These facts should alert us to the possibility that mental illness is, in part at least, a matter of

Mental illness is a matter of social definition

social definition and this definition is subject to changes stemming from such forces as growing public tolerance, professional fads, and changing governmental policies. In turn, these vague and shifting definitions make ascertaining the extent of mental illness in America difficult. Is there more or less illness or have definitions been more rigorously enforced, or have governments increased monies for treatment and incarceration, or are better records being kept than previously? These kinds of questions cannot be ignored when examining rates of mental illness in America.

RATES OF MENTAL ILLNESS IN AMERICA

Using categories similar to those of the American Psychiatric Association, how much mental illness exists in the United States? The only data available are those collected by the National Institute of Mental Health—a governmental subagency of Health, Education and Welfare—and these data are subject to many potential errors.[1] Yet, they are the best available and we will have to rely upon them in answering the questions about the scope of mental illness in America.

In Table 16.1 we can observe (for various years) the number of psychiatric case episodes, that is, the number of people seeking, or being forced to seek, a mental health expert or facility. There were just over 1,000 episodes per 100,000 of the population in 1955, whereas by 1971, there were almost 2,000. Thus, the rate of mental illness has doubled—at least by official statistics. We must be aware, however, that the number of psychiatric facilities available to the general public has also increased dramatically. Part of this increase is due to a growing awareness of the problem, and perhaps part from an actual increase in the incidence of mental illness. A good part of the increase, however, is due to the fact that, once available, people use

Table 16.1 **Rate of Psychiatric Care Episodes per 100,000 Population**

Year	Rate per 100,000
1971	1,967.8
1969	1,797.7
1967	1,604.3
1965	1,374.0
1955	1,032.2

SOURCE: National Institute for Mental Health, *Statistical Note 92,* table 1, GPO, 1973.

Table 16.2 **Percent of Inpatient and Outpatient Services**

Year	Inpatient	Outpatient	Total
1971	42.6%	57.4%	100%
1969	47.0	53.0	100
1967	52.9	47.1	100
1965	59.4	40.6	100
1955	77.4%	22.6%	100%

Source: NIMH, *Statistical Note 92*, table 5, 1973.

facilities, and it is at psychiatric facilities that episodes are recorded and national rates computed. No doubt many people needed psychiatric help in 1955 and could not get it, hence, their needs went unrecorded.

Much of this increase in psychiatric episodes is probably the result of the availability of outpatient facilities. Community psychiatric services are increasingly being used as a substitute for incarceration in mental hospitals. People who were, for good reason, afraid to enter a mental hospital as an inpatient have become willing to seek psychiatric help as an outpatient with a private therapist, a psychiatric social worker, a community mental health clinic, or the expanded outpatient services of most county hospitals. Table 16.2 reports this trend in outpatient treatment since 1955. As can be observed, 77 percent of all psychiatric episodes occurred as inpatients in hospitals in 1955, whereas by 1971, only 42 percent involved confinement to a hospital. Thus, over the last twenty years, people are increasingly treated outside the state mental hospital. The reasons for this are varied: (1) Professionals began to realize that confinement in a hospital was self-defeating and not in a patient's best interest (we will see why shortly); (2) the use of tranquilizer drugs reduces overt symptoms and enables people to remain in the community; and (3) it is impossible in terms of costs and logistics to confine all patients, thus, efforts have been made to help as many patients as possible in their homes and community.

What kind of mental illness is most prevalent? Who are these outpatients? An analysis of mental illness in America would require answers to these additional questions. In Tables 16.3 and 16.4, we can at least get a partial answer. A word of caution is necessary in interpreting the tables, however. The categories do not correspond exactly to those listed earlier. The National Institute for Mental Health (NIMH) tends to collapse categories, with the result that "depressive disorders" include both neurotic and psychotic depressions, while "all other categories" includes severe neuroses, personality disorders, and psychophysiological disorders. Yet, the data do offer a rough pic-

Outpatient facilities

Table 16.3 **Percent of Patient Care Episodes by Clinical Diagnosis**

Clinical Diagnosis	Percent
Mental retardation	3.1%
Organic brain syndromes	5.4
Schizophrenia	22.5
Other psychoses	1.5
Digressive disorders	15.4
Alcohol disorders	8.8
Drug disorders	2.9
All other disorders	32.4
Undiagnosed	8.0
Total	100.0%

SOURCE: NIMH, *Statistical Note 92*, table 5, 1973.

ture of the respective incidence of different forms of illness and the way these forms are treated.

As we can see from Table 16.3, schizophrenia—severe loss of touch with reality—accounts for 22.5 percent of the diagnosis, with another 1.5 percent concerned with other psychoses. Depressive disorders account for 15.4 percent, while the largest category is the residual "all other disorders" category. From Table 16.4, we see that 31 percent of inpatients are diagnosed as schizophrenics and 19 percent as "other psychoses." Thus, 50 percent of those incarcerated are diagnosed as psychotic in contrast to 28 percent who remain outpatients. The large number of "other disorders" and "undiagnosed" cases in outpatient facilities demonstrates that many nonpsychotic illnesses—most likely various forms of neuroses—can be handled with drugs and outpatient counseling. The comparatively small number of "other disorders" and "undiagnosed" among inpatients in hospitals probably

Schizophrenia is most commonly diagnosed

Table 16.4 **Outpatient and Inpatient Psychiatric Services by Clinical Diagnosis**

Clinical Diagnosis	Percent of Outpatients	Percent of Inpatients
Mentally retarded	3.3%	2.8%
Organic brain syndrome	2.5	9.3
Schizophrenic	15.7	31.8
Other psychoses	12.7	19.0
Depressive	1.5	1.6
Alcoholic	5.4	13.4
Drug abusers	2.1	4.0
Other	44.7	15.6
Undiagnosed	12.1%	2.5%
Total	100.0%	100.0%

SOURCE: NIMH, *Statistical Note 92*, table 5, 1973.

How deviant is "sick"? Is this man "mentally ill"? Who is to decide? Who should have the power to commit this man or any "deviant"?

reflects the bureaucratic and legal need to justify incarceration—schizophrenia or some other psychoses being the most acceptable label.

What do these data tell us about mental illness in America? More people than ever are seeking help; a majority of these can be helped as outpatients, with only those diagnosed as severely ill requiring incarceration. Is mental illness increasing in our industrial, urban world? The data cannot answer this question, since other forces can also account for the doubling of the "mental illness rate." It is certain, however, that emotional problems confront a very large number of people and that close to 5 million have sought help during the last year. A problem affecting so many inevitably generates a societal response. It is to the problems inhering in the cultural and structural features of this response that our analysis now turns.

The scope of maladjustment

THE CULTURAL REACTION TO MENTAL ILLNESS

Current beliefs about mental illness have changed from the once dominant conception that mental illness was a sign of sin to beliefs about mental illness as a "disease."[2] This view of mental illness has become codified into several related cultural tenets: (1) mentally ill people are "sick" and in need of "treatment"; (2) these sick people

Mental illness as a "disease"

can be dangerous; (3) people never really get over mental illness; and (4) mentally ill people must often be "cared for" for both "their own good" and for the "protection of society."

MENTAL ILLNESS AS A SICKNESS

Beliefs that some deviance is a sickness or disease places the care of "patients" in the hands of the medical profession who are "best suited to administer the cure." This definition has resulted in a "medical model" for the treatment of deviance and has created a vast market for medical personnel and facilities. In this context, it must be remembered that the definition of deviance as a disease or sickness is rather arbitrary. Some scholars have even contended that Americans have merely substituted the notion of sin for the labels "sickness" and "disease" without dramatic evidence that deviance involves a disease or illness (Szasz, 1960, 1970). There is no convincing evidence, these critics argue, that many deviants are sick or ill. What is clear, however, is that most Americans and key policy and funding agencies of government now operate under the belief that much deviance is a "disease and sickness" of the individual.

In many ways, this form of labeling is a reflection of the contradictions in dominant American values: freedom and individualism on the one hand and conformity on the other. Lack of conformity in a society that also values freedom to be an individual must invoke severe labels for acts of deviance. By proclaiming deviance a sin or a "disease," justification for a severe societal response can be made since a response repressing individual differences can now be done in the name of another value, humanitarianism. Thus, by proclaiming people sick, it becomes humane to suppress their deviance and does not violate their freedom to be a different individual. This application of values also helps justify the appropriateness of other beliefs about how to react to these "diseased deviants."

MENTALLY SICK PEOPLE CAN BE DANGEROUS

A number of opinion surveys reveal the suspicion and distrust of Americans toward people labeled mentally ill. J. C. Nunnally (1961) discovered over a decade ago that all classes and ages of Americans regard the mentally ill as "relatively dangerous, dirty, unpredictable, and worthless" (1961:51). There is a fear of mentally ill people—a sense that they can do unpredictable and dangerous things. Such a belief has been used, as we will see, to justify the often indiscriminate incarceration of "mental patients" in "hospitals" which, at times, differ very little from prisons.

Some of the "ill" are assumed dangerous. Here an ill person is confined to a straitjacket. Note, once again, the conditions under which this person is being "treated."

THE MENTALLY ILL ARE NEVER "REALLY CURED"

Americans believe that the unpredictable behavior of the mentally ill can reoccur, even after experts have pronounced an individual as "cured." The Thomas Eagleton affair in the 1972 presidential race amply documents this belief. Senator Eagleton was dropped from the Democratic ticket as public opinion polls began to document a large segment of the public as suspicious of his fitness to be vice president.

This belief in the danger of a sudden reoccurrence of a previous illness is often used to justify delays in releasing mental patients as well as activities designed to monitor the lives of the formerly ill who have been released.

THE MENTALLY ILL MUST BE CARED FOR

If deviance is an illness, then it must be treated. If it is an illness that is also dangerous to others, then society must suppress and incarcerate people for their own good as well as for society's. Americans believe that medical practitioners should have considerable control over the lives of patients in order to protect both society and the patient. And despite formal legal safeguards protecting the civil rights of those labeled mentally ill, this belief helps justify practices whereby medical personnel can readily incarcerate the "ill."

Such beliefs constitute a culture of mental illness, and as their stigmatizing nature would suggest, they have been used to legitimize a rather severe and often inhumane set of structural arrangements that not only suspend the civil rights of those incarcerated, but also force many to live under conditions that are hardly conducive to mental health. These beliefs, then, can only be fully understood by examining the structures in which they are sustained.

Beliefs about mental illness legitimize structural arrangements

THE STRUCTURE OF THE SOCIETAL REACTION

Who decides when someone is mentally ill? Usually either the individuals themselves or close friends and family decide that "something is wrong." There is typically a long period of denial or redefinition of symptoms as merely signs of being upset, but eventually, if symptoms persist, individuals become labeled as ill. Such a label sets into motion a societal reaction to the deviant that has potentially profound consequences: the individual can be incarcerated in a hospital; the patient can, in forty states, lose the right to vote; the individual can lose the right to hold political office in close to half of all states; and, the individual labeled mentally ill can be divorced in many states even though physical illness is not grounds for divorce.

Because the label mentally ill can suspend basic constitutional rights, most states have legal safeguards to protect the rights of the

Early reaction to the "ill" was often harsh and repressive.

ill. These laws are designed to keep individuals from illegally and incorrectly being confined to mental hospitals where, once confined, they lose many legal rights and are exposed to many abusive practices. Thus, in examining the societal reaction to mental illness, we should first focus on the efforts to legally protect the mentally ill and then to their experiences in mental hospitals. As we will come to see, legal rights are frequently illusionary; moreover, people's experiences in mental hospitals are often detrimental to the recovery of their mental health.

PROBLEMS IN MAINTAINING LEGAL SAFEGUARDS

A study of the Illinois system for protecting patients subject to commitment in the 1960s can perhaps illustrate the basic problem in protecting individuals in the face of medical "needs" to act informally and expeditiously (Kunter, 1967). Before a person can be involuntarily committed to a state institution, legal codes require: (1) a petition signed by a relative or friend stating their belief that the individual is mentally ill, (2) a physician's certificate stating that the individual actually is "mentally ill," (3) an examination by court-appointed doctors who are to submit a diagnosis to the court, and (4) a court hearing where the individual can request a jury.

On paper, these safeguards appear impressive, but in fact, they are routinely circumvented in practice. For example, in Cook County, Illinois (Chicago), certificates of insanity are routinely signed by staff physicians after an examination lasting only a few minutes. The court appointed doctor is also the *same one* originally signing the certificate, thus eliminating the safeguard of one doctor checking up on the other. Confinement in Cook County is recommended in 77 percent of the cases, with the burden of proving sanity thrust upon the patient in a three- to four-minute interview. At the court hearing patients are often so sedated by the physicians that they are unable to speak or defend themselves, and until recently, clinic personnel failed to notify individuals of their right to counsel or a jury trial.

The reality of legal safeguards

These practices are perhaps somewhat more extreme than in other counties, but they are not unusual, nor grossly exaggerated. The basic conflict is over legal due processes and the medical professions' desire to "protect the patient" and their clients—those seeking to commit the person. Moreover, the medical profession is not apt to seek a situation where conflicts in diagnosis occur, lest their general expertise to deal with the problem be questioned. And as we noted in Chapter 14 on crime, civil *and* criminal courts are heavily burdened, hence, the court has a need to expedite its caseload. Thus, there are a series of structural imperatives for "assuming insanity," once the label of mental illness is applied by members of the "normal" community. Such an assumption biases the commitment process in favor of society which, in accordance with dominant beliefs, "needs" to be protected against these "dangerous deviants."

Once committed, these biases are reinforced by the structure and operation of mental hospitals. The presumption of insanity remains and few efforts are made to help patients "get well."

PROBLEMS OF THE MENTAL HOSPITAL

In many ways mental hospitals are a response to contradictory pressures in the broader society: (1) the belief that society must be protected, (2) the belief that the "ill" must be treated, and (3) the desire to allocate as little money as possible to both tasks. The result is a system of underfinanced state and county mental hospitals which are charged with contradictory directives: cure the patient, protect society, and do not spend much money.

This situation has created a structure with several distinct roles: (1) the physicians in charge of administration and treatment, (2) the nurses in command of the daily implementation of drugs and other

Mental hospitals

The "recreation room" of a mental hospital of the 1890s. Note the crowding and the institutional character of the environment. How much of a "cure" can be achieved in such an environment?

medical prescriptions, and (3) the nonmedical staff—nurses aids and male attendants—in charge of implementing most of the day-to-day routine requirements of both the patients and medical staff. The nonmedical staff is by far the most numerous and they tend to be uneducated and poorly paid. There are few physicians and much of their time is spent monitoring records and performing other administrative tasks. Nurses tend to be intermediate in number and confine their duties to strictly "medical problems:" administering drugs, dealing with health problems, and reporting to doctors information from attendants. In this structure, there is an enormous cultural, educational, and prestige gap between the medical staff of doctors and nurses on the one hand and the nonmedical staff on the other. Communications is often difficult and brief, and yet, it is the nonmedical staff—the least trained—who have the most contact with and control over the patients, and who are thus in a position to assess "patient progress." The end result of this structural situation is for doctors to keep patients drugged and to have only brief contact with them. Nurses implement the drugging of patients, while attendants "deal with" outbursts and other problems of the ward.

In such a structure, little treatment can occur and patients can be said to be "getting better" when they repress symptoms and conform to the required daily routines of the hospital bureaucracy. Until a recent Supreme Court decision increased patient rights to petition to be released from hospitals, the fate of the patient was left to the discretion of doctors who have, on the whole, only the most cursory and indirect information on patients. Patients are often kept confined long after symptoms have been in remission. Moreover, the labeling of a patient as schizophrenic, for example, can become a self-fulfilling prophecy as doctors, nurses, and attendants interpret the patient's frustrations with incarceration as signs of schizophrenia rather than the normal emotions of anyone forced to stay where they do not wish to be.

Lack of treatment in mental hospitals

It is in this context that a study of what happened to "sane" people implanted, by a research psychologist, in a mental hospital is most illuminating (Rosenhan, 1973). In this study eight "normal" people were coached to seek admission to different mental hospitals with symptoms of hearing voices that were to say "empty," "hollow," and "thud." Beyond alleging these symptoms and falsifying names, vocations, and employment, no changes in their life histories were made. Immediately upon admission into the psychiatric ward, the pseudopatient ceased simulating *any* symptoms of abnormality. The patients talked freely, took notes of daily events, and were highly cooperative with the staff. Despite their normality, doctors, nurses, and attendants never detected it; patients were admitted, with only one

Being sane in insane places

The television and drugs passify the "ill" and constitute the major forms of "therapy" in mental hospitals.

exception, as schizophrenics and were later discharged with a diagnosis of schizophrenia "in remission." The only people to notice their "sanity" were other patients who said such things as, "you're not crazy. You're a journalist, or a professor. . . . You're checking up on the hospital."

There are several features of the experiences among these eight pseudopatients: (1) The label of schizophrenic was never revoked—thus assuring stigmatization for life. (2) Normality is never assumed in the hospital; the structure of the hospital is biased toward labeling a healthy person sick rather than a sick one healthy. Normal behavior can often be labeled abnormal, as was the case, for example, when a psychiatrist pointed to a group of patients sitting in front of the cafeteria one-half hour before lunch and noted the "oral-acquisitive" nature of their illnesses. (It apparently did not occur to the psychiatrist that there is little to look forward to in a psychiatric hospital besides eating.) (3) Staff and patients are highly segregated, with only minimal interaction. Those with the most expertise and power see the patients less than those with the least expertise and power. Moreover, many interactions between patients and doctors involved noncommunication, as was illustrated when a pseudopatient approached a doctor and asked "Pardon me, Dr. X. Could you tell me when I am eligible for grounds privileges?" The doctor replied, as he walked away, "Good morning, Dave. How are you today?" (4) Patients were often mistreated and abused, being beaten on occasion by attendants. Abusive language was commonly used to address patients. (5) Efforts were made to keep most patients highly sedated, and many would simply throw the pills into the toilet. (6) Patients were treated as "nonpersons" about whom the staff would talk as if they were not there.

The experiences of these normal people portray an environment which is highly custodial and hardly conducive to treatment and recovery. One of the interesting follow-up experiments to this study reveals another critical problem: How many people are misdiagnosed and forced to endure the environment of the mental hospital? The author of this study "informed" the staff that in the following three months, one or more pseudopatients would seek admission to their hospital. Of the 193 patients who were admitted, forty-one were defined as pseudopatients by at least one member of the staff. No pseudopatients were even sent, indicating that if labelers operated under the assumption of health, far fewer would be admitted to hospitals. Were these 41 sane? This can never be known, but it is clear that the expertise of medical experts is suspect and does not warrant the confidence or power that the public and courts accord them.

The inaccuracy of "expert" diagnoses

As the potential for mislabeling and the abusive effects of hospitals

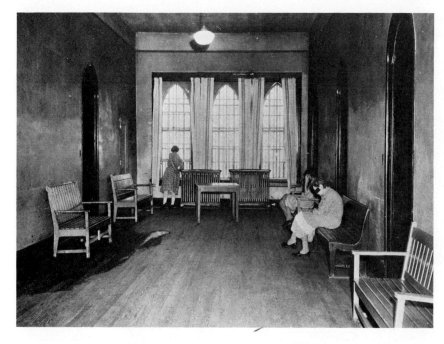

A sitting room of a mental "hospital." How much can people be helped in this kind of environment? The recognition of how little the "hospital" can do has stimulated efforts to keep people out of these hospitals.

on patient's mental health have become evident, efforts have been made to use a community, outpatient approach to mental illness (Table 16.2). Increasingly, community mental health clinics, crisis intervention centers, group therapies sponsored by church and community, sensitivity and human potential organizations, and a number of other efforts have been made to provide nonstigmatizing ways for people to seek solutions to their problems. Currently, these outpatient efforts are so diverse that they defy easy summary. What is clear, however, is that they pose a viable alternative to the abuses of inaccurate psychiatric labels and incarceration in hospitals.

THE REACTION TO MENTAL ILLNESS: CONTINUING DILEMMAS

With close to five million people seeking psychiatric help in a given year, and with untold numbers undoubtedly needing help, mental illness has become a big business. The government is committed in its funding policies to a medical definition of much deviance as illness; there are now thousands of professionals—psychoanalysts, psychiatrists, psychiatric social workers, clinical psychologists, to name but a few—whose careers and livelihood revolve around a

Mental illness is big business

Mental illness is now a "big business," creating economic interests that may go against the best interests of patients and society.

"mentally ill" population; and one-half of hospital admissions are now for mental illnesses, suggesting that many hospitals are financially dependent upon these "ill" patients.

Undoubtedly, many people need professional help. But what kind? And are current cultural beliefs and structural arrangements appropriate for dealing with the problem? It may be too late to ask such questions since the delivery of mental *health* services already revolves around an illness definition of the problem. Such a definition supports the interests of the medical profession, without any convincing evidence that most people with personal and social adjustment problems are sick or in need of medical treatment.

"Illnesses" support the health professions

These interests are legitimized by cultural beliefs which hold that many adjustment problems are "signs" of mental illness, that many of the mentally ill are dangerous, that they are never really cured, and that they must lose many civil liberties when being cared for by the medical professions. Only in the last decade have nonmedical, community outpatient services grown sufficiently to challenge these beliefs. Since the majority of psychiatric episodes are "treated" without incarceration, without great danger to the public, without suspension of people's civil liberties, and without stigmatizing labels, pressures for changes in beliefs and practices may be in their incipiency. Yet, these pressures must counter currently dominant beliefs as well as a psychiatric establishment committed to a medical model and "treatment" in mental hospitals. It is the dialectic between these two forces which ensures that the reaction to mental illness will continue to be one of America's enduring problems of culture and structure.

Pressures for a "nonillness" definition of adjustment problems

SUMMARY

In this chapter we sought to understand the reaction of American society to behaviors attributed to mental illness. This reaction is both a reflection and the cause of certain dominant beliefs. By all statistical evidence, mental illness is a problem affecting many millions of people, thus, the societal reaction means "big business" for the medical professions charged with resolving the problem.

As the data reveal, outpatient treatment of the "ill" has increased dramatically over the last decade. This shift in treatment away from confinement in mental hospitals is the result of the increasing use of drugs and the growing recognition that confinement to mental hospitals can be counterproductive.

Our analysis has concerned the problems of defining, diagnosing, and dealing with those who have behavioral adjustment problems in society. Whether these adjustment problems are an illness has yet to be determined. Presently, there appear relatively few safeguards to prevent hasty definitions of people as ill and in need of "treatment" in a mental "hospital." Aside from abusing people's civil rights, this lack of safeguards can expose individuals to the problems of the mental hospital which, as we have seen, are not well suited for treating and curing patients of their illnesses. One of the enduring problems of culture and structure in America will, therefore, be how to *define, protect, and help* those individuals who, for reasons that are still not totally understood, evidence *real and serious problems of behavioral adjustment*.

NOTES

1. For a comprehensive overview of mental health statistics, see Department of Health, Education, and Welfare, National Institute of Mental Health, Statistical Notes 80–100, Washington, D.C.: Government Printing, 1973; in particular, see "Statistical Note 92." For basic references on mental illness, see Gusman, 1970; Scheff, 1967, 1975; Clausen, 1972; Weinberg, 1967; Plog and Edgerton, 1969; Szasz, 1970; and Foucault, 1965.

2. For interesting accounts of the mental illness movement, see Szasz, 1960, 1970; Foucault, 1965; and Rosen, 1969.

REVIEW QUESTIONS

1. Why is the definition of mental illness somewhat arbitrary?
2. What would be the different consequences of defining a behavior as an "illness" as opposed to defining this same behavior as "an interpersonal adjustment problem"?
3. How do cultural beliefs influence the way American society deals with behavior adjustment problems?
4. What trends are evident in the societal reaction to those with adjustment problems? What prospects and problems are evident in these trends?
5. Discuss critically the question: Is there such a thing as mental illness?

GLOSSARY

insanity the lack of ability to distinguish right from wrong in committing an illegal act

mental illness behavior maladjustments defined by the medical profession charged with determining the existence of illness

mental retardation the definition and diagnosis of an individual by "experts" as having subnormal intellectual functioning

neurosis behavioral problems defined by experts as involving high levels of anxiety not related to organic causes, but which are not characterized as involving gross distortions of reality

organic brain syndromes cell damage to the brain that causes problematic behaviors for an individual

personality disorder a residual category used to label those behavioral adjustment problems that do not fall into other mental disorder categories

psychosis serious behavioral adjustment problems which involve gross distortions of reality; assumed by "experts" to be unrelated to impaired brain functioning

schizophrenia a type of psychosis involving a loss of conventional thought, the withdrawal from ordinary interaction, and the maintenance of unconventional conceptions of reality

BIBLIOGRAPHY

Abelson, P. H. "Methyl Mercury." *Science*, July 17, 1970.

Abrams, C. "Housing Policy—1937–1967. In B. J. Frieden and W. W. Nash, eds., *Shaping An Urban Future: Essays in Honor of Catherine Bauer Eurster*. Cambridge, Mass.: MIT Press, 1969.

———. *The City Is the Frontier*. New York: Harper & Row, Colophon Books, 1967.

———. "The Housing Problem and the Negro." In T. Parsons and K. Clark, eds., *The Negro American*. Boston: Houghton Mifflin, 1966.

Albini, J. L. *The America Mafia: Genesis of a Legend*. New York: Appleton, 1971.

Allen, F. *The Borderline of Criminal Justice*. Chicago: University of Chicago Press, 1964.

Allen, R. F., and Adair, C. H. *Violence and Riots in Urban America*. Worthington, Ohio: Charles A. Jones Publishing Co., 1969.

American Psychiatric Association. *Diagnostic and Statistical Manual of Mental Disorders*. 2d ed. Washington, D.C.: American Psychiatric Association, 1968.

Anderson, M. *The Federal Bulldozer*. New York: McGraw-Hill, 1964.

Appleman, P. *The Silent Explosion*. Boston: Beacon Press, 1965.

Banfield, E. C. *The Unheavenly City: The Nature and Future of Our Urban Crisis*. Boston: Little, Brown, 1970.

Banton, M. *The Policeman in the Community*. New York: Basic Books, 1964.

Bardwick, J. M. *Psychology of Women: A Study of Biocultural Conflicts*. New York: Harper & Row, 1971.

Batchelder, A. B. "Decline in Relative Income of Negro Men." *Quarterly Journal of Economics*, November 1964.

Battan, L. J. *The Unclean Sky: A Meteorologist Looks at Air Pollution*. New York: Doubleday, 1966.

Beegle, A. *Rural Social Systems*. Englewood Cliffs: Prentice-Hall, 1950.

Bell, G. R. *Escape from Addiction*. New York: McGraw-Hill, 1970.

Berelson, B. "Beyond Family Planning." *Science*, February 7, 1969.

Bevan, W.; Albert, R. S.; Loigeaux, R. R.; Mayfield, P. N.; and Wright, G. "Jury Behavior as a Function of the Prestige of the Foreman and the Nature of His Leadership." *Journal of Public Law*, Fall 1958.

Biderman, A. D. "Surveys of Population Samples for Estimating Crime." *Annals of the Academy of Political and Social Science* 84, November 1967.

Bird, C. *Born Female: The High Cost of Keeping Women Down.* Rev. ed. Pocket Books, 1971 (orig. published by David McKay, 1968).

Bittner, E. "The Police on Skid Row: A Study of Peace Keeping." *American Sociological Review*, October 1967.

Blake, N. M. *Water for the Cities.* Syracuse: Syracuse University Press, 1956.

Blankenship, W. C. "Head Librarians: How Many Men? How Many Women?" In Athena Theodore, ed., *The Professional Woman.* Cambridge, Mass.: Schenkman, 1971.

Blassingame, J. W. *The Slave Community: Plantation Life in the Ante-Bellum South.* New York: Oxford University Press, 1972.

Blau, F. D. "Women in the Labor Force: An Overview." In Jo Freeman, ed., *Women: A Feminist Perspective.* Palo Alto: Mayfield, 1975.

Blau, S. D., and Rodenbeck, J., eds. *The House We Live In: An Environmental Reader.* New York: Macmillan, 1971.

Blauner, R. *Racial Oppression in America.* New York: Harper & Row, 1972.

———. "The Dilemmas of The Black Urban Revolt." *Journal of Housing*, December 1967.

Blumberg, A. S. *Criminal Justice.* Chicago: Quadrangle Books, 1970.

Bordua, D. J., ed. *The Police.* New York: Wiley, 1967.

Boskoff, A. *The Sociology of Urban Regions.* 2d ed. New York: Appleton, 1970.

Boulding, K. E. "No Second Chance for Man." In *The Crisis of Survival*, edited by the editors of *The Progressive.* Glenview, Ill.: Scott, Foresman, 1970.

———. "The Economics of the Coming Spaceship Earth." In H. Jarret, ed., *Environmental Quality in a Growing Economy.* Baltimore: Johns Hopkins University Press, 1966.

Brinton, C. *The Anatomy of Revolution.* New York: Random House, Vintage Books, 1965.

Brophy, W. A., and Aberle, S. D. *Indian: America's Unfinished Business.* Norman: University of Oklahoma Press, 1966.

Bullock, H. A. "Significance of the Racial Factor in the Length of Prison Sentences." *Journal of Criminal Law, Criminology, and Police Science*, November–December 1961.

Bullock, P. "Employment Problems of the Mexican American." *Industrial Relations*, December 1964.

Burch, W. R. *Day Dreams and Nightmares–A Sociological Essay on the American Environment.* New York: Harper & Row, 1971.

Burch, W. R.; Cheek, N. H., Jr.; and Taylor, L. *Social Behavior, Natural Resources, and the Environment.* New York: Harper & Row, 1972.

Bureau of Census. *Current Population Reports*, no. 244. December, Washington, D.C.: Government Printing Office, 1972.

Burma, J. T., Ed. *Mexican Americans in The United States.* San Francisco: Canfield Press, 1970.

Campbell, A. "The Role of Family Planning in the Reduction of Poverty." *Journal of Marriage and the Family*, December 1968.

Campbell, A. K. *The States and Urban Crisis.* Englewood Cliffs: Prentice-Hall, 1970.

Campbell, R. R., and Wade, J. L., eds. *Society and Environment: The Coming Collision.* Boston: Allyn & Bacon, 1972.

Caplovitz, D. *The Poor Pay More.* New York: Free Press, 1963.

Carr, D. N. *Death of the Sweet Waters.* New York: Norton, 1966.

———. *The Breath of Life.* New York: Norton, 1965.

Carson, R. L. *The Silent Spring.* Boston: Houghton Mifflin, 1962.

———. *The Sea Around Us.* New York: Signet Library, 1954.

Carter, H., and Glick, P. C. *Marriage and Divorce: A Social and Economic Study.* Vital and Health Statistics Monographs, American Public Health Association Series, 1970.

Carter, R. M., and Wilkins, L. T. "Some Factors in Sentencing Policy." *Journal of Criminal Law, Criminology, and Police Science*, December 1967.

Cavan, R. S. *The American Family.* New York: Crowell, 1969.

Census Bureau. "Marital Status and Living

Arrangements: March 1974." *Current Population Reports*, no. 271. Washington, D.C.: U.S. Government Printing Office, October 1974.

Chafetz, J. S. *Masculine/Feminine or Human?* Itasca, Ill.: Peacock, 1974.

Chevigny, P. *Police Power*. New York: Pantheon Books, 1969.

Cicourel, A. V., and Kitsuse, J. I. *The Educational Decision-Makers*. Indianapolis: Bobbs-Merrill, 1963.

Clark, K. B. *Dark Ghetto: Dilemmas of Social Power*. New York: Harper & Row, 1965.

Clausen, J. A. "The Sociology of Mental Disorders." In H. Freeman, S. Levine, and L. G. Reeder, eds., *Handbook of Medical Sociology*. Englewood Cliffs: Prentice-Hall, 1972.

Clinard, M., and Quinney, R. *Criminal Behavior Systems*. New York: Holt, Rinehart & Winston, 1967.

Cloward, R. A., and Elman, R. M. "Poverty, Injustice, and the Welfare State." *The Nation*, February 1966.

Coffman, R. "Are Fertilizers Polluting Our Water Supply?" *Farm Journal*, May 1969.

Coleman, J. S. et al. *Equality of Educational Opportunity*. Washington, D.C.: Government Printing Office, 1966.

Commerce, Department of, U.S. *Social and Economic Conditions of Negroes in the United States*. Wash., D.C.: GPO, 1967.

Commoner, B. *Science and Survival*. New York: Viking Press, 1966.

Coombs, M.; Kron, R. E.; Collister, G.; and Anderson, K. E. *The Indian Child Goes To School*. Lawrence, Kans.: Haskell Press, 1958.

Cressey, D. R. *Criminal Organizations: Its Elementary Forms*. New York: Harper & Row, 1972.

———. *Theft of a Nation: The Operations of Organized Crime in America*. New York: Harper & Row, 1969.

Cumming, E.; Cumming, I.; and Edell, L. "Policeman as Philosopher, Guide, and Friend." *Social Problems*, Winter 1965.

Daly, H. E., ed. *Toward Steady-State Economy*. San Francisco: Freeman, 1973.

Daly, R. *The World Beneath the City*. New York: Lippincott, 1959.

Daniels, R., and Kitano, H. H. L. *American Racism: Explorations of the Nature of Prejudice*. Englewood Cliffs: Prentice-Hall, 1970.

Davies, J. C. "Toward A Theory of Revolution." *American Sociological Review*, November 1962.

Davis, A. *Social Class Influence Upon Learning*. Cambridge, Mass.: Harvard University Press, 1952.

Davis, J. P., ed. *The American Negro Reference Book*. Englewood Cliffs: Prentice-Hall, 1966.

Davis, K. "The American Family in Relation to Demographic Change." In C. F. Westoff and R. Parke, eds., *Demographic and Social Aspects of Population Growth*. Washington, D.C.: Government Printing Office, 1972.

———. "Population Policy: Will Current Programs Succeed?" *Science*, November 10, 1967.

Davis, W. H. "Overpopulated America." *The New Republic*, January 10, 1970.

Day, A. T. "Population Control and Personal Freedom: Are They Compatible?" *The Humanist*, November–December 1968.

Deckard, B. *The Women's Movement: Political, Socioeconomic, and Psychological Issues*. New York: Harper & Row, 1975.

de la Garza, R.; Kruszewski, Z. A.; and Arciniega, T. A. *Chicanos and Native Americans: The Territorial Minorities*. Englewood Cliffs: Prentice-Hall, 1973.

Dennison, G. *The Lives of Children*. New York: Random House, 1969.

Dentler, R. A. "For Local Control in the Schools." *Atlantic Monthly*, January 1968.

———. *Major American Social Problems*. Chicago: Rand McNally, 1967.

Detwyler, R., ed. *Man's Impact on Environment*. New York: Knopf, 1962.

deVilleneuve, R., ed. *The Enemy Is Us: A Rational Look at the Environmental Problem*. Minneapolis: Winston Press, 1973.

Dobb, M. *Studies in the Development of Capitalism*. London: Routledge, 1946.

Donlon, D. "The Negative Image of Women in Children's Literature." *Elementary English*, April 1972.

Duncan, O. D., and Schnore, A. "The Ecosystem." In C. A. Faris, ed., *Handbook of Sociology*. Chicago: Rand McNally, 1964.

Dynes, R., and Quarantelli, E. L. "What Looting in Civil Disturbances Really Means." *Trans-action*, May 1968.

Dynes, R. R.; Clark, A. C.; Dinitz, S.; and Ishino, I. *Social Problems: Dissensus and Deviation in an Industrial Society*. New York: Oxford University Press, 1964.

Eckert, R. E., and Stecklein, J. E. "Academic Women." In A. Theodore, ed., *The Professional Woman*. Cambridge: Schenkman, 1971.

Ehrlich, P. R. *The Population Bomb*. Rev. ed. New York: Ballantine, 1971.

––––––. "Eco-Catastrophe." *Ramparts*, September 1970.

Ehrlich, P. R., and Ehrlich, A. H. *Population, Resources, Environment: Issues in Human Ecology*. San Francisco: Freeman, 1970.

Ehrlich, P. R.; Holdren, J. P.; and Holm, R. W. *Man and the Ecosphere*. San Francisco: Freeman, 1971.

Elman, R. *The Poorhouse State*. New York: Random House, 1966.

Epstein, C. F. Fuchs. *Woman's Place: Options and Limits in Professional Careers*. Berkeley: University of California Press, 1971.

Erickson, K. *Wayward Puritans: A Study in the Sociology of Deviance*. New York: Wiley, 1966.

Esposito, J. C. *Vanishing Air: The Ralph Nader Study Group Report on Air Pollution*. New York: Grossman, 1970.

Esselstyn, T. C. "The Social Role of a County Sheriff." *Journal of Criminal Law, Criminology, and Police Science*, July–August 1953.

Falk, R. A. *This Endangered Planet: Prospects and Proposals for Human Survival*. New York: Random House, 1971.

Farley, R., and Taeuber, K. E. "Population Trends and Residential Segregation Since 1960." *Science*, March 1968.

Feagin, J. R., "We Still Believe that God Helps Those Who Help Themselves." *Psychology Today*, November 1972a.

––––––. "America's Welfare Stereotypes." *Social Science Quarterly*, March 1972b.

Feldstein, S. *The Poisoned Tongue: A Documentary History of American Racism and Prejudice*. New York: Morrow, 1972.

––––––. *Once A Slave: The Slaves View of Slavery*. New York: Morrow, 1971.

––––––. "Who Protests: The Social Bases of

Fernbach, F. L. "Policies Affecting Income Distribution." In M. S. Gordon, ed., *Poverty in America*. San Francisco: Chandler, 1965.

Flacks, R. "Social and Cultural Meanings of Student Revolt: Some Informal Comparative Observations." *Social Problems*, Winter 1970a.

––––––. "Who Protests: The Social Bases of the Student Movement." In J. Foster and D. Long, eds., *Protest! Student Activism in America*. New York: Morrow, 1970b.

––––––. "The Liberated Generation: An Exploration of the Roots of Student Protest." *Journal of Social Issues*, July 1967.

Fogel, R., and Engerman, S. *Time on the Cross*. Boston: Little, Brown, 1974.

Foucault, M. *Madness and Civilization*. New York: Mentor Books, 1965.

Franklin, J. H. *Reconstruction After the Civil War*. Chicago: University of Chicago Press, 1961.

––––––. *From Slavery to Freedom*. New York: Knopf, 1948.

Freeman, A. M. "Cleaning Up Foul Waters. I—Pollution Tax." *The New Republic*, June 20, 1970.

Freeman, H. E., and Jones, W. C. *Social Problems: Causes and Controls*. Chicago: Rand McNally, 1970.

Friedenberg, E. Z. "Status and Role in Education." *The Humanist*, September–October 1968.

––––––. *Coming of Age in America: Growth and Acquiescence*. New York: Random House, Vintage Books, 1963.

Gans, H. J. "Culture and Class in the Study of Poverty: An Approach to Anti-Poverty Research." In D. P. Moynihan, ed., *Understanding Poverty*. New York: Basic Books, 1969.

––––––. "Some Proposals for Government Policy in an Automating Society." *The Correspondent*, January–February 1964.

General Advisory Council for Education (England). *Children and Their Primary School.* London: Her Majesty's Stationery Office, 1967.

General Revenue Sharing. Washington, D.C.: U.S. Government Printing Office, September 24, 1973.

Genovese, E. D. *The Political Economy of Slavery.* New York: Vintage Books, 1965.

Gerver, I. "The Social Psychology of Witness Behavior with Special Reference to Criminal Courts." *Journal of Social Issues,* November 2, 1957.

Glasurd, B. A., and Smith, A. M., eds. *Promises to Keep: A Portrayal of Non-whites in the United States.* Chicago: Rand McNally, 1972.

Glazer, N. "Housing Problems and Housing Policies." *The Public Interest,* Spring, 1967.

Glazer, N., and Moynihan, D. P., eds. *Ethnicity: Theory and Experience.* Cambridge: Harvard University Press, 1975.

Goldberg, M. "Schools in Depressed Areas." In A. H. Passow, ed., *Education in Depressed Areas.* New York: Teachers College Press, Columbia University, 1963.

Goldfarb, R. *Ransom: A Critique of the American Bail System.* New York: Harper & Row, 1965.

Goldman, M. I. *Ecology and Economics: Controlling Pollution in the 70's.* Englewood Cliffs: Prentice-Hall, 1972.

———. "From Lake Erie to Lake Baikal—From Los Angeles to Tbilisi: The Convergence of Environmental Disruption." *Science.* October 2, 1970.

Goldman, M. I., ed. *Controlling Pollution.* Englewood Cliffs: Prentice-Hall, 1967.

Goldman, P., and Holt, D. "How Justice Works: The People vs. Donald Payne." *Newsweek,* March 8, 1971.

Goldsmith, J. R. "Los Angeles Smog." *Science Journal,* March 1969.

Goldsmith, S. F. "Changes in the Size Distribution of Income." In E. C. Budd, ed., *Inequity and Poverty.* New York: Norton, 1967.

Goode, W. J. *World Revolution and Family Patterns.* New York: Free Press, 1963.

Goodlad, J. I. "The Schools vs. Education." *Saturday Review,* April 19, 1969.

Goodman, P. "The Present Moment in Education." *New York Review of Books,* April 10, 1969.

Gordon, M. *Sick Cities.* Baltimore: Penguin Books, 1963.

Graham, F., Jr. "The Infernal Smog Machine." *Audubon,* September–October 1968.

———. *Disaster by Default: Politics and Water Pollution.* New York: Evans, 1966.

Grebler, L. *The Schooling Gap: Signs of Progress, Advanced Report 7.* Los Angeles: University of California Press, Mexican American Study Project, 1967.

———. "The Naturalization of Mexican Immigrants in the United States." *International Migration Review,* Fall 1966.

Grebler, L.; Moore, J. W.; and Guzman, R. *The Mexican American People.* New York: Free Press, 1970.

Greeley, A. M. *Why Can't They Be Like Us? America's White Ethnic Groups.* New York: Dutton, 1975.

———. *Ethnicity in the United States: A Preliminary Reconnaissance.* New York: Wiley, 1974.

Green, C. M. *The Rise of Urban America.* New York: Harper & Row, 1965.

Greer, S. *Urban Renewal and American Cities: The Dilemma of Democratic Intervention.* Indianapolis: Bobbs-Merrill, 1966.

Grier, E., and Grier, G. "Equality and Beyond: Housing and Segregation in the Great Society." *Daedalus,* Winter 1966.

Griffin, C. W., Jr. "America's Airborne Garbage." *Saturday Review,* May 22, 1965.

Grigsby, W. *Housing Markets and Public Policy.* Philadelphia: University of Pennsylvania Press, 1964.

Gusman, J. et al., eds. *Bibliography on Epistemology of Mental Disorders.* National Institute for Mental Health, Chevy Chase, Md.: National Clearinghouse for Mental Health Information, 1970.

Halleck, S. L. "A Critique of Current Psychiatric Roles in the Legal Process." *Wisconsin Law Review,* Spring 1966.

Hamilton, C. V. In C. V. Daley, ed., *Urban Violence.* Chicago: Center for Policy Study, 1969.

Hamilton, H. C. "The Negro Leaves the South." *Demography*, Winter 1964.

Hardin, G. "Parenthood: Right or Privilege?" *Science*, July 30, 1970.

———. "The Tragedy of the Commons." *Science*, February 16, 1968.

Hardin, G., ed. *Population, Evolution, and Birth Control*. San Francisco: Freeman, 1969.

Harr, C. *Federal Credit and Private Housing: The Mass Financing Dilemma*. New York: McGraw-Hill, 1960.

Harrington, M. "Eradicating Poverty." *Playboy*, January 1971.

———. "Introduction." In L. A. Ferman et al., eds., *Poverty in America*. Ann Arbor: University of Michigan Press, 1968.

———. *The Other America in the United States*. New York: Macmillan, 1963.

Havighurst, R. J., and Neugarten, B. L. *Society and Education*. Boston: Allyn & Bacon, 1967.

Health, Education, and Welfare, Department of, U.S. *Education Directory: Higher Education*. Washington, D.C., GPO, 1972.

———. "First Special Report to the U.S. Congress on Alcohol and Health." DHEW #72–9099. Washington, D.C.: Government Printing Office, 1971.

———. "First Special Report to U.S. Congress on Alcohol and Health." Washington, D.C.: GPO, 1971.

Helfrich, H. W., ed. *The Environmental Crisis—Man's Struggle to Live with Himself*. New Haven: Yale University Press, 1970.

Heller, C. S., ed. *Structured Social Inequality*. New York: Macmillan, 1969.

———. *Mexican American Youth: Forgotten at the Crossroads*. New York: Random House, 1966.

Hetzel, A. M., and Cappetta, M. "Teenagers: Marriages, Divorces, Parenthood, and Mortality." *Vital and Health Statistics*, series 21, No. 23, Washington, D.C.: National Center for Health Statistics, 1973.

Hill, G. "A Not So Silent Spring." In *The Crisis of Survival*, edited by the editors of *The Progressive*. Glenview, Ill.: Scott, Foresman, 1970.

Hirsch, W. *Scientists in American Society*. New York: Random House, 1968.

Hodge, R. W.; Treiman, D. J.; and Rossi, P. "A Comparative Study of Occupational Prestige." In R. Bendix and S. M. Lipset, eds., *Class, Status, and Power*. New York: Free Press, 1966.

Hodges, H. M. *Social Stratification: Class in America*. Cambridge, Mass.: Schenkman, 1964.

Hoffman, L. W. "Effects on Children: Summary and Discussion." In I. Nyc and L. W. Hoffman, *The Employed Woman in America*. Chicago: Rand McNally, 1963.

Hofstadter, R. "Spontaneous, Sporadic, and Disorganized." New York *Times* Magazine, April 28, 1968.

Holmstrom. L. L. *The Two-Career Family*. Cambridge, Mass.: Schenkman, 1972.

Horowitz, I. L. "Separate But Equal: Revolution and Counterrevolution in the American City." *Social Problems*, Winter 1970.

Horowitz, I. L., and Friedland, W. *The Knowledge Factory: Student Power and Academic Politics in America*. Chicago: Aldine, 1970.

Howard, W. E. "Jet Smoke: Conquest by Camouflage." In *The Crisis of Survival*, edited by the editors of *The Progressive*. Glenview, Ill.: Scott, Foresman, 1970.

Howe, F. "Sexual Stereotypes Start Early." *Saturday Review*, October 16, 1971.

Hunter, D. *The Slums: Challenge and Response*. New York: Free Press, 1965.

Ianni, F. A. J. "New Mafia: Black, Hispanic and Italian Styles." *Society*, March 1974.

———. *A Family Business: Kinship and Social Control in Organized Crime*. New York: Russell Sage, 1972.

Iltis, H. H. "The Optimum Human Environment." In *The Crisis of Survival*, edited by the editors of *The Progressive*. Glenview, Ill.: Scott, Foresman, 1970.

Inkeles, A., and Rossi, P. "National Comparisons of Occupational Prestige." *American Journal of Sociology*, January 1956.

Jacobs, J. *The Death and Life of Great American Cities*. New York: Random House, 1961.

Jacobs, P. "Keeping the Poor Poor." In J. Skolnick and E. Currie, eds., *Crisis in American Institutions.* Boston: Little, Brown, 1970.

Jacobs, W. R. *Dispossessing the American Indian.* New York: Scribners, 1972.

Janeway, E. *Man's World, Woman's Place.* New York: Delta, 1971.

Jencks, C. *Inequality: A Reassessment of the Effects of Family and Schooling in America.* New York: Basic Books, 1972.

———. "A Reappraisal of the Most Controversial Educational Document of Our Time." New York *Times* Magazine, August 10, 1969.

Johnson, C. S. *Growing Up in the Black Belt.* Washington, D.C.: American Council on Education, 1941.

Kadish, S. "The Crisis of Overcriminalization." *The Annals,* November 1967.

Kantrowitz, N. *Ethnic and Racial Segregation in the New York Metropolis: Residential Patterns Among White Ethnic Groups, Blacks, and Puerto Ricans.* New York: Praeger, 1973.

Karlen, H. M. *The Pattern of American Government.* Beverly Hills, Calif.: Glencoe Press, 1968.

Katz, M. "Legal Dimensions of Population Policy." *Social Science Quarterly,* December 1969.

Kauffman, R. "The Military Industrial Complex." New York *Times* Magazine, April 14, 1969.

Keniston, K. "The Fire Outside." *The Journal,* September–October 1970.

———. "Notes on Young Radicals." *Change,* November–December 1969a.

———. "You Have to Grow Up in Scarsdale to Know How Bad Things Really Are." New York *Times* Magazine, April 27, 1969b.

———. *Young Radicals.* New York: Harcourt Brace Jovanovich, 1968.

Kerner, O. et al. Kerner Commission Report. *See Report of the National Advisory Commission on Civil Disorders.*

Keuhn, L. L. *Organized Crime in America.* Unpublished manuscript. Olympia, Washington: The Evergreen State College, 1975.

Kidd, C. U. *Universities and Federal Research.* Cambridge, Mass.: Harvard University Press, 1959.

King, M. L., Jr. "Beyond the Los Angeles Riots: Next Stop: The North." *Saturday Review,* November 13, 1965.

Kitagawa, D. "The American Indian." In A. M. Rose and C. B. Rose, eds., *Minority Problems.* New York: Harper & Row, 1965.

Knowles, L. L., and Prewitt, K. *Institutional Racism in America.* Englewood Cliffs: Prentice-Hall, 1969.

Koat, R. "Some Implications of the Economic Impact of Disarmament on the Structure of American Industry." In Joint Economic Committee, *Economic Effect of Vietnam Spending.* Washington, D.C.: Government Printing Office, 1967.

Kolko, G. *Wealth and Power in America.* New York: Praeger, 1962.

Kormondy, E. J. *Concepts of Ecology.* Englewood Cliffs: Prentice-Hall, 1969.

Kosa, J., and Coker, R. E., Jr. "The Female Physician in Public Health: Conflict and Reconciliation of Sex and Professional Roles." *Sociology and Social Research* 49 (Winter), 1975.

Kotz, N. *Let Them Eat Promises: The Politics of Hunger in America.* Garden City, New York: Anchor Press, 1971.

Kozol, J. *Death at an Early Age.* New York: Houghton Mifflin, 1967.

Kramer, J. R. *The American Minority Community.* New York: Crowell, 1970.

Kristol, I. "Taxes, Poverty and Equality." *Public Interest,* September 1974.

Kunter, L. "The Illusion of Due Process in Commitment Proceedings." In T. J. Scheff, ed., *Mental Illness and Social Processes.* New York: Harper & Row, 1967.

Kuntz, R. F. "An Environmental Glossary." *Saturday Review,* January 2, 1971.

Kvistol, I. "The Lower Fifth." *New Leader,* February 17, 1964.

Lafave, W. R. *Arrest: The Decision to Take a Suspect into Custody.* Boston: Little, Brown, 1964.

Labor, Department of, U.S. *Manpower Report to the President.* Wash., D.C.: GPO, 1969.

Lampman, R. "Changes in the Share of Wealth Held by Top Wealth Holders." *Review of*

Economics and Statistics, November 1969.

———. "Changes in the Concentration of Wealth." In E. C. Budd, ed., *Inequity and Poverty*. New York: Norton, 1967.

———. "Income Distribution and Poverty." In M. S. Gordon, ed., *Poverty in America*. San Francisco: Chandler, 1965.

Landau, N. J., and Rheingold, P. D. *The Environmental Law Handbook*. New York: Friends of the Earth/Ballantine, 1971.

Landis, J. "The Trauma of Children When Parents Divorce." *Marriage and Family Living*, February 1960.

Lapp, R. E. *The Weapons Culture*. New York: Norton, 1968.

———. *Kill and Overkill*. New York: Basic Books, 1962.

Lenski, G. *Power and Privilege: A Theory of Social Stratification*. New York: McGraw-Hill, 1966.

Levitan, S. A. *The Design of Federal Antipoverty Strategy*. Ann Arbor: University of Michigan Press, 1967.

Levitan, S. A., and Hetrick, B. *Big Brothers and Indian Programs–With Reservations*. New York: McGraw-Hill, 1971.

Levy, B. "Do Teachers Sell Girls Short?" *NEA Journal*, December 1972.

Lewis, O. *The Study of Slum Culture–Backgrounds for La Vida*. New York: Random House, 1968.

Liberson, S. "An Empirical Study of Military-Industrial Linkages." *The American Journal of Sociology*, November 1971.

Lindesmith, A. R. "Dope Fiend Mythology." *Journal of Criminal Law, Criminology, and Police Science*, Winter 1940.

Linton, R. M. *Terracide: America's Destruction of Her Living Environment*. Boston: Little, Brown, 1970.

Lipset, S. M. "Youth and Politics." In R. K. Merton and R. Nisbet, eds., *Contemporary Social Problems*. 3d ed. New York: Harcourt Brace Jovanovich, 1971.

Lipset, S. M., and Raab, E. "The Non-Generation Gap." *Commentary*, August 1970.

Lohman, J. D. et al. *The Police and the Community*. Berkeley, Cal.: President's Commission on Law Enforcement and Administration of Justice, Field Survey No. 4, 1966.

Luce, C. F. "Energy: Economics of the Environment." In W. Helfrich, Jr., ed., *Agenda for Survival*. New Haven, Conn.: Yale University Press, 1970.

Maccoby, M. "Government, Scientists, and the Priorities of Science." *Dissent*, Winter, 1964.

McClane, A. J. "The Ultimate Open Sewer." *Field and Stream*, May 1968.

McClelland, D. C. *The Achieving Society*. New York: Free Press, 1961.

MacDonald, D. "Our Invisible Poor." In L. A. Ferman et al., eds., *Poverty in America*. Ann Arbor: University of Michigan Press, 1968.

McGrath, G. G.; Roessel, R.; Meador, B.; Helmstadter, G. C.; and Barnes, J. *Higher Education of Southwestern Indians with Reference to Success and Failure*. Tempe, Ariz.: Cooperative Research Project No. 939, University of Arizona Press, 1962.

McKinley, P. "Compulsory Eugenic Sterilization: For Whom Does the Bell Toll?" *Duquesne University Law Review*. February 1967.

McNamara, J. H. "Uncertainties in Police Work: The Relevance of Police Recruits' Background and Training." In D. J. Bordua, ed., *The Police: Six Sociological Essays*. New York: Wiley, 1967.

McWilliams, C. *North from Mexico*. Philadelphia: Lippincott, 1949.

Madsen, W. *Mexican Americans of South Texas*. New York: Holt, Rinehart & Winston, 1964.

Mankoff, M., and Majka, L. "Economic Sources of American Militarism." *Society*, May–June 1975.

Marquis, R. W. *Environmental Improvement: Air, Water and Soil*. Washington, D.C.: Graduate School Press, 1966.

Marx, K., and Engels, F. *Manifesto of the Communist Party*. New York: Appleton, 1955.

Mauss, A. *Social Problems as Social Movements*. Philadelphia: Lippincott, 1975.

Mayer, K. W., and Buckley, W. *Class and Society*. 3d ed. New York: Random House, 1970.

Mellanby, K. *Pesticides and Pollution*. New York: Collins, 1967.

Melman, S. *Pentagon Capitalism: The Political*

Economy of War. New York: McGraw-Hill, 1970.

Miles, R. E. "Whose Baby is the Population Bomb." *Population Bulletin*, February, 1970.

Miller, H. P. "Is the Income Gap Closed? No." In L. A Ferman et al., eds., *Poverty in America*. Ann Arbor: University of Michigan Press, 1968.

———. "Changes in the Number and Composition of the Poor." In M. S. Gordon, ed., *Poverty in America*. San Francisco: Chandler, 1965.

———. *Rich Man, Poor Man*. New York: Crowell, 1964.

Miller, S. M., and Roby, P. "Poverty: Changing Social Stratification." In D. P. Moynihan, ed., *On Understanding Poverty*. New York: Basic Books, 1969.

Miller, W. "The Elimination of the American Lower Class as a National Policy: A Critique of the Ideology of the Poverty Movement in the 1960s." In D. P. Moynihan, ed., *On Understanding Poverty*. New York: Basic Books, 1969.

———. "Focal Concerns of Lower Class Culture." In L. A. Ferman et al., eds., *Poverty in America*. Ann Arbor: University of Michigan Press, 1968.

———. "Lower Class Culture as a Generating Milieu of Gang Delinquency." *Journal of Social Issues*, 14 (March), 1958.

Mix. S. A. "Solid Wastes: Every Day, Another 800 Million Pounds." *Today's Health*, March 1966.

Moncrief, L. W. "The Cultural Basis for Our Environmental Crisis." *Science*, October 30, 1970.

Moore, J. W., with A. Cuéllar. *Mexican Americans*. Englewood Cliffs: Prentice-Hall, 1970.

Morris, R. E. "Witness Performance Under Stress: A Sociological Approach." *Journal of Social Issues*, November 1957.

Moynihan, D. P., ed. *On Understanding Poverty*. New York: Basic Books, 1969.

———. "Employment, Income, and the Ordeal of the Negro Family." *Daedalus*, Fall 1965.

Murphy, E. F. *Governing Nature*. Chicago: Quadrangle Books, 1967.

Nader, R. "Corporations and Pollution." In *The Crisis of Survival*, edited by the editors of *The Progressive*. Glenview, Ill.: Scott, Foresman, 1970.

Nagel, S. S. "Judicial Backgrounds and Criminal Cases." *Journal of Criminal Law, Criminology, and Police Science*, September 1962.

National Commission on Marijuana and Drug Abuse Report. Washington, D.C.: Government Printing Office, 1973.

National Welfare Rights Organization. *NWRO Proposals for a Guaranteed Adequate Income*. Washington, D.C.: NOW, 1969.

Neill, A. S. *Summerhill*. New York: Hart Publishing Co., 1960.

New Jersey Graduated Work Incentive Experiment. Washington, D.C.: Office of Economic Opportunity, 1971.

Newman, D. J. *Conviction: The Determination of Guilt or Innocence Without Trial*. Boston: Little, Brown, 1966.

———. "White Collar Crime." *Law and Contemporary Problems*, Autumn 1958.

———. "Pleading Guilty for Considerations: A Study of Bargain Justice." *Journal of Criminal Law, Criminology, and Police Science*, March–April 1956.

Newman, W. M. *American Pluralism, A Study of Minority Groups and Social Theory*. New York: Harper & Row, 1973.

Newsweek. "Justice on Trial." March 8, 1971.

Niederhoffer, A. *Behind the Shield: The Police in Urban Society*. Garden City, New York: Doubleday, 1968.

Nisbet, R. A. *The Quest for Community*. New York: Oxford University Press, 1953.

Novak, Michael. *The Rise of the Unmeltable Ethnics*. New York: Macmillan, 1972.

Nunnally, J. C., Jr. *Popular Conceptions of Mental Health*. New York: Holt, Rinehart & Winston, 1961.

Oakley, A. *Sex, Gender, and Society*. New York: Harper & Row, 1972.

Odum, E. "The Strategy of Ecosystem Development." *Science*, April 18, 1969.

———. *Fundamentals of Ecology*. 2d ed. Philadelphia: Saunders, 1959.

Office of Economic Opportunity. *Further Preliminary Results of the New Jersey Graduated*

Work Incentive Experiment. Washington, D.C.: OEO, 1971.

Orlans, H. *The Effects of Federal Programs on Higher Education.* Washington, D.C.: The Brookings Institution, 1962.

Ornati, O. "Poverty in America." In L. A. Ferman et al., eds., *Poverty in America.* Ann Arbor: University of Michigan Press, 1968.

_____. "Affluence and the Risk of Poverty." *Social Research*, Autumn 1964.

Orshansky, M. "Counting the Poor: Another Look at the Poverty Profile" and "Author's Note: Who Was Poor in 1966." In L. A. Ferman et al., eds., *Poverty in America.* Ann Arbor: University of Michigan Press, 1968.

_____. "Who's Who Among the Poor: A Demographic View of Poverty." *Social Security Bulletin*, July 1965.

Osborne, E. *The Limits of the Earth.* Boston: Little, Brown, 1953.

_____. *Our Plundered Planet.* Boston: Little, Brown, 1948.

Parker, G. G. "Survey of College Enrollments." *Intellect.* February and April 1973.

Parsons, T. "A Revised Analytical Approach to the Theory of Social Stratification." In R. Bendix and S. M. Lipset, eds., *Class, Status, and Power: A Reader in Social Stratification.* New York: Free Press, 1953.

Peterson, E. "The Atmosphere: A Clouded Horizon." *Environment*, April 1970.

Peterson, R. E. "The Student Left in American Higher Education." *Daedalus*, Winter 1968.

Pettigrew, T. F. "Issues in Urban America." In B. J. Frieden and W. W. Nash, Jr., eds., *Shaping an Urban Future: Essays in Honor of Catherine Bauer Wurster.* Cambridge: MIT Press, 1969.

Pinkney, A. *Black Americans.* Englewood Cliffs: Prentice-Hall, 1969.

Piven, F. F., and Cloward, R. A. *Regulating the Poor: The Functions of Public Welfare.* New York: Vintage Books, 1971.

Plog, S. C., and Edgerton, R. B., eds., *Changing Perspectives in Mental Illness.* New York: Holt, Rinehart & Winston, 1969.

Poloma, M. M. "Role Conflict and the Married Professional Woman." In C. Safilios-Rothschild, eds., *Toward a Sociology of Women.* Lexington, Mass.: Zerox Publishing, 1972.

Poloma, M. M., and Garland, T. N. "The Married Professional Woman: A Study in the Tolerance of Domestication." *Journal of Marriage and the Family*, Fall 1971.

President's Commission on Law Enforcement and Administration of Justice. *The Challenge of Crime in a Free Society.* Washington, D.C.: Government Printing Office, 1967.

_____. *Task Force Report: The Courts.* Washington, D.C.: Government Printing Office, 1967.

_____. *Task Force Report: Organized Crime.* Washington, D.C.: Government Printing Office, 1967.

_____. *Task Force Report: The Police.* Washington, D.C.: Government Printing Office, 1967.

Price, D. O., ed. *The 99th Hour–The Population Crisis in the United States.* Chapel Hill: The University of North Carolina Press, 1967.

Proceedings of the Conference on Revenue Sharing. Washington, D.C.: National Planning Association, December 1973.

Quinney, R. *The Social Reality of Crime.* Boston: Little, Brown, 1970.

_____. *Crime and Justice in Society.* Boston: Little, Brown, 1969.

_____. "The Study of White Collar Crime: Toward a Reorientation in Theory and Research." *Journal of Criminal Law, Criminology, and Police Science*, June 1964.

Rainwater, L. "The Problem of Lower-Class Culture and Poverty—War Strategy." In D. P. Moynihan, ed., *On Understanding Poverty*, New York: Basic Books, 1969.

_____. "Open Letter on White Justice and the Riots." *Trans-action*, September 1967.

Ramirez, S. *The Mexican American: A New Focus on Opportunity.* Washington, D.C.: Inter-Agency Committee on Mexican American Affairs, 1967.

Rapoport, R., and Rapoport, R. N. *Dual Career Families.* Baltimore: Penguin, 1971.

Ray, O. S. *Drugs, Society, and Human Behavior.* St. Louis: C. V. Mosbey Co., 1972.

Reagan, M. D. *The New Federalism.* New York: Oxford University Press, 1972.

Reich, C. *The Greening of America*. New York: Random House, 1970.

Report of the National Advisory Commission on Civil Disorders. Washington, D.C.: Government Printing Office, 1968. Paperback edition by Bantam Books, New York, 1968.

Report of the Special Senate Committee to Investigate Organized Crime in Interstate Commerce. 3d Interim Rep., Senate Rep. No. 307, 82d Cong., 1st sess., 1951.

Revelle, R. "Pollution and Cities." In J. Q. Wilson, ed., *The Metropolitan Enigma*. Cambridge, Mass.: Harvard University Press, 1968.

Ridgeway, J. *The Closed Corporation: American Universities in Crisis*. New York: Ballantine Books, 1968.

Rienow, R., and Leona, L. *Moment in the Sun: A Report on the Deteriorating Quality of the American Environment*. New York: Ballantine Books, 1969.

Robinson, W. S. "Bids, Probability, and Trial by Jury." *American Sociological Review*, February 1950.

Roby, P. "Structural and Internalized Barriers to Women in Higher Education." In Safilios-Rothschild, C., ed., *Toward a Sociology of Women*. Lexington, Mass.: Xerox College Publishing, 1972.

Rodman, H. "The Lower-Class Value Stretch." *Social Forces*, December 1963.

Rogers, D. *110 Livingston Street*. New York: Random House, 1968.

Roll, E. *A History of Economic Thought*. New York: Prentice-Hall, 1942.

Rosen, B. C. "The Achievement Syndrome." *American Sociological Review*, August 1956.

Rosen, G. *Madness in Society*. Chicago: University of Chicago Press, 1968.

Rosenberg, M. B.; Stupak, R. J.; and Willenber, D. "Military Professionalism and Political Invervention." *Society*, May–June 1975.

Rosenhan, D. L. "On Being Sane in Insane Places." *Science*, March 9, 1973.

Rosenthal, R., and Jacobson, L. *Pygmalion in the Classroom*. New York: Holt, Rinehart & Winston, 1968.

Rossi, P. H., and Blum, Z. D. "Class, Status, and Poverty." In D. P. Moynihan, ed., *On Understanding Poverty*. New York: Basic Books, 1969.

Rubenstein, R. E. *Rebels in Eden: Mass Political Violence in the United States*. Boston: Little, Brown, 1970.

Rudd, R. L. *Pesticides and the Living Landscape*. Madison: University of Wisconsin Press, 1964.

Safilios-Rothschild, C. *Women and Social Policy*. Englewood Cliffs: Prentice-Hall, 1974.

Savitz, L. *Dilemmas in Criminology*. New York: McGraw-Hill, 1967.

Schaffer, A.; Schaffer, R. C.; Ahrenholz, G. L.; and Prigmore, C. S. *Understanding Social Problems*. Columbus, Ohio: Merrill, 1970.

Scheff, T. J., ed. *Labeling Madness*. Englewood Cliffs: Prentice-Hall, 1975.

——. ed. *Mental Illness and Social Processes*. New York: Harper & Row, 1967.

Schermer, G. "Desegregating the Metropolitan Area." *The Public Interest*, June 1967.

Schlesinger, A. "The City in American History." In P. Hatt and A. Reiss, eds., *Reader in Urban Sociology*. 1st ed. New York: Free Press, 1951.

Schnore, L. F. "Social Class Among Nonwhites in Metropolitan Centers." *Demography*, February 1965.

Schorr, A. "Slums and Social Insecurity." Research Report No. 1, Division of Research and Statistics, Social Security Administration, Department of Health, Education, and Welfare, Washington, D.C.: Government Printing Office, 1963.

Schrag, C., and Kuehn, L. *Crime and Justice in America*. Pacific Palisades, Cal.: Goodyear Publishing, 1976.

Scientific American. Energy and Power. San Francisco: Freeman, 1971.

Scientific American. The Biosphere. San Francisco: Freeman, 1970.

Seligman, B. B. *Permanent Poverty: An American Syndrome*. Chicago: Quadrangle Books, 1970.

Seligman, B. B., ed. *Poverty as a Public Issue*. New York: Free Press of Glencoe, 1965.

Sewell, W. H. "Students and the University."

American Sociologist, May 1971.

Sexton, P. C. "City Schools." *The Annals,* March 1964.

Sherman, H. *Radical Political Economy.* New York: Basic Books, 1972.

_____. *Profits in the United States: An Introduction to a Study of Economic Concentration and Business Cycles.* Ithaca, New York: Cornell University Press, 1968.

Shoup, D. M. "The New American Militarism." *Atlantic Monthly,* August 1969.

Siegal, P. "On the Cost of Being Negro." *Sociological Inquiry,* Winter 1965.

Silberman, C. *Crisis in the Classroom.* New York: Random House, 1970.

Simkins, F. B. *A History of the South.* New York: Knopf, 1959.

Simon, R. J. *The Jury and the Defense of Insanity.* Boston: Little, Brown, 1967.

Sinclair, A. *The Emancipation of the American Woman.* New York: Harper & Row, 1965.

Skolnick, J. *The Politics of Protest.* New York: Simon & Schuster, 1969.

_____. *Justice Without Trial.* New York: Wiley, 1966.

Skolnick, J., and Currie, E. *Crisis in American Institutions.* Boston: Little, Brown, 1970.

Smelser, N. J. *The Sociology of Economic Life.* Englewood Cliffs: Prentice-Hall, 1963.

Smith. A. K. "Corporation and the Garrison-Managerial State." *Society,* May–June 1975.

Smith, B. *Police Systems in the United States.* 2d ed. New York: Harper & Row, 1960.

Solow, R. M. "The Measurement of Inequality." In E. C. Budd, ed., *Inequity and Poverty.* New York: Norton, 1967.

Sorensen, A.; Taeuber, K. E.; and Hollingsworth, L. J. "Indexes of Racial Residential Segregation for 109 Cities in the United States, 1940 to 1970." *Sociological Focus,* April 1975.

Sorokin, A. L. *American Indians and Federal Aid.* Washington, D.C.: The Brookings Institution, 1971.

Special Subcommittee on Indian Education. 90th Congress, part 2, Wash., D.C.: GPO, 1968.

Spicer, E. H. *Cycles of Conquest.* Tuscon, Ariz.: University of Arizona Press, 1962.

Sprout, H. "The Environmental Crisis in the Context of American Politics." In *The Crisis of Survival,* edited by the editors of *The Progressive.* Glenview, Ill.: Scott, Foresman, 1970.

Sprout, H., and Sprout, M. "Ecology and Politics in America: Some Issues and Alternatives." Morristown, N.J.: General Learning Press, 1971a.

_____. *Toward Politics of the Planet Earth.* Philadelphia: Van Nostrand Reinhold, 1971b.

Stampp, K. *The Peculiar Institution.* New York: Knopf, 1956.

Starnes, C. E. "Poverty and Inequality." In D. Zimmerman and L. Weider, eds., *Understanding Social Problems.* New York: Praeger, 1976.

Starobin, R. S. *Industrial Slavery in the Old South.* London: Oxford University Press, 1970.

Steif, W. "Why Birds Cough." In *The Crisis of Survival,* edited by the editors of *The Progressive.* Glenview, Ill.: Scott, Foresman, 1970.

Steiner, S. *La Raza: The Mexican Americans.* New York: Harper & Row, 1970.

_____. *The New Indians.* New York: Harper & Row, 1968.

Stern, A. C., ed. *Air Pollution.* New York: Academic Press, 1968.

Stern, P. M. *The Rape of the Taxpayer.* New York: Vintage Books, 1974.

_____. "How 381 Super-Rich Americans Managed Not to Pay a Cent in Taxes Last Year." New York *Times* Magazine, April 13, 1969.

Stockwell, E. G. *Population and People.* Chicago: Quadrangle Books, 1968.

Stoddard, E. R. *Mexican Americans.* New York: Random House, 1973.

Strauss, A. L. *Images of the American City.* New York: Free Press, 1961.

Strodtbeck, F. L.; James, R. M.; and Hawkins, C. "Social Status in Jury Deliberations." *American Sociological Review,* December 1957.

Study Commission on University Governance. "Education and Society: The Need for Reconsideration." In C. Foote and H. Mayer et al., eds., *The Culture of the University: Gov-*

ernance and Education. San Francisco: Jossey-Bass, 1968.

Surrey, S. S. *Pathways to Tax Reform.* Cambridge, Mass.: Harvard University Press, 1973.

Sutherland, E. H. *White Collar Crime.* New York: Holt, Rinehart & Winston, 1967.

_____. "White Collar Criminality. *American Sociological Review,* February 1940.

Sweezy, P. *The Theory of Capitalist Development.* New York: Monthly Review Press, 1942.

Szasz, T. S. *The Manufacture of Madness.* New York: Dell, 1970.

_____. *Psychiatric Justice.* New York: Macmillan, 1965.

_____. "The Myth of Mental Illness." *The American Psychologist,* February 1960.

Taeuber, C., and Taeuber, I. *The Changing Population of the United States.* New York: Wiley, 1958.

Taeuber, K. E. In K. Davis, ed., *The American Negro Reference Book. Englewood Cliffs: Prentice-Hall, 1966.*

Taeuber, K. E., and Taeuber, A. F. *Negroes in Cities: Residential Segregation and Neighborhood Change.* Chicago: Aldine, 1965.

Ten Broek, J. "The Two Nations: Differential Moral Values in Welfare Law and Administration." In M. Levitt and B. Rubenstein, eds., *Orthopsychiatry and the Law.* Detroit: Wayne State University Press, 1968.

Thernstrom. S. *Poverty and Progress.* Cambridge, Mass.: Harvard University Press, 1964.

Tompkins. D. C., ed. *Poverty in the United States During the Sixties: A Bibliography.* Berkeley, Cal., Institute of Governmental Studies, 1970.

Train, R. E. et al. *Environmental Quality: The First Annual Report of the Council on Environmental Quality.* Washington, D.C.: Government Printing Office, 1970.

Trowbridge, J. T. *The Desolate South: 1865–1866.* New York: Meredith Press, 1956.

Tumin, M. M. *Social Stratification: The Forms of Inequality.* Englewood Cliffs: Prentice-Hall, 1967.

Turner, J. H. "The Ecosystem: The Relationship between Nature and Society." In D. Zimmerman and L. Weider, eds., *Understanding Social Problems.* New York: Praeger, 1976a.

_____. "A Strategy for Reformulating the Dialectical and Functional Theories of Conflict." *Social Forces* 53 (March), 1976b.

_____. *American Society: Problems of Structure.* New York: Harper & Row, 1972a.

_____. *Patterns of Social Organization: A Survey of Social Institutions.* New York: McGraw-Hill, 1972b.

Turner, J. H., and Singleton, R. "White Racism: Oppression of Blacks in America." In D. Zimmerman and L. Weider, eds., *Understanding Social Problems.* New York: Praeger, 1976.

Turner, J. H., and Starnes, C. E. *Inequality: Privilege and Poverty in America.* Pacific Palisades, Cal.: Goodyear Publishing, 1976.

Vadakin, J. C. *Children, Poverty, and Family Allowances.* New York: Basic Books, 1968.

Valentine, C. A. *Culture of Poverty.* Chicago: University of Chicago Press, 1968.

Wald, G. "A Better World for Fewer Children." In *The Crisis of Survival,* edited by the editors of *The Progressive.* Glenview, Ill.: Scott, Foresman, 1970.

Waters, L. L. "Transient Mexican Agricultural Labor." *Southwest Social and Political Science Quarterly,* June 1941.

Weidenbaum, M. L. "Problems of Adjustment for Defense Industries." In E. Benoit and K. E. Boulding, eds., *Disarmament and the Economy.* New York: Harper & Row, 1963.

Weinberg, S. K., ed. *The Sociology of Mental Disorders: Analyses and Readings in Psychiatric Sociology.* Chicago: Aldine, 1967.

Weinsaig, M. H., and Doerr, D. W. *Drug Abuse: a Course for Educators.* Indianapolis: Butler University College of Pharmacy, 1969.

Wesley, C. "Indian Education." *Journal of American Indian Education,* January 1961.

Wesley, M. *The Tainted Sea.* New York: Coward-McCann, 1967.

Westley, W. "Violence and the Police." *American Journal of Sociology,* July 1953.

_____. *The Reduction of Intergroup Tensions.*

Bulletin No. 57. New York: Social Science Research Council, 1947.

Westoff, L. A., and Westoff, C. F. *From Now to Zero: Fertility, Contraception, and Abortion in America.* Boston: Little, Brown, 1971.

Wheaton et al., eds. *Urban Housing.* New York: Free Press, 1966.

Wheeler, H. "The Politics of Ecology." *Saturday Review,* March 7, 1970.

White, L., Jr. "The Historical Roots of Our Ecological Crisis." *Science,* March 10, 1967.

Whitehurst, C. *Women in America: The Oppressed Majority.* Pacific Palisades, Cal.: Goodyear Publishing Co., 1977.

Williams, R. M., Jr. *American Society.* 3d ed. New York: Knopf, 1970.

Wilson, J. Q. *Varieties of Police Behavior.* Cambridge, Mass.: Harvard University Press, 1968.

Wilson, O. W. *Police Administration.* New York: McGraw-Hill, 1950.

Wirth, L. *The Ghetto.* Chicago: University of Chicago Press, 1928.

Wolozin, H., ed. *The Economics of Air Pollution: A Symposium.* New York: Norton, 1966.

Woodward, C. V. *The Strange Career of Jim Crow.* New York: Oxford University Press, 1957.

———. *Reunion and Reaction.* Boston: Little, Brown, 1951.

Woodwell, G. M. "Toxic Substances and Ecological Cycles." *Scientific American,* March 1967.

Wright, Q. *A Study of War.* Chicago: University of Chicago Press, 1942.

Wurster, C. B. "The Dreary Deadlock of Public Housing." In W. C. Wheaton et al., eds., *Urban Housing.* New York: Free Press, 1966.

Wurster, C. F. "DDT and the Environment." In W. Helfrich, Jr., ed., *Agenda for Survival.* New Haven, Conn.: Yale University Press, 1971.

Yarmolinsky, A. *The Military Establishment.* New York: Harper & Row, 1971.

Zeitlin, M., ed. *American Society, Inc.* Chicago: Markham, 1970.

INDEX